BIBLIOTHECA HISTORICA

OR A Catalogue of 5000 volumes of books and manuscripts relating chiefly to the history and literature of North and South America among which is included the larger proportion of the extraordinary library of the late HENRY STEVENS Senior of Barnet Vt Founder and first President of the Vermont Historical & Antiquarian Society The whole comprising such a collection of ancient and modern books rich and rare useful and common as seldom occurs for sale in any country including many titles never before recorded in an American catalogue

EDITED WITH INTRODUCTION AND NOTES

BY HENRY STEVENS GMB FSA etc

SOMETIMES STUDENT IN YALE COLLEGE NOW RESIDING IN LONDON AT 4 TRAFALGAR SQUARE

To be sold by auction by Messrs LEONARD & Co at their Library Sales Room N° 50 Bromfield Street in Boston on Tuesday the 5th Wednesday the 6th Thursday the 7th and Friday the 8th day of April 1870 Sale each day to commence at 10 in the forenoon and 2 o'clock in the afternoon

BOSTON: H O HOUGHTON AND COMPANY

Cambridge: Riverside Press

1870

EXPLANATORY

THE BOOKS DESCRIBED IN THIS CATALOGUE are brought to auction, because the proprietors just now prefer the money to their books. It is presumed that the intelligent and discriminating purchasers will prefer the books to their money. Both parties may be thus equally benefited by the transaction. Hence an apology here for the seller would be as much out of place as one for the buyer. But this Library is so peculiar and so off the ordinary that some explanation seems desirable for the information of the buyers. The same explanation it is hoped may promote the interest of the sellers, the sale thus being made to realize Adam Smith's idea of fair trade, a good bargain for both parties.

The Catalogue is intended to be an alphabetical commonsense one, according to the well settled rules of bibliography, but many exceptions have been made to adapt it to circumstances and the convenience of sale by auction. Many lots are misplaced in consequence of the books coming in too late, and others to avoid as far as possible duplicates being sold the same day. The titles, especially those in foreign languages, were written by several hands, and at various times, with more or less fulness. The editor, therefore, not having, in most cases, the books before him to refer to, has had some difficulty in harmonizing and correcting the titles. No one can know better than himself the imperfections and shortcomings of this Catalogue, but his experience has taught him that it is better to let the generous reader have the pleasure of finding out the mistakes for himself rather than attempt to indicate and apologize for them. Let him that is free from errata in his own life point them out and crow. The writer will reciprocate on opportunity. No man ever yet, he thinks, printed a catalogue perfect in the eyes of others. The editor has printed enough of them to cause his youthful pride of accuracy to be completely taken out of him, and he is always willing to help take it out of others by encouraging them in the same laudable labors.

It has become a custom in this enlightened country to emphasize, at the expense of the seller, the importance of rare and valuable books by printing very long titles and filling out the pages with leads and blank spaces. The editor has ventured to depart somewhat from this custom, by endeavoring in most cases to render the titles short and concise, and then lead out the pages with notes in small type. He has done this for several reasons. First, by printing in two hundred and fifty pages what would otherwise occupy five hundred, the expense is less, which to a frugal mind is equivalent to virtue. Second, the Catalogue to his eye being more solid and compact presents a comelier appearance.

> Virtue to all complexions giveth grace,
> But Virtue gracèd is by a good face.

Third, having in the course of many years of bibliographical study and research picked up various isolated grains of knowledge respecting the early history, geography, and bibliography of this Western Hemisphere which he has not found it convenient hitherto to book in appropriate places, the writer has thought it well to pigeon-hole the facts here by inserting notes short and long in the Catalogue. That he may not be guilty any longer of the indiscretion of planting his corn where the crows will pull it up, as heretofore, he has caused to be printed on the back of the title Uncle Samuel's usual notice to the crows. To the intelligent collector whose object is to fill his head, this padding of small type will, it is hoped, be of no offence. The loud and indifferent collector whose noble object is to fill his shelves will doubtless readily pardon and skip this *minion* leading.

Fourth, and the previous reasons but lead up to this, because a very considerable proportion of the books described in this volume belonged to the library of his late honored father, the editor has thought by rendering it a trifle more than an ordinary sale catalogue, he might thereby erect an appropriate and affectionate memorial to one whose memory to him is dearer than can well be expressed on cold marble. He has aimed, therefore, to achieve for his parent a pious monument that, in warm and comfortable libraries, long after his books have been dispersed and the sale forgotten, may be referred to by intelligent bibliographers of American history, and be consulted by antiquaries with interest and respect. This Catalogue therefore has been made, after the manner of the old Vermont Farmer of Barnet, to stand square on its own taps, with a fashion of its own, full of odd titles, quaint conceits, originality, personal anecdote, disjointed historical connections, and general intelligence. Those who knew the mirth-loving, pains-taking Founder and first President of the Vermont Historical and Antiquarian Society, it is hoped, will recognize the effigies; those who did not are asked to take it on trust, calling to mind that all outside of the ordinary sale catalogue is intended as a filial memorial

STEPHANI ET AMICORUM.

HENRY STEVENS, Senior, was born at Barnet, Vermont, on the 13th day of December, 1791, and died on the old homestead, on the 30th of July, 1867, at the age of seventy-five, leaving his house full of books and historical manuscripts, the delight of his youth, the companions of his manhood, and the solace of his old age. His father was Enos Stevens, who from the age of twelve to fifteen was three years a captive among the St Francis Indians of Canada, was one of the original proprietors and first settlers of Barnet under a New Hampshire Grant, was married at the age of fifty and enriched his State with ten Green Mountain Boys and Girls. The father of Enos was Capt. Phineas Stevens, born at Sudbury, Massachusetts, in 1707, served his country in the Indian Wars, and in April 1747 defended successfully 'Fort N° Four' on Connecticut River against an attack of a large body of French and Indians, for which gallant action he was complimented with a sword by Admiral Sir Charles Knowles, whose fleet was then in Boston Harbor, the place thenceforward being called Charlestown, after Sir Charles. He was sent to Canada in 1752, by the Government of Massachusetts Bay, to redeem captives. Not finding enough of them for his money, and meeting with a New Hampshire young man named John Stark, he ventured to buy him on his own account of the Indians by exchanging a Shetland pony for which he paid 515 livres, and so restored to his friends the future hero of Bennington. Phineas was the son of Joseph, who was the son of Cyprian, who was the son of Cyprian senior, who was the son of Thomas of London, a supporter and friend of the Massachusetts Colony, who was the son of Thomas Stevens of Devonshire, one of the assignees of Sir Walter Raleigh of his Patent of Virginia, of March 1585.

To return, Henry and the late Thaddeus Stevens, born within seven miles of each other, were chums in boyhood at Peacham Academy, and warm friends through life. Leaving the Academy at the age of twelve with only a taste of books, and, as he expressed it, graduating at Nature's University, he became a self-taught man. The eldest of ten children, he became their guardian and educator. The father of a large family, he sought only to provide his children with education, leaving them to hoe their own rows. He was a farmer, an inn-keeper, a mill-owner, a landlord, and the squire by courtesy of Stevens Village. An antiquarian and a book collector, his house was the resort of the intelligent. He was a liberal and public-spirited citizen, a disinterested politician, an impartial justice, an industrious representative in the State Legislature, an obliging postmaster, a promoter of agriculture, and an advocate of temperance. A kind neighbor, he pastured the widow's cow, protected the fatherless, and annually supplemented his minister-tax with one load of hay and two bushels of white beans. He was a collector and reader of newspapers, a hoarder of pamphlets, and a gatherer of the unconsidered trifles of the day. He lectured on Temperance, Agriculture, and Education, and contended that Vermont should be manured all over with school-houses. He was a strong advocate of internal improvements and domestic manufactures. Through life he was a wool-grower and a protectionist, and his clothes were homespun. In knowledge of the statistics of his county few were his equals, and none was his superior in the history of his own State and the early Green Mountain Boys. He was a confidential agent of the Secretary of the Treasury at Washington, for collecting information respecting the New England manufactures, and the State of Vermont owes to him the collection and arrangement of her Historical Papers.

Many of his books and historical pamphlets like those from Washington's library, found their way through the writer into the library of the British Museum. In February, 1857, some 2000 volumes of Vermont newspapers, 3000 tracts, and many of his valuable historical manuscripts were burnt with the State House at Montpelier, an irreparable loss to himself and to posterity. His widow now possesses about 250 large quarto and folio volumes of historical manuscripts relating to the New Hampshire Grants, to Vermont, and to the Controversy with New York, among which are the Ethan and Ira Allen papers, the papers of the first three Surveyors-general, miscellaneous correspondence, etc. All the rest of his library not otherwise appropriated is included in this Catalogue. In many volumes will be found his book-plate, comprising the arms of Vermont over his name and address, and these lines: —

In Paradise, the tree
Of knowledge was the pride;
By God's supreme decree,
The man who eat — *then died.*

But Heaven in mercy since
Does him who tastes forgive;
To *know*, is no offence;
Now, he who eats — *shall live.*

Mr Stevens represented Barnet two years in the State

Legislature. He was no speaker, but generally managed to carry his point by force of native talent and ingenious surprise. At one time the Legislature was at a dead-lock in the appointment of some officer and neither party would yield. The opposition contended that the candidate was not equal to the place. The gentleman from Barnet gained the floor. "Mr Speaker," said he, "may I ask if this candidate is the man who unarmed recently hugged a bear to death." "He is." "Then, sir, I think he is not the man to flinch under any circumstances, — he shall have my vote," and amid roars of laughter the candidate was unanimously elected. Years after he generally attended the Legislature, a self-elected member of the Third House. For several years the Third House was regularly organized and held its daily sessions like the other two branches. The printed journals and proceeding are full of wit and humor. Mr Stevens was annually elected chairman of the *Committee on Useless Information and Antiquarian Lower*. With a mind well stored with wise saws and modern instances he frequently brought down the House by a knack Samson never dreamed of. His occasional reports are said to have drawn crowds and applause. In his historical mousings in garrets, among sequestered hen-coops and old barrels, he chanced to light upon about a bushel of old Continental and State money, redeemed but never properly cancelled. This he called his "Antiquarian Currency," and with it bought in his travels through the country vast numbers of old books, papers, tracts, etc. Educated in the good old school of unswerving integrity and no trowsers-pockets, he could not bear to see the rising generation standing around the stores, the taverns, and the railway stations, wearing whiskers, chewing tobacco, with hands in their breeches. The less hopeless of these youths he delighted to rescue. In his pocket-book the writer found the following: —

$20. BURLINGTON, June 2d, A. D. 1860.

In consideration of Twenty Dollars of Antiquarian Money received of my friend Henry Stevens, I promise upon honor to keep my hands out of my trowsers-pockets for the space of two months, except in case of necessity. W. B. RICH.

To the remnants of the library of such a man are added the remainders of the gatherings of years, from all parts of Europe and America, of one of his sons; the whole forming the unique collection brought together and described in this Catalogue. It is hardly fair, however, to call this compound a Library, since it is too miscellaneous, too disintegrated, and too incoherent. But it is just the collection by its dispersion to help fill important gaps in public and private libraries. It is in many respects unlike any other collection ever brought together in this country. The first impulse of a librarian or bibliographer reading the Catalogue, will most likely be to ask, if all this remain, what must have been the library before it was *picked?* There is scarcely a book herein described that is not deserving of a place in any of our large public libraries; and yet most of the good standard every-day works, such as "no library should be without," and which everybody wants, are not here. That is just it. The remainder of a picked library in this country is frequently found to be equivalent to a weeded library. The part left is often the best. The American bibliographers and librarians, with notable exceptions, are gregarious and are inclined to be too imitative, running in grooves. There is the Obadiah Rich groove, the Ternaux-Compans groove, and the Ander Schiffahrt groove. Books described by these worthies go off like hot cakes, and are found in dozens of libraries, public and private; but it is only the rare cognoscenti, the knowing ones of a thousand, who ferret out the unknown and undescribed books and secure them. One may safely assert that not one quarter of the titles of the books pertaining to the discovery, exploration, and development of our Continent, are recorded in these and other manuals. The very fact that a book of this kind is not so recorded is a sufficient reason why it, like folly, should be shot as it flies.

One often hears librarians and book collectors talk of trash, and sees them, not unfrequently, decline as such the plums of history offered them, because, forsooth, they do not find them described in their own favorite manuals, or because they are translations, or written in a language they cannot read. Sirs, there is no such thing as trash in our historical literature, or in the historical literature of any language, so far as it relates to America. You may, if you please, apply that disparaging term to a funeral sermon on my grandmother, and I may, if I please, entertain a like opinion of the one on yours; yet both of these documents might very properly be preserved in the public libraries of a nation whose hopes and prospects are backed by its genealogy, its biography, and its history. It is amazing to see how light is the mental pabulum that best nourishes some minds, while others require nothing less hearty than the Novum Organon Baconis. No American probably ever wrote or owned a book so weak but there might be found another American with a mind just strong enough to thrive upon it. With these views the writer unhesitatingly declares his belief that this collection, well suited to varying tastes and capacities, is as nearly exempt from trash as any one probably ever offered by auction to the American public. The collection is miscellaneous and valuable; but the proprietors have no twinges of conscience about breaking it. The books are good ones and generally in good condition, many well bound and some even in extravagant bindings, or they are in a good state for binding — large, clean, and uncut. Some of the books, it is true, are not adapted to the capacities of all collectors, any more than all collectors are fitted to possess some of the books; but the books on an average are probably of as high a quality as the average of the collectors. The proprietors, therefore, on the whole, can with confidence recommend the library (ut vulgo) as one eminently well calculated for dispersion. Incomplete in itself, it will go far towards completing others, and filling up those inconvenient chinks which every earnest student of American history finds in our libraries, and will continue to find until librarians and committees turn over a new leaf, and give their attention to the collection of the true sources of American history, regardless of the language in which they are written, measuring their purchases rather by the capacities of their purses and shelves than by their knowledge of the subjects. It is proverbial that the better and more conscientious of the American historians break down with their labors before they have collected their materials, or they are driven abroad to mouse out in foreign countries and foreign languages what ought to be at home at their service in the public libraries. It is requiring too much of our historians, besides their reference books and general tools, to oblige them to procure for themselves these thousand-and-one expensive out-of-the-way helps. They should belong to the public, and should be collected rather than the common every-day ones, if all cannot be had.

When it is fairly comprehended by our curators, with their large funds and hungry alcoves, that probably more than five sixths of all the books pertaining to the discovery, exploration, and development of our young Hemisphere born since the Printing-Press, are in the languages of Spain, Portugal, Italy, Holland, and France, it is not unlikely that even committees who cannot read a word of these languages, or librarians who cannot catalogue the books, rather than other Motleys should be driven abroad in search of what ought to be found at home, will venture to buy such books on trust, on the new and growing principle that a public library should *lead* and not *follow* the wants of scholars. The narrow remark, hitherto often heard, that Dutch books are not read, and the Portuguese ones never called for, will probably not much longer be repeated by librarians who make any pretensions to the collection of materials of American history. One might as well attempt to write the history of New England without a knowledge of the English language, as a history of New York without the Dutch, or of Brazil without the Portuguese, of Mexico without the Spanish, or Canada without the French. A very considerable proportion of our earliest and best geographical books are in Latin and no other language. Many of our earliest maps are by German geographers; and in order to comprehend their lines and see as they saw, the modern historian must divest himself of his native shackles, stand in their shoes, take the same inland views, and study under the same circumstances. He must read the same reports of the navigators, in the same languages, and he will most likely by this process see the blunders that very early confused the geographers, and have since puzzled the historians. Bring all these books, maps, and languages together, and the sun will rise. We shall then ascertain our historical bearings, and know whither and how far we have drifted these four hundred years. Our moorings to the apron-strings of the Old World will be cut, and the two hemispheres will revolve as loving companions and equals in the waltz of the spheres. It is difficult at this late day to attempt anything like a complete collection of the history and literature of the Old World, but it is unpardonable to neglect that of the New. The mere difficulty of language is not insurmountable. Did not an editor of the North American Review learn the Spanish language that he might write understandingly of the South American Republics? And would not Southey's History of Brazil have been a far better book had he given the same prominence to the numerous Dutch works on his subject that he did to the Portuguese?

Some folks affect to despise translations, and divers editions. It is not so with the true historian and experienced researcher. A good translation is itself occasionally a useful comment on the original work, and moreover, the translator being often better up in the subject treated than the author himself, sometimes corrects many errors, and makes valuable additions. There are dozens of such examples recorded in this Catalogue, *f. i.* see N° 878 Hearne, and N° 1562 Pike. Again, other important books are known to us only through translations, as N° 460, the Life of Columbus by his son. A comparison of the English and French editions of N° 249, Bouquet's Account of the Expedition against the Ohio Indians, is a notable instance in favor of the translation, which contains a valuable Life of Bouquet, not in the original. The superiority of many Dutch editions over the original works is proverbial. The plates and maps are almost always far superior, and the translator is generally an expert. The French, English, German, Spanish, Swedish, and American books relating to America translated into Dutch are very numerous, and generally, in some respects, possess points superior to the originals, insomuch that, as far as the department of American history is concerned, all such books should be accessible somewhere in America. On the other hand, translations are important sometimes from their very badness or untrustworthiness, and should be preserved in our most important libraries as a means of tracing to their true source misstatements and falsehoods. How many misstatements are attributed to Herrera, which can be traced no nearer that author than Capt. John Stevens' English translation and abridgment, in six volumes? It is absolutely necessary to study this latter book to see where so many English and American authors have taken incorrect facts. So of many French and German translations which are the parents of errors sworn on to the original authors.

Worse still, it is not unfrequently necessary for an historian to be acquainted with a book only to be certain that it is good for nothing. There are many such in this Catalogue, and some of them will very properly bring good prices too. They have good titles, and read well. Such a book is Peters' History of Connecticut, N° 486, a book of not half the historical value of Knickerbocker's New York, and without any of its wit. Yet it has often been quoted by French and German authors as true history. The writer has before him a remarkable book of this good-for-nothing kind, of excessive rarity if not unique. It was reprinted some years ago at Rouen, in fifty copies, which reprint is now almost as rare as the original. The original will be sought, now that its title has got into catalogues, as ardently as if it had any historical value. The title is, "Relation du Voyage des Dames Religieuses Ursulines de Roüen, a la Nouvelle Orleans. Parties de France le 22. Fevrier 1727. & arrivez à la Louisienne le 23. Juillet de la même année. Les noms desquelles Dames Religieuses sont marquez dans ladite Relation. 100 pp.

Small octavo. Chez Antoine le Prevost, Rouen, 1728." The editor, in behalf of his numerous notes, historical, biographical, explanatory, geographical, bibliographical, gossipy, and personal, desires it to be understood that they are to be taken at what they are worth, he having given them only where he had something to say, or some duty to perform either to himself or to the public, and that they are not designed to force up the prices of the particular lots to which they are attached; but are intended rather to shed a bibliographical flavor over the entire Catalogue. Most of the better and rarer lots of known and prime importance are recorded without comment, as Mather's Magnalia, Hazard's State Papers, etc., the titles sufficiently explaining themselves. On the other hand, many of the more elaborate notes, some of them not complimentary to the books, will cost far more in printing than the lots will sell for. Neither has he indulged in overmuch bibliographical quiddling about the mechanical and manufacturing points of the books, as to the quantity of the paper, the quality of the binding, the brilliancy of impressions, the crushed levant (whatever that new-fangled term may mean) and the number of copies of certain recent reprints, the inertia of which on shelves it is hard to overcome.

It is not easy to convey any adequate idea of a large uncommon collection, like this, short of a patient reading of the entire Catalogue from end to end. The editor therefore has exercised his ingenuity to sweeten the labor, and thinks perhaps it may bait the attention of the indifferent reader to be informed that in the General Histories of North and South America there are many works of authors such as Acosta, Anglerius, Apollonius, Barcia, Barlæus, Benzoni, Clavigero, Eden, Hazard, Herrera, Labat, Laet, Lafitau, Las Casas, Peter Martyr, De Solis, Garcilasso de la Vega, etc. In local and particular history of Colonies, States, cities, towns, villages and parishes, the titles are too many to specify here. In bibliography, the reader is invited to consult the Catalogue under Asher, Bibliotheca Chethamensis, Blades, British Museum, Catalogues, Collier, Fry, Harrisse, Macray's

Bodleian Library, Moule, Nutt, Quaritch, Rothelin, Stevens, Whiting, Boturini, and the notes under several of the Mexican titles. For rare and valuable Manuscripts, he is referred to Benedict Arnold's characteristic Autograph Letters from Ticonderoga, Fay's urgent letter to the Green Mountain Boys to reinforce General Gates against Burgoyne; Gorton's Answer to Morton's New Englands Memorial, the original Autograph MS written in 1669; Riccio's MS account of Hernandes' Natural History of New Spain; and the Original Book of Minutes of the Corporation for New England in London for thirty years, 1655–1685, under N° 1399. For the Indian languages of America, see under Avila, Juan de la Anunciacion, Mexico, 1575; Paredes, Tapia Zenteno, Villegas, etc. Works pertaining to Canada, Acadia, and the British Provinces generally are numerous, some of which, as rare as they are important, may be seen under Canada, Champlain, Charlevoix, Cornutus, Denys, Examen, Hennepin, Joutel, LaHontan, LeBeau, LeClercq, LeJeune, Mackenzie, Memoires, Montcalm, Nova Scotia, Relation, Shea's Publications, Shirley, Tanner, Thevenot, Thevet, Tupper, and Vimont. Pertaining to New England, California, New York, Pennsylvania, Virginia, Florida, the Mississippi Valley, the Great West and North West, the works are numerous; and equally so on Mexico, and other parts of Spanish America, as Brazil, Paraguay, Peru, etc. The works pertaining to Washington, Franklin, and Hamilton, are well represented, and so are the departments of early geography and discovery, atlases, maps, the Indians, slavery, colonies, the old French War, the Stamp Act, the Revolution, tobacco, statistics, etc. Though last not least, there is a large number of works on the natural history of this Continent, not the least curious of which is N° 2435, wherein the learned author endeavors to account for the introduction and rapid increase of Asses in the New World. He says nothing however about their being found among either bibliographers or book collectors.

H. S.

Boston, Feb. 22, 1870.

Arrangement of the Sale

FORENOONS AT 10 AFTERNOONS AT 2 O'CLOCK

1870

Tuesday Forenoon, April 5th N°s 1 to 353

Tuesday Afternoon, April 5th N°s 354 to 631

Wednesday Forenoon, April 6th N°s 632 to 973

Wednesday Afternoon, April 6th N°s 974 to 1271

Thursday Forenoon, April 7th N°s 1272 to 1609

Thursday Afternoon, April 7th N°s 1614 to 1896

Friday Forenoon, April 8th N°s 1897 to 2284

Friday Afternoon, April 8th N°s 2285 to 2545

Bibliotheca Historica.

TUESDAY FORENOON.

1 ABBOT (ABIEL) An Eulogy on George Washington, delivered at Haverhill, 22 February, 1800. With the Farewell Address. *Fine copy, sized paper, uncut, white vellum, by Pratt.* 8° *A. H. Moore, Haverhill,* 1800

2 ABBOTT (George) A briefe Description of the whole World. *Fine portrait, calf.* 12° *London,* 1634

Pp. 240 to 329 relate to America.

3 ABINGDON (Earl of) Thoughts on the Letter of Edmund Burke, on the Affairs of America. *Half mor.* 8° *Oxford,* 1777

4 ABINGDON (Earl of) Thoughts on the Letter of Edmund Burke on the Affairs of America. 6th edition. *Half roan.* 8° *Oxford,* 1777

This 6th Edition contains an Explanatory Dedication of xci pages, not in any of the earlier editions.

5 ABLYN (CORNELIUS) DIE NIEUWE WEERELT DER LANDTSCHAPPEN ENDE EYLANDEN, *etc.* *Black letter, fine copy, vellum.* *Folio, Antwerpen,* 1563

This EXCESSIVELY RARE volume, in the dialect of Brabant, contains the following Voyages and Travels: 1. The Voyages of Cadamosto; 2. The first three Voyages of Columbus; 3. The Voyage of Alonzo Niño; 4. The Voyage of Vincent Pinzon; 5. The four Voyages of Vespucci; 6. The Voyage of Pedro Alvarez Cabral; 7. The Relations of Joseph the Indian; 8. Letters of Emanuel, King of Portugal to Leo X concerning the Conquests and Discoveries of the Portuguese in the East Indies; 9. The Itinerary of Ludovico de Varthema; 10. The Description of the Holy Land in the thirteenth century, by Brocard, the Monk; 11. The Voyages of Marco Polo; 12. Relation of Haython respecting the Tartars; 13. Two Books upon Asiatic and European Sarmatia, by Mathew Miechow; 14. An Account of the Embassy of Paulus Jovius to Russia; 15. Peter Martyr's account of the Newfound Islands; 16. Stella's Antiquities of Prussia; 17. Maximilianus Transilvanus; 18. Cortes's Second and Third Relations; 19. History of the Canary Islands, 1543; 20. Martyr's Legatio Babilonica, etc.

6 ABRESCH (F. L.) Animadversiones ad Æschylum; accedunt Annotationes ad quædam Loca, N. Testamenti. [*"Not often to be met with."*—EBERT.] *Calf.* 8° *Medioburgi,* 1743

7 ACCOUNT of the European Settlements in America. *Maps.* 2 *vols., calf.* 8° *London,* 1757

8 ACCOUNT (An) of the European Settlements in America. [By E. Burke ?] 2 *vols, calf.* 12° *London,* 1766

9 ACOSTA (JOSEPH DE, *of the Society of Jesus*) DE NATVRA NOVI ORBIS libri dvo. Et de promvlgatione Evangelii apud Barbaros, sive, de procvranda Indorum salute, Libri sex. *Vellum.* 8° *Col. Agrip.* 1596

This copy of Acosta is a rare curiosity, it having been through the Inquisition and thoroughly expurgated. It probably belonged once to some Convent library in Spain or Mexico, where the monks could not afford to destroy their books altogether. So the official *Corrigidor* simply ran his pen through the wicked, dangerous or objectionable words, sentences, or paragraphs, and left the book on the shelves. In this copy, probably one-tenth of the whole work is partially erased with pale-brown ink, in little snatches, throughout the volume, but not so as to prevent its being read.

" Some flowrets of Eden ye still inherit,
But the trail of the serpent is over them all."

10 ACOSTA (JOSEPH DE) De Natvra Novi Orbis Libri duo, etc. *Another and fine copy. Vellum.* 8° *Col. Agr.* 1596

11 ACOSTA (JOSEPH DE) Histoire Natvrelle et Moralle des Indes, tant Orientalles, qu' Occidentales ; traduit par Regnault Cauxois. *First Edition in French. Vellum.* 8° *Paris,* 1600

12 ACOSTA (Joseph de) Histoire Natvrelle et Moralle des Indes. *Another copy, calf.* 8° *Paris,* 1600

13 ACOSTA (Joseph de) Histoire Naturelle et Moralle des Indes, tant Orientalles qu' Occidentales. Derniere Edition. *Half calf.* 8° *Paris,* 1606

14 ADAM (*Rev.* T.) Private Thoughts on Religion ; extracted from his Diary. 12° *Poughkeepsie,* 1814

15 ADAMS (C. B. *State Geologist*) First Annual Report on the Geology of the State of Vermont. 8° *Burlington,* 1845

16 ADAMS (Hannah) A view of Religions of the various religious Denominations, alphabetically arranged. 2d edition, with large additions. *Calf.* 8° *J. W. Folsom, Boston,* [*n. d.*]

17 ADAMS (Hannah) Memoir, written by herself; with additional Notices by a Friend. *Portrait, cloth.* 12° *Boston,* 1832

18 ADAMS (John) A Defence of the Constitutions of Government of the United States of America. *First English Edition. Calf.* 8° *London,* 1787

19 ADAMS (John) Constitutions of Government. A Defence of the United States of America. *First English Enlarged Edition. Portrait, 3 vols. calf; fine copy.* 8° *London,* 1794

20 ADAMS (John) Defence of the Constitutions of Government of the United States of America. *New edition ; 3 vols, calf.* 8° *London,* 1794

21 ADAMS (John) Défense des Constitutions Americaines, ou De la nécessité d'une balance dans les pouvoirs d'un gouvernement libre. . . . . Avec des notes et observations de M. de la Croix. 2 tom. *Half calf.* 8° *Paris,* 1792

22 ADAMS (John Quincy) A Letter to Harrison Gray Otis, on the present state of our National Affairs. *Uncut, sewed.* 8° *G. W. Nichols, Walpole, N. H, May,* 1808

23 ADAMS (Samuel) An Oration delivered at the State House, in Philadelphia, to a very numerous Audience ; on Thursday the 1st of August, 1776. *Half roan.* 8° *London,* 1776

24 ADDITIONS to Plain Truth, addressed to the Inhabitants of America, containing further Remarks on a late Pamphlet entitled "Common Sense." *Half morocco.* 8° *Philadelphia*, 1776

25 ADDRESS (The) of the People of Great Britain to the Inhabitants of America. *Half roan.* 8° *London*, 1775

26 ADDRESS (The) of the People of Great Britain to the Inhabitants of America. *Half roan.* 8° *T. Cadell, London*, 1775

27 AELREDUS. OPERA Omnia, ope et studio R. Gibboni, FIRST EDITION, *scarce. Calf.* 4° *Duaci*, 1631

28 AGASSIZ (Louis) A Journey in Brazil, by Professor and Mrs. Louis Agassiz. *Illustrated, cloth.* 8° *Boston*, 1868

29 ALBERTI Stadensis Chronicon a condito Orbe usque ad annum 1256. *Calf.* 4° *Helmaestadii*, 1587

30 ALDEN (TIMOTHY) Sermon in Portsmouth, 5 Jan. 1800, on the death of George Washington. *Fine copy, sized paper, clean, vellum by Pratt.* 8° *Portsmouth, N. H.*, 1800

31 ALDEN (Timothy) Account of the several Religious Societies in Portsmouth, N. H., from their first Establishment, and of the Ministers of each to January 1st, 1805. 8° *Boston*, 1808

32 ALEXANDER (Caleb) Grammatical System of the English Language. 12° *Thomas and Andrews, Boston*, 1793

33 ALI BEY. Extracts from a journal of Travels in North America, consisting of an Account of Boston and its vicinity. *Boards uncut.* 12° *Boston*, 1818

34 ALLEN (Col. Ethan) Narrative of his Captivity; written by Himself. 12° *Burlington*, 1846

35 ALLEN (IRA) THE NATURAL AND POLITICAL HISTORY OF THE STATE OF VERMONT. *Map, good copy, half calf.* SCARCE. 8° *London*, 1798

36 ALLEN (Ira) *Four Olive-Branch tracts, viz:*

1 A Concise Summary of the Second Volume of the OLIVE BRANCH, a book containing an account of Governor Chittenden's giving written instructions to Gen. Ira Allen in 1795, to purchase military stores in Europe, for the militia of Vermont, etc. 24 pp. *uncut.* 8° *For the author, Philadelphia, April*, 1807

2 Statements applicable to the cause of the OLIVE BRANCH, which was a cargo of cannon and arms purchased by the authority of the Governor of Vermont to supply the militia thereof, captured on its passage from Ostend in France, to New York, by an English man-of-war (in 1796,) *etc.* *Uncut.* 8o *For the author, Philadelphia, July*, 1807

3 Ira Allen's Address to the Freemen of Vermont and Legislature thereof respecting a cargo of military stores captured by the British, etc. *Uncut.* *For the author, Philadelphia, Aug.* 1808

4 Extracts from *Select Speeches* lately published in Philadelphia, applicable to the cause of the Olive Branch. 4 *rare tracts, in* 1 *vol.* 8o.

37 ALLIN (John) An Exact Relation of the most Execrable Attempts of John Allin committed on the Person of His Excellency Francis Lord Willoughby of Parham, Captain-general of the continent of Guiana, and of all the Caribby-Islands, and our Lord Proprietor. *Half morocco, uncut.* 4° *R. Lowndes, London*, 1665

38 ALMANACS. 3 *vols. complete, but sallow as greenbacks*, 8°, *viz:* —
1 STAFFORD'S ALMANACK for 1784. Adapted to the Horizon and Meridian of New Haven, but may serve indifferently for all the towns in Connecticut. [With two pages of remarkable events.] *Uncut.* *T. & S. Green, New Haven, n. d.*
2 AN ASTRONOMICAL EPHEMERIS Calendar, or Almanack for 1785, adapted to the Horizon and Meridian of Hartford, but may serve indifferently for all Towns in New England. By N. Strong of Yale College. *Hudson & Goodwin, Hartford.*
3 WEBSTER'S CALENDAR: or the Albany Almanack for 1786, being the tenth and eleventh of American Independency, calculated for the Meridian of Albany. By Ebin W. Judd. *Uncut.* *Charles Webster, Albany, n. d.*

39 ALOE. A true account of the Aloe Americana in Mr. Cowell's Garden at Hoxton. *Half roan.* 8° *London*, 1729

40 ALSOP (R.) A Poem; sacred to the Memory of George Washington, adapted to the 22d of Feb. 1800. *Vellum, uncut.* 8° *Hartford*, 1800

41 ALTING (H.) THEOLOGIA Elenctica Nova. 4° *Amstelod.* 1654

42 ALTING (H.) THEOLOGIA Problematica Nova. *Calf.* 4° *Amstelod.* 1662

43 AMBROSIUS (Episcopus) Expositio super Apocalypsin. Nunc primum in lucem edita. *Calf.* *Folio, Lutetia*, 1554

44 AMERICA. An Account of the European Settlements in America. A new edition, *maps*, 2 vols. *Half maroon mor. uncut.* 8° *London*, 1808

45 AMERICA. An Application of some General Political Rules to the Present State of Great Britain, Ireland and America. *Half morocco.* 8° *London*, 1766

46 AMERICA. CONSIDERATIONS on the Propriety of Imposing Taxes in the British Colonies, for the Purpose of raising a Revenue, by Act of Parliament. *Half morocco. Scarce.* 8° *John Holt, New York*, 1765

47 AMERICA. Constitutions of the several Independent States of America, the Declaration of Independence, *etc.* *Calf.* 8° *Dublin*, 1783

48 AMERICA. The Contest in America between Great Britain and France, with its consequences and importance. An Account of the Views and Designs of the French in all parts of America, in which a proper Barrier between the two nations in North America is pointed out. By an Impartial Hand. SCARCE. *Vellum.* 8° *London*, 1757

49 AMERICA. Le Déstin de l'Amerique ou dialogues pittoresques. *Half brown mor.* 8° *London*, [1778]

50 AMERICA. The History of America, in two books. I. The General History of America. II. History of the late Revolution. 2d edit. 12° *Dobson, Philadelphia*, 1795

51 AMERICA. Narrative of the Official Conduct of Valentine Morris, late Governor in chief of the Island of St. Vincent and its Dependencies. Written by himself. *Half morocco uncut. Scarce.* 8° *London*, 1777

52 AMERICAN CONGRESS. An Answer to the Declaration of the American Congress. *Half morocco.* 8° *London*, 1776

53 AMERICAN CONGRESS. An Answer to the Declaration of the American Congress. 4th edition. *Half morocco uncut.* 8° *London,* 1776

54 AMERICAN CONGRESS. An Answer to the Declaration of the American Congress. 5th edition. *Half morocco uncut.* 8° *London,* 1776

55 AMERICAN ANTIQUARIAN SOCIETY. Catalogue of Books in their Library at Worcester. *Half maroon morocco uncut.* *Royal* 8° *Worcester,* 1837

56 AMERICAN Journal of Medical Sciences. No. 1, Nov. 1827, No. 13, 14, 15, 17 to 25, 28, 46, 47, 49, 50, 51, 52, (Aug. 1840.) New Series No. 2, (April 1841,) No. 4, 7, 9, 11, 12, 13, 14, 16 and 24, (Oct. 1846,) *in all* 30 *numbers. Uncut.* 8° *Philadelphia,* 1827–1846

57 AMERICAN Journal of Medical Sciences. Nos. 14 and 15. Feb. and May, 1831.

58 AMERICAN MUSEUM, OR REPOSITORY OF ANCIENT AND MODERN FUGITIVE PIECES, ETC. Prose and Poetical. 11 *vols. elegant half-green mor. uncut, fine clean copy.* 8° *Phil.* 1787–92

59 AMERICAN MUSEUM; or, Repository of Fugitive Pieces. 2d edition. 7 *vols. calf, uncut.* 8° *Phila.* 1787–1790

60 AMERICAN PREACHER. Select Discourses from the American Preacher. 2 *vols. Half purple morocco, uncut.* *Edinburgh,* 1796–1801

61 AMERICAN REMEMBRANCER, or an Impartial Collection of Essays, Resolves, Speeches, etc., relative to the Treaty with Great Britain, with the accompanying Documents. 2 *vols.* in 1. 8° *Phila.* 1795

62 AMERICAN REVOLUTION. 10 *Tracts in* 1 *vol. Half morocco. contents lettered.* 8°

1. De Tumultibus Americanis, *Oxon.* 1776
2. The Claim of the American Loyalists Reviewed, *Lond.* 1788
3. The Case and Claim of the American Royalists, *ib. n. d.*
4. Grant, Proposals . . to form Colonies in Canada, *scarce,* *np. n. d.*
5. Observations on the Treaty with America, . . *ib.* 1780
6. Payne. Letter to the Abbé Raynal, *Reprint, Lond.* 1780
7. Reply to the Observations of Lt. Gen. Wm. Howe, *ib.* 1782
8. Letters to a Nobleman on the Conduct of the War, *ib.* 1779
9. Letter to Lord Howe on his Naval Conduct, etc., *ib.* 1779
10. Examination of Jos. Galloway, late Speaker of Penn[a]. *ib.* 1779

63 AMERICAN Review of History and Politics, and General Repository of Literature and State Papers. 3 *vols. Calf.* 8° *London,* 1810–12

64 AMERICAN State Papers, a Collection of Original and Authentic Documents relative to the War between the United States and Great Britain. Washington's Official Letters to Congress, *Vol.* I. 8° *London,* 1795

65 AMERICAN State Papers, communicated to Congress by the President, 1805 to 1807. *Boards.* 8° *Boston,* 1808

66 AMERICAN STATES. Observations on the Commerce of the American States, with Appendix. *Half morocco, uncut.* 8° *London,* 1783

67 American War. History of the War in America, between Great Britain and her Colonies, from its Commencement to the Conclusion, in 1783. To which is added a Collection of Interesting and Authentic Papers. 3 *vols. half morocco, uncut.* 8° *Dublin,* 1779–85

Vol. 3 is a supplemental volume, and is of very considerable rarity.

68 Amérique Délivrée (L') Esquisse d' un Poeme sur l'Indépendance de l'Amérique. *Thick paper, vol.* 2, *half calf, gilt.* 8° *Amst.* 1783

69 Ames (Fisher) Oration at the Old South Meeting House, February 8, 1800, before the Governor and Legislature of Massachusetts, on the Sublime Virtues of Gen. George Washington. 8° *Boston,* 1800

70 Ames (William, *Puritan of Amsterdam*) De Conscientia, Libri V. *Title-page wanting. Small* 8°

71 Amyraldus (M.) Paraphrasis in Psalmos Davidis, una cum Annotationibus et Argumentis. *Calf.* 4° *Salmvrii.* 1662

72 Anbury (Thomas) Voyages dans les Parties Intérieures de l'Amerique. *Map,* 2 *vols, half bound.* 8° *Paris,* 1790

73 Anbury (Thomas) Journal d'un voyage fait dans l'Interieur de l'Amerique septentrionale. Ouvrage dans lequel on donne des détails precieux sur l'insurrection des Anglo-Americains, et sur la Chute disastreuse de leur papier-monnoie. Traduit de l'Anglois et enrichie des notes par M. Noël. *Avec carte and figures.* 2 *vols. sheep.* 8° *Paris,* 1793

74 Andrews (J.) History of the War with America, France, Spain and Holland; commencing in 1775, and ending in 1783, *Portraits, Maps and Charts,* 4 *vols. half calf.* 8° *London,* 1786

75 ANGLERIUS (Petrus Martyr) De Rebus Oceanicis et Orbe novo decades III. Eivsdem praeterea Legationis Babylonicae libri III. *Vellum, fine copy,* scarce, *folio, Apud Jo. Bebelium, Basileæ,* 1533

For other works by this author, see Martyr (Peter).

76 Annals and Memoirs of the Royal Society of Northern Antiquaries. First series. 8° *Copenhagen,* 1837

77 Annual Register, or a View of History, Politics and Literature, complete from the commencement 1758 to 1817, inclusive. 59 *vols. calf.* 8° *London,* 1795–1818

78 Anson (*Com.* George) Journal of a Voyage to the South Seas, and round the Globe, in H. M. Ship Centurion, by Pascoe Thomas. *Calf.* 8° *London,* 1745

79 Anson (*George*) Journal, &c., *another copy, calf,* 8° *London,* 1745

80 Anson (George) A Voyage round the World, 1740–4, compiled by R. Walter. 2d Edit. *Maps, calf gilt.* 8° *London,* 1748

81 Anson (George) A Voyage Round the World, compiled by Richard Walter. 6th Edit. *Maps, calf gilt.* 8° *London,* 1749

82 ANSON (George) A VOYAGE ROUND THE WORLD in the Years 1840–44. Compiled from his Papers and Materials, by R. Walter. *Maps and* 42 *Copper Plates. Calf.* 4° *London*, 1776

83 ANSWER (An) to the Declaration of the American Congress, 5th Edition. *Half roan.* 8° *T. Cadell, London*, 1776

84 ANSWER (An) to the Declaration. *Another copy.* 5th Edition. 8° *London*, 1776

85 ANSWER to the Dissenters' Pleas for Separation. 3d Edition. 8° *Cambridge*, 1701

86 ANTILLES. Histoire et Commerce des Antilles Anglois. *Calf, gilt.* 12° [*n. p.*], 1758

87 APOCATASTASIS (The); or Progress Backwards. A New "Tract for the Times." [By Prof. Marsh of Vermont.] *Cloth.* 8° *Burlington*, 1854

88 APOCRYPHAL New Testament. Third Edition, with Prefaces and Tables, Notes and References. *Half morocco uncut.* 8° *London*, 1821

89 APOLLONIUS (LEVINIUS) DE PERUUIÆ, REGIONIS, inter Noui Orbis provincias celeberrimæ inventione, *etc. No map. Calf gilt.* 8° *Antv.* 1567

90 APOSTOLIUS (M.) Paroemiæ; cum Pantini Versione, ejusque et Doctorum Notis. *Calf.* 4° *Elzevir, Lugd. Batav.*, 1619

91 APPEAL (An) to the Justice and Interests of the People of Great Britain in the present dispute with America. *Half roan.* 8° *London*, 1774

92 APOLLODORUS. De Deorum origine Libri III. Graece et Latine. *Vellum.* 8° *Ex Officina Commel*, 1599

93 APOSTOLORUM et Sanctorum Conciliorum Decreta. *Boards.* 4° *Parisiis*, 1540

94 ARMINIUS (J.) Examen Libelli quem Gul. Perkinsius edidit de Predestinationis modo et ordine. 8° *Lugd. Batav.* 1612

95 ARND (Johann) Des Gottseligen und Hocherleuchteten Lehrens Herr. Johann Arnds Weiland General-Superintendentens des Fürstenthums Lüneburg, Paradiesz-Gärtlein, zur uebung des wahren Christenthums durch Geistreiche Gebäter, &c. *Wants pp.* 169–172, *and last leaf.* 16° *Christoph Saur, Germantown (Penn.)* 1765

96 ARNOLD (BENEDICT, *Traitor*) A LONG AUTOGRAPH DRAFT OF A LETTER to the Committee of the Green Mountain Boys sitting at Charlestown, N° 4, defending himself from the charge of plundering the property of Major Skene, at Skenesborough (now Whitehall, N. Y.), a day or two before the taking of Ticonderoga, on the 10th of May, 1775, with a copy of his Orders to Capt. Herrick, the 8th of May, 1775. Two documents of very considerable historical interest. They bear three Autograph Signatures of the Traitor. One "Bened^t" (*the rest torn off*). 2d, "B Arnold," and 3d, "Benedict Arnold." The documents are endorsed by the late Henry

Stevens, Senior, Founder and first President of the Vermont Historical and Antiquarian Society, "Benedict Arnold's Reply to the Charlestown Letter, Ticonderoga, 1775."

The following are copies of these important historical Documents:

Gentlemen, Ticonderoga, July. 6 1775.

Col°. Hinman has Just shewn me a Letter, Dated at Charlston June 30, & Signed by a number of Gentlemen, which Sems evidently Calculated (by Cpl. Coughran, or some other Person) to, Asperse my Character by Intimating, I, gave orders or rather Countenanced the Plundering Major Skenes House, &c. To Convince you of my Inocency in the Matter, herewith you have a Coppy my Orders to Capt Herrick, the Officer I sent to take Possession of the Majors, Vessel, Boats, &c. Neither have I ben at Skensborough, nor did I know of Doctr Sterne's receiving, any Plunder there Untill after his return from St. Johns & he was gone home. Nor do I recollect ever, speaking to him or hearing him say any thing in regard to, Major Skenes Effects. Neither have I ever given the least Countenance to Plundering but Positive Orders to the Contrary, & I now declare on my honour I have, never received Directly or Indirectly, Six pence worth of Any kind of Plunder, except the Property of Capt. Friend Taken in the Sloop great Part of which is returned, & I have wrote to the Continental Congress, in regard to the remainder, & am Determined to Abide their Decision. I am Gentn. Your Vy Obt S. . . .

Benedt . . . .

To The Gentlemen at Charlstown who Directed to Colo. Hinman.

N B. I had forgot to mention about 4lb. or 6lb. of small Beads, delivered me by Capt. Brown, taken at Skensborogh, *Supposed the Kings Property* in Major Skenes hands, to Distribute to the Indians this I Distributed Among the Caughyawaga Indians. B Arnold.

[*The Enclosure on a separate sheet.*]

Capt Herrick. Castleton, 8th may 1775

Sr You will proceed Emediately to Skenesborough and then then take Possession of all the Boats & Craft you Can find also the Stores of Powder Ball Arms &c. and monies in the hands of Major Philip Skeen, which are publick property and Seize the Body of said Skeen and him Keep in Safe Custody untill Further Orders or Remove him where you think he may be Keep in Safety and Seize and, Examen his papers and Such as are of a Publick nature to Detain and you are To Consult with the Gentlemen of the Committe who Goes with you Observing to Use the Famaly with Politeness in perticuler the Young Ladies and Injor no private Property belonging To any Person.

To Capt Samll Herreck. Benedt Arnold, Comandr & Chairman of Committe of Warr.

A True Coppy of The orders From Coll. Arnold To Capt. Herrick Taking July 5th 1775 at Ticonderoga. Test. Benedict Arnold,

97 Arnold (Josias Lyndon of *St Johnsbury Vermont*) Poems. 12° *Providence*, 1797

98 Arrianus. De Expeditione Alex. Magni Historiarum Libri VIII. *Calf.* *Folio, H. Stephanus*, 1575

99 Asher (George M.) A Bibliographical and Historical Essay on the Dutch Books and Pamphlets relating to New-Netherland, and to the Dutch West-India Company and to its possessions in Brasil, Angola, etc. As also on the maps, charts, etc., of New-Netherland, with facsimiles of the map of New-Netherland by N. I. Visscher, and of the three existing views of New Amsterdam. Compiled from the Dutch public and private libraries, and from the Collection of Mr. Frederick Muller in Amsterdam. *Complete, sewed, uncut.* 4° *Frederick Muller, Amsterdam*, 1868

One of the fullest and most accurate bibliographical works known on any subject.

100 Asplund (John) The Annual Register of the Baptist Denomination in North-America, to the 1st of November 1790,

containing an Account of the Churches and their Constitutions, Proceedings, &c., [with additions and corrections continued to page 70.] *Fine copy, uncut.*
4° *Preface dated Southampton County, July* 14, 1791

101 ASSEMBLY'S Shorter Catechism explained. By Way of Question and Answer. 8° *Edinburgh*, 1777

102 ATKINS (JOHN) A Voyage to Guinea, Brasil, and the West Indies. *Calf.* 8° *London*, 1735

103 ATKYNS (SIR R.) An Enquiry into the Power of Dispensing with Penal Statutes; with Animadversions on a Book writ by Sir Edward Herbert, etc. 4° *London*, 1689

104 ATLAS des Departmens de la France, et de ses Colonies, par Perrol et Achin. *Numerous maps. Half roan.* *Oblong* 4° *Paris*, n. d.

105 ATLAS. KAART-BOEK der Zee van Vereenigde Nederlanden. *Boards.* *Atlas folio, Amsterdam, n. d.*

106 ATLAS van het alrude Holland. IX *Landkaarten.* *Folio, Graavenhaage*, 1745

107 ATWOOD (Thomas) The History of the Island of Dominica. *Calf, gilt.* 8° *London*, 1791

108 AUDIN (J. M. V.) History of the life, works and doctrines of John Calvin. *Calf.* 8° *Louisville, Ky. n. d.*

109 AUSTIN (W.) Letters from London, written during the Years 1802–3. 8° *Boston*, 1804

110 AUTOGRAPH SOUVENIR, a Collection of Autograph Letters, interesting Documents executed in fac-simile, by F. G. Netherclift; with Transcriptions and occasional Translations by R. Sims, of the British Museum. *Cloth, gilt.* 4° *London*, 1865

111 AVILA (EL P. F. FRANCISCO DE) ARTE DE LA LENGUA MEXICANA, y brevis platicas de los Mysterios de N. Santa Fee Catholica, y otros para exortacion de su obligacion á los Indios. *Scarce. Vellum.* 16° *Mexico*, 1717

112 B*** (M. de *i. e. Beherens*) Histoire de l'Expedition de Trois Vaisseaux: aux Terres Australes en 1721. 2 vols, *calf, gilt.* 12° *La Haye*, 1739

This is an account of the famous expedition of Roggevein, which sailed from the Texel in August, 1721.

113 BACK (*Kapitan* G.) Reise durch Nord-Amerika in den Jahrein, 1833–5, aus dems Englischen von Dr. Karl Andrée. *Frontispiece, boards.* 8° *Leipzig*, 1836

114 BAILEY (M.) Histoire de l'Astronomie Moderne, depuis la Fondation de l'Ecole d'Alexandrie. 2 *volumes, calf.* 4° *Paris*, 1778

115 BAILEY (N.) Antiquities of London and Westmiuster. Third edition. 12° *London*, 1737

116 BAKEWELL (R.) Introduction to Geology. *Plates, cloth.* 8° *London*, 1838

BUCKLE's copy with his bookplate and manuscript notes.

117 BALCARCEL y FORMENTO (DOMINGO) y MALO (Feliz Venancio). LAGRYMAS DE LA PAZ, VERTIDAS EN LAS EXEQUIAS DEL SEÑOR D. FERNANDO DE BORBON, por Excelencia el Justo, VI. Monarchia, de los que con tan esclarecido nombre ilustraron la Monarchia Española: Celebradas en el Metropolitano Templo de esta Imperial Corte de Mexico: *vi* and 98 *pages.* 4° *En Mexico,* 1762

In the same volume are the following: —

TORRES (Ludovicus Antonius de) Laudatio Funebris Ferdinandi VI. Hispaniarum, et Indiarum Regis. Habita Mexici etc. Title and xxii pages.

VALLEJO (Francisco Antonio Fernandez) Oracion Funebre en las Solemnes exequias, que en la muerte de la Augusta, y Cath. Magestad, de el Sr. D. Fernando de Borbon, etc. Se celebraron en Mexico. Mexico, 1760. *3 vols. in* 1. *Vellum. Impressio en Mexico en el Imprenta de el Real,* 1762–60.

THIS EXCESSIVELY RARE AND CURIOUS VOLUME contains 31 emblematical copperplate engravings by ANTONIO MORENO, a Mexican artist. As an American Book of Emblems and Epigrams, as well as a Mexican work of art and poesy, it is deserving of more than a passing notice.

118 BALL (JOHN) A Treatise of Faith. Divided into two Parts: the first shewing the Nature, the second, the Life of Faith. *Calf.* 4° *London,* 1637

119 BANCROFT (Edward) GUIANA, an Essay on the Natural History of Guiana, with an Account of the Religion, Manners and Customs of its Indian Inhabitants. *Calf.* 8° *Lond.* 1769

120 BANCROFT (Edward) Proeve over de Naturlyke Geschiedenis van Guiana. *Half morocco, uncut.* 8° *Utrecht,* 1772

121 BANCROFT (Edward) Proeve over de Naturlyke Geschiedenis van Guiana. *Half morocco uncut.* 8° *Utrecht,* 1782

122 BANCROFT (George) Memorial Address on the Life and Character of Abraham Lincoln. *Cloth.* 8° *Washington,* 1866

123 BAPTIST Mission. Brief narrative of the Baptist Missions in India. *Half red morocco, gilt.* 8° *London,* 1808

124 BARBARITIES of the Enemy, exposed in a Report of the Committee of the House of Representatives, with accompanying Documents. 12° *Worcester,* 1814

125 BARBE de MARBOIS (M.) Histoire de la Louisiane, et de sa Cession aux Etats-Unis de l'Amerique. *Map,* 8° *Paris,* 1829

126 BARCIA (D. ANDRES GONZALES) HISTORIDORES PRIMITIVOS DE LAS INDIAS OCCIDENTALES. Illustrados con eruditas Notas, y copiosas Indices.
3 *vols, fine copy, vellum,* *Folio, Madrid,* 1749

This highly important Collection of the earliest and best Spanish works on the Discovery and History of America, has now become exceedingly rare. The learned and enterprising editor died while the various works were passing through the press. They are all printed as separate and distinct works. Some of the parts were sold separately and others were not cared for. The labor of Collection was posthumous. It is therefore difficult to tell precisely how the several pieces should be arranged, or what constitutes an entirely complete set, as the printing occupied more than twenty years. This set is bound in three volumes, and contains, Vol. I. 1. The Life of Christopher Columbus by his son Ferdinand, retranslated into Spanish from the Italian of Alfonso de Ulloa, 128 pp.; 2. The Second, Third and Fourth Relations of Cortes (the first lost) 156 pp.; 3. Three Relations sent to Cortes by Alvarado and Godoy, pp. 157–173. 4. Historical Summary of the Natural History of the Indies by Oviedo, 57 pp. and

9 pp. Index; 5. The Marquis of Lorito's Apologetical Examination of the voyages, travels and wonderful escapes of Alvar Nuñez Cabeça de Vaca in reply to the criticism of Caspar Plautus, a Monk at Litiz, who wrote under the pseudonym of Honorius Philoponus, *Madrid*, 1736, 50 pp.; 6. Relation of Alvar Nuñez Cabeça de Vaca, 43 + 9 pp.; Commentaries of the same upon his success as Governor of Rio de la Plata, 70 + 2 pp. Vol. II. General History of the West Indies and the Conquest of Mexico, by Francisco Lopez de Gomara, 226 + 30 + 214 + 23 pp. Vol. III. 1. Zarate's Discovery and Conquest of Peru, 4 + 176 + 14 pp.; 2. True Relation of the Conquest of Peru by F. de Xeres, pp. 176–237 + 7 pp.; 3. The History and Discovery of Rio de la Plata by Ulrich Schmeidel, translated from the Latin, which is a translation from the German, 31 + 9 pp.; 4. Argentina and the Conquest of Rio de la Plata, and Parts of Peru, Tecumen, Brasil, &c., by D. Marten del Barco Centenera, a poem in 28 cantos, 107 + 17 pp. 5. Voyage round the World by Simon Perez de Torres, 45 pp.; 6. Abstract of the Relation of a Voyage of some St. Malo Merchants from Moka in Arabia, etc.

127 BARDWELL (H.) Memoir of Rev. Gordon Hall. *Frontispiece, cloth.* 12° *New York*, 1841

128 BARING, (ALEX.) Inquiry into the Causes and Consequences of the Orders in Council; and an Examination of the Conduct of Great Britain towards the Neutral Commerce of America, *uncut.* 8° *New York*, 1808

129 BARLÆUS (CASPAR) Rervm per Octennivm in Brasilia, historia, etc. *Map and plates, vellum,* 8° *Clivis*, 1660

This work contains a vocabulary of CHILIAN and Latin on pp. 474–491.

130 BARLÆUS (CASPAR) Rervm per Octennivm in Brasilia historia, etc. cui acces. G. Pisonis Tractatus de Aeribus etc. in Brasilia. Editio secunda. *Map and plates vellum.* 8° *Clivis*, 1660

131 BARLOW (Joel) The Vision of Columbus: A Poem. *Calf.* 12° *C. Dilly, London*, 1787

132 BARLOW (Joel) Advice to the Privileged orders in the several States of Europe, resulting from the Necessity and propriety of a General Revolution in the Principle of Government. 2d edition. 2 *Parts, half roan.* 8° *Lond.* 1792–1795

133 BARLOW (JOEL) The Political Writings. New Edition. 12° *New York*, 1796

134 BARLOW (JOEL) THE COLUMBIAD, a Poem. *Calf,* *Roy.* 8° *London*, 1809

135 BARNARD (JOHN, *Pastor of a Church in Marblehead*) Sermons on several subjects. *Calf.* 8° *London*, 1727

136 BARNS (R.) Vitæ Romanorum Pontificorum, cum Indice. *Calf.* 8° *Basileæ, n. d.*

137 BARRERE (Pierre) Nouvelle Relation de la France Equinoxiale, contenant la description des côtes de la Guiane; de l'Isle de Cayenne, etc. *Map and plates, calf.* 8° *Paris*, 1743

The Author of this excellent little book resided three years in the Countries which he so accurately describes, having been sent out there by the King as a Doctor of Medicine.

138 BARRINGTON (James) The Possibility of Approaching the North Pole asserted. New Edition, with Appendix, by Col. Beaufoy. *Map, half calf.* 8° *London*, 1818

139 BARROW (*Sir* John) The Life of Richard Earl Howe, K. G., Admiral of the Fleet, *etc.* *Portrait, cloth.* 8° *London*, 1838

140 BARROW (*Sir* John) Life of Admiral George Lord Anson. *Portrait, cloth.* 8° *London,* 1839

141 BARROW (*Sir* John) An Autobiographical Memoir, containing Observations and Reminiscences, at Home and Abroad, from early Life to advanced Age. *Portrait, half calf.* 8° *London,* 1847

142 BARRY (Ed.) El Espiritu del Despotismo. 12° *Filadelfia,* 1822

143 BARTH (H.) TRAVELS AND DISCOVERIES IN NORTH AND CENTRAL AFRICA: being a Journal of an Expedition undertaken under the Auspices of H. B. M's Government in the year 1849–55. *Illustrated with Maps and numerous Engravings.* 3 *vols. cloth,* *thick* 8° *London,* 1857

144 BARTHES AND LOWELL. Catalogue des Livres Français, etc. *Half morocco.* 8° *London,* 1857

145 BARTLETT (J.) Address to the Charlestown Branch of the Washington Benevolent Society. *Uncut.* 8° *Charlestown,* 1813

146 BARTRAM (WILLIAM) TRAVELS through North and South Carolina, Georgia, East and West Florida, the Cherokee Country, etc. *Portrait and Map.* 8° *Phila.* 1791

147 BARTRAM (William) Travels, etc. *Another copy.* 8° *Phila.* 1791

148 BARTRAM (William) Travels through North and South Carolina, Georgia, East and West Florida, etc. *Map and plates, half calf.* 8° *London,* 1792

149 BARTRAM (William) Reizen door Noord-en Zuid-Carolina, Georgia, Oost-en West-Florida; De Landen der Cherokees, der Muscogulges, etc. *Half crimson morocco, uncut.* 8° *Haarlem,* 1794

150 BARTRAM (William) Voyage dans les Parties Sud de l'Amerique Septentionale, Savoir, les Carolines, la Georgie, les Florides, le pays de Cherokees, etc. *Map and plates,* 2 *vols. Calf gilt, fine copy.* 8° *Paris,* 1801

151 BASCOM (*Rev.* Jonathan, *of Orleans*) An Oration delivered Feb. 22, 1800, the day of public Mourning for the Death of General George Washington. *Fine copy, sized paper, uncut, bound in white vellum, by Pratt.* 8° *S. Hall, Boston,* 1800

152 BATTLE of Bunker or Breed's Hill: a Particular Account of, by a Citizen of Boston. *Uncut.* 8° *Boston,* 1825

152* BAXTER (Richard) Poetical Fragments: Heart Improvement with God and It Self. The Concordant Discord of a Broken-healed Heart. Sorrowing-rejoicing, Fearing-hoping, Dying-living, etc. *Third edit.*

16° *London,* 1699, *with additions, etc., London,* 1700

A scarce edition. In the Preface is an allusion to the New England Version of the Psalms, commonly called the Bay Psalms.

153 BEAUMONT (W.) On the Gastric Juice and Physiology of Digestion. 8° *Plattsburgh,* 1833

154 Beckmann (J.) Litteratur der alteren Reisebeschreibungen. *2 vols. half roan.* 8° *Gottingen*, 1807

155 Beecher (H. W.) Life Thoughts. *Cloth*, 12° *Boston*, 1859

156 Beecher (Lyman) Sermon at Woolcot, Con., Sept. 21, 1814, at the Installation of the Rev. John Keyes. *Uncut.* 8° *Andover*, 1805

157 Behme (J.) Concerning the Election of Grace, or of God's Will towards Man, commonly called Predestination. *Calf.* 4° *London*, 1655

158 Behrens (M. de) Histoire de l'Expedition de Trois vaisseaux, envoyés par la Compagnie des Indes Occidentales aux Terres Australes en 1721. 2 *vls in one, cf.* 8° *A la Haye*, 1739

159 Bellamy (J.) Letters and Dialogues, between Theron, Paulinus and Aspasio. *Calf.* 8° *London*, 1761

160 Bellamy (J.) Letters, etc. *Another copy. Calf.* 8° *London*, 1761

161 Bellarminus (R.) Recognitio Librorum Omnium, ab ipso edita. *sm.* 8° *Ingolstadii*, 1608

162 Bellarminus (R.) Descriptio Librorum ab ipso edita. *Half bound.* *sm.* 8° *Ingolstadii*, 1608

163 BELLVM CHRISTIANORVM Principvm, praecipve Gallorvm, contra Saracenos, anno 1088, pro terra sancta gestum: autore Roberto Momacho.
Carolus Verardus de expugnatione regni Granatæ, *etc.*
Christophorus Colom de prima insularum, in mari Indico sitarum lustratione, *etc.*
De legatione regis Aethiopiæ ad Clementem VII. ac Regẽ Portugalliæ, *etc.*
Joan. Baptista Egnatius de origine Turcarum.
Pomponius Lætus de exortu Moamethis.
Fine copy, calf, *folio, Henricus Petrus Basileæ*, 1533

This rare book has hitherto been valued by American Collectors, mainly because it contains an early reprint of the celebrated Letter of Columbus, written from Lisbon, in March, 1493, to Raphael Sanxis, respecting his discovery by a western route of certain Islands of India beyond the Ganges. But the collection of these six documents in one volume has a peculiar appropriateness in exhibiting, in a striking manner, the grand features of the gigantic struggle of seven hundred years between the Christians and Mohammedans. Mohammedanism withstood the Crusades and the subsequent wars, but it yielded after the fall of Granada, when Columbus gave a new world to Christendom, and the Portuguese went forth to explore and Christianize the East.

164 Belknap (Jeremy) The History of New Hampshire. *Map, 3 vols.* 8° *Boston*, 1791–2

165 Belknap (J.) History of New Hampshire. Vol. II. *sheep.* 8° *I. Thomas, Boston*, 1791

166 [Belknap (Jeremy) The Foresters; an American Tale: being a sequel to the History of John Bull, the Clothier, *with a copperplate frontispiece engraved by Semour, primitive sheep.* 12° *I. Thomas and E. T. Andrews, Boston*, 1792

167 BENEZET (Anthony) Historical Account of Guinea and the Slave Trade, with a Representation of the Injustice and Dangerous Tendency of Tolerating Slavery, by Granville Sharp. *Half maroon morocco, uncut.* 12° *London,* 1772

168 BENNET (R. G.) en Van Wijk (J.) Verhandeling over de Nederlandsche ontdekkingen en Amerika, Australië, de Indiën en de Poolanden. *Half morocco, uncut.* 8° *Utrecht,* 1827

169 BENNET AND VAN WIJK. *Another copy, Half calf.* 8° *Utrecht,* 1827

170 BENTHAM (Jeremy) Defence of Usury. 18° *Phila.* 1796

171 BENZONI (GIROLAMO) LA HISTORIA DEL MONDO NVOVO di M. Girolamo Benzoni Milanese. La qval tratta dell' Isole, & Mari nuouamente ritrouate, & delle nuove Città da lui proprio vedute, per acqua & per terra in quattordeci anni. FIRST EDITION, *excessively rare, fine copy. Portrait and many woodcuts.* 8° *Venetia Per Anni* XX [1565]

Benzoni was the first regular European traveller in the New World who published his travels. His journeys occupied him fourteen years. His book is considered one of the best of the original works. The 16 wood-cuts were all reproduced by DeBry in his great work, in 1592.

172 BENZONI (GIROLAMO) LA HISTORIA DEL MONDO NVOVO. La qual tratta delle Isole, & mari nouamente ritrouati, et delle nuove Città da lui proprio Vedute, per acqua & per terra in quattordeci anni. Nouvamente ristampata, et illustrata con la giunta d'alcune cose notabile dell' Isole di Canaria. *Wood-cuts. Fine clean copy. Vellum.* 8° *Venetia,* 1572

173 BENZONI (GIROLAMO) NOVÆ NOVI ORBIS Historiæ, id est Rerum ab Hispanis in India Occidentali hactenus gestarum: Opera Urbani Calvetonis ex Italicis. *Vellum.* 8° *Geneva,* 1586

To this edition is added "De Galorum in Floridam expeditione."

174 BENZONI (GIROLAMO) NOVÆ NOVI ORBIS HISTORIÆ Libri Tres, Urbani Calvetonis opera, Commentariis descripti, Latini facti; adjuncta est, DE GALLORUM IN FLORIDAM EXPEDITIONE, *morocco, gilt, fine copy.* 8° *apud hæredes Eust. Vignon, Genevæ,* 1600

175 BERGOMENSIS (JACOBUS PHILIPPUS) SUPPLEMENTUM SUPPLEMENTI CHRONICARUM, Incip. ab exordio mundi usque in Annum Salutis, 1502. *In the original vellum, fine copy.* *Folio, Venetiis,* 1503

The highest interest and importance attach to this beautiful volume from the fact that it is the earliest book in which there is a full account of the First Voyage of Columbus, after the great discoverer's own letter, in 1493. It passed through many editions, but this is the first in which appears the Chapter *De quatuor permaximis insulis in india extra orbem nuper inventis* [*per Christophorum Columbum.*] Anything printed prior to the first Decade of Peter Martyr, in 1511 is of priceless value in early American History. This edition though alluded to by the learned French Bibliographer, Monsieur Harrisse, is not described by him, that of 1506 being the first recorded by him.

176 BERGOMENSIS (JACOBUS PHILIPPUS) SUPPLEMENTUM CHRONICARUM, AB ORIGINE MUNDI. *Wood-cuts and ornamental capitals.* *Folio, Venetiis,* 1513

A beautiful specimen of early printing, clean and in perfect condition. This edition also contains the early account of the discovery of India by sailing west.

177 BERJEAU (J. PH.) Catalogue Illustré des Livres Xylographiques. *Wood-cuts.* 8° *Londres,* 1865

178 BERKEL (ADRIAN VAN) AMERIKAANISCHE VOYAGIEN Behelzende een Reis na Rio de Berbice gelegen op het vaste Land van Guiana aande Wildekust van America, Mitgaters een andere na de Colonie van Surinamme, &c. *Fine copy with frontispiece and plates. Vellum.* 4° *J. ten Hoorn, Amst.* 1695

179 BERNHARD (HERTOG &c.) Reize naar en door Noord-Amerika. 1825–6. *Plates.* 2 *vols, boards.* 8° *Dordrecht,* 1829

180 BESSER (W. S.) Primitiæ Floræ Galiciæ Austriacæ utriusque. 2 *vols, boards uncut.* 12° *Viennæ,* 1809

181 BEZA (Theodore) Epistolae Theologicæ. Secunda editio. 8° *Genevæ,* 1575

182 BEZERRA e LIMA (Joaó Antonio) Elogio do Padre D. Luiz Caetano de Lima. 4° *Lisboa,* 1759

183 BIBLIA HEBRAICA eorundum Latina interpretatio Xantis Pagnini, reconter Bened. Ariæ Montani, &c. [*The right edit. see* BRUNET, I. 857] *half calf.* *Folio, Plantin, Antv.* 1584

184 BIBLIA HEBRAICA cum notis D. E. Jablonski, *inlaid.* 4 *vols, interleaved, half morocco, fine copy.* *Folio, Berolini,* 1699

185 BIBLIA HEBRAICA, a J. Leusden: recens, a Van der Hooght. *Calf.* *Thick* 8° *Amstelred.* 1705

186 BIBLIA SACRA LATINA. 2 *vols. Calf.* 8° *Rob. Stephani, Lut. Paris.* 1545

187 BIBLIA SACRA LATINA, interprete Sebastiano Castalione. *Fine large copy, but pierced by small worm.* *Folio, Basiliæ,* 1566

188 BIBLIA SACRA LATINA. 2 *vols. Folio,* *Oliv. Rob. Stephani, Paris,* 1557

189 BIBLIA SACRA LATINA, interprete S. Pagnini, *&c. fine copy.* *Folio, Basiliæ,* 1564

190 BIBLIA SACRA LATINA, curâ F. Junii. SCARCE. *Folio, London,* 1593.

191 BIBLIA SACRA quae praeter Antiquae Latinae versionis amend., &c., opera A. Osandri. *Pig skin. Scarce.* *Folio, Tubingen,* 1600

192 BIBLIA SACRA LATINA. . . . Scholiis Tremelio & Junio. SCARCE. *Folio, Hanoviæ,* 1624

193 BIBLIA SACRA LATINA, Vulgatae Editionis, &c. *Folio, Antverpiæ,* 1630

194 BIBLIA SACRA LATINA, cum Comment. JACOBO GORDONO. 3 *vols. fine copy, calf.* SCARCE. *Folio, Paris,* 1632

195 BIBLIA MAGNA COMMENTARIUM litteralium Gagnæi, Esti, et al. edente J. de la Haye. 5 large volumes. *Fine copy, old calf,* SCARCE. *Folio, Paris,* 1643

196 BIBLE (*Auth. version*) Genevan notes, with Common Prayer and Psalms. *Half calf.* *Folio, Amst.* 1708–1711

197 BIBLE. La Sainte Bible, revue sur les textes Hebrewe et Grecis. 4° *Amsterdam*, 1712

198 BIBLE. BIBLIA, DAS IST DIE GANZE HEILIGE SCHRIFT, *etc.* 8° *Philadelphia, zu finden bey Ernst Ludwig Baisch, in der zweyten Strasse nahe bye der Rees-Strasse*, 1775.

So far as known this is the only copy now extant of this edition. It was probably printed at Neutlingen in Germany and sent over to Mr. Baisch in Philadelphia, who printed a new title and issued it among his countrymen in Pennsylvania. Dr. O'Callaghan's description, page 28, was made from this copy.

199 BIBLE. DANIEL, with a brief explication, by Hugh Broughton. *Very scarce.* 4° *Hanaw*, 1607

200 BIBLE. Translated from the Septuagint and the Greek, by Charles Thomson, late Secretary to the Congress of the United States. 4 *vols, calf,* 8° *Philad.* 1808

201 BIBLIOTHECA VETERUM PATRUM . . . Graeco-Latino. Per LaBigne. 2 *vols. Fine copy, calf.* *Folio, Paris*, 1624

This scarce work is a necessary addition to any edition of the Latin Fathers.

202 BIBLIOTHECA CHETHAMENSIS; sive Bibliothecæ publicæ Mancuniensis, ab Humfredo Chetham fundatae. Edidit Joan Radcliffe. 2 *vols half roan, uncut.* 8° *Mancunii*, 1791

203 BIGELOW (TIMOTHY) EULOGY ON WASHINGTON Pronounced before the Masonic Fraternity at the Old South Meeting House, Feb. 11, 1800. *Vellum uncut.* 8° *Boston*, 1800

204 BILLINGS (Joseph) An Account of a Geographical and Astronomical Expedition to the Northern Parts of Russia, in the Years 1785 etc. to 1794. *Map and Plates, calf, fine copy.* 4° *London*, 1802

205 BILSON (THOMAS) The Trve Difference between Christian Svbiection and unchristian Rebellion wherein the Princes Lawful Power and indepriveable Right to beare the Sword are defended against the Popes censures, etc. *Black Letter, half bound.* *thick* 8° *London*, 1586

206 BIRCH (T.) Life of the Hon. Robert Boyle. *Calf.* 8° *London*, 1744

This valuable volume contains several original letters never before published, of the New England Apostle John Eliot.

207 BIRCH (T.) Historical View of the Negotiations between the Courts of England, France and Brussells, from 1592 to 1617. *Calf.* 8° *London*, 1749

208 BIRKBECK (Morris) Notes on a Journey in America, from the Coasts of Virginia to the Territory of Illinois. *Map, half morocco, uncut.* 8° *London*, 1818

209 BIRKBECK (Morris) Notes on a Journey in America from the Coast of Virginia to the Territory of Illinois. 2d edit. *Large Map, half red morocco, uncut.* 8° *London*, 1818

210 BIRKBECK (Morris) Notes on a Journey in America. 4th edit. *London*, 1818. Letters from Illinois. 3d edit. 2 *vols in one. Calf gilt.* 8° *London*, 1818

211 BISCHOFF (J.) History of the Woolen and Worsted Manufactures, and the Natural and Commercial History of Sheep, from the earliest Records. 2 *vols, cloth,* 8° *London,* 1842

212 BISHOP (Abraham) Oration in Wallingford 11th March, 1801, before the Republicans of Connecticut at their General Thanksgiving for the Election of Thomas Jefferson to the Presidency, and of Aaron Burr to the Vice Presidency. *Uncut.* 8° *Anthony Haswell, Bennington,* 1801

213 BISHOP (J. L.) History of American Manufactures, from 1608 to 1860. Vol. I. *Cloth.* 8° *Philadelphia,* 1861

214 BISSELIUS (Joannes é Soc. Jesu) Argonauticon Americanorum, sive Historiae, Periculorum Petri de Victoria ac Sociorum eius Libri XV. 16° *Monachii,* 1648

215 BISSELIUS (Joannes) Argonauticon Americanorum. *Vellum.* 16° *Gedani,* 1698

216 BISSELIUS (J.) Argonauticon Americanorum, sive Historiæ Periculorum Petri de Victoria ac Sociorum ejus. *Vellum.* *Gedani,* 1698

217 BLACKMORE (Sir R.) Creation, a Philosophical Poem. Third edition, *calf,* SCARCE *edition.* 12° *London,* 1695

218 BLADES (WILLIAM) A CATALOGUE OF BOOKS printed by, or ascribed to the Press of William Caxton, in which is included the press-mark of every Copy contained in the Library of the British Museum. *Uncut, fine paper sewed.* 4° *London,* 1865

PRIVATELY PRINTED, only 50 copies. Of which 20 were for the author's friends, 15 for sale in England, and 15 for sale in America. Price, £1.10.0 in London.

219 BLAIR (Hugh) Sentimental Beauties, from his Writings, with Additions by W. H. Reid. *Calf.* 12° *London,* 1809

220 Blair (H.) Sermons. First complete American Edition. *Portrait.* 2 *vols.* 8° *Baltimore,* 1814

221 BLAIZE DE MONTLUC. The Commentaries of Messire Blaize de Montluc Mareschal of France, wherein are describ'd all the Combats, Rencounters, Battels, Sieges, etc., with other signal and remarkable Feats of War. *Portrait, calf,* *Folio, London,* 1674

222 BLIGH (William) Voyage a la Mer du Sud, pour introduire, aux Indes Occidentales, l'Arbre à Pain, et d'autres Plantes utiles; Avec une relation de la Révolte à bord de son Vaisseau, *etc.* Traduit de l'Anglais par F. Soulés. *Maps, half calf.* 8° *Paris,* 1792

223 BLOUNT (CHARLES) THE MISCELLANEOUS WORKS OF. Containing, I. The Oracles of Reason, 1693. II. Anama Mundi: or, the Opinions of the Ancients concerning Man's Soul after this Life, 1679. III. Great is Diana: or, the Original of Priestcraft, 1695. IV. An Appeal from the Country to the City for his Majesty's Person, liberty and property, 1695. V. A Just Vindication of Learning and

Liberty of the Press, 1695. A Dialogue between King William and King James on the Banks of the Boyn, the day before the Battle (in verse), 1695. To which is prefixed the Life of the Author. *In one volume, with separate and collective title-pages; fine copy in blue morocco, contents lettered.* VERY RARE IN THIS STATE. 8° *London*, 1679–1695

This volume is from the library of the late H. T. BUCKLE, bearing his No. 2,623, on his bookplate. On the fly-leaf is carefully pasted, in the handwriting of Buckle, an analysis of the volume, with a biographical sketch, beginning, "Charles Blount was born in 1654, and in 1693 shot himself in consequence of the absolute refusal of his late wife's sister to marry him." Considerable interest attaches to this volume from the fact that it has been charged upon ETHAN ALLEN that his VERMONT BIBLE, or *Oracles of Reason*, printed at Bennington in 1788, was stolen in substance from Blount. It is not charged that Allen ever saw Blount's Oracles, but that among his friends he numbered one Thomas Young, a free-thinking, roving Englishman, who acted as verger to Blount's monuments, but had not the courage or power to book or publish his tenets. In Allen he found a willing disciple, ambitious of literary eminence. Blount believed in God, one and indivisible; in the authenticity of the Scriptures; and in a future state of rewards and punishments; but denied Original Sin. Allen figures up at about the same total.

"Old Ethan once said with significant nod,
Though I hold not with Jesus, I know there's a God;
There's a devil also; you will see him some day,
In a whirlwind of fire take Levi away."

Blount himself is accused of stealing and translating his *Oracles* from a French book called *The Hypothesis of the Præ-Adamites*. Where the anonymous author stole *his* Oracles is not stated. In this volume is a great deal, both by Blount and his editor, about the right and wrong of marrying a deceased wife's sister. He would, she wouldn't. So still arguing from the same monitor within, and believing, that "I myself am King of Me," shot himself; and hence his friendly editor's defence of suicide. All these things and much more, the purchaser of this curious volume, if he finds the thread, may spin out by himself.

224 BLOUNT (THOMAS) Law Dictionary. Second edition. *Half calf.* *Folio, London*, 1691

225 BOEHLEN (J. VAN) REIZ naar de Oost-en Westkust van Zuid-Amerika, Sandwichs-en Philippijnsche Eilanden, China en de Javen 1826–7–8 en 9. *Maps and Plates.* 3 *vols, half green morocco, fine uncut copy.* 8° *Amsterdam*, 1835

226 BOETHIUS (A. M.) Consolationis Philosophiæ Libri V. Anglo-Saxoniæ Redditi ab Alfredo. *Frontispiece. Calf.* 8° *Oxoniæ*, 1698

227 BOHN'S ANTIQUARIAN LIBRARY. Matthew Paris's English History, from 1235 to 1273. Translated by Rev. J. A. Giles. 2 *vols;* Matthew of Westminster's Chronicle, Translated by C. D. Yonge. 2 *vols.* 4 *vols, cloth.* *Post* 8° *London*, 1853

228 BONNET (J. E.) Etats Unis de l'Amerique, a la Fin du XVIIIe Siècle. 2 *vols in* 1, *boards.* 8° *Paris, n. d.*

229 BOOK OF COMMON PRAYER, and administration of the Sacraments etc. according to the use of the Protestant Episcopal Church of the United States of America: together with the Psalter, or Psalms of David. By Direction of the General Convention. 12° *New York, by Hugh Gaine*, 1793

Attached to this edition is "The Whole Book of Psalms in Metre; with Hymns suited to the Feasts and Fasts of the Church and other Occasions of Public Worship. 12° *Hugh Gaine, New York*, 1793

230 BOOKSELLER. Three hundred and fifty years' Retrospection of an Old Bookseller; containing an Account of the Origin and progress of Printing, type-founding, and Engraving, etc. *Portrait* of John Dunton, born 1659 — died 1733.
Half calf. 8° *Cork, for the author*, 1835

231 B[oss] (V. D.) LEBEN DER SEE-HELDEN . . angefangen mit Cristoforo Colombo. Entdechem der Newen Welt etc.
Vellum. 4° *Nuremberg*, 1681

A valuable book upon the early voyages of Columbus, Vespucci, Magellan, DaGama, d'Almeida, Albuquerque, Andrea Dorea, Drake, Cavendish, the Dutch Voyagers, etc. etc., with many portraits, plates, and maps.

232 BOSSU (M.) Nouveaux Voyages aux Indes Occidentales, contenant une Relation des differens Peuples qui habitent les environs du grand Fleuve Saint Louis appelé vulgairement le Mississippi. *Plates.* 2 *vols in* 1. *Half calf.* 8° *Paris*, 1768

233 BOSSU (M.) Nieuwe Reizen naer Noord-Amerika. *Frontispieces.* 2 *vols, half blue morocco, uncut.* 12° *Amsterdam*, 1769

234 BOSSU (M.) Travels through that part of North America formerly called Louisiana. Translated by J. R. Forster.
2 *vols, calf.* 8° *London*, 1771

235 BORDA (Andreas de) PRACTICA DE CONFESSORES DE MONJAS, en que se explican los quatro Votos de Obediencia, Pobreza. Casstidad, y Clausura por modo de Decalogo. *Fine copy, vellum. Folios* 39-52 *wormed.*
8° *Mexico, por Francisco de Ribera Calderon*, 1708

236 BORDLEY FAMILY of Maryland. Biographical Sketches of, by Mrs. E. Bordley Gibson. Part I. 8° *Philadelphia*, 1865

237 BOSMAN (W.) DESCRIPTION OF THE COAST OF GUINEA, divided into the Gold, the Slave, and the Ivory Coasts. *Map and Engravings. Calf.* 8° *London*, 1721

238 BOSTON DIRECTORY (The) containing the Names of the Inhabitants, their occupations, places of Business, and Dwelling-houses. Also a List of the Civil Government of Massachusetts, and of the Town Officers, Public Offices, Banks, etc. Likewise a Table of Duties on Stamped Paper, Vellum, etc. (conformably to the Stamp Act, passed July 6, '97.) And a List of all the Stages that run from Boston, with the places at which they put up, etc., to which is prefixed a General Description of Boston. Ornamented with a Plan of the Town from actual survey. *Half calf, fine clean copy, plan missing.*
12° *Printed by Rhoades & Laughton, for John West*, 1798

From this small book, in which the compiler has justly shown great pride in his subject, we learn that BOSTON, the capital of the State of Massachusetts, having 18,038 inhabitants in 1790, with Hull, Chelsea, and Hingham constitutes the County of Suffolk. It has 97 streets, 36 lanes, 26 alleys, besides 18 courts, etc., most of them irregular, "and not very convenient." State Street, however, is very spacious, "and being on a line with Long Wharf, where strangers usually land, exhibits a flattering idea of the town." The foreign and domestic trade of Boston is very considerable, "to support which there are three Banks," viz: The *Union*, discount day Tuesday; the *Massachusetts*, discount day Monday; and the *U. S. Branch*, discount days Mondays *and* Thursdays. "The principal manufactures consist of rum, loaf sugar, beer, sail-cloth, cordage, wool and cotton cards, playing cards, pot and pearl ashes, paper hangings, hats, plate, glass, tobacco, and chocolate. There are 30 distilleries, 2 breweries, 8 sugar-houses, and eleven ropewalks." The intercourse with the country is considerable, and increasing. Already "on the great road between this and New Haven, distant 164 miles," to say nothing of the considerable portions of the world beyond, there are now 20 coaches and 100 horses employed. "Attempts have been made to change the government of the Town from its present form to that of a city; but this measure, not according with the Democratic spirit of the people, has as yet failed." By a MS. note of a former possessor we learn that "SAMUEL ADAMS, retailer, etc., Elliot Street, is Town Crier," with his office at 71 Newbury Street, while from page 136 we learn that Abraham Adams, leather-dresser and breeches-maker, 72 Newbury Street is "*Informer of Deer*," while Daniel Bell and George Hamlin are the *Hogreeves*. The names of the *Fence Viewers*, the *Cullers of Dry Fish*, the *Surveyors of Hemp*, and other Public Officers are all given on pp. 135–137. On pp. 146–8 is a full list of the stage coaches to and from the town, from which it is apparent that facilities of travel are not slight. Mail coaches for New York three times a week, through in three days and one hour. To Albany twice a week, through in three days and six hours. Coaches to Providence, Salem, Marblehead, Dedham, Quincy, Dorchester and Milton, Medford and Watertown, *every* day (Sundays excepted), while to Cambridge and Roxbury go two stages every day.

239 BOSTON DIRECTORY for the years 1821, 1822, 1823, 1826, 1827, 1829, 1830, 1831, 1833, 1834, 1835, 1836, 1837, 1838, 1839, 1840, 1841, 1842, 1844 and 1845. (All with the maps except 1823, 1841, and 1845.) 20 *vols.* 12° *Boston*, 1821–45

240 BOSTON. The Boston Almanac for the years 1839 to 1851. By S. N. Dickinson. 13 *vols, cloth.* 16° *Boston*, 1839–51

241 BOSTON. The Boston Almanac for 1844, 1845, 1847, 1849, 1859, and 1862. 6 *vols, cloth.* 16°

242 BOSTON. RECEIPTS AND EXPENDITURES of the City of Boston from 1819 to 1856 inclusive. 6 *vols*, AN EXCESSIVELY RARE COLLECTION, *half morocco uncut.* 8° *Boston.*

243 BOSTON ORATIONS, Delivered at the Request of the Inhabitants to Commemorate the Evening of the Fifth of March, 1770. 12° *Printed by Peter Edes, Boston.*

244 BOSWELL (James) Life of Dr. Samuel Johnson, with Notes and Biographical Illustrations, by Malone. *Cloth.* 12° *Whittingham, Cheswick*, 1830

Complete in one pocket volume, in pearl type; a beautiful edition, now become scarce.

245 BOUDINOT (Elias) A Star in the West; or, a humble Attempt to discover the long-lost Ten Tribes of Israel. *Fine copy. Calf.* 8° *D. Fenton, Trenton, N. J.*, 1816

246 BOUGAINVILLE (M. de) Voyage autour du Monde, en 1766–9. 2 *vols in* 1, *calf.* 12° *Neuchatel*, 1773

247 BOULTON (Thomas) The Voyage, a Poem in seven Parts: Containing Reflections upon A Farewell, Calm, Moderate Breezes, Hard Gale, Shipwreck, Deliverance and Return. Parts 1 to 6. 8° *Printed for the author, Boston*, 1773

Dedicated to Governor Wanton, of Rhode Island. *Scarce.*

248 BOUTON (N.) Two Sermons in Commemoration of the Organizing of the First Church in Concord, N. H., and the settlement of the first Minister, Nov. 18, 1730. *Map.* 8° *Concord*, 1831

249 BOUQUET (HENRY) AN HISTORICAL ACCOUNT OF THE EXPEDITION AGAINST THE OHIO INDIANS in the year 1764. Including the Transactions with the Indians relative to the delivery of their Prisoners, with an account of the Battle of Bushy-Run, etc. *Very fine large and clean copy, with the three maps, and with the two copper-plates after Benj. West.* 4° *London*, 1766

250 BOWDITCH (H. J.) Consumption in New England; or, Locality one of its chief Causes. *Half roan.* 8° *Boston*, 1862

251 BOWDLER (Thomas) Life and Character of Lieut. Gen. Villettes, with Letters written in France in 1814. Postscript to the Letters written in France in 1814. *Portrait, half calf.* 8° *London*, 1815

252 BOWMAN'S Sermon, Preach'd at Wakefield, versify'd. By C. H. Crambo. 8° *Dublin*, 1731

253 BRACKENRIDGE (H. M.) Recollections of Persons and Places in the West. *Boards.* 8° *Philadelphia, n. d.*

254 BRACKENRIDGE (H. H.) Modern Chivalry. *2 vols.* 18° *Phila.* 1804

255 BRACKENRIDGE (H. M.) Views of Louisiana. 12° *Baltimore*, 1817

256 BRACKENRIDGE (H. M.) History of the Late War between United States and Great Britain, containing a minute account of the various Military and Naval Operations. 4th edition, revised. *Half black morocco, gilt.* 12° *Baltimore*, 1818

257 BRADBURY (John, *F. L. S. London*) Travels in the Interior of North America, 1809–1811. *Half rus.* 8° *Liverpool*, 1817

258 BRADLEY (Mrs. Eliza) An authentic Narrative of the Shipwreck and Sufferings of, *with large* COLORED *wood-cut.* 8° *G. Clark, Boston*, 1821

259 BRAND (Gerhard) Leben und Thaten des Fürcreflichen und Sonderbahren See-Helden Herrn-Michaelis de Ruiter, Admirael, etc. *Many beautiful plates. Vellum.* *Folio, Amsterdam*, 1687

This volume contains much incidentally pertaining to the East and West Indies.

260 BRASIL. De Instellinge van de Generale Compagnie ghemaeckt in Portugael na Brasil, toelatinge, met de Acte van Sijn Maiesteyt, 10 Meert, 1649. SCARCE. [See Asher N°. 257.] *Fine copy, uncut, polished calf by Francis Bedford.* 4° *Amsterdam* [1649]

261 BRATTLE (MAJ. GEN. W.) Two printed broadsides or posters, the one a letter to Gen. Gage, the Commander-in-Chief at Boston, dated Cambridge, Aug. 20, 1774, concerning Capt. Minot's Minute Men at Concord, the removing of the stocks of Powder, etc.; and the other. A Letter to the Public, dated Boston, Sept. 2, 1774, explaining his relations and correspondence with Gen. Gage, and alluding to the threatenings he had received; his banishment from his own home, etc.

EXCESSIVELY SCARCE WAIFS. *Folded and bound together in a 4° volume in white vellum, by Pratt.* 4° *Boston,* 1774

262 BRAY (Thomas D. D.) An Essay towards promoting knowledge in all Parts of his Majesty's Dominions, at Home and Abroad [America]. *Vellum by Pratt.* 4° *Boston,* 1707

263 BRIDGEWATER Centennial Celebration, June 3, 1856. 8° *Boston,* 1856

264 BRIGGS (William) Military History of Europe, etc., from the Commencement of the War with Spain, 1739, to the Treaty of Aix la Chapelle, 1748. *Calf.* 8° *London,* 1755

Contains much about America.

265 BRISSOT DE WARVILLE (J. P.) New Travels in the United States of America, performed 1788. Translated from the French. *Half calf.* 8° *London,* 1792

266 BRISSOT (WARVILLE J. P.) Niewe Reize in de Vereeingde Staaten van Noord-Amerika. 3 *vols, half brown morocco, uncut; fine copy.* 8° *Amsterdam, n. d.*

267 BRITAIN. Present State of Great Britain and America. *Calf.* 8° *London,* 1767

268 BRITANNIA TRIUMPHANT; or, an Account of the Sea-Fights and Victories of the English Nation under the following Commanders, viz: Earl of Cumberland, Drake, Raleigh, Prince Rupert, Albemarle, York, Howe, Osborn, Keppel, Hawke, Anson, Cornish, Pocock, Rooke, Boscawen, Draper, Moore, and Wolfe. To which is prefixed a large Introduction, containing a History of Navigation, etc. By a Society of Naval Gentlemen. 2d edit. *Calf, scarce.* 8° *R. James, Lond.* 1776

This important book, relating chiefly to affairs in America, deserves to be better known in this country. It contains portraits of the Earl of Cumberland, Drake, Raleigh, Howe, and Boscawen.

269 BRITANNISCHE RYK IN AMERIKA. Vervattende Terre-Neuf, Niew-Schotlandt, Niew-Engelandt, Niew-York, Niew-Jersey, Pensylvanie, Marilandt, Virginie, Carolina en Hudsons-Bai. *Maps, calf.* 4° *Amsterdam,* 1721

270 BRITISH EMPIRE. Political Essays concerning the Present State of the British Empire. *Calf.* 4° *London,* 1772

Essay V. pp. 226–479 is on the British Colonies, chiefly in America.

271 BRITISH MUSEUM. A List of the Books of Reference in the Reading Room of the British Museum. *Cloth.* 8° *Lond.* 1859

This catalogue, containing about 30,000 volumes of the books most used, or oftenest called for, in the British Museum, and hence placed in the Reading Room where every reader may help himself, is perhaps one of the best guides there is for the formation of large public libraries.

272 BRODHEAD (John R.) Final Report of the Agent appointed by the Governor of New York to procure and transcribe documents in Europe, relative to the Colonial History of N. York, with Calendars of the London, Holland, and Paris Document. *Scarce. Sheep.* 8° *Albany,* 1845

273 BRODHEAD (J. R.) History of the State of New York. First Period, 1609–1664. *Cloth.* 8° *London,* 1853

274 BROMLEY (Thomas) The Way to the Sabbath of Rest, or the Soul's Progress in the Work of the New Birth.
Calf. 8° *Germantown, Penn.* 1759

275 BRONSON (A.) Plain Exhibition of Methodist Episcopacy.
Cloth. 12° *Burlington,* 1844

276 BROWN (C.) Narrative of the Expedition to South America, in 1817. *Half maroon morocco gilt,* 8° *Lond.* 1819

277 BROWN (J.) View of the Figures, and Explication of the Metaphors in Scripture. First American edition. 12° *Middlebury, Vt.* 1812

278 BROWN (W.) CHANCERY REPORTS; copious Notes and References to American and later English Cases, by C. Perkins. 4 *vols.* 8° *Boston,* 1844

279 BUCANIERS. The History of the Bucaniers of America.
Fine copy, calf extra. 16° *London,* 1810

280 BUENOS-AYRES. A Relation of Mr. R. M's Voyage to Buenos Ayres. *Map, calf.* 12° *London,* 1716

281 BULKELEY (PETER, *of Concord in N. E.*) THE GOSPEL COVENANT; or the Covenant of Grace opened. *Fine copy, calf.* 4° *M. S. for Benjamin Allen, London,* 1646

282 BUNYAN (John) Solomon's Temple Spiritualized.
12° *Hartford,* 1802

283 BUNYAN (John) Heart's Ease in Heart Trouble. Or a Sovereign Remedy against all Trouble of Heart, that Christ's Disciples are subject to. 16° *W. Fessenden, Brattleb.* 1813

284 BUNYAN (John) The Visions of John Bunyan; being his last Remains; giving an account of the Glories of Heaven, the Terrors of Hell, and of the World to Come. *Clean copy.* 12° *Thomas Hubbard, Norwich, (Con.)* 1795

285 BURNS (Robert) Poems chiefly in the Scottish Dialect. 2 *volumes in* 1. *A scarce edition,* 12° *W. Magee, Belfast,* 1793

286 BURCHARD (Rev. J.) Sermons, Addresses and Exhortations, with Appendix, by C. G. Eastman.
2 *copies.* 12° *Burlington,* 1836

287 BURCHETT (J.) Memoirs of Transactions at Sea, during the War with France, 1688–97. *Calf.* 8° *London,* 1703

288 BURGOYNE (LIEUT. GEN. JOHN) A STATE OF THE EXPEDITION FROM CANADA, as laid before the House of Commons; with a Collection of authentic Documents. *Maps, half calf.* 4° *London,* 1780

Fine copy with all the Maps.

289 BURGOYNE (LIEUT. GEN. John) Letter from, to his Constituents upon his late Resignation; with the Correspondences relative to his Return to America. 5th edition.
8° *London,* 1779

290 BURKE (Edmund) Account of the European Settlements in America. Map. 2 *volumes, calf.* 8° *London,* 1757

291 BURKE (E.) Account etc., 2d Edition, 2 *volumes, calf.* 8° *London,* 1758

292 BURKE (E.) Account etc., 4th Edition, 2 *volumes, calf.* 8° *London,* 1765

293 BURKE (E.) Account etc., New Edition, 2 *volumes, calf.* 8° *London,* 1766

294 BURKE (E.) Account etc., 5th Edition, 2 *volumes, calf.* 8° *London,* 1770

295 BURKE (E.) Account etc., 6th Edition, 2 *volumes, calf.* 8° *London,* 1777

296 BURK (William) Histoire des Colonies Européennes dans l'Amerique. 2 *vols in* 1. *Calf.* 8° *Paris,* 1767

297 BURNEY (J.) Chronological History of the Discoveries in the South Sea, or Pacific Ocean. *Maps. Calf.* 4° *London,* 1803

298 BURNEY (W.) The British Neptune. A History of the Achievements of the Royal Navy. *Plates.* 12° *London,* 1807

299 BUSBY (Thomas) Concert Room and Orchestra Anecdotes of Music and Musicians, Ancient and Modern. With Engravings. 3 *vols, calf.* 12° *London,* 1825

300 BUTLER (B. F.) Address at West Point, on the Military Profession of the Western States. 8° *New York.* 1839

301 BUTLER (C.) History of Groton, including Pepperell and Shirley, from the first Grant in 1655, with Appendices. *Cloth.* 8° *Boston,* 1848

302 BUTLER (G.) Fortune's Foot-Ball, or the Adventures of Mercutio. 2 *vols in* 1, SCARCE. 12° *Harrisburgh,* 1797

303 BYRON (John) The Narrative of the Expedition round the world, containing an account of the distresses suffered on the coast of Patagonia, 1740–1746. Also the Loss of the Wager. Written by himself; frontispiece. 8° *London,* 1768
Voyage round the World, in the ship *Dolphin,* Com. Byron, with Description of the Straits of Magellan, and the Patagonians. By an Officer on Board. *Portraits.* 2 *vols in* 1. *Calf.* 8° *London,* 1767

304 BYRON (John) Narrative, containing an Account of the great Distresses suffered by Himself and Companions on the Coast of Patagonia, 1740–6, etc. Second edit. *Calf.* 8° *Lond.* 1768

305 CABINET Annual Register, and Historical, Political, Biographical, and Miscellaneous Chronicle. *Cloth.* 12° *London,* 1833

306 CABRERA (P. T.) RUINS OF AN ANCIENT CITY, discovered near Palenque in Guatemala, Spanish America; Translated from the original Manuscript of Capt. Don Antonio Del Rio; followed by Teatro Critico Americano, or a Critical Research into the History of the Americans. *Half mor.* 4° *Lond.* 1822

307 CAINES (George) An Enquiry into the Law Merchant of the United States, or Lex Mercatoria Americana.
Calf. 8° *New York*, 1802

308 CALAMY (E.) An Elegant and Learned Discourse of the Light of Nature; with severall other Treaties.
Calf. 4° *London*, 1654

309 CALCAGNINUS CŒLIUS. OPERA, cum Indicæ, *in the original Gothic binding.* *Folio*, *Froben*, *Basileæ*, 1544

This important work consists of his Letters, Judicium Vocalium, Treatise on Egyptian Affairs, Essays on Cicero's Offices, de perenni Motu Terræ, and others.

310 CALIFORNIA. NOTICIA DE LA CALIFORNIA, y de su Conquista Temporal y Espiritual hasta el Tiempo presente; sacada de la Historia Manuscrita formada en Mexico año de 1739, por el Padro Miguel Venegas. *Maps and plates.* 3 *vols, calf.* 4° *Madrid*, 1757

311 CALIFORNIA. Geographical Memoir upon Upper California. By John Charles Fremont. 8° *Washington*, 1848

312 CALIFORNIA. Report of the Debates in the Convention of California, on the Formation of the State Constitution. By J. Ross Browne, 1849. 8° *Washington*, 1850

313 CALIFORNIA State Library. Catalogue of the California State Library. By W. C. Stratton. *Half calf.* 8° *Sacramento*, 1866

314 CAMDEN SOCIETY PUBLICATIONS. 26 *vols, cloth.* 4° *London*, 1839–49

PLUMPTON CORRESPONDENCE. A Series of Letters, chiefly Domestick, written in the Reigns of Edward IV., Richard III., Henry VII., and Henry VIII. Edited by Thomas Stapleton; with Notices Historical and Biographical, 1839.

ANNALS OF THE FIRST FOUR YEARS OF THE REIGN OF QUEEN ELIZABETH. By Sir John Hayward, Knt. Edited from a Manuscript in the Harleian Collection, by John Bruce, 1840.

ECCLESIASTICAL DOCUMENTS: viz. I. A Brief History of the Bishopric of Somerset from its first Foundation to 1174. II. Charters from the Library of Dr. Fox Macro. Now first published by the Rev. Joseph Hunter, 1840.

SPECULI BRITANNIÆ PARS; An Historical and Geographical Description of the County of Essex, by John Norden, 1594. Edited from the Original Manuscript, by Sir H. Ellis, 1840.

KEMP'S NINE DAIES WONDER; Performed in a Daunce from London to Norwich. With Introduction and Notes, by Rev. Alex. Dyce, 1840.

THE EGERTON PAPERS. A Collection of Public and Private Documents chiefly illustrative of the Times of Elizabeth and James I., from the Original Manuscript. Edited by J. Payne Collyer, 1840.

NARRATIVES ILLUSTRATIVE OF THE CONTESTS IN IRELAND in 1641 and 1690. Edited by T. Crofton Croker, 1841.

CHRONICLE OF WILLIAM DE RISHANGER of the Barons' Wars. The Miracles of Simon de Montfort. Edited from Manuscripts in the Cottonian Library, by J. O. Halliwell, 1840.

SECOND BOOK OF THE TRAVELS OF NICANDER NUCIUS, of Corcyra. Edited from the Original Greek Manuscript, with English Translation, by Rev. J. A. Cramer. 1841.

THREE EARLY ENGLISH METRICAL ROMANCES, with an Introduction and Glossary. Edited by John Robson, 1842.

PRIVATE DIARY OF MR. JOHN DEE, and the Catalogue of his Library of Manuscripts. Edited from the Original Manuscripts by J. O. Halliwell, 1842.

AN APOLOGY FOR LOLLARD DOCTRINES, attributed to Wicliffe. Now first printed from a Manuscript in the Library of Trinity College, Dublin, with Introduction and Notes, by J. Henthorn Todd, D.D., 1842.

Rutland Papers. Original Documents Illustrative of the Times of Henry VII. and VIII., from the Private Archives of the Duke of Rutland. By W. Jerdan, 1842.

Diary of Dr. Thomas Cartwright, Bishop of Chester. From the Original MS. in the possession of the Rev. Joseph Hunter, 1843.

Original Letters of Eminent Literary Men of the Sixteenth, Seventeenth, and Eighteenth Centuries. With Notes and Illustrations, by Sir H. Ellis, 1843.

Three Chapters of Letters relating to the Suppression of Monasteries. Edited from the Originals in the British Museum, by Thos. Wright, 1843.

Correspondence of Robert Dudley, Earl of Leycester, during his Government of the Low Countries in the years 1585-6. Edited by J. Bruce, 1844.

The French Chronicle of London. Croniques de London depuis l'an 44. Hen. III. jusqu'a l'an 17 Edw. III. Edited from a MS. in the Cottonian Library, by G. J. Aungier, 1844.

Three Books of Polydore Vergil's English History, comprising the Reigns of Henry VI., Edward IV., and Richard III. Edited by Sir H. Ellis, 1844.

The Thornton Romances. The Early English Metrical Romances of Perceval, Isumbras, Eglamour, and Degravant. Edited from MSS. at Lincoln and Cambridge, by J. O. Halliwell, 1844.

Verney Papers. Notes of the Proceedings of the Long Parliament, temp. Charles I., from Original Memoranda taken in the House by Sir Ralph Verney. Edited by J. Bruce, 1845.

Letters from James, Earl of Perth, to his Sister, the Countess of Errol, etc. Edited by W. Jerdan, 1845.

De Antiquis Legibus Liber. Cronica Maiorum et Vicecomitum Londoniarum, 1178 ad annum 1274, cum Appendice, curante Thomª Stapleton, 1846.

Polydore Vergil's English History. Vol. I. containing the first eight Books comprising the Period prior to the Norman Conquest. Edited by Sir H. Ellis, 1846.

The Camden Miscellany. Volume the First, 1847. I. Register and Chronicle of the Abbey of Aberconway. II. Chronicle of the Rebellion in Lincolnshire, 1470. III. Bull of Pope Innocent VIII. on the Marriage of Henry VIII. with Elizabeth of York. IV. Journal of the Siege of Rouen, 1591, etc.

Certaine Considerations upon the Government of England. By Sir Roger Twysden Knt. Edited from the unpublished Manuscript, by J. M. Kemble, 1849.

315 Camden (William) Annales Rerum Anglicarum et Hibernicarvm. *Vellum.* *Thick* 8° *Elzevir, Lugd. Batav.* 1625

316 Camerarius (J.) Commentarii utriusque Linguæ. *Calf.* *Folio, Basileæ,* 1551

317 Campbell (W. W.) Annals of Tryon County; or the Border Warfare of New York, during the Revolution. *Boards.* 8° *New York,* 1833

318 Campe (J. H.) Pizarro or the Conquest of Peru. New Edit., trans. by E. Helme. *Half roan.* 12° *London,* 1826

319 Canada. Debates of the House of Commons in the year 1774 on the Canada Bill. *Map, cloth, uncut.* 8° *London,* 1839

320 Canadian Freeholder (The) Showing the Sentiments of the Bulk of the Freeholders of Canada concerning the late Quebec-Act, with some remarks on the Boston-Charter-Act &c. 3 *vols,* (*vol.* 3 *very rare*) *half calf.* 8° *London,* 1777-9

321 Cancelada (Juan Lopez) Guia de varias Curiosidades que comprehenden los Sucesos Memorables del Presente Siglo. *Fine copy, calf.* 16° *Mexico,* 1808

With Portrait of Prince Ferdinand, engraved by *Larren, and with several pages of statistics and tables engraved on copper.*

322 Candid and Impartial Considerations on the Nature of the Sugar Trade. *Half morocco.* 8° *London,* 1763

323 CANDID Examination of the Mutual Claims of Great Britain and the Colonies, with a Plan of Accommodation on Constitutional Principles.
Half morocco. 8° *James Rivington, New York,* 1775

324 CANDIDUS. Plain Truth to the Inhabitants of America, containing Remarks on a late Pamphlet entitled Common Sense.
Half roan. 8° *London,* 1776

325 CANOVAI (STANISLAO) ELOGIO DI AMERIGO VESPUCCI che riporto il premio dalla Accademia di Cortona nel di 15 Ottobre 1788. Con una Dissertazione Giustificativa di questo celebre Navigatore. *Half morocco.* 4° *Firenze,* 1790

This book passed through four editions, with many changes and alterations, and was the cause of a vast amount of research and discussion relative to the earliest discoveries in America, and by many authors. The claims of Canovai in behalf of Vespucci were vehemently opposed.

326 CANOVAI (STANISLAO) Elogio di Amerigo Vespucci, 4th Edit.
Fine Copy. Half gr. morocco gilt, uncut. 8° *Firenz.* 1798

327 CAPEL (D.) Vorstellungen des Norden, oder Bericht von einigen Nordländern, und absonderlich von dem so genandten Grünlande, etc. *Hamburg,* 1675.—Ein kurtzer Discours von der Schiff-Fahrt by dem Nord-Pol nach Japan, China, und so weiter, *with a copperplate map of the surroundings of the North Pole. 2 vols in 1, fine copies in white vellum, by Pratt. Scarce in this condition.* 4° *Hamburg,* 1676

This important work is divided into two books the first in 11 and the second in five chapters. Book I. gives an account of all that is known of voyages towards the North Pole; Mercator's opinion; that of Isaac Pontanus; the voyages of the Hollanders from Amsterdam 1594–1609; Spitzbergen; and ch. 11, the voyages of Captains Winwood, and of Henry Hudson westward to America. Book II. treats of the voyages of the Zeni, of Dietman Blefkens, 1563, of Greenland, with an abstract of H. Megisser's valuable book of 1613, and G. N. Schurtz's Narrative.

328 CARDENAS y CANO (GABRIEL de) [*i. e.* ANDRES GONZALES BARCIA] Ensayo Cronologico, para la Historia General de la Florida. *Vellum.* *Folio, Madrid,* 1723

329 CAREY (H. C.) and J. Lea. The Geography, History, and Statistics of America and the West Indies. *Map and plates, uncut, half cloth.* 8° *London,* [1824]

330 CARLI (L. *Comte*) LETTRES AMERICAINES; pour servir de suite aux Memoires de D. Ulloa. 2 *vols.* 8° *Paris,* 1788

331 CARLI. Another copy. 2 *vols, half blue morocco, uncut.* 8° *Paris,* 1788

332 CARROLL (*Abp.*) An Address to the Roman Catholics of the United States of America, *and other tracts in* 1 *vol.*
Half calf. 8° *Annapolis printed, Worcester reprinted,* 1785

333 CARTHAGENA. An Account of the Expedition to Carthagena with Explanatory Notes and Observations [by Dr. Smollet.]
Calf. 8° *London,* 1743

334 Carthagena. An Account of the Expedition to Carthagena.
Half roan. 8° *London,* 1743

335 CARTHAGENA. Original Papers relating to the Expedition to Carthagena. *Half roan.* 8° *London,* 1744

336 CARTHAGENA. 4 *tracts in* 1 *vol.* *Calf.* 8°
An Account of the Expedition to Carthagena. *London*, 1743
Original Papers relating to the Expedition to Carthagena. *London*, 1744
Original Papers relating to the Expedition to Cuba. *London*, 1744
Original Papers relating to the Expedition to Panama. *London*, 1744

337 CARTILLA Y DOCTRINA ESPIRITUAL, para la crianza, y educacion de los Novicios, que tomaren el habito en la Orden de N. P. S. Francisco: En la qual brevemente se les enseña lo que deben hacer, conforme à la Doctrina de N. Serafico Dr. San Buenaventura. Reimprime se à solicitud del R. P. Fray Juan Bautista Dosal, Padre de S. Joseph de Yucatan etc. *Fine copy, vellum.* 8° *Felipe de Zuniga, Mexico*, 1775

338 CARVER (Jonathan) Travels though the Interior parts of North America, 1766–1768, 2d edit. *Fine copy.* LARGE PAPER, *maps and plates.* 8° *London*, 1779

339 CARVER (J.) Travels through the Interior Parts of North America, in the years 1766–1767, and 1768. With Copper-plates. *Calf, gilt.* 8° *Dublin*, 1779

340 CARVER (J.) Travels through the Interior Parts of North America 1766–1768. *Calf.* 8° *Dublin*, 1779

341 CARVER (JONATHAN) Three Years' Travels through the Interior Parts of North America, *with extra map and plates inserted from Cooke's Voyages. Half calf.* 8° *Edinburgh*, 1798

342 CARVER (JONATHAN) REIZE door de Binnenlanden van Noord-Amerika . . . . naar den Derden Druk uit het Engelsch door J. D. Pasteur. *Maps and colored plates.* 2 *vols, half calf.* 8° *Leyden*, 1796

343 CASAUBON (I.) Ad Polybii Hist. Librum Primum Commentarii. *Calf.* 4° *Parisiis*, 1617

344 CASAUX (Marques de) Considerations sur quelques Parties du Mechanisme. *Tree-calf.* 8° *Londres*, 1785

345 CASCALES (FR.) Discursos Historicos de Murcia. *Engraved Title.* SCARCE. *Half calf. Many plates of arms of Families in Spain.* *Folio, Murcia*, 1621

346 CASE (A) decided in the Supreme Court of the United States in Feb. 1793 "Whether a State be liable to be sued by a Private Citizen of Another State." *Half roan, uncut.* 8° *Philadelphia*, 1793

347 CASE Decided in the Supreme Court of the United States Feb. 1793, "Whether a State be liable to be Sued by a Private Citizen of another State." *Uncut.* 8° *Boston*, 1793

348 CASKET (The) A Miscellany consisting of Unpublished Poems. *Neat half calf, uncut.* 8° *Murray, London*, 1829

349 CASPIPINA'S Letters; containing Observations on a variety of Subjects, to which is added the Life and Character of Wm. Penn. 2 *vols, half calf.* 12° *Bath*, 1777

350 CASPIPINA'S Letters; on a variety of Subjects, to which is added, the Life of Wm. Penn. 2 *vols, tree calf.* 12° *Bath*, 1787
By the Rev. Mr. Duché the first Chaplain to the Congress.

351 CASSELL (JOH. PHIL. *of Bremen*) OBSERVATIO HISTORICA de Frisonum Navigatione fortuita in Americam Sec. XI. facta. Ob solennium lustrationem Ludi Ref. Fridericeani et Orationes in ea habendas, edita, a Joh. Phil. Cassell, R.
Uncut. 4° *J. C. Seigeler, Magdeburge*, 1741

The author in this rare tract discusses the statements of Adam of Bremen respecting the discovery of America by the Danes, in the eleventh century. Dr. Kohl has recently revived the fables of this mediæval author, and built up a goodly historical structure on their foundation.

352 CASTLE BUILDERS (The): or the History of William Stephens of the Isle of Wight, Esq., lately deceased. A Political Novel. *Scarce, calf.* 8° *London*, 1759

This William Stephens resided sixteen years in Georgia, and was the first Secretary of that Colony and keeper of its BLACK BOOK, a list of the disreputable characters that were induced to become voluntary and involuntary emigrants on the pious founding of that Colony. Into this book were posted their antecedents, and their actions and behaviour for three years after landing in Georgia. This Black Book still exists in England and contains a mine of valuable American genealogical materials. Few families in this country can boast of genealogical trees of harder wood; or can trace more minute historical and genealogical particulars of their English ancestors than those who have descended from some of the early emigrants to Georgia, whose names were so carefully recorded by William Stephens, the First Historian of that Colony. These volumes with other early records of Georgia, filling 21 folio volumes, were once, under promise of secrecy, deposited with the writer for four hours, and offered for £500. He offered £300 and lost the prize. When by death the obligation of secrecy was removed he invited the distinguished baronet who now possesses the collection, to breakfast, and communicated to him the circumstances. Within three days the collection changed hands, and now slumbers in the West of England. When it shall wake to the public use, this book and everything else pertaining to William Stephens will awaken to new interest.

353 CASTRO (JOÃO DE, *Fourth Vice Roy of India.*) Vida de Dom Ioão de Castro, quarto Viso-Rey da India, Escrita por JACINTO FREYRE DE ANDRADA, Impressa por ordem de seu Neto o Bispo Dom Francisco de Castro, Inquisidor Geral neste Reyno, do Conselho de Estado de Sua Magestade, E agora terceira vez impressa. *Fine copy, old calf.*
Folio, Lisboa, Officina Real dos Herd. di M. Deslandes, 1703

This Life of De Castro, by Andrada, is of very considerable importance to the American historian, inasmuch as herein are described the struggles between Spain and Portugal for mastery, both in Brazil and the East Indies.

TUESDAY AFTERNOON.

354 CATALOGUE of the Library of the late George Offor, comprising rare early Bibles, the Works of John Bunyan, rare Horæ, etc. Sold by Sotheby, Wilkinson & Hodge, June 1865. *Half morocco, gilt.* 8° *London*, 1865

355 CATALOGUE. Bangs, Brother & Co., George Cowin's Library; Books on America. *Interleaved and priced. Half morocco.* 8° *New York*, 1853

356 CATALOGUE of the Library of Dr. Kloss of Franckfort, including many original and unpublished Manuscripts, and printed Books with MS. Annotations by Philip Melancthon. *Neat half calf, uncut.* 8° *London*, 1835

357 CATALOGUE of the Pennsylvania State Library; compiled and classified by Wallace De Witt. *Cloth.* 8° *Harrisburg*, 1859

358 CATALOGUE of the Library of the University of Vermont, Burlington. 8° *Burlington*, 1854

359 CATALOGUES. A Collection of 12 Catalogues of Books, rare tracts, History and Literature of America, &c. Sold by auction by Messrs. Puttick & Simpson, 1855–1860, *bound in 1 vol, half roan.* 8° *London*, 1855–60

360 CATALOGUE. BIBLIOTHECA AMERICANA. A Catalogue of Books relating to the History and Literature of America. Sold by Puttick and Simpson, March 6–9 and 20–23. Two Parts, *bound in one volume.* LARGE PAPER, *cloth, uncut.* *Royal* 8° *London*, 1861

This, one of the most carefully prepared auction Catalogues ever issued in London, contains 2415 lots with full collations of every work. It fills vi + 273 pages.

361 CATALOGUE. BIBLIOTHECA AMERICANA. Catalogue Raisonné d'une très-précieuse Collection de livres anciens et modernes sur l'Amérique et les Philippines. Rédigé par Ch. LeClerc. *Sold by auction in Paris, Jan.* 15–25, 1867, *vii* + 407 *pp. Half red morocco, uncut.* 8° *Maisonneuve, Paris*, 1867

This Catalogue, made on the model of the preceding, contains a careful collation of each book, and in many instances analyses and important notes.

362 CATCOTT (Alexander) A Treatise on the Deluge. *Calf.* 8° *London*, 1768

363 CATCOTT (Alexander) A Treatise on the Deluge. 2d edition. *Calf.* 8° *London*, 1768

This Book contains incidentally some remarkable statements and inferences respecting the effects of the Flood in America.

364 CAYENNE. Tableau de Cayenne, ou de la Guianne Francaise. *Half calf, uncut.* 8° *Paris,* 1799

365 CAYETANO DE CABRERA Y QUINTERO (Don) ESCUDO DE ARMAS DE MEXICO: Celestial Proteccion de esta Ciudad, de la Nueva España y de casi todo el Nuevo Mundo, Maria Santissima, en su portentosa Imagen del Mexicano Guadalupe, milagrosamente apparecida en el Palacio Arzobispal el año de 1531, y jurada su principal Patrona el passada de 1737, etc. *Fine large clean and perfect copy, with the quaint copperplate frontispiece, designed by Joseph de Ibarra, and engraved by Balthasar Troncoso of Mexico in* 1743. 18 *prel. leaves* + 522 *pp.* + *Indice,* 24 *pp. Vellum.*
Folio, Mexico, por la Viuda de Jos. Bernardo de Hogal, 1746

An extraordinary Book, brimful of the marvellous in Religion, law, medicine, history, and politics. All the authors, native and foreign, who have written on Mexico, are here laid under contribution, the religious elements predominating, but the historical not excluded. There is much respecting the conversion and education of the various tribes of Indians, and the institutions founded for their benefit.

366 CAYLUS (Madame) Les Souvenirs 1770. Voyages d'un Philosophe, 1769. Discours prononcés par M. Poivre. *In* 1 *volume. Calf.* 8° 1769

367 CHURCH of ROME. A short Refutation of the Principal Errors of the Church of Rome, whereby a Protestant of a mean and ordinary capacity may be enabled to defend his Religion against the most subtle Papist. 2d edition, with additions. 12° *M. Downing, London,* 1735

368 CICERO (M. T.) Cato Major, or discourse on Old Age. . . . . With explanatory notes by BENJ. FRANKLIN. *Half calf.* 8° *London,* 1778

369 CICERO (M. T.) Opera quæ supersunt Omnia. 20 *vols, calf, a beautiful and scarce edition.* 16° *Rob. et And. Foulés, Glasg.* 1749

370 CLARENDON'S History of the Rebellion and Civil Wars of England. 6 *volumes. Fine copy, calf extra.* 8° *Oxford,* 1819

371 CLARK (T.) Naval History of the United States, from the Commencement of the Revolutionary War. 2 *volumes.* 12° *Phila.* 1814

372 Clark (Dr. G. S.) Hebrew Criticism and Poetry. *Calf.* 8° *London,* 1810

373 CLARKE (John) Corderii etc., or a Select Century of the Colloquies of Corderius, with an English translation. New edition, *fine copy.* 12° *Isaiah Thomas, Boston,* 1789

374 Clarke (*Rev.* J.) Discourses to Young Persons. 12° *Boston,* 1804

375 CLARKE (M. St. Clair) Cases of Contested Elections in Congress from 1789 to 1834. 8° *Washington,* 1834

376 CLARKSON (T.) Essay on the Slavery and Commerce of the Human Species; Translated from a Latin Dissertation which obtained the first Prize in the University of Cambridge, 1785. *Calf.* 8° *London,* 1785

377 CLAVIGERO (FRANCISCO SAVERIO) STORIA ANTICHA DEL MESSICO. *Maps and numerous engravings.* 4 *vols, half morocco, uncut, very fine copy.* 4° *In Cesena,* 1780

CLAVIGERO was a native of Vera Cruz (born 1731, died at Bologna, 1787), a Jesuit and a thorough antiquarian, who spent thirty years of active research into the archæology and antiquities of Mexico. His book, originally published in Italian, is a mine of precious historical documents, and contains valuable lists of others in the Mendoza, the Vatican and the Boturini collections. All the other books that have been elaborated since on the same subject, instead of superseding Clavigero's, have tended rather to magnify its importance.

378 CLAVIGERO (F. S.) The History of Mexico, collected from Spanish and Mexican Historians. Translated from the original Italian by C. Cullen. *Maps and plates,* 2 *vols, calf.* 4° *London,* 1787

379 CLAVIGERO (F. S.) Historia Antiqua de Megico; traducida del Italiano por Joaquin De Mora. *Maps and plates,* 2 *vols, half roan.* *Royal* 8° *Londres,* 1826

380 CLAVIGERO (F. S.) Geschichte von Mexico. 2 *vols, maps and many plates, half morocco, gilt, uncut.* 8° *Leip.* 1789–90

This German translation of Clavigero was made from the English by Cullen, who took his from the original Italian. The German editor has added notes and illustrations. Many of the archæological blunders of German writers on Mexico are traceable to this double translation.

381 CLAY (Henry) Obituary Addresses on, in the House of Representatives, June 30, 1852. *Cloth.* 8° *Washington,* 1852

382 CLEMENTIUS Clementinus Amerinus. Lucubrationes, Praeterea adjecimus Rihardum de signis febrium, Antonium et Christ. Barsisium de Febribus.
Folio, Henricus Petrus, Basileae, 1535

383 CLINTON (Sir Henry) Narrative relative to his conduct in North America. 3d edition. *London,* [*n. d.*]
Cornwallis. Answer to that part of the Narrative of Sir H. Clinton relating to Cornwallis. *London,* 1783
Reply (A) to Sir H. Clinton's Narrative. 2d edition.
3 *vols in one, half calf.* 8° *London,* 1783

384 CLOPPENBURCH (JEAN EVERHARDT) LE MIROIR DE LA CRUELLE, & HORRIBLE TYRANNIE ESPAGNOLE perpetree au Pays Bas, par le Tyran Duc de Albe, & aultres Com̃andeurs de par le Roy Philippe le deuxiesme. 4° *Amst.* 1620
Le Miroir de la Tyrannie Espagnole perpetree aux Indes Occidentales. Par un Evesque BARTHOLOME DE LAS CASAS. 2 *vols in one; many copperplates; fine copy, old calf extra.*
4° *J. E. Cloppenburg, Amsterdam,* 1620

385 CHABERT (M. de) Voyage dans l'Amerique Septentrionale, en 1750–51, pour rectifier les Cartes des Cotes de l'Acadie, de l'Isle Royale et de l'Isle de Terre-neuve. *Maps and charts; half morocco; fine uncut copy.* 4° *Paris,* 1753

386 CHALKLEY (THOMAS) A Collection of the Works of, in Two Parts. *Calf.* 8° *Printed by* BEN. FRANKLIN, *Phila.* 1749

387 CHALKLEY (THOMAS) A Collection of the Works, in Two Parts. *Calf.* 8° *Printed by* B. FRANKLIN, *Phila.* 1749

388 CHALKLEY (Thomas) The Works of T. C., containing his Epistles and other Writings. *Calf.* 8° *London*, 1751

389 CHALMERS (George) An Estimate of the Comparative strength of Great Britain, and of the Loss of her Trade from every War since the Revolution. New edition, continued to 1810. *Half calf.* 8° *London*, 1810

390 CHALMERS (Geo.) Estimate, etc. *Another copy. Calf.* 8° *London*, 1810

391 CHALMERS (Geo.) Opinions of eminent Lawyers on various Points of Jurisprudence, chiefly concerning the Colonies, Fisheries, and Commerce of G. Britain. 8° *Burlington*, 1858

392 CHAMPLAIN (SAMUEL DE) LES VOYAGES DE LA NOVVELLE FRANCE OCCIDENTALE, DICTE CANADA, faits par le Sr de Champlain Xainctongeois, Captaine pour le Roy en la Marine du Ponant, & toutes les Descouvertes qu'il a faites en ce païs depuis l'an 1603, jusques en l'an 1629 . . . . Ensemble vne Cart generalle de la description dudit pays faict en son Meridien selon la declinaison de la guide Aymant, & en Catechisme ou Instruction traduicte du Francois au language des peuples Sauuages de quelque contrée, avec ce qui s'est passé en ladite Nouuelle France en l'année 1631. *An unusually large and fine copy, measuring* $9\frac{3}{4}$ *by* $6\frac{3}{4}$ *inches, with several rough leaves, in every way a desirable and perfect copy, except that the large map is M. Tross's excellent replica, instead of the original.* VELLUM. *In this condition a book of the highest degree of rarity.* 4° *Clavde Collet, Paris*, 1632

393 CHAMPLAIN (S. de) Les Voyages, etc. *Another copy, wanting the large map, and otherwise slightly imperfect towards the end, with some leaves mutilated, but a good working copy.* 4° *Paris*, 1632

394 CHANDON ET DELANDINE. NOUVEAU DICTIONNAIRE HISTORIQUE, avec des Tables Chronologiques, etc. 13 *vols, calf.* 8° *Lyon*, 1804

395 CHANNING (Henry) Sermon at New London, Dec. 20th, 1786, occasioned by the Execution of Hannah Ocuish, a Mulatto Girl, for the murder of Eunice Bolles. *Uncut, but mutilated.* 8° *T. Green, New London*, 1786

396 CHAPIN (*Revd.* Alonzo B.) Glastenbury for 200 Years, a Centennial Discourse May 18th, A. D. 1853. With an Appendix. *Half brown morocco, uncut.* 8° *Hartford*, 1853

397 CHAPMAN (W.) ON CANAL NAVIGATION; with Investigation of MR. ROBERT FULTON'S Plan of Wheel-Boats. *Plates, half bound.* 4° *London*, 1797

Considering the date of this book, it is one of considerable interest.

398 CHAPPE D'AUTEROCHE (M.) A Voyage to California, to observe the transit of Venus, etc. *Half blue morocco, gilt, uncut. Plan of Mexico.* 8° *London*, 1778

399 CHAPPELL (Lieut. E.) Narrative of a Voyage to Hudson's Bay in H. M. Ship Rosamond. *Map and plates, half calf.* 8° *London,* 1817

400 CHARACTERS. Containing an Impartial Review of the public conduct and abilities of the most eminent personages in the Parliament of Great Britain: considered as Statesmen, Senators, and Public Speakers. Revised and corrected by the Author, since the original publication in the Gazetteer, *xvi + 152 pp. Half calf.* 8° *London,* 1777

Nineteen characters are held up to public view in this interesting volume, viz: Lords Mansfield, Camden, Lyttelton, Chatham, Germain, Hillsborough, Suffolk, Shelburne, Sandwich and North; Dukes of Grafton and Richmond; and Messrs. Thurloe, Burke, Barré, Wedderburne, Fox, Ellis, and Dunning, besides many others incidentally. A large portion of the contents pertains to American affairs.

401 CHARLEVOIX (LE P. FRANÇOIS XAVIER) HISTOIRE DE L'ISLE ESPAGNOLE ou de S. Domingue, ecrite particulierement sur des Memoires Manuscrits du P. Jean-Baptiste le Pers, Jesuite. *Maps, 2 vols.* 4° *Pralard, Paris,* 1730

402 CHARLEVOIX (*Le P. F. X.*) Histoire de S. Domingue. Another edition. *Maps and plates, 4 vols, old calf.* 8° *Amsterdam,* 1733

403 CHARLEVOIX (Le P.) HISTOIRE DE LA NOUVELLE FRANCE, [Canada] avec le Journal d'un voyage fait par ordre du Roy dans l'Amerique Septentrionale. *Maps and plates, 6 vols, calf, gilt.* 8° *Chez Ganeau, Paris,* 1744

404 CHARLEVOIX (Le P.) HISTOIRE DE LA NOUVELLE FRANCE, avec le Journal d'un Voyage dans l'Amerique Septentrionale. *Maps and plates, fine copy, 6 vols, calf, gilt.* 8° *Chez Nyon, Paris,* 1744

405 CHARLEVOIX (Le P.) HISTOIRE DE LA NOUVELLE FRANCE; avec le Journal d'un Voyage fait par ordre du Roi dans l'Amerique Septentrionale. 6 *vols, maps and plates, calf.* 8° *Chez Didot, Paris,* 1744

406 CHARLEVOIX (Le P.) All the Maps and Plates of the six duodecimo volumes of Pere Charlevoix's Histoire de la Nouvelle France. Collected and bound in one volume *in calf, gilt, and lettered, Tom. vii.* 12° *Paris,* 1744

A valuable companion volume to any edition of Charlevoix's Canada. The opportunity of securing these maps and plates in this form seldoms occurs.

407 CHARLEVOIX (Le P.) HISTORIA PARAGUAIENSIS; ex Gallico, Latina. Cum Animadversionibus et Supplemento. *Half vellum.* A VERY SCARCE EDITION. *Folio, Venetiis,* 1779

408 CHAS (J.) ET LEBRUN. Histoire Politique et Philosophique de la Revolution de l'Amerique Septentrionale. *Half calf, uncut.* 8° *Paris,* (1801)

409 CHASTELLUX (Le Marquis de) VOYAGES dans l'Amerique Septentrionale, 1780–82. *Maps, 2 vols.* 8° *Paris,* 1786

410 CHASTELLUX (Marquis de) Travels in North America in 1780, '81, '82, with Notes. *Map, 2 vols, calf. Fine copy.* 8° *London,* 1787

411 CHASTELLUX (Marquis de) Travels in North America in 1780, 1781, and 1782. Translated from the French by an English Gentleman, with Notes. *Map and plates, 2 vols, calf.* 8° *London*, 1787

412 CHAUNCY (Charles) Seasonable Thoughts on the State of Religion in New England. 8° *Boston*, 1743

413 CHAUNCY (Charles) A Complete View of Episcopacy. 8° *Boston*, 1771

414 CHAUNCY (Charles) The Benevolence of the Deity, fairly and impartially Considered. *Half russia.* 8° *Powars and Willis, Boston*, 1784

415 CHAUNCY (Charles) The Benevolence of the Deity, fairly and impartially Considered. *Half morocco, uncut.* 8° *Powars & Willis, Boston*, 1784

416 CHAUNCY (Isaac) The Doctrine which is Godliness; with a brief Account of the Church Order of the Gospel according to the Scriptures. *Calf.* 8° *London*, 1737

417 CHECKLEY (JOHN) A SHORT AND EASIE METHOD WITH THE DEISTS. Wherein the Certainty of the Christian Religion is demonstrated, by infallible Proof from Four Rules, which are Incompatible to any Imposture that ever yet has been or that can possibly be. In a letter to a Friend. The Eighth Edition, pp. 1–41. 8° *London: Printed by J. Applebee, and Sold by* JOHN CHECKLEY, *at the Sign of the Crown and Blue Gate, over against the West-End of the Town-House in Boston*, 1723

Besides the above title this volume contains:

1 Checkley (J.) A Discourse concerning Episcopacy, pp. 41–127.
2 The Epistle of St. Ignatius to the Trallians, pp. 128–132.
3 Checkley (J.) The Speech of Mr. John Checkley upon his Tryal at Boston in New England, for publishing *A Short and Easie Method with the Deists*, &c. to which is added The Jury's Verdict, His Plea in Arrest of Judgment, and the Sentence of the Court. 2d edit. *London*, 1728
4. Checkley (J.) A Specimen of a True Dissenting Catechism upon Right True-Blue Dissenting Principles, &c.

Splendid copy, bound in one volume, in Bedford's best polished calf extra, gilt edges.

Considerable interest attaches to this very rare book, in consequence of the alarm that it raised in New England, and the litigation that ensued. The book itself is Leslie's well known *Short and Easie Method*, but in reprinting it Checkley appended a Discourse concerning Episcopacy, wherein he endeavors to prove that Dissenters not being Episcopally ordained, are no ministers, etc., and comments rather harshly upon the Church Courses of New England. This gave great offence and Checkley was prosecuted in 1724 in the Inferior Court of Boston for publishing "a false and scandalous libel." He was convicted, but appealed to the Superior Court, where after a long speech in his own defence, the jury brought in a verdict against him. Checkley then put in a "Plea in arrest of Judgment," which is given in extenso in his speech, but the Court sentenced him to pay £50 to the king, and give security for his good behavior. The whole story is told in the above books, in Thomas's History of Printing, and in Stevens's Nuggets, No. 535.

418 CHESTERTON (Geo. L.) A Narrative of Proceedings in Venezuela . . . in the Years 1819–20. *Half calf.* 8° *Lond.* 1820

419 CHILD (Sir Josiah) A New Discourse of Trade, of Companies of Merchants, of Navigation, Naturalization of Strangers,

Woolen Manufactures, and the Balance of Trade and the Nature of Plantations. 4th edition. *Calf gilt.* 8° *Lond. n. d.*

The American political economist and historian should not fail to consult the various editions of this work.

420 CHILD (Sir J.) A New Discourse of Trade, and Nature of Plantations. *Calf.* 8° *London,* 1694

421 CHILD (Sir J.) A New Discourse of Trade. *Calf.* 8° *Lond.* 1698

422 CHINA. Histoire Generale ou Annales de la Chine; traduites du Tong-Kren-Kang-mon, par la feu Pere Joseph-Anne-Marie de Moyriac de Mailla. *Maps and Plates,* 4 *vols, calf.* 4° *Paris,* 1777

423 CHIPMAN (Daniel) Memoir of Thomas Chittenden, first Governor of Vermont. *Cloth.* 12° *Middlebury,* 1849

424 CHIPMAN (Daniel) Life of Hon. Nathaniel Chipman; with Selections from his Miscellaneous Papers. *Cloth.* 8° *Boston,* 1846

425 CHIPMAN (D.) On the Law of Contracts. 8° *Middlebury,* 1822

426 CHIPMAN (Nathaniel) Sketches of the Principles of Government. First Edition. 12° *Rutland,* 1793

427 CHIQUITOS (*Tribe of Indians in Paraguay*) Erbauliche . . Geschichten derer Chiqvitos . . in Paraguaria. . . *Frontispiece,* SCARCE, *vellum.* 8° *Wien,* 1729

428 CHOICE Notes from "Notes and Queries," History. *Cloth.* 12° *London,* 1858

429 CHRISTIAN HISTORY, Containing Accounts of the Revival and Propagation of Religion in Great Britain and America in 1743. [Edited by Thomas Prince, of Boston.] *Calf.* 8° *S. Kneeland, Boston, N. E.* 1744

430 CHRONICLE OF EVENTS, Discoveries and Improvements, for the Popular Diffusion of Useful Knowledge. *Illustrated with Maps and Engravings. Cloth.* 8° *Boston.*

431 CHURCH (DR. BENJAMIN) AN ORATION DELIVERED MARCH FIFTH, 1773, AT THE REQUEST OF THE INHABITANTS OF THE TOWN OF BOSTON, to Commemorate the Bloody Tragedy of the Fifth of March, 1770. THE FOURTH EDITION. *Very fine large clean copy, sized paper, rough leaves bound in white forrel, by Pratt.* 4° *Printed by J. Greenleaf, Boston,* 1773.

432 CHURCH (Thomas) History of King Philip's War; also of Expeditions against the French and Indians, 1689–1704, by his Son, Thos. Church. With Appendix, etc., by S. G. Drake. *Frontispiece.* 12° *Boston,* 1825

433 CHURCH (Thomas) History of Philip's War, commonly called the Great Indian War of 1675–6. Also of the French and Indian Wars at the Eastward, 1689–90–92–96 and 1704. With Notes and Appendix by S. G. Drake. Second Edition *with Plates.* 12° *Boston,* 1827

434 Clinton (Sir Henry) Answer to that part of the Narrative of Lieut. Gen. Sir Henry Clinton, which relates to the Conduct of Lieut. Gen. Earl Cornwallis, during the Campaign in North America in 1781. 8° *London,* 1783

435 Cobbett (William) Paper against Gold. *Cloth.* 12° *New York,* 1834

436 Cockburn (James) A Review of the General and Particular Causes which have produced the late Disorders and Divisions in the Yearly Meeting of Friends, held in Philadelphia, etc. *Calf.* 8° *Philad.* 1829

437 Cocker (Edward) Decimal Arithmetic. *Old calf.* 8° *London,* 1685

The early editions of Cocker are rare and much sought for. "According to Cocker" is English for "According to Gunter."

438 Cohen (M. M.) Notices of Florida and the Campaigns. *Map, boards.* 12° *Charleston, S. C.* 1836

439 COLDEN (Cadwallader) An Explication of the first Causes of Action in Matter and of the Cause of Gravitation. *Polished calf,* 8° *New York printed, London reprinted,* 1746

440 Colden (Cadwallader) History of five Indian Nations of Canada. *Map, calf,* 2d edition. 8° *London,* 1750

This second edition is identical with the first London edition, except this new title. The original dedication to Governor Burnet in the first New York edition is here changed to General Oglethorpe. There are some other liberties taken in the London editions which led the author when he found them out to protest against them.

441 Colden (Cadw.) The History of the Five Indian Nations of Canada. *Map,* 3d edition. 2 *vols, calf.* 8° *London,* 1755

442 Collection of Curious Observations, on the Manners, Customs, etc., of the several Nations of Asia, Africa, and America. Translated from the French, first printed 1749, by J. Dunn. 2 *vols, calf.* 8° *London,* 1750

443 Collection of Interesting Papers relative to the Dispute between Great Britain and America. *Half russia.* 8° *J. Almon, London,* 1777

This rare volume is usually called the Prior Documents of Almon's Remembrancer.

444 Collection of Memorials concerning divers deceased Ministers and others of the People called Quakers, in Pennsylvania, New Jersey and Parts adjacent. 8° *London,* 1788

445 Collection of Scarce and valuable Treatises upon Metals, Mines and Minerals; being a Translation from the Learned Albaro, Alonso Babba and others. *Calf.* *Small* 8° *London,* 1739

446 Colliber (*Samuel*) Columna Rostrata; or a Critical History of the English Sea-Affairs. *Calf.* 8° *London,* 1727

Considerable portions of this book pertain to American affairs.

447 Collier (J. Payne) A Bibliographical and Critical Account of the Rarest Books in the English Language, alphabetically arranged, which, during the last fifty

years, have come under the observation of J. P. Collier, F. S. A. THE ORIGINAL EDITION PUBLISHED AT 3 GUINEAS. 2 *vols, half roan, cloth sides, uncut.* 8° *Joseph Lilly, London,* 1865

448 COLLINSON (Peter, *Friend and Correspondent of Franklin*) Some Account of the late Peter Collinson. In a letter to a Friend, *with a brilliant impression of Miller's line engraved portrait. Privately* PRINTED. *Half morocco.* 4° *London,* 1770

On pp. 6–7 is an interesting Letter from Franklin.

449 COLMAN (BENJAMIN) The Honour and Happiness of the Virtuous Woman; considered in the two Relations of a Wife and Mother, upon the Death of Mrs. Elizabeth Hirst, consort of Grove Hirst, Esq., who died July 10, 1716, aged 35. *Fine copy in polished calf, by Bedford.* 16° *B. Green, Boston,* 1716

450 COLMAN (Benj.) The Holy Walk and Glorious Translation of Blessed Enoch, a Sermon Preached at the Lecture in Boston Two Days after the Death of the Reverend and Learned Cotton Mather who departed this Life Feb'y 13th, 1728. *Half calf.* 12° *Boston,* 1728

451 COLMAN (George) Prose on several Occasions; accompanied with some Pieces in Verse. *Portrait, 3 vols, calf.* 8° *London,* 1787

452 COLMAN (GEORGE *the Younger*) BLUE BEARD: a Dramatic Romance, as altered for the New York Theatre: With Additional Songs by Wm. Dunlap, Esq. *D. Longworth, New York,* 1802

The Voice of Nature, a Drama in Three Acts, translated and altered from the French Melo-Drama called, The Judgment of Solomon. By William Dunlap, Esq. As performed at the New York Theatre. Printed from the prompt book. *Scarce.* *Longworth, New York,* 1803

The Child of Nature, a Dramatic Piece, from the French of Madame of Sillery, formerly of Genlis. *Scarce.* *W. Spotswood, Philadelphia,* 1790

The Committee, A Comedy by R. Howard. 4 *vols in* 1, *half sheep.* 16° *London,* 1792

453 COLOM (JACOBUS) NOVA TOTIUS TERRARUM ORBIS Geographica ac Hydrographica Tabula. *Engraved Title, and* 23 *folded Maps.* *Folio, Amst.* [1663]

An excessively rare marine atlas in which are many maps of parts of America. Those of New Netherland, and New York Harbor are particularly interesting.

454 COLOMBIA: being a Geographical, Statistical, Agricultural, Commercial and Political Account of that Country. *Portrait. Half morocco.* 8° *London,* 1822

455 COLOMBIA: being a Geographical, Statistical and Political Account of that Country. 2 *vols, half russia.* 8° *London,* 1822

456 COLOMESIUS (P.) Observationes Sacræ: acced. Paralipomenæ de Scriptoribus Ecclesiast, etc. *Calf.* 8° *Londini,* 1688

457 Columbia. Herinneringen uit eene dreijarige dienst bij den Allervernial endsten en Moord dadigsten oorlog . . in Columbia. 2 *vols, half brown morocco gilt, uncut.* 8° *Gorinchem,* 1829

458 Columbian Eloquence, being the Speeches of the most celebrated American Orators, delivered in the Trial of the Hon. Sam. Chase before the U. S. Senate. *Vol. I.* 12° *Baltimore,* 1806

459 COLUMBUS. Eyn schön hübsch lesen von etlichen inszlen die do in Kurtzen zyten funden synd durch dẽ Künig von hispania, vnd sagt võ groszen wunderlichen dingen die in dẽ selbẽ inszlen synd. *In best gros grained brown levant morocco by Pratt.* 4° *Getruckt zü straszburg uff gruneck võ meister Bartolomesz küstler ym iar,* 1497

This is believed to be the first book in the German language relating to the discoveries in the new world. It is apparently made up from Columbus' first Letter of 1493. The original is so rare that it has been sold in London for 25 guineas. The present copy is one of five reproduced in marvellous fac-simile by the elder John Harris, so well done as to defy detection.

460 COLUMBUS. Historie del Sig. Don Fernando Colombo. Nelle quali s' hà particolare, & vera relatione della Vita, & de' fatti dell' Ammiraglio Don Christoforo Colombo suo Padre. Et dello scoprimento, ch' egli fece dell' Indie Occidentali, dette Mondo Nvovo, possedute dal Potentissimo Rè Catolico. *Vellum.* 8° *G. Bordoni, Milano,* 1614

This edition contains a long dedication by Cæsar Parona, dated Milan, 4 June, 1614, and four verses by the same author. Also Letter of Columbus, dated Genoa, Dec. 8, 1502; of Diego Columbus, Dec. 8, 1511, and the Will of the Admiral dated 1498, with Codicils of 1498, 1502 and 1506.

461 COLUMBUS. Historie del Sig. Don Fernando Colombo. *Another copy. Vellum.* 8° *Milano,* 1614

462 Columbus. Histoire de Christophe Colomb, suivie de sa Correspondence, d'Eclaircissemens et de Pièces curieuses et inédites, Traduite de l'Italien de Bossi, par M. C. M. Urbano. *Portrait.* 2d Edition. *Calf.* 8° *Paris,* 1825

463 Comestor (Petrus) Historia Scolastica Sacre Scripture. *Black letter.* *Folio, Jehan Petit, Parisiis,* 1513

A beautiful specimen of early printing, having the printer's Device and Mark on the title-page.

464 Comly (John) A New Spelling Book. *Boards.* 16° *Philad.* 1821

465 Commelyn (I.) Histoire de la Vie et Actes memorables de Frederic Henry, de Nassau, Prince d'Orange. *Maps and plates, vellum.* *Folio, Amsterdam,* 1656

466 Commuck (T.) Indian Melodies. Harmonized by Thos. Hastings. *Ob.* 4° *New York,* 1845

467 Compendium Logicæ Secundum Principia D. Renati Cartesii Plerumque Efformatum, et Catechistice Propositum. *Sewed. Cut askew and stained. Uncommon.* 12° *Bostoni in Nov-Anglia, Excusum,* 1735

On the fly leaf is this autograph, "Joseph Green Ejus liber 1743." On page 5

Joseph has written "from the knowledge of a thing we may argue the essence of a thing," and from his knowledge of Latin he has with his pen corrected innumerable typographical errors. The printing of Latin correctly at that day in Boston must have been as difficult as Ander Schiffahrt found it at a later period in New York.

468 Concanen (M.) and A. Morgan. History and Antiquities of the Parish of St. Saviour's, Southwark. *Russia.* 8° *London*, 1795

469 Concilia Illustrata, &c. 4 *volumes, fine copy, calf.* *Thick* 4° *Norib*, 1675

470 Conciliatory Address to the people of Great Britain and of the Colonies. *Half roan.* 8° *London*, 1775

471 Condamine (M. de la) Bekort verhaal van een Reyse gedaan in 't binnelands gedcelto van Zuyd Amerika. *Half morocco, uncut.* 8° *Amsterdam*, 1746

472 Condamine (La) Relation d'un Voyage dans l'interieur de l'Amerique Meridionale. *Nouv. Ed. Map and Plate. Calf.* 8° *Maestricht*, 1778

473 Confession (The) of Faith, Together with the Larger Catechism: Composed by the Assembly of Divines then sitting at Westminster, with the Sum of Christian Doctrine, etc. (*wants last leaf*). *Vellum, by Pratt, clean copy with rough leaves.* 12° *Kneeland & Henchman, Boston*, 1723

474 Congress. An Answer to the Declaration of the American Congress. Fifth Edition. 8° *London*, 1776

475 Congress. Extracts from the Votes and Proceedings of the American Continental Congress at Philadelphia, 5th Sept. 1774. Containing the Bill of Rights, a list of Grievances, etc. *Half roan.* 8° *Boston*, 1774

476 Congress. Journal of the Congress at Philadelphia, Sept. 5, 1774. *Half roan.* 8° *London*, 1775

477 Congress. Extracts from the Votes and Proceedings of the American Continental Congress, Held at Philadelphia, Sept. 5, 1774. Terrible Tractoration, *and other Tracts, in* 1 *volume.* 8°

478 Congress Canvassed (The) or an Examination into the Conduct of the Delegates at their Grand Convention, held in Philadelphia, Sept. 1, 1774, by A. W. *Farmer. Half morocco.* *London*, 8° 1774

479 Congress (The) Canvassed: or an Examination into the Conduct of the Delegates at their Grand Convention, held in Philadelphia, Sept. 1, 1774, by A. W. *Farmer. Half roan.* 8° *London*, 1775

480 Congress. Proceedings and Debates of the First House of Representatives of the United States, with Index. Reported by Thos. Lloyd. *Vol. I.* 8° *New York*, 1789

481 Congress. Register of Debates in Congress with copious Index. *Vol. I. boards uncut.* *Imp.* 8° *Washington*, 1825

482 CONGRESSIONAL REGISTER, or History of the Proceedings and Debates of the First House of Representatives of the United States of America.
Volumes II and III. 8° *New York*, 1790
The third volume is very rare.

483 CONNECTICUT. Blue Laws; the Code of 1650.
Boards. 12° *Hartford, n. d.*

484 CONNECTICUT REGISTER. Green's Register, For the State of Connecticut; with an Almanack for the Years 1794, 1799, 1802, 1804, 1805, 1806, 1809, 1810, 1811, 1812, 1813, 1814, 1815, 1817, 1818, 1819, and 1820. 17 *vols, in good order.*
15° *T. Green, New London*, [1794–1820]

485 CONNECTICUT REGISTER for the years 1813, 1815, 1817, 1819, 1833, 1835, 1838, 1839, and 1851. 9 *vols, clean,* 16° *T. Green, New London*, 1813–1851

486 CONNECTICUT. General History of, from its first Settlement to the Revolution. By a Gentleman of the Province, 1781. By the Rev. Samuel Peters. *Plates.* 12° *New Haven*, 1829

487 CONNECTICUT. Letters from the English Kings and Queens, Charles II. etc., to the Governors of Connecticut, from 1635 to 1749. By R. R. Hinman. 12° *Hartford*, 1836

488 CONNECTICUT. Collections of the Connecticut Historical Society. *Vol. I. cloth.* 8° *Hartford*, 1860

489 CONNECTICUT. Collections of the Connecticut Historical Society. *Vol. I. cloth.* 8° *Hartford*, 1860

490 CONSIDERATIONS on the Measures carrying on with respect to the British Colonies in North America. 8° *Boston*, 1774

491 CONSIDERATIONS on the Propriety of Imposing Taxes in the British Colonies. [By Mr. Dulaney, Chief Justice of Maryland.] *Half morocco.* 8° *London*, 1776

492 CONSIDERATIONS on the Propriety of Taxing the British Colonies, for the Purpose of raising a Revenue, by Act of Parliament, by Mr. Dulaney of Maryland. *Half morocco.* 8° *Reprinted, London*, 1776

493 CONSOLATORY Thoughts on American Independence showing the great Advantage that will arise from it to the Manufactures, the Agriculture, and Commercial Interest of Britain and Ireland. By a Merchant. *Half roan.* 8° *Edinb.* 1782

494 CONSTITUTIONS OF THE SEVERAL INDEPENDENT STATES of AMERICA, the Declaration of Independence, etc. *Boards uncut.* 8° *Philadelphia*, 1781
FIRST EDITION, only two hundred copies printed by order of the Continental Congress.

495 CONSTITUTIONS of the Several Independent States of America; the Declaration of Independence, Articles of Confederation, etc., arranged with Preface and Dedication by Rev. W. Jackson. *Calf.* 8° *London*, 1783

496 CONSTITUTIONS. *Another Copy. Portrait of Washington. Boards.* 8° *London*, 1783

497 CONSTITUTIONS of the several Independent States of America, Declaration of Independence, Articles of Confederation, etc. Second Edition. 12° *Boston*, 1785

498 CONSTITUTION of the United States, Declaration of Independence, Prominent Political Acts of Washington, etc. 12° *Washington*, 1846

499 CONSTITUTION of the United States, etc., by W. Hickey. 12° *Philadelphia*, 1847

500 CONTEST (The) In America between Great Britain and France, with its Consequences and Importance. SCARCE. *Calf.* 8° *London*, 1757

501 CONTEST with the Colonies: the Interest of the Merchants and Manufacturers of Great Britain, Stated and Considered. *Half morocco.* 8° *London*, 1774

502 CONTESTED Elections in Congress, from 1789 to 1834. 8° *Washington*, 1834

503 CONTINHO (Da Cunha de Azeredo) Essay on the Commerce of the Portuguese Colonies in South America, especially the Brazils. 8° *London*, 1807

504 COOK'S VOYAGES. Plates to Cook's Voyages. *Maps, Portraits, and Plates. Half calf, uncut.* *Folio, London*, 1776

A fine set in thick paper, (plates not folded,) very rare in this State.

505 COOKE (Edward) Voyage to the South Sea and Round the World in 1708–1711. 2 *vols, fine copy.* 8° *London*, 1712

506 COOLIDGE and Mansfield. History and Description of New England. Vol. I. Maine, New Hampshire, and Vermont. *Illustrated.* 8° *Boston*, 1859

507 COOPER (Thomas) Some Information respecting America. *Half calf.* 8° *London*, 1794

508 COOPER (Thomas) Some Information respecting America. Second Edition. *Half russia.* 8° *London*, 1795

508* CORNARO (Lewis) Discourses on a sober and temperate Life. Translated from the Italian Original. *Fine copy, calf.* 16° *Philadelphia, Dobson*, 1791

509 CORNUTUS (JACOBUS) IAC. CORNVTI DOCTORIS MEDICI PARISIENSIS CANADENSIVM PLANTARVM, aliarumque nondum editarum Historia. Cui aductum est ad calcem Enchiridion Botanicvm Parisiense, etc. *Fine large clean copy, with many full-page copper-plates representing Canadian Plants.* SCARCE. 4° *Apud Simonem Le Moyne, Parisiis*, 1635

510 CORNWALLIS (Earl) An Answer to that part of the narrative of Lieutenant-General Sir Henry Clinton, which relates to the conduct of Lieutenant-General Earl Cornwallis, during the Campaign in North America, 1781. *Half green morocco, gilt, uncut.* 8° *London*, 1783

511 CORNWALLIS (Earl) Answer to Sir Henry Clinton, in relation to the conduct of Lieutenant General Earl Cornwallis, during the Campaign in North America in 1781. *Half green morocco, uncut.* 8° *London*, 1783

512 CORONELLI (VINCENZO) ISOLARIO DESCRITTIONE DI TUTTE L' ISOLE, colce asservationi degli Scogli Sirti Scagni e Secche del Globo Terracqueo. *Numerous portraits, plates, and maps. Calf extra.* *Atlas Folio, Venetia*, 1696

513 CORREO MERCANTEL de España y sus Indias, 1792–4. 4 *vols, half calf, uncut.* 4° *Madrid*, 1792–4

514 CORRESPONDENCE between Governour Sullivan and Col. Pickering, in which the latter vindicates Himself against the groundless Charges and Insinuations made by the Governour and others. *Uncut.* 8° *Boston*, 1808

515 CORTÉS (Fernando) Correspondance, avec l' Empereur Chas. Quint, sur la Conquete de Mexique. *Frontispiece. Calf gilt. Fine copy.* 8° *Francfort*, 1779

516 CORTES (Hernando) Brieven van Ferdinand Cortes aan Keizer Karel V., wegens de Verovering van Mexico. *Map* 2 *vols, half morocco, uncut.* 8° *Amsterdam*, 1780

517 CORTES (Hernando) Brieven van Ferdinand Cortes aan Keizer Karl V., wegens de Verovering van Mexico. 2 *vols, half crimson morocco, uncut.* 8° *Amsterdam*, 1780

518 CORTES (FERDINAND) Brieven . . aan Karel V. 2 *vols in* 1, *half calf, uncut.* 8° *Amsterdam*, 1780

519 CORTES (Hernando) The Despatches of, translated with Introduction and Notes. By George Folsom. *Half green morocco.* 8° *New York*, 1843

520 COTTON (JOHN, *Teacher to the Church of Boston in New England*) THE CHURCH'S RESURRECTION, or the Opening of the Fift and Sixt verses of the 20th Chap. of the Revelation. *Half morocco.* 4° *London*, 1642

521 COTTON (John) The Keyes of the Kingdom of Heaven, and Power thereof, according to the Word of God. 12° *London*, 1644, *Reprinted, Boston*, 1852

522 COTTONI POSTHUMA; Divers choice Pieces of that Renowned Antiquary, Sir Robert Cotton. Preserved from the injury of Time, etc., by J. Howell, Esq. 8° *London*, 1651

523 COWPER (William) Table Talk and other Poems. *Neat calf.* 18° *Whittingham, Chiswick*, 1825

523* COW-POX. A concise view of all the most important facts which have hitherto appeared concerning the Cow-Pox. 3d edition, corrected and enlarged. *Boards.* 12° *Charlestown, for E. & S. Larkin*, 1801

524 COXE (Tench) A View of the United States of America, in a series of Papers written at various times between the years 1787 and 1794. *Calf.* 8° *Phila.* 1794

525 COXE (Wm.) Die neuen Entdeckungen der Russen, zwischen Asien und Amerika. *Half maroon morocco, uncut.* 8° *Leipzig,* 1783

526 COXE (William) An Account of the Russian Discoveries between Asia and America. 3d edit. revised and corrected. *Maps.* *London,* 1787

527 CRAIG (N. B.) History of Pittsburgh. *Maps, cloth.* 12° *Pittsburgh,* 1851

528 CRANZ (D.) Historie Van Groenland of eigenlijk van de Kuste der Straate Davis. *Half bound, uncut.* 8° *Amsterdam,* 1767

529 CUJACIUS (JACOBUS) OPERA OMNIA. 10 *vols, calf.* *Folio, Paris,* 1663

530 Cullen (W.) Synopsis and Nosology. 12° *Hartford,* 1792

531 ÇURITA (GERONOMO) ANALES DE LA CORONA DE ARAGON. 7 *Volumes, calf.* *Folio, En Çaragoça,* 1610–21

"Ouvrage tres estimé des Espagnols. L'edition que nous citons est la troisieme et cella que l'on prefere. On doit trouver a la fin du 6e vol. deux f. contenant les errata et la souscription et aussi Apologia de Ambrosio de Morales. Le 7e vol. contient l'index des six premiers." — *Brunet.* This history of the Kingdom of Aragon is indispensable to a full understanding of early American discovery.

532 CUSHING (CALEB) History and Present State of Newburyport. *Boards, uncut.* 12° *Newburyport,* 1826

533 DALRYMPLE (Alexander) An Historical Collection of the Several Voyages and Discoveries in the South Pacific Ocean. *Maps and plates,* 2 *vols in* 1, *calf.* 4° *London,* 1770–71

534 DAMPIER (WILLIAM) COLLECTION OF VOYAGES, in four Volumes containing, I. Dampier's Voyages round the World. II. Voyages of Lionel Wafer. III. Dampier's Expedition by Funnel. IV. Cowley's Voyage. V. Sharp's Journey to the Isthmus of Darien. VI. Wood's Voyage thro' the Straits of Magellan, and VII. Robert's Adventures among the Corsairs of the Levant. 4 *vols, very fine copy in old calf gilt, maps and plates.* 8° *London,* 1729

535 DAMPIER (Wm.) NOUVEAU VOYAGE autour du Monde. *Maps and plates,* 5 *vols, calf.* 8° *Rouen,* 1715

536 DAMPIER (Wm.) Nouveau Voyage autour du Monde. *Maps and plates, 4th edition,* 5 *vols, calf gilt.* 12° *Amsterdam,* 1723

537 DANA (James, *of New Haven*) Sermon at East Hartford, Dec. 23, 1801, at the Ordination of Rev. Andrew Yates. *Uncut.* 8° *Hartford,* 1802

538 DANA (S. L.) A Muck Manual for Farmers. 12° *Howel,* 1842

539 D'ANVILLE (M.) Compendium of Ancient Geography. Translated from the French. 2 *vols, russia.* 8° *London,* 1810

540 DARBY (William) Tour from New York to Detroit. *Map, boards, uncut.* 8° *New York,* 1819

541 DARBY (W.) Tour from the City of New York to Detroit, in the Michigan Territory. *Maps, half green morocco, uncut.* 8° *New York,* 1819

542 DARTMOUTH COLLEGE. Observations on Facts, vindicating the Rights of Dartmouth College and Moors' Charity School to the Grant made by the Legislature of Vermont in June 1785. *Uncut.* 8° [*Windsor, Vt.* 1807]

543 DARTMOUTH COLLEGE. A Vindication of the Official Conduct of the Trustees of Dartmouth College. Published by the Trustees. *Uncut.* 8° *Concord,* 1815

544 DASSIÉ (le Sieur, *C. R.*) Le Routier des Indes Orientales et Occidentales; traitant des Saisons propres à y faire Voyage: Une Description des Anchrages, Profondeurs de plusieurs Havres & Ports de Mer. Avec 26 differentes Navigations. *Fine copy.* SCARCE. 4° *Paris,* 1667

545 DAVIES (Charles) Elements of Descriptive Geometry. 2d edition. *Calf.* 8° *New York,* 1832

546 DAVIES (JOHN) The History of Barbadoes, St. Christophers, Mevis, St. Vincents, Antego, Martinico, Montserrat and the rest of the Caribby-Islands, in all 28. In two books. *Fine copy, calf,* *Folio, London,* 1666

547 DAVIS (A.) Antiquities of Central America, and the Discovery of New England by the Northmen, 500 years before Columbus. Eleventh edition. 8° *Rochester,* 1843

548 DAVIS (JOHN) AN EULOGY ON GENERAL GEORGE WASHINGTON, at Boston, Feb. 19, 1800, before the American Academy of Arts and Sciences. *A matchless copy, on sized paper, perfectly uncut, clean, bound in white vellum, by Pratt.* 4° *W. Spotswood, Boston,* 1800

549 DAWSON (J.) Lexicon Novi Testamenti. 8° *Londini,* 1809

550 DAWSON (R.) On Spermatorrhœa and Urinary Deposits. *Half calf.* 8° *London,* 1851

551 DAY (Thomas) FOUR TRACTS: Reflections on the Present State of England, and the Independence of America, *etc.* *Calf.* 8° *London,* 1785

552 DEAN (Amos) Lectures on Phrenology. *Cloth.* 12° *Albany,* 1834

553 DEBATES IN CONGRESS on the Bill for repealing the Law "For the more Convenient Organization of the Courts of the United States." *Calf.* 8° *Albany,* 1802

554 DEBATES of the House of Commons, 1774, on the Canada Bill; Reported by Sir H. Cavendish. *Map, cloth.* 8° *London,* 1839

555 DEDHAM. Historical Address, Second Centennial Anniversary Address before the Citizens of Dedham Sept. 21st, 1836. By F. S. Haven. *Uncut.* 8° *Dedham,* 1837

556 DEFENSA de los diez y seis cargos hechos por el Señor J. de Valdenebro, Corregidor de la Coruña sobre la causa que se formó por ultrajar, por acriminar bajo el asustador titulo de crimen de Estado à V. de Fronda, Consul General, que frié cerca de las Estados-Unidos de la America, &c. *Calf.* 16° *Pamplona,* 1820

557 De Forest (J. W.) History of the Indians of Connecticut, from the earliest known Period to 1850. *Map, cloth.* 8° 1852

558 Delaplaine's (Joseph) Repository of the Lives and Portraits of distinguished American Characters. *Uncut, boards.* 4° *Philadelphia, n. d.*

559 De Laune (T.) A Plea for the Non-Conformists. *Old calf.* 12° *London,* 1712

560 Delirius (Mart. Ant.) Syntagma Tragœdiæ Latinæ, in tres partes distinctum. *Calf.* 4° *Lut. Paris.* 1620

561 Dellaway (*Rev.* J.) Discourses upon Architecture in England; with an Appendix of Notes and Illustrations, and an Historical Account of Master and Free Masons. *Cloth.* 8° *London.*

562 Denys (M. *Gouv. Lieut. Gen. et Proprietaire de toutes les Terres & Isles qui sont depuis le Cap de Campseaux, jusques au Cap des Roziers,* i. e. *New Brunswick & Gaspé*) Description Geographique et historique des costes de l'Amerique septentrionale. Avec l' Histoire Naturelle des Peuples des Animaux, des Arbres & Plantes de l'Amerique Septentrionale, & des ses divres Climats. Avec un Description exacte de la Pesche des Moluës, tant sur le Grand-Banc qu' à la Coste, &c. 2 *vols, fine copy.*
Excessively scarce. 16° *Loüis Billaine, Paris,* 1672

Gov. Denys was the William Penn of that large tract of land bordering on the Gulf of St. Lawrence, now the Province of New Brunswick and Eastern Canada, south of the River St. Lawrence. This country the Governor explored and surveyed himself, and hence his book is among the best and most authentic materials we have relating to those Provinces.

563 De Pauw (M.) Recherches Philosophiques sur les Americains. 3 *vols, half calf.* 8° *Cleve,* 1782

564 De Pauw (M.) Selections from with Additions by Daniel Webb, Esq., with Sequel to the Selections, in Notes. *Half calf.* 8° *Bath,* 1795

565 De-Rossi (J. B.) De Hebraicæ Typographiæ Origine ac Primitiis, seu antiquis ac rarissimis Hebraicorum Librorum. *Calf.* Seculi XV. 4° *Ex Regio Typogr. Parmae,* 1776

566 De Saulcy (F.) Journey round the Dead Sea, and in the Bible Lands in 1850–51, including an Account of the Discovery of the Sites of Sodom and Gomorrah. *Map.* 2 *vols, cloth.* 8° *London,* 1854

567 De Solis (Antonio) History of the Conquest of Mexico, by the Spaniards, Translated by Townsend. Revised Edition. *Maps and plates,* 2 *vols, calf.* 8° *London,* 1753

568 DE VRIES (David Peterson) Voyages from Holland to America, A. D. 1632 to 1644. Translated from the Dutch, by Henry C. Murphy. *Portrait. Cloth. Scarce.* 4° *New York,* 1853

Only 250 *copies printed* for Mr. James Lenox.

569 D'EWES (Sir S.) Autobiography and Correspondence of, during the Reigns of James I. and Charles I. Edited by J. O. Halliwell. *Portraits.* 2 *vols, cloth.* 8° *London,* 1845

570 DIALOGUES of the Dead. Second Edition. *Calf.* 8° *London,* 1760

Among the Dialogues is one between an English Duellist and a North American Savage, and another between Fernando Cortes and William Penn.

571 DIAZ DEL CASTILLO (Bernal) History of the Conquest of Mexico. Translated from the original Spanish by M. Keatinge. *Map, half morocco.* 4° *London,* 1800

572 DIBDIN, (REV. T. F.) INTRODUCTION to the Rare and Valuable Editions of the Greek and Latin Classics. Fourth Edition, greatly enlarged. 2 *vols, half calf.* 8° *London,* 1827

573 DICKINSON (JONATHAN) The True Scripture Doctrine concerning some Important Points of Christian Faith; in five Discourses. 12° *Printed by S. Rogers, Boston,* 1741

574 DICKINSON (Jonathan *President of the College of New Jersey*) Familiar Letters to a Gentleman. 4*th edition, half calf.* 12° *Edinburgh,* 1784

575 DICTIONARY. AN ALVEARIE or quadruple Dictionarie, English, Greek, Latin and French. *Scarce.* *Folio, London,* 1580

576 DICTIONNAIRE Francois Latin &c. *Old calf.* *Folio, R. Etienne, Paris,* 1549

577 DICTIONARIUM Latino-Graecum. 4° *C. Stephanus, Paris,* 1554

578 DICTIONARIUM Latino-Gallicum, ex omnibus Latinitatis Autoribus collection. *Calf.* 8° *Parisiis,* 1704

579 DIGNITY of Human Nature; or a brief Account of the certain and established Means for attaining the true End of our Existence, by J. B. *Calf.* 4° *London,* 1754

580 DISRAELI (ISAAC) Amenities of Literature; edited by the Hon. B. Disraeli. 2 *vols, cloth.* 8° *London,* 1859

581 DITSON (G. L.) The Para Papers on France, Egypt and Ethiopia. *Uncut.* 8° *Paris,* 1838

582 DIXON (George) VOYAGE Autour du Monde et principalement a la Cote Nord-Ouest de l'Amerique en 1785, 6, 7, 8, par les Capitaines Portlock et Dixon. *Maps and plates. Half calf, uncut.* 4° *Paris,* 1789

583 DOBRIZHOFFER (MARTIN) HISTORIA de Abiponibus, equestri, bellicosaque Paraquariæ Natione. *Map and engravings.* 3 *vols, half maroon morocco, uncut, fine copy. Scarce.* 8° *Viennae,* 1784

584 DOBSON (John) Chronological Annals of the War, from April 1755 to the Peace of 1763. *Calf.* SCARCE. 8° *Oxford,* 1763

This volume contains an interesting summary of the events in West Virginia, and on the Ohio, prior to the Defeat of Braddock, 9th July, 1755, chiefly under the management of Mr. Washington.

585 DODD (Rev. W.) Thoughts in Prison; his Last Prayer, and other Miscellaneous Pieces. 4° *Boston,* 1778

586 DODGE (Nehemiah, *of Middletown*) A Discourse at Lebanon, 4 Mch, 1805, in honor of the election of Thomas Jefferson. *Half roan.* 8° *Norwich, Conn.* 1805

587 DODONÆUS (REMBERTUS) STIRPIVM Historiæ Pemptades Sex, sive Libri XXX. *Engraved Title and numerous woodcuts, calf.* *Folio, Ex officina Plantiniana, Antverpiae,* 1616

588 DOMINICA. The History of the Island of Dominica. *Half gr. mor. uncut.* 8° *London,* 1791

589 DONCK (ADRIEN VANDER) BESCHRYVINGE VAN NIEUW-NEDERLANT, &c. [Description of New Netherland (in its present state) including the Nature, character, Situation and fruitfulness of the said Land; together with the profitable and fortunate accidents to be found there for the support of man (whether native or foreign). Also the manners and unusual qualities of the savages or Aborigines of the Land. And a particular Account of the marvellous nature and habits of the Beavre: to which is added a discussion on the situation of New Netherland, between a Netherland Patriot and a New Netherlander. Described by Adrian Vander Donck, Doctor of Laws, who still resides in New Netherland.]
FIRST EDITION, *with an engraved view of* "t'Fort nieuw Amsterdam op de Manhatens" *on page* 9, *not in the second edition. Fine large, clean and perfect copy, in white vellum by Pratt, see* ASHER, N. 7. 4° *Evert Nieuwenhof, Amsterdam,* 1655

What "*the first folio*" is to an English Collector, a *Vander Donck* is to the American. When he has once screwed his courage to the price of a VANDER DONCK, he seldom flinches at any other rare work that may turn up. This first edition usually commands from £12 to £20 in Europe.

590 DON QUIXOTE at College; or a History of the Gallant Adventures, lately Achieved by the combined Students of Harvard University, with some facetious reasonings. By a Senior. *Uncut.* 8° *Boston,* 1807

591 DOUGLASS (William) Summary, Historical, etc. of the British Settlements in North America. *Map,* 2 *vols, calf.* 8° *London,* 1755

592 DOUGLASS (W.) A Summary of the First Planting, Progressive Improvements and Present State of the British Settlements in North America. *Map,* 2 *vols, calf, fine copy.* 8° *London,* 1755

593 DOUGLASS (William) *Another edition,* 2 *vols, fine copy, calf.* 8° *London,* 1760

594 DOUGLASS (William) A Summary Historical, &c., of the British Settlements in North America. 2 *vols, calf.* 8° *London,* 1760

595 DOWNING (SIR GEORGE *one of the First Graduates of Harvard College.*) DEDUCTIE INGESTELT tot onderrichtinge vanden Coningh van Groot Brittannien op verscheyden Poincten vervatt in seeckere Antwoorde van wegen Syne maj-

esteyt gegeven aenden Ambassedeur vande Heeren Staten Generael. *Morocco.* 4° *Graven Hage, Nov.* 1664

596 DRAKE (MRS. JOANA) TRODDEN DOWN STRENGTH, by the God of Strength, or, Mrs. Drake Revived, showing her strange and rare Case, great and manifold afflictions, for tenne years together. Related by her friend Hart On-hi. *Vellum, short copy, some leaves clipped.* 16° *London,* 1647

The interest to New Englanders of this curious book centres not in the main subject but in what is incidentally told of one of her spiritual advisers. Mrs. Drake was a half crazed religious enthusiast, whose spiritual health required constant wrestling with Satan and Doctors of Divinity. Possessed of property, her husband procured the Rev. Mr. Dod, who for three years disputed constantly with all her temptations and objections, "and was able to answer all," but being obliged to leave, he looked about for another helper. "In which interim, notice was given unto him of one Mr. HOOKER then at Cambridge, now in New England: A great Scholar, an acute Disputant, a strong learned, a wise modest man, every way rarely qualified; who being a Non-conformitan in judgment, not willing to trouble himselfe with *Presentative* Livings, was contented and persuaded by Mr. Dod to accept of that poore Living of 40*l.* per annum; Mr. Drake her Husband being a worthy well-beloved Gentleman, and able to procure his liberty, and retaine him still in the same: This worthy man accepted of the place, having withall, his dyet and lodging at Esher Mr. Drake's house." p. 117. "This man, Mr. Hooker being a good, acute, *smart* Preacher when he listed, besides that information Mr. Dod had given him, was so wise, first to try her spirit," etc. p. 119. "For Mr. Hooker being newly come from the University had a new answering methode (though the same things) wherewith shee was mervellously delighted," etc. p. 120. Mr. Hooker lived long in this family, till she imagined "her time on earth was but of small continuance. About which time it fell out, that Mr. Hooker also having acted his part with her, and done his best, to comfort, uphold and rectifie her spirit, so fitting her for mercy, as nothing remained to be done but a full gaile of spirituall winde to blow upon her, to bring forth her fruit, that by God's providence he was married unto her waiting-woman: After which both of them having lived some time after with her, and he cal'd to be Lecturer at Chelmsford in Essex, they both left her," etc. These early glimpses of one of the most honored of our New England fathers, are refreshing.

597 DRAKE (*Sir* FRANCIS) and NORRIS (*Sir* JOHN) Warhafftige vnd gründtliche Historia desz Zugs, Welchen die Edele vnd Gestrenge Herrn, Norwitz vnd Drak (nach jhrer glücklechen widerkunfft ausz den Occidentalischen Insulen) ausz vergünstigung der Durchleuchtigsten vñ Vnvberwindlichsten, Elisabeth, Konigin ausz Engelland, &c., in Portugal fürgenommen haben: In welcher auszführlich angezeigt wirdt, was gemaldte Obersten von Tag zu Tag gehandelt, vnd wider den Fiendt erhalten haben. 30 *pp. fine copy. With a spirited full length wood-cut portrait of Norris on the reverse of the title.* EXCESSIVELY RARE. 4° *Franckfort am Mäyn,* 1590

This is an account of the celebrated Expedition, unfortunate for England, under Sir Francis Drake and Sir John Norris against Portugal.

598 DRAKE (Sir Francis) The English Hero: or, Sir Francis Drake Reviv'd. Being a full account of the Dangerous Voyages, admiralle Adventures, Notable Discoveries &c., 1572–1595. The 8th edition enlarged. By R. B. *Sallow, calf.* 16° *Nath. Crouch, London,* 1710

599 DRAKE (Sir Fr.) The English Hero, or Sir Francis Drake Reviv'd. 9th Edit. By R. B. *Half calf.* 12° *N. Crouch, London,* 1716

600 DRAKE (Sir F.) The English Hero: or, Sir Francis Drake reviv'd. 16th Edition, *portrait.* 16° *London,* 1762

601 DRAKE (Sir Francis) The English Hero, or Sir Francis Drake Revived, with an account of his dangerous voyages, etc., 16th Edition, *wanting pp.* 5–14, *morocco.* 16° *C. Hitch, London,* 1762

602 DRAKE (Samuel G.) Sketches of Northwood, New Hampshire (MS. Notes by the Author). From the Historical Society's Collections. *Interleaved, half calf.* 8°

603 DRAPER (E. A.) An Address . . on the Case of Gen[l] Pictou, late Governor of Trinidad; with Observations on the Conduct of Wm. Fullarton, Esq., and the Right Hon. John Sullivan. *Half calf.* 8° *London,* 1806

604 DRUMMOND (W., of Hawthornden) The Poetical Works, Edited by W. B. Turnbull. *Portrait. Cloth.* 12° *London,* 1856

605 DRUSIUS (Joannes) Quæstionvm Ebraicarvm Libri tres. 8° *Franckeræ,* 1599

606 DRUSIUS (J.) Quæstionum Ebraicarum Libri tres. *Portrait, calf.* 8° *Franckeræ,* 1599

607 DRUSIUS (J.) Annotationvm in totum Jesu Christi Testamentum libri decem. *Calf.* 4° *Franckeræ,* 1612

608 DRUSIUS (J.) Veterum Interpretum Græcorum in totum Vet. Test. collecta, cum notis. *Calf.* 4° *Arnhemiae,* 1622

609 DUBOCCAGE (Madame) La Colombiade, ou La Foi portée au Nouveau Monde. Poëme. *Copper-plates, fine copy. Half brown mor. uncut.* 8° *Paris,* 1756

610 DUCHÉ (Jacob, *Chaplain of the Continental Congress*) Caspipina's Letters; with Life of William Penn. 2 *vols in* 1, *calf gilt.* 12° *Bath,* 1777

611 DUCHÉ (Jacob) Discourses on Various Subjects. 3d edition. *Frontispiece.* 2 *vols, half mor. uncut.* 8° *London,* 1790

612 DUDLEY OBSERVATORY, *Albany.* Inauguration, Aug. 28, 1856. Eulogy by W. Hunt. — Remarks by Prof. Bache. — Mrs. Dudley's Letter. — The Uses of Astronomy, by Edward Everett, etc. 8° *Albany,* 1856

613 DUMMER (Jeremiah) A Defence of the New-England Charters. 8° *London, n. d.*

614 DUMMER (Jer.) A Defence of the New England Charters. *Half roan.* 8° *London,* 1770

615 DUNN (H.) Guatimala, or the United Provinces of Central America in 1827–8. *Boards.* 8° *New York,* 1828

616 DUNTON (John) Life and Errors. 2 *vols, half mor. uncut, with many portraits and other extra illustrations inserted.* 8° *London,* 1817

617 DU PERIER (M.) Histoire Universelle des Voyages, faits par

Mer et par Terre dans l'Ancien et dans le Nouveau Monde. *Plates, calf.* 8° *Paris,* 1707

This volume relates entirely to America.

618 DU PRATZ (LE PAGE) Histoire de la Louisiane, contenant la Decouverte de ce vaste Pays; l'Histoire Naturelle; les Moeurs, Coutumes etc., avec deux Voyages dans le Nord du nouveau Mexique etc. *Maps and* 40 *Plates.* 3 *vols.* 8° *Paris,* 1758

619 DUTANT (J.) The Salvation of the Saints, by the Appearances of Christ. 1. Now in Heaven. 2. Hereafter from Heaven. *Portrait, calf.* 8° *London,* 1653

620 DWIGHT (TIMOTHY, *D. D.*) THE CONQUEST OF CANAAN, a Poem in Eleven Books. 12° *Hartford,* 1785

621 DWIGHT (T. *D. D.*) GREENFIELD HILL, a Poem in Seven Parts. 8° *New York,* 1794

622 DWIGHT, (T. *D. D.*) Greenfield Hill; a Poem, in Seven Parts. *Boards.* 8° *New York,* 1794

623 DWIGHT (*President* T.) Fourth of July Discourse, 1798. Illustrating the Duty of Americans at the Present Crisis. *Uncut.* 8° *New Haven,* 1798

624 DWIGHT (Theodore) History of the Hartford Convention; with a Review of the Policy of the United States Government, which led to the War of 1812. *Half morocco.* 8° *Boston,* 1833

625 ECHARD (Lawrence) The Gazetteer's, or Newsman's Interpreter. Being a Geographical Index of all the considerable Provinces, Cities, &c., in Europe. 15th edition, corrected, and very much enlarged. *Two Parts in* 1 *vol. calf.* 8° *London,* 1741

626 EAST INDIA COMPANY (DUTCH.) BEGIN ENDE Voortgangh van de Vereenighde Nederlantsche Geoctroyeerde Oost-Indische Compagnie. Vervatende de voornaemste Reysen, by de Inwoonderen der selver Provincien derwaerts gedaen. Alles Nevens de beschrijvinghen der Rijcken, Eylanden, Havenen, Revieren, Stroomen, Rheeden, Winden, Diepten ende Oidiepten, *etc.*

[*Anglicè.* The Origin and Progress of the chartered East India Company of the United Netherlands, containing the principal voyages undertaken by the Dutch, comprising descriptions of the empires, islands, ports, rivers, roads, winds, etc., as also the religion, manners, customs, government, &c. Illustrated with maps and copperplates. Divided into 2 volumes, of which the first contains 14 Parts [and the second twelve] the larger part inedited.]

Very fine copy in vellum, with clasps, 2 *vols.* *Oblong* 4°, *Amsterdam,* 1646

When the collectors, bibliographers, librarians and public libraries of this country shall turn their attention to the collection of the true sources of early American history, regardless of the language in which they are written, this magnificent collection of voyages, compiled by ISAAC COMMELIN of Amsterdam, will be better appreciated than it is now. A mere glance at the table of Contents will show its inestimable value to the historian and geographer of the East as well as the West. When it is comprehended that more than one half of these important voyages are here printed for the first time, even Committees who cannot read a word of the language in which they are printed, and Librarians who cannot catalogue the works, will venture to buy them on trust, on the new and growing principle that a public library should *lead* and not *follow* the demands of scholars. Isaac Commelin was born in Amsterdam in 1598, and died there in 1676. He was an author of some eminence, but this is his *magnum opus*, rivalling, if not exceeding in intrinsic value the better known and more famous collection of DeBry and Hulsurs. These two volumes contain the following voyages:—

1 Voyages to the North in 1594–95, written by G. de Veer, with appendix containing the Voyage of Henry Hudson in 1609
2 Voyages of Cornelis de Houtman to the East Indies, 1595–1600
3 Voyage of Van Neck and Van Warwijck to the E. Indies 1598–1600, with vocabulary of Java and Malacca
4 Voyage round the world by Sebald de Weert, 1598–99
5 Voyage of Oliver van Noort round the world, 1598–1603
6 Voyage to the E. Indies under Pieter Both and Paul van Caerden, 1599–1601
7 Second Voyage of Van Neck and Van Foreest to the E. I. 1600–1604
8 Voyage of S. vander Hagen, Seneschel, and J. van Heemskerk to the E. I. 1599–1603
9 Voyages of Harmensz, van Warwijck & S. de Weert to the E. I. 1601–1604
10 First Voyage of J. van Spilbergen to the East, with description of Java by Pontanus, 1601-1604
11 Voyage to the East I. by van Warwijck and de Weert, 1602–1604
12 Second Voyage of van der Hagen and P. van Solt to the E. I. 1603–1606
13 Voyage of C. Matelief, 1605–1608, and Letters of J. l'Hermite, May 1607
14 Voyage of Paulus van Caerden to the East, 1606–1609
15 Voyage of P. W. Verhoeff to the East, 1607–1616
16 Voyage of P. vanden Broecke to the Coasts of Africa and to the East, 1605–1630
17 Description of Hindostan by J. van Twist, 1638
18 Second Voyage of J. van Spilbergen round the World, 1614–1618, and of Schouten and Lemaire, 1615–1617
19 Voyage of J. l'Hermite round the World, 1623–26, and other papers
20 Voyage of W. Schram, and meeting with C. Compaen, 1626, of van Rechteren, 1628–32. Naval combat off Goa, 1639
21 Voyage of H. Hagenaer, 1631–37, Caron's Japan, 1636, Martyrs of Japan by Gysbertsz, *etc.*

627 EAST INDIES. Historie van Oost Indien, vervattende, behalven de Zeer nette beschrÿving der vergelegene landen, een omstandig verhaal van het wedervaren der Franschen aldaar. *Plates. Half vellum.* 12° *Amsterdam,* 1696

628 Eaton (Amos) Philosophical Instructor or Webster's Elements of Natural Philosophy, etc. 8° *Albany,* 1824

629 Economy of Human Life; Translated from an Indian Manuscript. 18° *Richmond,* 1825

630 Ecton (J.) Thesaurus Rerum Ecclesiasticarum; being an Account of the Valuations of all the Ecclesiastical Benefices in the several Dioceses of England and Wales. *Calf.* 4° *London,* 1763

631 Ecuyer (W. S.) Lettres d'un Cultivateur Americain, 1770–81. Traduites de l'Anglois. 2 *vols.* 8° *Paris,* 1785

WEDNESDAY FORENOON.

632 EDEN (RICHARDE) THE DECADES OF THE NEW WORLDE OR WEST INDIA, Conteynyng the navigations and conquestes of the Spanyardes, with the particular description of the moste ryche and large landes and Ilandes lately found in the west Ocean perteynyng to the inheritance of the kinges of Spayne. Wrytten in the Latine tongue by Peter Martyr of Angleria, and translated into Englysshe by Rycharde Eden.
Half calf. 4° *Londini. In ædibus Gulielmi Powell,* 1555

FIRST EDITION. Fine large clean and perfect copy, measuring 7½ by 5¼ inches. Pierced by a worm, but when sized, mended and bound by a Bedford or a Pratt will make a matchless copy. The great historical importance of this book is not yet fully appreciated. Besides the first three Decades of Peter Martyr it contains a translation of that Author's paper on the recently discovered Islands, first printed in 1521 to supply the loss of Cortes's First Relation. It also contains the Bull of Pope Alexander (in Latin and English) dividing the world between Spain and Portugal; as well as translations of the most important parts pertaining to maritime discovery and the new world, of Ziegler, Paulus Jovius, Vespucci, Maximilianus Transylvanus, Oviedo, Gomara, Andreas de Corsali, Cadamosto, Butrigarius, the Classic Authors, etc.

633 EDINBURGH ADVERTISER (The) for the Year 1774. *Half blue morocco gilt, uncut.* 4° *Edinburgh,* 1774

A VERY RARE volume of Scotch Newspapers, containing much about America at the beginning of the Revolution.

634 EDWARD (D. B.) History of Texas. 12° *Cincinnati,* 1836

635 EDWARDS (Bryan) Historical Survey of the French Colony in the Island of St. Domingo. *Half calf.* 4° *London,* 1797

636 EDWARDS (Bryan) History of the British Colonies in the West Indies; with Historical Survey of St. Domingo. *Map.* 8° *London,* 1798

637 EDWARDS (Bryan) The History, Civil and Commercial, of the British Colonies in the West Indies. *Map, half calf.* 8° *London,* 1798

638 EDWARDS (Bryan) The History of the British Colonies of the West Indies. 3 vols, 3d edition, LARGE PAPER, *calf.* 8° *London,* 1801

639 EDWARDS (Bryan) Burgerlyke Handelkundige Geschiedenis van de Engelsche Volkplantingen in de West-Indien. 6 *vols, half blue mor. gilt, uncut.* 8° *Haerlem,* 1794–99

640 EDWARDS (Bryan) Burgerlyke en Handelkundige Geschiedenis van de Engelsche Volkplantingen in de West-Indien, uit het Engelsche. 6 *vols, half calf, uncut.* 8° *Haarlem,* 1794–99

641 EDWARDS (Bryan) Geschiedkundige Beschouwing van St. Domingo. *Half blue morocco, uncut.* 8° *Haarlem,* 1802

642 EDWARDS (Jonathan, *of Northampton*) The Distinguishing Marks of a Work of the Spirit of God. A Discourse at New Haven Sept. 10, 1741, the day after Commencement. Published with great enlargements, with a Preface [of 18 pages] by Rev. W. Cooper of Boston. *Sallow, rough leaves.* 12° *Kneeland & Green, Boston,* 1741
With three autographs of Winslow Tracy, Dec. 8, 1741, and one of Lucy Carver.

643 EDWARDS (Jonathan) Some Thoughts concerning the present Revival of Religion in New England. 12° *Boston, N. E.* 1742

644 EDWARDS (Jonathan) Enquiry into the modern prevailing Notions of that Freedom of Will supposed to be essential to Moral Agency, *etc. Calf.* 8° *Boston, N. E.* 1754

645 EDWARDS (Jonathan) The Great Christian Doctrine of Original Sin defended. 8° *Boston, N. E.* 1758

646 EDWARDS (Jonathan) A Treatise concerning Religious Affections, in Three Parts. *Boards.* 8° *Boston,* 1763

647 EDWARDS (Jonathan) The Life and Character of, Together with a number of his Sermons. 2 *vols, half calf.* 8° *Boston,* 1765

648 EDWARDS (Jonathan) The Life of the late Rev. Jonathan Edwards. 8° *S. Kneeland, Boston,* 1765
Sermons on various important subjects. 2 *vols in* 1, *gilt-calf, fine copies.* 8° *S. Kneeland, Boston,* 1765

649 EDWARDS (Jonathan) History of the Work of Redemption, containing the Outlines of a Body of Divinity, entirely new. 8° *New York,* 1786

650 EDWARDS (Jonathan) An Account of the Life of the late Reverend Mr. David Brainerd, Minister of the Gospel and Missionary to the Indians who died at Northampton, in New England, Oct. 9, 1747, in the 30th year of his age. Chiefly taken from his Diary and other private writings written for his own use. *Calf.* 8° *Edinburgh,* 1765

651 EDWARDS (Jonathan) An Account of the Life of David Brainerd, with his Journal; also Mr. Beatty's Journal of a Two Months' Tour. *Calf.* 8° *Edinburgh,* 1798

652 EDWARDS (Jonathan) Account of the Life of David Brainerd with Mr. Brainerd's Journal. To this edition is added Mr. Beatty's Mission to the westward of the Alleghany mountains. *Half calf.* 8° *Edinburgh,* 1798

653 ELLIS (Henry) Voyage to Hudson's Bay in 1746–47. *Map, calf.* 8° *London,* 1748

654 Ellis (Henry) Voyage à la Baye de Hudson fait en 1746 & 1747; pour la Decouverte du Passage de Nord-Ouest. 2 *vols in* 1. *Maps and plates, calf, fine copy.* 8° *Paris,* 1749

655 Ellis (Henry) Voyage à la Baye de Hudson, 1746–47 traduit et augmenté de quelques Remarques. *Half olive morocco, gilt, uncut.* 8° *Leide,* 1750

656 Ellis (Henry) Voyage a la Baye de Hudson, fait en 1746–7, par les Navires *le Dobbs-Galley et la California* pour la Decouverte d'un Passage au Nord Ouest. *Plates, half morocco, uncut.* 8° *Paris,* 1750

657 Ellis (John) Directions for bringing over Seeds and Plants from the East Indies, and other distant Countries. *Calf.* 4° *London,* 1770

658 Ellis (*Rev.* W.) Three Visits to Madagascar during the Years 1853–54–56. *Illustrated, cloth.* 8° *London,* 1858

659 EMBLEMS. El Espejo de la Muerte, en que se notan los Medios de preparase para Morir, por Consideraciones sobre la Cena, la Passion y la Muerte de Jesu Christo, con muy Curiosas Empresas Emblematicas. Explicadas por Don Carlos Bundets. *Fine copy, calf.* 4° *Jorgio Gallet, Amberes,* 1700

This very desirable volume of Emblems contains forty-two exquisite line engravings on copper, each filling a quarto page, being poetical representations of Death. The editor says they need only to be seen to be appreciated as the work of a master, but he declines to give the name of the artist, but says that the designs are due to a monk of the order of Saint Francis.

659* Emerson (R. W.) Centennial Discourse, delivered before the Citizens of Concord 12th Sept. 1835. *Uncut.* 8° *Concord,* 1835

660 Emigration from Ireland into the United States. 8° 1828

661 Emigrant's (The) Guide to and Description of the United States of America; by S. H. Collins. 4th edition. *Map.* 16° *Hull* [1830]

662 Emory (Lieut. Col.) Reconnoissance in Mexico and New California. 8° *Washington,* 1848

663 Enchiridion Cosmographicus: dass ist ein Handbuchlein der gantzen welt gelegenheit. *Black letter, half roan,* 4° *Colln am Rhein,* 1604

664 English Colonies. Geschichte der Englischen Kolonien in Nord-Amerika, bes auf den Frieden 1763. 2 *vols, half morocco.* 8° *Leipzig,* 1777

665 English Liberties, or the Free-Born Subject's Inheritance, compiled first by Henry Care, and continued with large Additions by W. N. Fifth Edition. *Small* 8° *Printed by James Franklin, Boston,* 1721

This book was printed when Benjamin Franklin was an apprentice to, and had principal charge of his brother James' business.

666 Epictetus. Enchiridion: una cum Cebetis Tabula, Græcé et Latiné, cum Notis Casauboni. *Calf.* 8° *Londini,* 1659

667 Episcopacy Examined, and Re-examined. *Cloth.* 12° *New York,* 1835

668 ENS (GASPAR) WEST-VUND OST INDISCHER LUSTGART; Eygentliche Erzehlung Wannvnd von wemdie Newe Welterfunden. *Polished calf gilt, by Bedford.* 4° *Collen*, 1618

Gaspar Ens was one of the Editors employed by the DeBrys in their Collection of Voyages, 1590-1634, and was well read in the history and bibliography of the New World. This volume is a Summary of the most interesting sources of American History.

669 EPITOME of Mr. Forsyth's Treatise on Fruit Trees; also Notes on American Gardening and Fruits, etc. by an American Farmer. *Plates.* 8° *Philadelphia*, 1803

670 ERASMUS (D.) Life of, with an Account of his Writings. From the larger Work of Dr. Jorten, by A. Laycey. *Portrait after Holbein; half calf.* 8° *London*, 1805

671 ERCILLA (Don Alonzo) La Araucana. *Portrait*, 2 *vols in* 1, *neat calf.* 8° *Madrid*, 1776

672 ERSKINE (*Rev.* Ralph) Gospel Sonnets: or Spiritual Songs. In six parts. Second American Edition from the 24th English Edition. To which is now prefixed, an Account of the Author's Life and Writings. *Fine clean copy.* 12° *Worcester, Isaiah Thomas, Jun. Feb.* 1798

673 ESPINOZA (FRAY ISIDORO DE) Compendio de la Vida Mirabillosa del gloriosissimo Padre S. Francisco de Assis, Patriarcha, y Fundador primero del Orden de los Menores: Deducido de la Chronica Seraphica, y entresacado de lo que escribiò el Il. Sr. D. F. Damian Cornejo, Por Fray I. de Espinosa, Indigno Frayle Menor. *Calf, fine copy*, EXCESSIVELY RARE. 4° *Mexico, por Joseph Bernardo de Hogal*, 1735

The Compiler of this handsome volume (of 770 pages, with 9 preliminary and 18 sequent leaves of tables and indexes) was a Franciscan Missionary of high standing in Mexico, being the President of the New Hospice of St Ferdinando. There is a full length portrait of St Francis engraved in Mexico by Sotomaior.

673* ESSAY (An) on the Nature and Glory of the Gospel of Jesus Christ: on Spiritual Blindness, and Divine Illumination. A Supplement to the Author's Letters and Dialogues, *etc.* 4 *copies, fine and clean.* 12° *Isaiah Thomas, Worcester*, 1797

674 EURIPIDES. Tragœdiæ, Graece et Latine, cum Brodaei Annotationibus, *etc.* *Calf.* *Thick* 4° *Parisii*, 1561

674* EURIPIDES. Tragœdiæ, quae extant; cum Latina G. Canteri Interpretatione. *Calf.* 4° *P. Stephanus*, 1602

675 EURIPIDES. Tragœdiæ, Græce et Latine. Edidit G. Canterus. *Thick* 8° *Noribergæ*, 1697

676 EUROPEAN SETTLEMENTS. Account of the European Settlements in America. Fifth Edition, 2 *vols, calf, maps.* 8° *London*, 1770

677 EVELYN (John) Navigation and Commerce, their Original and Progress. *Half morocco, title mounted.* 8° *London*, 1674

678 EVELYN (John) Kalendarium Hortense, or the Gardener's Almanac. Eighth Edition. *Frontispiece, calf.* 12° *London*, 1791

679 EXÁMEN SUCINCTO SOBRE LOS ANTIGUOS LIMITES de la Acadia sobre las estipulaciones del Tratado de Utrecht, relations a èllos. 52 *pp. in double columns, in French and Spanish. Fine copy, calf.* 8° [*Madrid?* 1751?]

A small book of great rarity and historical importance. It contains a valuable map of the country from Virginia to Newfoundland, in which is set forth the divers conflicting claims of both the French and the English. The entire district of Maine, from the River Sagadahoc to the head of the Bay of Fundy, is marked as pertaining to the government of the Sieur CHARNIZAI, granted in 1638. The book is a small neat volume, without date or place of imprint. It was probably privately printed for the use of the Commissioners.

679* EXAMINATION. A further Examination of our present American Measures. *Half calf.* 8° *Bath,* 1776

680 EXEGESIS Historica Regni Sueciae. *Half bound.* 4° *Stokholmiæ,* 1620

681 EXPLICACION DE LA BULA de la Santa Cruzada, que para la Mayor commodidad de los Reverendos Parrocos, y utilidad de todos los Fieles, manda dar a luz el Ill. Sr. Comissario General de la misma Santa Cruzada. *Fine copy, vellum.* 8° *Toledo,* 1758

On the utility, facility, and necessity of this Holy Bull, see pp. 13 and following. This Bull was sold for half a dollar, mostly in Mexico. Without it priests are said to have refused to give absolution.

682 EXPOSITION (An) of the Causes and Character of the Late War between the United States and Great Britain [Attributed to the pen of Mr. Secretary Dallas]. *Uncut.* 8° *Wm. Slade, Middlebury, Vt. July* 4, 1815

683 EXTRACTS from the Votes and Proceedings of the American Continental Congress, held at Philadelphia Sept. 5th, 1774. 8° *Hartford,* [1774]

684 EXTRACTS from the Votes and Proceedings of the American Continental Congress, held at Philadelphia Sept. 5th, 1774. *Half morocco.* 8° *Boston,* 1774

685 EXQUEMELIN (A. O.) DE AMERICAENSCHE ZEE-ROOVERS Behelsende een Partinent Verhael van alle de Roverye en Onmenselijcke Vreetheeden die de Engelsche en Franse Roovers tegens de Spanijaerden in America Gepleeght hebben. *A remarkably fine large and perfectly* UNCUT *copy, measuring nearly* 9 *by* 7 *inches. Complete with the beautiful engraved title, four portraits, six copperplates and two maps.* 4° *Jan ten Hoorn, Amsterdam,* 1678

FIRST EDITION, rare in any state, but UNIQUE in this condition. Perhaps no book in any language was ever the parent of so many imitations, and the source of so many fictions as this, the Original of the BUCANIERS OF AMERICA.

686 FAGRSKINNA, Kortfattet. Norske Konge-Saga: af P. A. Munch, og C. R. Unger. *Uncut.* 8° *Christiania,* 1847

687 FAIRBANKS (Jason) Report of the Trial of, for the Murder of Miss Elizabeth Fales. At the Supreme Court, Dedham, August, 1801. 3d edit. 8° *Boston,* 1801

688 FALKLAND ISLANDS. Thoughts on the late Transactions respecting Falkland's Islands. *Half mor.* 8° *New York*, 1771

689 FANCOURT (C. St. John) History of Yucatan, from its Discovery to the Close of the 17th Century. *Map. Cloth.* 8° *London*, 1854

690 FARMER and MOORE. New Hampshire Gazetteer. *Map and Engravings.* 12° *Concord*, 1823

691 FARMER and MOORE. COLLECTIONS, Historical and Miscellaneous, and Monthly Literary Journal. *Vol. III. Boards, uncut.* 8° *Concord, N. H.* 1824

This third volume in this state is very scarce.

692 FAUX (W.) Memorable Days in America, being a Journal of a Tour to the United States, including an Account of Mr. Birkbeck's Settlement in Illinois. *Half calf, gilt.* 8° *London*, 1823

693 FAY (JOSEPH, *Secretary to the Council of Safety at Bennington, Vt.*) AN ORIGINAL AUTOGRAPH LETTER, dated "In Council of Safety, Bennington, 21 Sept. 1777. To all Gentlemen concerned," enclosing a copy of a dispatch just received from GENERAL GATES, which the General requests may be forwarded to the Green Mountain Boys without a moment's delay. *In good preservation, one page* *Folio*, 1777

This spirited appeal to the GREEN MOUNTAIN BOYS ends thus: — "It seems that your assistance can never be more wanted than at this critical moment. The armies are now in such Position as renders it impracticable for the Enemy to avoid an Action, and it is a thing almost impossible for them to Retreat. Therefore if you should now instantly give your assistance you may have it in your power to do yourselves and country a greater service. So favorable a prospect of Success in the Northern Department never before appeared. Pray exert yourselves this once, and the matter cannot detain you long." The Boys did exert themselves, nor were they long detained by Burgoyne. That distinguished General retired to Cambridge and the Boys returned to the mountains.

694 FEARON (B.) Narrative of a Journey of Five Thousand Miles through the Eastern and Western States of America; with Remarks on Mr. Birkbeck's "Notes" and "Letters." *Calf.* 8° *London*, 1818

695 FEARON (Henry Bradshaw) Narrative of a Journey of 5000 Miles through the Eastern and Western States. Third edition. *Half morocco.* 8° *London*, 1819

696 FEDERAL Ready Reckoner, or Trader's Guide. 12° *Worcester*, 1795

697 FENELON (F.) The Adventures of Telemachus; with a Poem on a Rural Retreat, by the same Author; and likewise by another Hand, the Adventures of Aristonous. Translated by Mr. Ozell. *Plates, 2 vols, calf.* 8° *London*, 1735

698 FERNANDEZ DE SAN SALVADOR (DR. D. AUGUSTIN POMPOSO) Los Jesuitas quitados y Restituedos al Mundo. HISTORIA DE LA ANTIQUA CALIFORNIA. *Scarce.* 12° *Mariana Ontiveros, Mexico*, 1816

699 FFIRTH (John) Truth Vindicated; or, a Scriptural Essay wherein the Vulgar and frivolous cavils, commonly urged

against the Methodist Episcopal Church, are briefly considered. The 2d edition, revised. 24° *New York, Daniel Hitt,* 1810

700 Ficoroni (Fr.) Le Memorie ritrovate nel Territorio della prima, e seconda Citta di Labico, ei loro giusti Siti. *Plates. Half calf.* 4° *Roma,* 1745

701 Filesacus (J.) De Pœnitentia Syntagma. *Small* 8° *Parisiis,* 1633

702 Finlay (Hugh, *Surveyor of Post Roads of North America,*) Journal kept during his Survey of the Post Offices between Falmouth and Savannah, 13 September 1773, to 26 June, 1774. 150 *copies printed, uncut.* 4° *F. H. Norton, Brooklyn,* 1867

703 FIRMIN (Giles, *Sometime of New England*) Of Schism, Parochial Congregations in England, and Ordination by Imposition of Hands. Wherein Dr. Owen's Discovery of Schism is examined, with Mr. Noyes of New England his Arguments against Imposition of hands in Ordination. 8° *Lond.* 1658

A presentation copy "For the reverend and my very dear friend Mr. Argar, Minister in Braintree." Throughout this book the author makes frequent references to the New England Fathers, Hooker, Norton, and others.

704 FIRMIN (Giles) The Real Christian, or a Treatise of Effectual Calling, &c. *Corner of pp.* 181–2 *torn off. Calf.* 8° *Rogers & Fowle, Boston,* 1742

The biographers who seek personal gossip about our early New England Fathers should not neglect to consult the several works of Giles Firmin, a Suffolkman, educated at Old Cambridge, who came to New England in 1634 (?) and subsequently practiced as a physician at Ipswich, where he married a daughter of Master Nathaniel Ward, "The Simple Cobler of Agawam in America." He returned to England and became "Minister of the Gospel at Shalford in Essex," from whence he was ejected in 1662 for Nonconformity. He then resumed his practice as a Physician and lived on till 1697. In neither profession was it his practice, as he says, to administer "a rowsing vomit" to his patients "when they had need of other kind of Physic."

705 Fischer (C. A.) Tafereelen van Brasilië. *Half maroon morocco, uncut,* 8° *Haarlem,* 1819

706 Fischer (C. A.) Tafereelen van Brasilië. *Half calf.* 8° *Haarlem,* 1819

707 Fisher (A.) Journal of a Voyage of Discovery to the Arctic Regions, in the Hecla and Griper, 1819–20. *Map. Half calf.* 8° *London,* 1821

708 Fisher (William) New Travels among the Indians of North America. *Portraits. Calf.* 12° *Philadelphia,* 1812

709 Fisk (E.) Anniversary Sermons in the First Congregational Church, Wrentham, June 14, 1846. 8° *Boston,* 1846

710 Fitzherbert (N.) Oxoniensis in Anglia Academiæ Descriptio. 12° *Romæ,* 1602

711 Fitzherbert (N.) Oxoniensis, *etc. Another copy.* 12° *Romæ,* 1602

712 Fleet's Pocket Almanack for the Year 1793, calculated chiefly for the use of the Commonwealth of Massachusetts, Boston, the Metropolis. To which is annexed the Massachusetts Register, &c. 16° *Boston, F. & J. Fleet.*

713 FLEMING (Philippe) Oostende Vermaerde, gheweldighe lanckduyrighe ende Bloedighe Belegheringhe, Bestorminghe ende Stoute Aenvallen, etc., etc. *Many portraits, plates and maps.* 12 + 598 *pp.* 4° *Graven Hage,* 1621

This book is called the New Troy or the Wonderful Siege of Ostend, 1597–1604.

714 FLINT (A.) Sermon at East Haddam, Oct. 23, 1816, at the Ordination of Rev. Isaac Parsons. *Uncut.* 8° *Hartford,* 1816

715 FLINT (Timothy) Recollections of the last Ten Years, passed in occasional Residences in the Valley of the Mississippi. *Half calf.* 8° *Boston,* 1826

716 FLINT (Timothy) Indian Wars of the West. 12° *Cincinnati,* 1833

717 FOCHER (JOANNES, *Minorita*) ITINERARIVM CATHOLICVM Proficientium, ad infideles cõuertendos. Fratere Ioãe Focher minorita autore. Nuper summa cura & diligẽntia auctũ, expurgatum, limatũ ac prælo mãdatũ, per fratrem Didacum Valadesium, ejusdem instituti, ac provintiæ Sancti Euangelij in noua Hyspania, professorem. Ad Reverendissimom Patrem, F. Franciscum Guzmanum, omnium Indiarum maris Occeani Commissarium generalium. *Vellum.* 8° *Hispali, Apud Alfonsum Scribanum,* 1574

This EXCESSIVELY RARE book of viii prelim + 99 folioed + 9 leaves of Index, is wholly unknown to the American historian, though it has played no inconsiderable part in the conversion of the Indians of Mexico, especially the Nation of the *Chichimecas.* Fray Focher was a Frenchman, but his book on the conversion of infidels generally was abridged, altered and adapted by the Mexican Missionaries to their use among the Indians. This fine copy unfortunately wants the ninth leaf of Index.

718 FLORENCIA (FRANCISCO DE, *de la Compañia de Jesus*). LA MILAGROSA INVENCION de un Thesoro escondido en un Campo . . . . patente y a en el Santuario de los Remedios en su Admirable Imagen de Ntra Señora, Defensora de los Españoles, avogada de los Indios, Conquistadora de Mexico, *etc.* Noticias de su Origen, y venidas a Mexico, etc. *Very fine clean copy, in the original vellum.* SCARCE. 4° *En Sevilla,* 1745

719 FLORES (JUAN DE) THE HISTORIE OF AVRELIO AND OF ISABELL, doughter of the Kinge of Schotlande, nyeuley translatede In foure langagies, Frenche, Italien, Spanishe, and Inglishe [*colophon*] Fue Impressa en muy noble villa de *Anuers, en casa de Iuan Latio Año de* 1556.

FIRST EDITION, OF THE HIGHEST RARITY. *Fine copy, in small* 8°

JUAN FLORES was one of the very earliest of the Romance writers of Spain, more than three quarters of a century before Cervantes. He seems to have exhausted his inventive powers with this story. It first appeared in 1521, under the title of *La Historia de Grisel y Mirabella.* The same year it came out at Milan in Italian. In 1530 it reappeared in French as *Le jugement Damour.* In 1535 it came out under the new title of *La Deplovrable fin de flamete,* appearing in many editions, and finally after having been translated into English and again in French, it appeared in this beautiful form in four languages, in four columns, side by side as the *Historia de Aurelio y de Ysabela.* It has been printed in several editions and languages since, but none is comparable to this in rarity, beauty, or quaintness of language and orthography. That Shakespeare drew inspiration from this little book in his *Tempest*, has been many times asserted. The following is a sample of the English: "If me cõinge (madame) geueth you plesour wherfore of itt hope you vengeãce, and satisfaction of the foshippe that you beare me: this desiere I gretley to vnderstande: for if y had beane myndede to haue kepte me peace of manney of yowre workes, you haue now taken frome the goodnesse for to saie a grete parte of the secretes of the ladies, that be to me knowen," etc.

720 FORBES (A.) CALIFORNIA; a History of Upper and Lower California, from their first Discovery to the Present Time, with Appendix. *Map and numerous engravings. Cloth.* 8° *Lond.* 1839

721 FORBES (A.) California, etc. *Another copy. Map and engravings. Half morocco, uncut.* 8° *London,* 1839

722 FORCE (Peter) TRACTS and other Papers, relating principally to the Origin, Settlement, and Progress of the Colonies in America from the Discovery of the Continent to the Year 1776. 2 *vols, cloth, uncut.* 8° *Washington,* 1836–8

723 FOREIGN COUNTRIES. Commercial Regulations of the Foreign Countries with which the United States have Commercial Intercourse. *Boards, uncut.* 8° *Washington,* 1819

724 FORREST (Edwin) Fourth of July Oration. 8° *N. York,* 1838

725 FORREST Divorce Case. Report of the Trial of Catherine N. Forrest *vs* Edwin Forrest for Divorce, December, 1851. *Uncut.* 8° *New York,* 1851

726 FORSTER (Johan Reinhold) REISE UM DIE WELT 1772–1775. Beschrieben von George Forster. 2 *vols, half calf.* 4° *Berlin,* 1778–80

George Forster, the son of J. R. Forster, who accompanied Capt. Cook in his voyages, edited and published these volumes. It was to this same George Forster, and to this same work that Humboldt, in his Cosmos acknowledges his indebtedness more than to all other sources, for his early love of nature and tropical beauty. This original edition is uncommon.

727 FORT PILLOW Massacre. Reports of the Committee on the Conduct of the War. 8° *cloth.*

728 FOSTER (Dan) Examination of a late Publication, entitled the Doctrine of Eternal Misery, by Nathan Strong. 8° *Walpole, N. H.* 1803

729 FOSTER (J. Y.) NEW JERSEY and the Rebellion: a History of the Services of the Troops and People of New Jersey in aid of the Union Cause. *Cloth.* *Thick* 8° *Newark,* 1868

730 FOTHERGILL (John, *Friend, and friend of Franklin*) An Account of the Life and Travels of, to which are added divers Epistles to Friends in Great Britain and America. *Calf.* 8° *London,* 1753

731 FOUNDATION of the Faith assailed in Oxford: a Letter to the Archbishop of Canterbury. 8° *London,* 1831

732 FOUR LETTERS; being an interesting Correspondence between John Adams and Samuel Adams, on the important Subject of Government. *Uncut.* 8° *Boston,* 1802

733 FOX (C. J.) History of the old Township of Dunstable, including Nashua, Nashville, Hollis, Hudson, etc. *Map and Engravings. Cloth.* 8° *Nashua,* 1846

734 Fox (Charles James) Letter to the Electors of the City and Liberty of Westminster. *Half morocco.* 8° *London,* 1793

735 Fox (Eben *of Roxbury, Mass.*), Revolutionary Adventures. *Portrait. Cloth.* 18° *Boston,* 1838

736 FOXE (John) Acts and Monuments of the Martyrs. *Vol. II.* Black letter, very fine, *large and clean copy. Calf.* *Folio, London,* 1610

737 Francis (C.) Historical Sketch of Watertown, Mass., from its first Settlement to the close of its Second Century. 8° *Cambridge,* 1830

738 FRANCK (Sebastian) Weltbuch, naemlich in Asiam, Aphricam, Europam und Americam. *Black letter, vellum.* *Folio,* 1542

Considering the early date of this work, and the amount of matter in it, it must be regarded as one of the most important historical books on America at that time. It passed through several editions and translations.

739 FRANCK (Sebastian) VVerelt-boeck. Spieghel. *Fine clean copy.* A very scarce edition. *Vellum, uncut.* *Folio, Amsterdam,* 1595

740 Francklyn (G.) An Answer to Rev. Mr. Clarkson's Essay on the Slavery and Commerce of the Human Species, particularly the African. From a Gentleman in Jamaica to his friend in London. The treatment of Slaves in the West Indies. Showing the Antiquity, Universality, and Lawfulness of Slavery, as ever having been one of the States and Conditions of Mankind. *Uncut, boards.* 8° *The Logographic Press, London,* 1789

741 Franklin (Benj.) The Complete Works; now first collected, with Memoirs of his early Life, written by Himself. *Portrait and Vignettes. 3 vols, half calf.* 8° *London, n. d.*

742 FRANKLIN (Benjamin) Remedio Natural para precaverse de los Rayos, y de sus funestos efectos. Secreto tan util, como curioso, sacado de las repetidas observaciones, y experiencias, que sobre la analogia de la electricidad con la materia de los rayos, ha estampado en Madrid año de 1757, en su *Diario Philosophico* Don Juan Galisteo, tom. I. num. 6. 8*pp.* 4° [*At end*] *Reimpresso en Mexico,* [1758 ?]

This tract treats of Dr. Franklin's discovery of the use of the lightning rod, and the use of the electrical machine, as set forth in his publication in London in 1751, how the matter was immediately taken up in France and Spain, and subsequently in Mexico, particularly in Pueblo de los Angeles where there is usually much lightning. The writer differs from Franklin and other philosophers as to the form and shape of the lightning rods. Instead of being pointed or square, as discussed in the Royal Society of London, this writer thinks the form of a cross would better secure the desired protection. The Holy Cross always strikes certain terror into the malignant spirits of the clouds, so that if Franklin's steel points were arranged in the form of a cross they would become a more secure protection against the insults of the lightning!

743 Franklin (Benj.) Experiments and Observations on Electricity. 5th edition, *half green morocco, gilt, uncut.* 4° *London,* 1774

744 FRANKLIN (Benj.) Political, Miscellaneous, and Philosophical Pieces; with Notes and Index. *Plates.* 2 *vols, calf.* 4° *London,* 1779

745 FRANKLIN (Benj.) Political, Miscellaneous, and Philosophical Pieces, with Notes and Index. *Portrait and plates. Half green morocco, uncut.* 8° *London,* 1779

746 FRANKLIN (Benj.) Political, Miscellaneous, and Philosophical Pieces, with Notes and Index. *Portrait and plates, calf.* 8° *London,* 1779

747 FRANKLIN (Benj.) SÄMMTLICHE WERKE aus dem Englischen und Französischen ubersetzt, von G. T. Wenzel. *Portrait,* 3 *vols, half red morocco uncut.* 8° *Dresden,* 1780

748 FRANKLIN (Benj.) Osservazione a chiunque desideri passare in America. *Half green morocco, gilt uncut.* 8° *Padova,* 1785

749 FRANKLIN (Benj.) The Life of Benjamin Franklin. Written by himself. *Good copy.* 12° *Cushing & Carlton, Salem,* 1796

750 FRANKLIN (Benj.) Nach gelassene Schriften und Correspondenz, nebst seinem Leben. 5 *vols, half red mor. uncut. Fine copy.* 8° *Weimar,* 1817

751 FRANKLIN (Benj.) Der Weg zum Glück, oder Leben und Meynungen des Dr. Benjamin Franklin von ihm selbst geschrieben. *Fine copy, scarce.* 16° *Reading, Pa., bey Heinrich B. Sage,* 1820

752 FRANSHAM (John) The Entertaining Traveller. *Plates,* 2 *vols, calf.* 8° *London,* 1767

753 FREZIER (M.) Relation du Voyage de la Mer du Sud aux Côtes du Chily et du Perou, Faits pendant les années 1712, 1713 & 1714. Dediée à S. A. R. Monseigneur le Duc d'Orleans Regent du Royaume. Par M. Frezier, Ingenieur Ordinaire du Roy. Ouvrage enrichi de quantité de Planche en Taille-douce. *Fine copy, calf.* 4° *Paris, Chez Jean-Geoffròy Nyon,* 1716

754 FREZIER (M.) Relation du Voyage de la Mer du Sud, aux Cotes du Chili, du Perou, et du Bresil 1712–14. *Maps and plates,* 2 *vols, half calf.* 8° *Amst.* 1717

755 FREZIER (M.) Relation du Voyage de la Mer du Sud, aux Cotes du Chili, du Perou et de Bresil. *Maps and Plates,* 2 *vols, calf.* 8° *Amsterdam,* 1717

756 FREZIER (Mr.) Voyage to the South Sea, and along the Coasts of Chili and Peru in the Years 1712–13 and 14; with a Postscript by Dr. Edmand Halley. 37 *maps and plates, calf.* 4° *London,* 1717

757 FREZIER (M.) Reis-Beschryving door de Zuid-Zee, langs de Kusten van Chili, Peru en Brazil 1712–14. *Numerous maps and plates, vellum.* 4° *Amsterdam,* 1718

758 FREZIER (M.) Relation du Voyage de la Mer du Sud, aux Cotes du Chily et du Perou 1712, 13, 14. *Calf, plates.* 4° *Paris,* 1746

759 Free Enquiry (A) into the causes both real and pretended for laying the Embargo. By a Citizen of Vermont. 8° *C. Spear, Windsor, Vt.* 1808

760 Free-Masonry. Principles of Free-Masonry Delineated. *Calf.* 12° *Exeter,* 1777

761 Fremont (J. C.) Report of an Exploration between the Missouri River and the Rocky Mountains. 8° *Washington,* 1843

762 Fremont (John Charles) Geographical Memoir upon Upper California, in illustration of his Map of Oregon and California. 8° *Washington,* 1848

763 FRENCH EAST INDIA COMPANY. 4 *very rare tracts in* 1 *vol. vellum.* 16° 1665–6, *viz :*

Relation de la Conduite presante de la Cour de France: &c. 106 *pp.* *Fribourg,* 1665

Discovrs d'vn fidele Sviet dv Roy tovchant l'Establissement d'vne Compagnie Françoise pour le Commerce des Indes Orientales. 60 *pp.* *Paris,* 1666

Articles et Conditions sur lesquelles les Marchands Negotiants du Royaume supplient pour l'Etablissement d'une Compagnie pour le Commerce des Indes Orientales. 23 *pp.* *Paris,* 1665

Relation de l'Etablissement de la Compagnie François pour le Commerce des Indes Orientales. 132 *pp.* *Amsterdam,* 1666

764 Frisbie (Levi) An Oration at Ipswich, the 29th of April 1783, on account of the Peace between Great Britain and the United States of America. *Uncut.* 4° *E. Russell, Boston,* 1783

765 FRY (Francis) A Description of the Great Bible 1539, and the 6 editions of Cranmer's Bible 1540 and 1541, also the editions in large folio of the authorized version 1611, 1613, 1617, 1634, 1640, with illustrations and original leaves from the several editions. *Folio, London,* 1865

A few copies only published at £5 5*s.* each.

766 Fry (Francis, F. S. A.) The Bible by Coverdale, 1535. Remarks on the Titles; the Year of Publication, the Preliminary, the Water-marks, etc., with fac similes. Published a £3 3 0. *Half morocco,* *Imp.* 8° *London,* 1867

This is one of the few copies printed upon pure white vellum. Few books are better entitled to the honor of a *vellum* issue than this historical and bibliographical account of the first printed Bible in the English language. Notwithstanding the most active bibliographical research for the past two hundred years, it is not even now known where or by whom Miles Coverdale's English Bible was printed.

767 GAGE (Thomas) New Survey of the West Indies; or the English Americain his Travail by Sea and Land. *Second Edition, with maps, half calf.* *Folio, London,* 1655

768 Gage (Thomas) Nieuwe ende seer naeuwkeurige Reyse Door de Spanische West Indien. *Maps and plates ; half brown morocco.* 4° *Utrecht,* 1682

769 Gage (Thomas) Voyages dans la Nouvelle Espagne, avec la Description del a Ville de Mexique. *Map and plates,* 2 *vols, half blue morocco, uncut.* 8° *Amsterdam,* 1695

770 GAGE (Thomas) Les Voyages dans la nouvelle Espagne, avec la Description de la Ville de Mexique. 4 *vols in* 2, *calf.* 8° *Amsterdam*, 1721

771 GALL (Ludwig) Meine auswanderung nach den Vereinigten-Staten in Nord Amerika, in 1819 und 1820. *Frontispieces*, 2 *vols, half calf.* 8° *Trier*, 1822

772 GALLOWAY (JOSEPH, *Late Speaker of the House of Assembly of Pennsylvania, and later Tory refugee in London*) A Candid Examination of the Mutual Claims of Great Britain, and the Colonies: With a Plan of Accommodation on Constitutional Principles. *Fine copy, rough leaves.* 8° *New York by* JAMES RIVINGTON, 1775

In the same volume are the following other scarce tracts by Mr. Galloway, viz:

2. A REPLY to an Address to the Author of a Pamphlet, entitled, "A Candid Examination," &c. By the author of the Candid Examination. *Fine copy, rough leaves.* *New York by* JAMES RIVINGTON, 1775
3. THE EXAMINATION of Joseph Galloway, before the House of Commons in a Committee on the American Papers. 2d Edit. *London, J. Wilkie*, 1780
4. LETTER to a Nobleman, on the Conduct of the War in the Middle Colonies. 2d Edit. With a Plan of the operations of the British and Rebel Army in the Campaign 1777 on the Delaware River. *London, J. Wilkie*, 1779
5. A LETTER to the Right Honorable Lord Viscount H—e, on his naval conduct in the American War. *London, J. Wilkie*, 1779
6. COOL Thoughts on the Consequences to Great Britain of American Independence. On the Expence of Great Britain in the settlement and Defence of the American Colonies. On the value and importance of the American colonies, &c. *London, J. Wilkie*, 1780
7. Historical and Political Reflections on the Rise and Progress of the American Rebellion, &c. *London, J. Wilkie*, 1780

In all seven rare octavo tracts, all large and clean copies, richly bound in one volume, in old red morocco gilt edges. Throughout the volume are many manuscript corrections, probably by the hand of the author. The volume is lettered "Galloway's American Tracts," and if there were any doubt before, this will probably settle the authorship of the anonymous tracts.

773 GARAY (José de) An Account of the Isthmus of Tehuantepec. 8° *London*, 1846

774 GARCIA AB HORTO. Aromatum et simplicium aliquot Medicamentorum apud Indos nascentium Historia; in Epitomen contractu, à Car. Clusio. *Plates, vellum.* 8° *C. Plantin, Antverpiae*, 1674

775 GARCIA ab Horto. Aromatum et Simplicivm aliquot medicamentorum apud Indos nascentium Historia. *Wood-cuts, vellum.* 8° *Ex Officina Plant. Antverpiæ*, 1593

776 GARCIA (GREGORIO) Origen de los Indios de el Nuevo Mundo, Indias Occidentales, etc. *Calf.* *Folio, Madrid*, 1729

777 GARCILASSO DE LA VEGA (El Yuca) Histoire des Guerres Civiles des Espagnols dans les Indes. Traduite par J. Baudoin. 4 *vols, map and plates. Calf.* 8° *Amsterdam*, 1706

778 GARCILASO DE LA VEGA (El Yuca) La Florida: Historia del Adelantado, Hernando de Soto, y de otros Heroicos Caballeros, Espanoles, e Indios. *Half vellum.* *Folio, Madrid*, 1723

779 GARCILLASSO DE LA VEGA (El Yuca) Histoire de la Conquete de la Florida. Nouv. Ed. *Map and plates. 2 vols, calf.* 8° *La Haye*, 1735

780 GARDINER (Capt.) An Account of the Expedition to the West Indies against Martinico with the Reduction of Guadelupe. 3d Edition. In French and English. *Half calf.* 4° *John Baskerville, Birmingham*, 1762

781 GAULE (J.) The Mag-astro-mancer, or the Magicall-Astrologicall-Diviner Posed and Puzzled. *Calf.* 4° *London*, 1652

782 GAZETTEER. The North American and the West-Indian Gazetteer. Colonies and Islands. *Half calf.* 8° *Lond.* 1776

From this book it appears that KING PHILIP of Spain [not Pokonoket] died at Bristol in Rhode Island. See under BRISTOL.

783 GEBELEN (M. Count de) Histoire Naturelle de la Parole. *Plates, half calf.* 8° *Paris*, 1776

784 GEE (Joshua) The Trade and Navigation of Great Britain Considered. 8° *London*, 1738

785 GEE (Joshua) The Trade and Navigation of Great Britain Considered. Fourth Edition. *Calf.* 8° *London*, 1738

786 GEE (Joshua) The Trade and Navigation of Great Britain Considered. Fifth Edition. *Calf.* 8° *Glasgow*, 1750

787 GEE (Joshua) The Trade and Navigation of Great Britain Considered. New Edition. *Calf.* 8° *London*, 1768

788 GEIJER (E. G.) History of the Swedes. Translated with Introduction and Notes by J. H. Turner. First Portion is from the Earliest Period to the Accession of Charles the Tenth. *Cloth.* 8° *London.*

789 GENERAL Collection of Treatys, Declarations of War, Manifestos, etc., relating to Peace and War from 1648 to the present Time. *Calf.* 8° *London*, 1710

790 GENTLEMAN'S Law Magazine, containing a variety of the most useful Practical Forms of Writing. 12° *Middlebury, Vt.* 1804

One of the rarest books printed in Vermont.

791 GENTLEMAN'S MAGAZINE and Historical Chronicle from 1735 to 1838. 96 *vols.* 8° *London.*

From 1735 to 1782 16 vols, irregular; from 1787 to 1825 inclusive, complete with the exception of Part II. 1806, 76 vols. New Series from July 1836 to June 1838, 4 vols.

792 GIBBS (M.) Practical Forms and Precedents. Second Edition. 8° *New York*, 1854

793 GIBSON (Edm. *Bp. of London*) Two Letters to Families in the English Plantations abroad, and to Missionaries there on Instruction of the Negroes. *Half roan, closely cut.* 8° *London*, 1727

794 GILBERT (Thomas) Voyage from New South Wales to Canton in 1798. *With Views of the Islands discovered. Half green, morocco, uncut.* 4° *London*, 1789

795 GILL (John) Exposition of the Book of Solomon's Song; to which is added the Targum. *Half calf.* *Folio, London*, 1728

796 GILLELAND (J. C.) History of the Late War between the United States and Great Britain; containing an accurate account of the most important engagements by Sea and Land, with geographical sketches. *Sheep.* 12° *Baltimore,* 1817

797 GILLIES (JOHN) Historical Collections relating to remarkable periods of the Success of the Gospel. 2 *vols, uncut, half brown morocco.* 8° *Glasgow,* 1754

Page 328, Success of the Gospel in America. Pages 348–351 purport to be extracts "from Turner's Remarkable Providences, Part I. Ch. 18," containing the reports of the Speeches of the Indians collected and taken down by Daniel Gookin, and translated into English by Eliot. A large part of the second volume relates to America.

798 GILLIES (John) Memoirs of the Life of George Whitefield. *Calf, title MS.* 12° 1798

799 GILPIN (William) of Queen's College, Oxford, Life of Bernard Gilpin. Second Edition. *Calf.* 8° *London,* 1753

800 GILPIN (W.) Observations, relative chiefly to Picturesque Beauty, made in the year 1776, in several Parts of Great Britain; particularly the High-lands of Scotland. *Illustrated with numerous Engravings.* 2 *vols, calf.* 8° *London,* 1789

801 GISBORNE (Lionel) The Isthmus of Darien in 1852. Journal of the Expedition of Inquiry for the Junction of the Atlantic and Pacific Oceans. 4 *Maps, cloth.* 8° *London,* 1853

802 GIUSTINIANO (AGOSTINO) CASTIGATISSIMI ANNALI della Ecclesia et Illustrissima Republica di Genoa; con la loro copiosa Tavola. *Engraved title, calf gilt.* *Folio, Genoa,* 1537

"Par commun." — *Brunet.* This volume contains early references to Columbus.

803 GLASTENBURY for Two Hundred Years, a Centennial Discourse, May 18th 1853, by Rev. Alonzo B. Chapin, with Appendix. *Cloth.* 8° *Hartford,* 1853

804 GLOVER (Mr.) Substance of the Evidence on the petition presented by the West India Planters to the House of Commons, 16 March, 1775. *Half roan.* 8° *London, n. d.*

805 GOLDEN CABINET (The) being the Laboratory, or handmaid to the Arts, containing such Branches of Useful Knowledge, as nearly concerns all kinds of people, from the squire to the peasant. The 3 Parts.
Sheep. 12° *Phil. W. Spotswood,* 1793

806 GOLDSMITH (Oliver) The Vicar of Wakefield.
2 *vols in* 1. 12° *E. Bushnell, Norwich, Ct.* 1791

807 GOMARA (FRANCESCO LOPEZ DE) HISTORIA de las Conquistas de Hernando Cortès traducida al Mexicano y aprobada por verdadera por D. Juan Bautista de San Anton Muñon Chimalpain Quauhtlehuanitzin, Indio Mexicano. Publicada por C. M. de Bustamante. 2 *vols.* 4° *Mèxico,* 1826

808 GONÇALES DE MENDOZA. Histoire dv Grand Royavme de la Chine, contentant trois Voyages fait vers iceluy en l'an 1577–79–81. Trad. par Luc de la Porte.
Vellum. 8° *Paris,* 1588

809 GONÇALEZ DE MENDOZA. Histoire dv Grande Royavme de la Chine. *Calf.* 8° *Paris,* 1589

810 GOODHUE (Rev. J. F.) History of the Town of Shoreham, Vermont, from the Date of its Charter, 1761, with Historical Accounts of the County of Addison, by S. Swift. *Portraits. Cloth.* 8° *Middlebury,* 1861

811 GOODWIN (N.) Genealogical Notes, or Contributions to the Family History of some of the First Settlers of Connecticut and Massachusetts. *Cloth.* 8° *Hartford,* 1856

812 GOODWIN (N.) Another Copy. *Cloth.* 8° *Hartford,* 1856

813 GORTON (SAMUEL, *of Rhode Island*) A COPIE OF AN ANSWER SENT TO NATHANIEL MORTON OF NEW PLIMOUTH CONCERNING SOME PART OF HIS BOOKE INTULED NEW ENGLANDS MEMORIALL, *dated* Warwick, June 30th, 1669, *and signed* ꝑ me SAMUELL GORTON. *The original Autograph Manuscript in the well-known beautiful penmanship of Gorton, on six large pages, very closely written with about 75 lines on a page, in good preservation, and richly bound in red morocco by Pratt in his best style.* *Folio,* 1669

THIS IMPORTANT HISTORICAL MANUSCRIPT, one of the *archetypa* of the Old Colony is deserving of a permanent abiding place. Notwithstanding its vicissitudes it has seen good company. It bears the endorsements of THOMAS PRINCE and GOVERNOR HUTCHINSON, showing that it has been under the hands of those distinguished historians. In 1842 the writer purchased it in Connecticut, and soon after lent it for a short time to Col. PETER FORCE who made good use of it. It next, in 1844, passed into the hands of EDWARD A. CROWNINSHIELD at a cost of $50, in our golden days. After having rested there for fifteen years it passed over to London with Mr. Crowninshield's library, being estimated in that purchase at fifteen guineas. It has since been richly bound at a cost of two guineas, and is now looking out for another situation, having re-crossed the Atlantic.

814 GOSTLING (W.) A Walk in and about Canterbury, with many Observations, etc. *Map. Calf.* 8° *Canterbury,* 1779

815 GOTTFRIED (J. L.) NEWE ARCHONTOLOGIA COSMICA, das ist Beschreibung aller Kayserthumhen Konigreichen und Republicken der gantzen Welt, die Keinen Hohern erkennen. *Maps and numerous fine Views, by Merian. Vellum.* *Folio, Franckfurt,* 1646

816 GRAHAM (JOHN A.) DESCRIPTIVE SKETCH of the Present State of Vermont. *Portrait. Marbled calf.* 12° *London,* 1797

817 GRAINGER (J.) The Sugar-Cane; a Poem, in four Books, with Notes. 8° *London,* 1766

818 GRANADOS Y GALVEZ (JOSEPH JOAQUIN) Tardes Americanas, Gobierno Gentil y Catolicon: Breve y particular Noticia de toda la Historia Indiana: sucesos, cosos notables, y cosas ignoradas, desde la entrada de la Gran Nacion Tulteca á esta tierra de Anahuac, hasta los presentes tiempos. Trabajadas por un Indio, y un Español. *Vellum.* EXCESSIVELY RARE AND IMPORTANT.
4° *Mexico, D. Felipe de Zuñega y Ontiveros,* 1778

See NUGGETS No. 1286. The author of this interesting history of Mexico was stationed in the Province of Michoican, and was guardian of the Convent of Xiquilpan, Valladolid, and Rioverde, and Superintendent of all the Missions among the Indians in that Department. The book is in the form of a dialogue between an Indian and a Spaniard. There is a good deal respecting early Mexican Archæology and Antiquities, especially respecting the Mexican Calendar, the names of the Kings of the Empire of Tezcuco, etc.

19 GRAY (F. C.) Oration before the Legislature of Massachusetts, on the hundredth Anniversary of the Birth of George Washington. *Uncut.* 8° *Boston*, 1800

820 GRAY-CAP (A), for a Green-head in a Dialogue between Father and Son. First American Edit. *Calf.* 12° *Phil. S. Longcope*, 1798

821 GRESWELL (Rev. W. P.) ANNALS OF PARISIAN TYPOGRAPHY, containing an Account of the earliest Typographical Establishments of Paris; and Notices and Illustrations of the most remarkable Productions of the Parisian Gothic Press; *Cuts of Printer's Marks. Half morocco, uncut.* LARGE PAPER. 8° *London*, 1818

822 Griffet (H.) Traité de Preuves, de la verité de l'Histoire. *Calf.* 8° *Liege*, 1770

823 GRIFFITH (W.) Annual Law Register of the United States, for 1821–2. Vol. III. and Vol. IV. 2 copies, 3 vols. *Uncut.* 8° *Burlington, N. J.* 1822

824 GROAN (A) from a True Blue Presbyterian, who is no Lover of Independency, nor an Admirer of High Flown Presbetry; who would drown the ignorant zealous Professor, and pour burning Coals on the lukewarm Laodicean Temper. *Sewed.* 8° *Edinb.* 1735

825 GROTIUS (Hugo) Excerpta ex Tragœdiis et Comœdiis Græcis quæ exstant, tenvo quæ periervnt. Latinis versibus reddita cum Notis et Indice. *Calf.* 4° *Parisiis*, 1626

826 GRYNAEUS (SIMON) NOVVS ORBIS Regionvm ac Insvlarvm, etc. *Old calf.* *Folio, Basiliæ*, 1537

A grand old book of reference, containing, in a fair Latin version the Voyages, 1 of Codamosto, 2 Columbus, 3 Alonzo Niño, 4 Vincent Pinzon, 5 Americus Vespucci, 6 Pedro Alvarez Cabral, 7 Joseph the Indian, 8 the Portuguese to India described in a letter of Emanuel to Leo X, 9 Varthema, 10 the Holy Land by Brocard, 11 Marco Polo, 12 Haython's Tartars, 13 Sarmatia by Matthew Miechow, 14 Muscovie by Paulus Jovius, 15 Peter Martyr's New Islands, 16 Stella's Prussia, 17 Maximilian of Transilvania, his Account of Magellan's Voyage.

827 GUIANA. An Essay on the Natural History of Guiana in South America; with Account of the Religion, Manners and Customs of its Indian Inhabitants. *Boards.* 8° *London*, 1769

828 GUICCIARDINI (Jr.) Historia d'Italia . . . gli ultimi quattro libri. MENTIONS COLUMBUS. *Vellum.* 4° *Venezia*, 1564

829 GUILLERMIN (Gilbert) Précis Historique des derniers Evénements de la Partie de l'Est de Saint-Domingue, depuis le 10 Aout 1808 jusqu'a la Capitulation. *Map and Engravings. Half mor. uncut.* 8° *Paris*, 1811

830 GUMILLA (Joseph) HISTOIRE Naturelle, Civile et Geographique DE L' ORINOQUE, et des principales Rivieres qui s'y jettent. Traduit de l'Espagnol, par M. Eidous. *Map, 3 vols, calf. An important work.* 8° *Avignon*, 1758

831 HADDON (WALTER) Contra Hieron. Osorium eiusq; odiosas Insectationes pro Euangelicæ Veritates necessaria Defensione, Responsio apologetica, continuata per J. Foxum. *Wants the Title Page; commencing with B i. Calf.* 4° *J. Day, London,* 1577

"Q. Elizabeth being asked whether she preferred Haddon or Buchanan as men of learning? she replied, Buchananum omnibus antepono, Haddonum nemini postpono." — *Lowndes.*

832 HACKE (William) A Collection of Original Voyages. *Maps, calf.* 8° *London,* 1698

833 HACKETT (J.) Narrative of the Expedition which sailed from England in 1817, to Join the South American Patriots. *Half morocco.* 8° *London,* 1818

834 HALE (Salma) History of the United States. 2d Edition. *Half calf.* 8° *London,* 1827

835 HALE (Samuel) Annals of the Town of Keene, from its Settlement in 1734 to 1815. *Map, cloth.* 8° *Keene,* 1851

836 HALES (J. G.) Survey of Boston, and its Vicinity. *Frontispiece and map, half roan.* 12° *Boston,* 1821

837 HALIBURTON (T. C.) Historical and Statistical Account of Nova Scotia. *Map and engravings,* 2 *vols, half morocco, fine uncut copy.* 8° *Halifax,* 1829

838 HALL (BASIL) Extracts from a Journal written on the Coasts of Chili, Peru, and Mexico, in the years 1820, 1821, 1822. *Third Edition. Map,* 2 *vols, half mor.* 8° *Edinburgh,* 1824

From the library of Louis Philippe at Neuilly.

839 HALL (Basil) Voyage au Chili, au Pérou, et au Mexique. 2 *vols, half calf.* 8° *Paris,* 1825

840 HALL (Basil) Extracts from a Journal written on the coasts of Chili, Peru and Mexico, in the years 1820–1, 2. 4th Edition. 2 *vols, map, half calf.* 8° *Edinburgh,* 1825

841 HALL (Basil) DAGBOCK gehouden op eene Reize lanjs de Kusten van Chili, Peru en Mexico 1820–22. 2 *vols, half brown morocco, uncut.* 8° *Delft,* 1826

842 HALL (Basil) Voyage au Chili, au Pérou, et au Mexique. 2 *vols in* 1, *boards.* 16° *La Haye,* 1835

843 HALL (Basil) Voyage dans les États-Unis de l'Amerique du Nord, et dans le Haut et le Bas-Canada. *Map,* 2 *vols, half calf.* 8° *Paris,* 1854

844 HALLIDAY (J.) LIFE OF WILLIAM LATE EARL OF MANSFIELD. *Portrait, half maroon morocco.* 4° *London,* 1797

Contains observations relating incidentally to America and its bibliography.

845 HAMILTON. MEMOIRS OF LADY HAMILTON, with Illustrative Anecdotes of many of her most particular Friends and distinguished Contemporaries. *Portrait after Romney; boards, uncut.* LARGE PAPER, *fine copy.* 8° *London,* 1815

Rigidly suppressed in London, but reprinted the same year in New York. This London edition has become very rare, especially in the fine condition of the present copy.

846 HAMILTON (ALEXANDER, *Late Secretary of the Treasury*) OBSERVATIONS on Certain Documents contained in No. V. & VI. of "*The History of the United States for the year* 1796," in which the charge of Speculation against Alexander Hamilton, late Secretary of the Treasury, is fully refuted. WRITTEN BY HIMSELF. *Clean copy on a foul subject, rough leaves, sewed.* 8° *John Fenno, Philadelphia,* 1797

"Written by himself," or this little book of 96 pages would most likely have been pronounced the greatest libel upon the greatest man New York ever produced. It has been claimed to the honor of his friends that they endeavored to suppress it. It was copyrighted, and never reprinted until recently, but scarce as it has become, it is now part of the literature of the land. The author writes on p. 5 : "Merely because I *retained* an opinion once common to me and the most influencial of those who opposed me, *That the public debt ought to be provided for on the basis of the contract upon which it was created,* I have been wickedly accused with wantonly increasing the public burthen many millions, in order to promote a stock-jobbing interest of myself and friends." Having been cleared of all these accusations by Committees of Congress composed mainly of his most intelligent and active enemies, he was finally charged with "a connection with one James Reynolds for purposes of improper pecuniary speculation." To extricate himself from this jimfiscal corner Mr. Hamilton wrote this book. Clear himself he did, most assuredly, of the charge, but in doing so it has been thought by some that he sawed off a leg to cure a corn. "My real crime," confesses the late Secretary not without a blush, "is an amorous connection with his [Reynolds] wife for a considerable time, with his privaty and connivance," and that was how he came to be the private banker of Mr. James Reynolds, the husband of Mrs. Reynolds, "from whose conversation it was quickly apparent that other than pecuniary consolation would be acceptable," p. 18. Truth never appeared so naked as in these confessions of Alexander Hamilton.

847 HAMILTON (Alexander) Report of the Secretary of the Treasury in the United States, on manufactures Dec. 5 1791. *Half roan.* 8° *London,* 1793

848 HAMILTON (Alex.) Letter to Major Gen. Alex. Hamilton, containing Observations on his Letter, concerning the Public Conduct and Character of John Adams. *Vellum.* 8° *New York,* 1800

849 HAMILTON (Alex.) Letter concerning the Public Conduct and Character of John Adams. New Edition with Preface. *Vellum, fine copy.* 8° *Boston,* 1809

850 HAMILTON (Alex.) Letter from, concerning the Public Conduct and Character of John Adams Esq., written in the year 1800. *Vellum, fine uncut copy.* 8° *Boston,* 1809

851 HAMILTON (Alex.) Another, New Edition with a Preface. *Vellum, uncut.* 8° *Boston,* 1809

852 HAMILTON (F.) Account of the Kingdom of Nepal, and of the Territories annexed to this Dominion by the House of Gorkha. *Illustrated with Engravings. Calf.* 4° *Edinb.* 1819

853 HANCOCK (JOHN) AN ORATION; DELIVERED MARCH 5, 1774, AT THE REQUEST OF THE INHABITANTS OF THE TOWN OF BOSTON: To Commemorate the Bloody Tragedy of the Fifth of March 1770. *Very large & beautiful copy, sized paper, in white forrel by Pratt.* 4° *Edes and Gill, Boston,* 1774

854 HANSEN (Leonardus) Vita mirabilis et Mors pretiosa venerabilis Sororis Rosæ de S. Maria Limensis. *Boards.* 16° *Rome*, 1664

855 HARDY (F.) Memoirs of the Political and Private Life of James Caulfield, Earl of Charlemont. *Portrait. Second Edition, 2 vols, calf.* 8° *London*, 1812

856 HARLEIAN COLLECTION OF VOYAGES AND TRAVELS, compiled from the Library of the Earl of Oxford, interspersed and illustrated with Notes. *Maps and plates, 2 vols.* *Folio, London*, 1745-7

This Collection forms a Supplement to the Churchill Collection.

857 HARRIS (T. M.) Journal of a Tour into the Territory Northwest of the Alleghany Mountains, in 1803. *Half bound.* 8° *Boston*, 1805

858 HARRIS (William) Historical and Critical Account of the Lives and Writings of James I, Charles I, Cromwell, and Charles II. New Edition. 5 *vols, half calf.* 8° *London*, 1814

859 HARRISSE (*Monsieur* HENRI, *Avocat*) BIBLIOTHECA AMERICANA VETUSTISSIMA. A Description of Works relating to America published between the years 1492 and 1551. LARGE PAPER, 99 *copies printed, uncut, and not cut open. Unbound.* 4° *Geo. P. Philes, Publisher, New York*, 1866

860 HARRISSE (HENRI) BIBLIOTHECA AMERICANA VETUSTISSIMA, 1492–1551. 400 *copies printed, uncut and not cut open or bound.* *Im.* 8° *G. P. Philes, New York*, 1866

"NO LIBRARY IS COMPLETE WITHOUT IT."

Some six or eight months after the publication of this *Magnum Opus* in New York it was taken up warmly by the members of the Geographical Society of Paris, and, after the manner of that learned Body, referred to a Committee to examine and report upon it. The report was drawn up by that distinguished geographer, savant, and man of sense, M. ERNEST DESJARDINS, and read at the sitting of the Central Commission, the 18 Jan. 1867, and published in the *Bulletin* of the following April. Monsieur HARRISSE had permission accorded to him to have 500 copies struck off separately, at his own expense (*Bulletin*, p. 406). From this elaborate Report, the following translated extracts will mingle amusement with instruction. "Permit me, Gentlemen," says M. Desjardins, "to greet with pleasure, on its appearance, THE FIRST WORK OF SOLID ERUDITION WHICH AMERICAN SCIENCE HAS PRODUCED, and which is due to the patient research, to the ardent love of high historical studies, and to the criticism as sagacious as methodical, of a young savant, M. HARRISSE, a Frenchman by origin. I am happy to add that the first duty of your reporter is to render to the author, in the name of the Geographical Society of Paris, an homage, let us rather say a justice, which to the present hour, has not been rendered to him elsewhere than in France. I am not here to examine for what reason the country to which this useful work does so much honor has remained indifferent to the publication of this new and unique repertory which will henceforth serve as the necessary guide to the future historians of the discovery and conquest of the New World." . . . . "The well known impartiality of our Society makes it my duty to declare at once that there has not hitherto been published a more useful book for the preparation of the American history of the sixteenth century, and I hasten to add that this judgment, for it is not a personal opinion, is already confirmed by the special men of both worlds, who pass as the best arbiters in these matters, M. ICAZBALCETA of Mexico, whose most complete approbation without any restriction, I have now before me; M. d'AVEZAC, a judge so competent in learned bibliography, who has presented M. Harrisse's works to the Academy of Inscriptions and Belles Lettres (Session of the 10th Aug. 1866) accompanying this homage with explanations so luminous and praises so merited; M. VIVIEN DE SAINT-MARTIN, who reserves to them a worthy place in his *Année géographique;* M. LE DUC DE MONTPENSIER, who interests himself so much in the history of discoveries, and particularly in whatever touches Christopher Columbus ; MM. GAYANGOS and ZARCO DEL VALLE, of Madrid, not to cite the favorable testimonies of savants who are particularly known to me. M. Harrisse has, as we see, something in the applause of such judges to support unjust or flimsy criticism, and to have confidence in a work to which the future belongs." . . . . "That which cannot enough be praised in this immense work, is the vigorous method which the author has followed, and which it will be permitted to us to call by its true name, the French Method. He has not lost sight, even in his long dissertations, that he is a bibliographer, as such, charged with offering to the erudite public all the documents, and accompanying them with their historical justification, never thinking that he was permitted to set forth his own opinion. He applied himself to correct all the errors running through the history, but always in bringing forward proofs by facts, and never conjecture by reasoning. Every book is described *de visu*," etc. — "It will be understood that M. Harrisse's work, in spite of the exceptional interest which the numerous dissertations it comprises present, is not one of those which can be read consecutively and all at a breath. I shall add that there are very few readers sufficiently competent in each of the branches of American history to discover the errors of a man so learned as M. Harrisse." . . . . "I must still add, to be just, that M. Harrisse has applied to the accomplishment of his task as much abnegation as zeal and intelligence. He has given, without pretending to derive from it any material fruit, all his time to the editing and typographical direction of an admirable collection, the FIRST SPECIMEN OF AMERICAN ERUDITION, and the repertory henceforth indispensable to all serious study of the conquest of America," — and so on through a dozen pages. It will perhaps be an act of simple justice to *one* of the half dozen "arbiters" named above to add that he told the writer, that his indorsement and recommendation of the book consisted in a barely civil acknowledgment of a presentation copy with a few commonplace compliments. He could not, he thought, under the circumstances, have written less, and was consequently much surprised at the use made of his letter.

As there are two sides to the Atlantic, so there appear to be two opinions as to the merits of this book. M. Harrisse throughout his work had played swagger to a certain Vermonter who had for some time resided abroad, and to whom he was much indebted. M. Harrisse undertook to befoul him with many untruthful flings, insomuch that in the *London Athenæum* of the 6th of Oct. 1866, this G. M. B. felt it a duty to himself as well as to the public to apply publicly the *beech seal*, a remedy which the early Green Mountain Boys always found effectual with trespassing Yorkers. After bringing him to with a blank cartridge and cursorily examining his papers, and taking poor ANDER SCHIFFAHRT under his protection, this obscure writer concludes his four columns with the following brief summary. "The book at bottom is not a bad one; but the author has made it a mere fact-bag and crammed it with no end of extraneous matter. Like the jackdaw he does not appear to be able to resist anything *bright*, but picks it up regardless of its use or relevancy. The style of printing the titles in *apparent* facsimile misleads, and is a mistake. The collations are often obscure and not precise enough. There is a distressing want of uniformity in the orthography of names of places and persons. The mis-spelling of names is astounding. It is no exaggeration to say that the *errata* of names alone will make a list of 500. Two persons are made of one ; one is made of two. Some are created altogether, witness Ander Schiffahrt. Chronology is set at defiance. Geography is obscured. History is in a muddle. Grammar and the Queen's English tortured, if not murdered. Acknowledgments are generally wanting where most required, and often given where not deserved. The index, though extremely full, is not trustworthy, names being left out of it purposely, or certainly not by accident. Evidences of bad temper are abundant, and flippant flings, which can always be parried, are plenty. M. Harrisse quotes largely at second-hand, and omits to mention the books most used. His general and particular scholarship is lamentably deficient, his pedantry and plagiarism manifest, his want of courtesy to predecessors and fellow-laborers, his spite and obscure vision as to the wants of others, are apparent thoughout. These are some of the faults which should be looked to in a future edition. I hear with feeling akin to national pride that the author of the BIBLIOTHECA AMERICANA VETUSTISSIMA is not an American, and that therefore this book cannot fairly be charged to American scholarship." One hundred extra copies of this number of the

Athenæum went to the chief geographers and bibliographers of Paris, and hence, after due button-holing of the great and the learned the beech-seal was removed and a son of France stood before the world whitewashed by the Geographical Society of Paris. Who will whitewash the whitewasher?

861 HARROP (Mr.) The History of the Irish Rebellion in the year 1798, &c. 2 *vols in one, calf, gilt.* 8° *Philadelphia,* 1815

862 HARTFORD CONVENTION. Proceedings of a Convention of Delegates, convened at Hartford, Conn. Dec. 15th, 1814. *Second Edition.* 8° *Boston,* 1815

863 HARTFORD CONVENTION. Proceedings of a Convention of Delegates from the States of Massachusetts, Connecticut, etc, convened at Hartford, Conn. December 15th, 1814. *Uncut.* 8° *Hanover,* 1815

864 HARTLEY (T.) A Discourse on Mistakes concerning Religion, Enthusiasm, Experiences, etc. 8° *Reprinted by C. Sower, Germantown,* 1759

865 HARTSINCK (JAN JACOB) BESCHRYVING VAN GUIANA of de Weldekust in Zuid-America. *Maps and plates.* 2 *vols, half morocco, uncut.* 4° *Amsterdam,* 1770

866 HASENMULLER (M. E.) Historia Jesvitici Ordinis, cum duplici Polycarpi Lysars Prefatione. *Calf.* 8° *Francofurti,* 1595

867 HAVEN (Samuel F.) An Historical Address at Dedham, 21st Sept. 1836, being the Second Centennial Anniversary of the Incorporation of that Town. *Uncut.* 8° *Dedham,* 1837

868 HAWKIN (R. B.) Account of the Public Charities of the Town of Bedford. *Portrait, half calf.* 8° *Bedford,* 1828

869 HAWKINS (SIR R.) Observations of, in his Voyage into the South Sea in the Year 1593. Edited by Capt. Drinkwater Bethume. *Cloth.* 8° *Printed for the Hakluyt Society, Lond.* 1847

870 HAWKSWORTH (JOHN) GESCHICHTE DER SEE–REISEN und Entdeckungen im Sued-Meer von Commodore Byron, Cap. Wallis, Carteret und Coock, im Dolphin, der Swallow, und dem Endeavour ubersetzt von G. F. Schiller. *Maps and plates.* 3 *vols, calf.* 4° *Berlin,* 1774

871 HAWKSWORTH (J.) Relation des Voyages, exécutés par Byron, Carteret, Wallis et Cook, d'apres les Journaux tenus par les differens Commandans et les Papiers de M. Banks. *Map and plates.* 4 *vols, calf.* 4° *Paris,* 1774

872 HAWKSWORTH (J.) RELATION DES VOYAGES autour du Monde, exécutés par le Commodore Byron, et les Capitaines Carteret, Wallis et Cook. 4 *vols, calf.* 8° *Paris,* 1774

873 HAZARD (EBENEZER) HISTORICAL COLLECTIONS CONSISTING OF STATE PAPERS, and other authentic Documents: intended as materials for an History of the United States of America. 2 volumes. A MATCHLESS COPY, *sized paper, pure and clean, perfectly* UNCUT, *gilt tops, bound in best gros grained, red morocco gilt backs, by Bedford. The sizing and binding alone cost* $35. 4° *T. Dobson, for the author, Philadelphia,* 1792–94

EXCESSIVELY RARE IN THIS CONDITION.

374 HAYWARD (J.) New England Gazetteer. 12° *Boston*, 1839

375 HEARNE (Samuel) A Journey from Prince of Wales's Fort in Hudson's Bay to the Northern Ocean, for the Discovery of Copper Mines, a north west Passage, &c. in 1769–1772. *Fine copy, on Large Paper, uncut, half red morocco, maps.* *Roy.* 4° *London*, 1795

376 HEARNE (Samuel) A Journey from Prince of Wales Fort into the Northern Ocean, 1769–72. *Maps.* 8° *Dublin*, 1796

377 HEARNE (S.) Landreis van't Prins van Wallis Fort aan Hudsons Bai, naar den Noorder-Ocean, in 1769–73. *Map*, 2 *vols in* 1, *half calf, uncut.* 8° *Den Haage*, 1798

378 HEARNE (SAMUEL) VOYAGE DU FORT DU PRINCE DE GALLES dans la Baie de Hudson, a l'Ocean Nord. *Map and plates.* 2 *vols, calf, fine copy.* 8° *Paris*, 1799

The interesting tradition which has drifted down to us through Albert Gallatin, about the romantic manner in which La Perouse, the celebrated French navigator, caused the publication of the invaluable Journal of Hearne, which he found in a pigeon-hole in Fort Prince of Wales, after it had been surrendered to him, is traced to and confirmed in the prologomena of this French translation.

379 HEBERT (R.) The Poetical Works. *Portrait, neat calf.* 12° *London*, 1854

380 HEEREN (A. H. L.) Political System of Europe and its Colonies from the Discovery of America, to the Independence of the American Continent. 2 *vols.* 8° *Northampton*, 1829

381 HELMS (Ant. Zach.) Voyage dans l'Amerique Méridonale, par Buenos Ayres et Potosi jusqu'a Lima. *Cloth.* 8° *Paris*, 1812

382 HELPS (ARTHUR) THE SPANISH CONQUEST in America; and its Relation to the History of Slavery and to the government of Colonies. *Vols* 1, 2, 3. *Cloth.* 8° *London*, 1855–57

383 HEMMENWAY (MOSES) SEVEN SERMONS, on the Obligation and Encouragement of the Unregenerate to labour for the Meat which endureth to everlasting Life. *Unbound.* 8° *Boston, N. E.* 1767

384 HEMMENWAY (Moses, *of the First Church in Welles*) A Vindication of the power of the Unregenerate. Against the Exceptions of Rev. Mr. Samuel Hopkins. *Calf.* 8° *J. Kneeland, Boston*, 1772

385 HEMMENWAY (Abby Maria) Vermont Gazetteer, A Historical Magazine, a Digest of the History of each Town, Nos. 1 to 6. 8° *Ludlow, Vt. July* 1860 *to Aug.* 1863

386 HENNEPIN (R. P. LOUIS) NOUVELLE DECOUVERTE D'UN TRES GRAND PAYS DANS L'AMERIQUE, entre le Nouveau Mexique et la Mer Glaciale; avec un Voyage quil contient une Relation exacte de l'Origine, Mœurs, Coutumes etc. des Caraibes par le Sieur De la Borde. *Maps and Plates. Calf, rare.* 8° *Amsterdam*, 1704

387 HENNEPIN (LOUIS) VOYAGE, ou Nouvelle Decouverte d'un tres grand Pays dans l'Amerique entre le Nouveau Mexique et la Mer Glaciale. *Maps and Plates. Old calf, very fine copy, scarce.* 8° *Amsterdam*, 1704

888 HENRY (John Joseph) An Accurate and Interesting Account of the hardships and sufferings of the Band of Heroes who traversed the Wilderness in the campaign against Quebec in 1775. *Sheep.* 12° *William Greer, Lancaster, Pa.* 1812

889 HERBERT (THOMAS) A Description of the Persian Monarchy Now beinge the Orientall Indyes. *Curious Plates. Calf.* *Folio, London,* 1634

On page 217 begins "A Discourse and proofe that Madoc ap Owen Gwynedd first found out that Continent now call'd America."

890 HERBERT (Thomas) A Description of the Persian Monarchy, Now beinge the Orientall Indyes. A Relation of some Yeares Travaile, begvnne 1626. *Plates. Calf. Folio, London,* 1634

891 HERNANDEZ (FRANCISCO) DE MATERIA MEDICA NOUÆ HISPANIÆ Philippi Secundi Hispanearum ac Indiarum Regio invictissimi iussu collecta a Doctore Francisco Hernando noui Orbis primario, ac in ordinem digesta a Doctore NARDO ANTONIO RECIO eiusdem Maiestatis medico, libris quatuor. 4°

THE ORIGINAL AUTOGRAPH MANUSCRIPT of Dr. Nardo Antonio Reccio, comprising about 450 closely written quarto pages, bound in old red morocco, with the Arms of Cardinal Zelanda, from whose library the volume came. Hernandes the celebrated Naturalist was sent to New Spain by Philip the Second about 1595, where he remained exploring for several years, and returned to Europe with an herbarium the very richness and magnitude of which overwhelmed the men of science. A small 4o volume, containing a synopsis of the work, was printed in Mexico in 1604. After the death of Hernandes the collections were placed in the hands of Dr. Nardo Antonio Reccio, who with many collaborateurs completed, edited, and printed the great work at Rome, in folio, in 1628, but for some reason which has not yet been fully explained, was not published till 1651. The above MS is of the highest historical and scientific importance. It is not the work as finally printed.

892 HERRERA (ANTONIO DE) HISTORIA GENERAL de los Castellanos en las Islas i Tierra Firme del mar Oceano. Descripcion de las Indias Occidentalis. *Bound in 4 vols, fine copy, calf.* *Folio, Madrid,* 1730

893 HEURES. LES PRESENTE HEURES A LUSAIGE DE ROMME FURẼT A- | CHEUES LE. X X. IOUR DE DECẼBRE. LAN MIL CINC CENS & DEUX | POUR SIMON VOSTRE: Libraire demourãt a Paris a la rue | neuue nostre dame a lenseigne sainct Jehan leuãgeliste. |

8° *Phil. Pigouchet, pour Simon Vostre, Paris,* 1502

A Book to delight the eye and unbutton the pocket of the collector of fine Books. This is an edition not mentioned by BRUNET, whose publisher, M. Fermin Dedot, has paid special attention to this department of bibliography. The present copy is in small octavo, measuring 7½ by 4½ inches, 92 leaves, in Gothic type, with signatures *a* to *l* in eights, and *m* in four leaves. On the title page is Philipe Pigouchet, the printer's device, and the date in full, 1502, and on the reverse an Almanac for 20 years, 1501-20. There are 15 exquisite full-paged woodcuts, and every page throughout the volume is surrounded by beautiful borders, composed of woodcuts large and small, representing scriptural subjects, arabesques, hunting parties, love scenes, the story of Susanna and the Elders, scenes from the life of Joseph, of Mary, and of Christ; grotesques, and games of old and young; boys at play at blind man's buff, tennis and hocky; the dance of death, etc. etc in endless variety and indiscriminate order. It is a charming specimen of the best style and best time of SIMON VOSTRE's wonderful art and taste; in perfect preservation, in the original calf binding, somewhat worn, with gaufred gilt edges, and in a brown morocco case. None of the woodcuts are colored.

894 HEY (Richard) Observations on the Nature of Civil Liberty and the Principles of Goverment. *Half roan.* 8° *T. Cadell, London,* 1776

The author does not intend his book to be an answer to Dr. Price's on same subject, though both have a bearing on American questions.

895 HEYTHUYSEN (F.) The Equity Draftsman. *Boards.* 8° *New York,* 1819

896 HICKERINGILL (CAPT. EDM.) JAMAICA VIEWED: with all the Ports, Harbours, and their several soundings, Towns, etc. 3d edition. *Map. Very fine copy, polished calf, by F. Bedford.* 4° *B. Bragg, London,* 1705

897 HICKESIUS (GEORGE) INSTITUTIONES GRAMMATICÆ ANGLO-SAXONIÆ et Moeso-Gothicæ. 4° *Oxon,* 1689.
JONAS (Runolphus) GRAMMATICA ISLANDICA Rudimenta. 2 *vols in* 1. 4° *Oxon,* 1688

898 HILDRETH (Richard) Geschiedenis van de Vereenigde Staten van Noord America. 6 *vols, half green mor. gilt, uncut.* 8° *Gravenhage,* 1854–8

This edition is translated out of the *American* with a Preface, and with notes, by M. Keijzer of Delft, a monument of Dutch enterprise deserving of respect and commendation.

899 HINMAN (Royal R.) Letters from the English Kings and Queens to the Governors of the Colony of Connecticut, with the Answers thereto from 1635 to 1749. 12° *Hartford,* 1836

900 HINMAN (R. R.) Historical Collection of the Part sustained by Connecticut during the War of the Revolution, with Appendix containing important Letters etc. *Cloth.* 8° *Hartford,* 1842

901 HINTON (J. H.) HISTORY AND TOPOGRAPHY OF THE UNITED STATES. New and improved Edition by S. L. Knapp. *Illustrated with numerous engravings.* 2 *vols, half mor.* 4° *Boston,* 1835

This American Edition, edited with many corrections and additions by S. L. Knapp, is far superior to the English Edition.

902 HIPPISLEY (G.) Narrative of the Expedition to the Rivers Orinoco and Apuré in South America; which sailed from England in November 1817. 8° *London,* 1819

903 HISTOIRE DES DROGVES, Espiceries, et de certains Medicames simples qui naissent dans les Indes et en l'Amerique. *Woodcuts,* seconde edition. 8° *Lyons,* 1619

A curious and rare work in four parts, by Garcie du Jardin, Christ. de la Coste, and Nicholas Monardus, translated by Ant. Colin.

904 HISTORIÆ ROMANÆ SCRIPTORES, partim Græci, partim Latini, in vnum velut corpus redacti. 2 *vols, calf.* 8° *Henricus Stephanus, Paris,* 1568

905 HISTORICAL Magazine and Notes and Queries concerning the Antiquities, History and Biography of America. Vol. I. Nos. 1, 4, 5, 8. III. No. 1, 2, 3, 4, 6, 7. IV. No. 2, 3. VII. No. 11, and Vol. VIII. No. 8. New Series Vol. I. No. 3. Vol. II. No. 6. In all 16 numbers, *uncut.* 4° *New York, Jan.* 1857–*Nov.* 1867

906 HISTORICAL MAGAZINE, &c. Vol. I. No. 4, April 1857 & Vol. III. No. 4, April 1858. 4°

907 HISTOIRE et Commerce des Colonies Angloises, dans l'Amerique Septentrionale. Ou l'on trouve l'état actuel de leur population, & des détails curieux sur la constitution de leur gouvernement, principalement sur celui de la Nouvelle-Angleterre, de la Pensilvanie, de la Caroline, & de la Géorgie. Nouv. Ed. *Half red morocco.* SCARCE. 12° *A La Haye,* 1755

908 HISTORY of the Reign of Queen Anne, Digested into Annals. Year the Fourth. *Calf.* 8° *London,* 1706

909 HISTORY (The) of the Island of Dominica. By Thomas Atwood. *Half calf.* 8° *London,* 1791

910 HISTORY. A short history of the Opposition, [relating chiefly to American Affairs.] 3d Edit. *Half roan.* 8° *London,* 1779

911 HISTORY (A) of the War with America, France, Spain and Holland. Begun in the Year 1775 and ended in 1783. VERY RARE. *Calf.* 8° *London,* 1787

912 HISTORY (The) of the United States from their first settlement as Colonies. *Half calf.* 8° *London,* 1826

913 HISTORY of Modern Europe, 1802–15, in a series of Letters from a Nobleman to his Son. *Boards, uncut.* 8° *Keene, N. H.* 1822

914 HITCHCOCK (E.) Report on a Re-Examination of the Economical Geology of Massachusetts. *Uncut.* 8° *Boston,* 1838

915 HOBART (J. H. *Bishop of New York, &c.*) Sermons on Redemption. 2 *vols, half mor. gilt, uncut.* 8° *London,* 1824

916 HOBART (A.) Historical Sketch of Abington, Mass. with an Appendix. *Cloth.* 8° *Boston,* 1839

917 HODGES (*Rev.* C. W.) Sermons. *Portrait, cloth.* 12° *Burlington,* 1850

918 HODGSON (A.) Remarks during a Journey through North America in the Years 1819–21. 8° *New York,* 1823

919 HODGSON (A.) LETTERS from North America, written during a Tour in the United States and Canada. 2 *vols, neat, half calf.* 8° *London,* 1824

920 HOLMES (ABIEL) LIFE OF EZRA STILES D. D. President of Yale College. *Portrait.* 8° *Thomas & Andrews, Boston,* 1798

921 HOLMSBY (*Capt.* John) The Voyages, Travels, and Wonderful Discoveries in his voyage to the Southern Ocean in 1739. *Calf.* 12° *London, F. & J. Noble, n. d.*

922 HOLY, Sacred and Divine Roll and Book from the Lord God of Heaven, Revealed in the United Society at New Lebanon, N. Y. *Boards.* 12° *Canterbury, N. H.* 1843

923 HOLYOKE (E.) SERMON Preach'd to the Convention of Ministers of the Province of the Massachusetts Bay N. E. at Boston on Thursday, May 28, 1741. 8° *Boston,* 1741

924 HOLYOKE (Thomas) A Large Dictionary. *Folio, London,* 1677

925 HOMER. ILIAS ET ODYSSEA; Graece; opera J. Micylii et J Camerarii recognitum. *Calf.* *Folio, Basileæ*, 1541

926 HOMER & EUSTATHIUS. Ἐυσταθιου Ἀρχιεπισκοπου Θεσσαλονικης Παρεκβολαι εἰς την Ὁμηρου Ἰλιαδα. 2 *vols in* 1, *the* ILIAD *complete, fine large clean copy.* *Thick folio, Romæ*, 1542

This first edition of the Commentaries of Eustathius, in Greek, on the Iliad of Homer, in fine condition, like the present copy, has become very rare. It is one of the most beautiful books ever printed. The companion volumes containing the Odissea, published eight years later, are less attractive.

927 HOMERI ILIAS. FRANCISCI XAVERII ALEGRII Americani Veracrucensis HOMERI ILIAS Latino carmine expressa, cui accedit ejusdem ALEXANDRIAS, sive de expugnatione Tyri ab Alexandro Macedone. 2 *vols, very fine copy in vellum.* 4° *Bononiæ, Typis Ferdinandi Pisarri*, 1776

Who ever before heard of an American translation of the Iliad? Vera Cruz forever! for one of her sons nearly a century ago gave to the world this translation of the whole 24 Books of the Iliad into Latin hexameters, and added thereto his *Alexandrias*, nearly 100 pages more, which had lain full tweuty years in his pigeon-holes in Mexico. The volumes are very handsomely printed, and tastefully decorated with copperplate head and tail pieces, engraved, probably, expressly for this work. The fourth Book of the *Alexandrias* ends with the following allusion to Mexico:

Hactenus Æmathios Vatem memorasse triumphos
Sit satis, arboream recubat dum lentus ad umbram,
Qua per Mexiceos lequidus perlabitur agros
Anthius, ac placidis fœcundat jugera limphis,
Et Guadalupæi surgunt felicia templi
Culmina, pinnatoque minantur in æthera clivo.
Fors olim tua, Diva parens, graviore cothurno
Signa canam, laudesque tuas procul ultima Thule
Audiet, ac positis numen venerabitur aris.

928 HOPKINS (Bp. J. H.) The Primitive Church, compared with the Protestant Episcopal of the present Day. 12° *Burlgt'n*, 1835

929 HORATIUS, cum Commentariis etc. J. C. Messenii, Lucilii Satyrarum quae supersunt Reliquiæ, a F. I. F. Dousa cum Notis etc. in 1 vol. *Fol. ex officina Plantin. Lug. Bat.* 1597

930 HORATIUS. Cum erudito Torrentii Commentario; item P. Nannii Alemariani in Artem Poeticam. *Folio, Antv.* 1608

931 HORNIUS (GEORGIUS) DE ORIGINIBUS AMERICANIS Libri quatuor. *Vellum.* 8° *Hagae-Cometis*, 1653

932 HORNIUS (G.) Historia Naturalis et Civilis. *Calf.* 8° *Lugd. Batav.* 1670

933 HOSKINS (N.) History of the State of Vermont, from its Discovery to the Year 1830. 12° *Vergennes*, 1831

934 HOTTINGERUS (J. H.) Historia Orientalis, ex variis Orientalium Monumentis collecta. *Calf.* 4° *Tiguri*, 1651

935 HOWE (*Sir* William) The Narrative of Lt. Gen. Sir Wm. Howe, relative to his conduct during his late command of the King's Troops in North America. *Half roan.* 4° *Lond.* 1780

936 HOWE (ROBERT, *Lord*) A Letter from Cicero to the Right Hon. Lord Viscount H—e: occasioned by his late Speech in the House of Commons. *Half roan.* *J. Bew. London*, 1781

A thorough roasting and toasting of the two brothers Lord and Sir William Howe, commanding in America for their blunders, selfishness, and misconduct, especially at Brooklyn on Long Island, at White Plains, the Brandywine, Germantown, Valley Forge, Princeton, New York, on the Raritan, the Delaware, etc.

937 HOWE (ROBERT, *Lord*) A CANDID AND IMPARTIAL NARRATIVE of the Transactions of the Fleet, under the command of Lord Howe, from the arrival of the Toulon Squadron, on the coast of America, to the time of his Lordship's departure for England. With Observations. By an Officer then serving in the Fleet. The 2nd Edition, revised and corrected. With a Plan of the Situation of the Fleet, within Sandy Hook. *Very rare, especially with the Plan, fine copy.* 8° *London, for J. Almon* [1779]

938 HOWISON (John) Sketches of Upper Canada, domestic, local, and characteristic. *Half brown mor.* 8° *Edinburgh,* 1821

939 HUBBARD (John) The American Reader, containing a Selection of narration, harrangues, addresses, orations, dialogues odes, hymns, poems, &c. 3d Edit. 8° *Walpole, N. H. Thomas & Thomas,* 1807

940 HUBBARD (William) A Narrative of the Indian Wars in New England, from the first Planting thereof in 1607 to the Year 1677. *Unbound.* 12° *Printed by John Trumbull, Norwich, Con. n. d.*

941 HUBBARD (William) A narrative of the Indian Wars in New England. *Calf, scarce, sheep.* 12° *Brattleborough, W. Fessenden,* 1814

942 HUDSON'S BAY. Voyage de la Baye de Hudson, 1746–7, pour la Docouverte du Passage de Nord-Ouest. Par M. H. Ellis. *Plates,* 2 *vols in* 1, *Vellum.* 12° *Paris,* 1749

943 HUGHES (REV. GRIFFITH) THE NATURAL HISTORY OF BARBADOES. In Ten Books. *Plates. Calf,* LARGE PAPER. *Folio, London,* 1750

944 HUGHES (W. C.) The American Miller and Millwright's Assistant. 12° *Detroit,* 1850

945 HULL (Gen. William) Defence of, written by Himself. *Boards, uncut.* 12° *Boston,* 1814

946 HUTTON, (Charles) Miscellanea Mathematica. *Half calf.* 8° *London,* 1775

947 HUTTON (Wm.) Life, written by Himself, including a particular Account of the Riots at Birmingham in 1791. *Portrait, russia gilt.* 8° *London,* 1817

948 HUMBOLDT (ALEX. VON) EXAMEN CRITIQUE de l'Histoire de la Géographie du Nouveau Continent et des progrès de l'Astronomie nautique aux quinzième et seizième siècles. *Uncut, sewed,* 5 *vols.* 8° *Paris,* 1836–39

949 HUMBOLDT (ALEX. VON) Essai Politique sur la Royaume de la Nouvelle Espagne. 5 *vols, half morocco, uncut, fine copy.* 8° *Paris,* 1811

950 HUMBOLDT (Alex. von) Tableaux de la Nature, Traduits par J. B. B. Eyries. 2 *vols, calf.* 12° *Paris,* 1808

951 HUMBOLDT (A. von) Aspects of Nature. Translated by Mrs. Sabine. 2 *vols.* 8° *London,* 1849

952 HUMPHREYS (Col. David) Miscellaneous Works. *Portrait.* 8° *New York,* 1804

953 HUMPHREYS (*Col.* David) Life of Maj.-Gen. Israel Putnam; with Appendix containing Sketch of the Battle of Bunker Hill, by S. Sweet. *Portrait.* 12° *Boston,* 1818

954 HUMPHREYS (David) Historical Account of the Incorporated Society, for the Propagation of the Gospel in Foreign Parts. *Calf.* 8° *London,* 1730

955 HUMPHREYS (D.) Another copy. *Calf.* 8° *London,* 1730

956 HUNGARY. HVNGARICARUM RERUM SCRIPTORES varii, Historici, Geographici, Quidam nunc primum editi, Indicibus, *etc.* SCARCE. *Calf. Folio, Francofvrti,* 1600

957 HUNTER (J. D.) MEMOIRS of a Captivity among the Indians of North America from Childhood to the Age of Nineteen, with Anecdotes descriptive of their Manners and Customs. *Half calf.* 8° *London,* 1823

958 HUNTER (J. D.) *Another,* New Edition, *with Portrait. Neat half calf, uncut.* 8° *London,* 1823

959 HUNTER'S New Picture of Edinburgh. *Map and Engravings. Boards.* 18° *Edinburgh*

960 HUNTT (H.) A Visit to the Red Sulphur Spring of Virginia during the Summer of 1837. *Uncut.* 8° *Washington,* 1838

961 HUTCHINS (THOMAS) A TOPOGRAPHICAL DESCRIPTION OF VIRGINIA, Pennsylvania, Maryland, and North Carolina, comprehending the rivers Ohio, Kenhawa, Sioto, Cherokee, Wabash, Illinois, Missisippi, etc. With a Plan of the Rapids of the Ohio, a Plan of the several villages in the Illinois country, a Table of the Distances between Fort Pit and the Mouth of the Ohio, all engraved on Copper. And an Appendix, containing Mr. Patrick Kennedy's Journal up the Illinois River, and a correct List of the different Nations and Tribes of Indians, etc. *Fine copy of an important book, now become very rare.* 8° *London, for the Author,* 1778

962 HUTCHINSON (SAMUEL, *of Boston, in New England*) A DECLARATION of a Future Glorious Estate of a church to be here upon Earth, at Christ's Personal appearance for the Restitution of all things, a Thousand Years before the Ultimate Day of the General Judgment. 36 *pp. half roan.* 4° *London,* 1667

Samuel Hutchinson, the author of this extraordinary and rare compilation, was a brother of William, the father of Anne Hutchinson, the strong-minded of New England 200 years ago. He was a Fifth-monarchy man, and has here not only set forth his own views both in prose and verse, but has collected the opinions of competent writers of the old world and the new upon the establishment of the Fifth Kingdom, that of Christ, the new Heaven and the new Earth. His principal paper is "A Letter sent to a Friend in Old England concerning the Personal Monarchical Reign of Christ with the Saints here upon Earth, being an Answer to a Letter sent from *Old* England to *New* in 1659." He does not go so far as a subsequent American writer of this latitude, and intimate that New England is to be the New-Jerusalem.

963 HUTCHINSON (Gov. Thomas) HISTORY OF THE COLONY OF MASSACHUSETTS BAY. *2d Ed.* *2 vols, calf, fine copy.* 8° *London*, 1765–1767

964 HUTCHINSON (THOMAS) HISTORY OF THE COLONY OF MASSACHUSETTS–BAY from the first Settlement in 1628. *Second Edition.* *2 vols, calf, fine copy.* 8° *London*, 1760–67

The date on the first vol. is 1760, in error for 1765.

965 HUTCHINSON (THOMAS) HISTORY OF THE COLONY OF MASSACHUSETTS–BAY from 1628 to 1691. *Second Edition.* 8° *London*, 1765

966 HUTCHINSON (Thomas) The Letters of Governor Hutchinson and Lt. Gov. Oliver. *2d Ed.* *Half roan.* 8° *London*, 1774

967 HYGINUS ET POLYBIUS. De Castris Romanis quæ exstant. *Plates.* 4° *Amstelod.* 1660

968 IDEAS NECESSARIAS a todo Pueblo Americano Independente, que quiera ser libre. *Fine copy, calf.* 12° *Puebla, Mexico*, 1823

969 ILLINOIS REGIMENT. A List of Officers of the Illinois Regiment, and of Crockett's Regiment. A List of Non-Commissioned Officers and Soldiers of the Illinois Regiment, and the Western Army. *Uncut.* 4° *n. d.*

970 IMLAY (GEORGE) Topographical Description of the Western Territory of North America; with Account of the Discovery, Settlement, and present State of Kentucky, etc. *Maps, half maroon morocco, uncut.* 8° *London*, 1793

971 IMPARTIAL HISTORY (An) of the War in America, between Great Britain and her Colonies, from its commencement to the end of the year 1779. With an Appendix, containing a collection of interesting and authentic Papers, tending to elucidate the History. *Map, calf.* 8° *London*, 1780

972 INDEX BIBLICUS Multijugus: or, a Table to the Holy Scripture. *Calf.* 8° *London*, 1672

973 INDIA in the Fifteenth Century; a Collection of Voyages to India, from Latin, Persian, Russian, and Italian sources. Edited with Introduction, by R. H. Major. *Cloth, uncut.* 8° *London, for the Hakluyt Society*, 1857

WEDNESDAY AFTERNOON.

974 INDIA ORIENTALIS. Historia Indiæ Orientalis, ex variis auctoribus collecta et iuxta seriem topographicam Regnorum, Prouinciarum & Insularum, per Africæ, Asiæque littora, ad extremos vsque Iaponios deducta, qua Regionvm, et Insvlarvm situs & commoditas, *etc.* Auctore M. GOTARDO ARTHVS Dantiscano. *Vellum.* SCARCE.
8° *Colon. Agrip. sumptibus Wilhelmi Lutzenkirch,* 1608

Master GOTARD ARTHUS of Dantzig was one of DeBry's editors, and was therefore well read in the early voyages of the Portuguese, the Spanish, the Dutch and others, to the East Indies by the routes of both capes. He resided at Frankfort, and finished this work in September, 1605, after the first seven Parts of DeBry's India had been published. In a condensed form this work is perhaps one of the best summaries there is of all the various East India voyages up to 1605, and therefore to the geographer and bibliographer it is of very considerable value. Chapter 35 treats of the Molucca Islands and the divers routes thither, especially that by the Straits of Magellan. The book, in enabling the American historian to trace the gradual and mysterious separation of the new hemisphere from the old, entitles it to a prominent place among books on America.

975 INDIAN AFFAIRS. A Report to the Secretary of State of the United States, on Indian Affairs. By Jedediah Morse. *Map and portrait. Half morocco, uncut.* 8° *New Haven,* 1822

976 INDIANS. A brief Account of the Proceedings of the Committee appointed 1795 by the Yearly Meeting of Friends of Pennsylvania, New Jersey, &c. for promoting the Improvement and gradual Civilization of the Indian Natives. *London,* 1806
Ditto of the Yearly Meeting held in Baltimore, &c.
2 tracts. 8° *London,* 1806

977 INDIANA. The Soldier of Indiana, in the War for the Union. 8° *Indianapolis,* 1864

978 INFANTRY Tactics, Abstract of, for Use of the Militia of the United States. 12° *Boston,* 1830

979 INQUIRY (An) into the present state of the British Navy, with reflections on the late War with America. By an Englishman. *Half calf.* 8° *London,* 1815

980 INSTRUCTIONS to the Envoys Extraordinary and Ministers Plenipotentiary of the U. States of America to the French Republic, their Letters of Credence and full Powers, and the Despatches received from Them relative to their Mission.
8° *Philadelphia, n. d.*

981 INTEREST of Great Britain Considered, with regard to her Colonies, and the Acquisitions of Canada and Guadaloupe etc. *Half calf.* 8° *London,* 1761

982 INTEREST (The) of the Merchants and Manufacturers of G. Britain in the present Contest with the Colonies. *Half roan.* 8° *London,* 1774

983 IRVING (WASHINGTON) Diedrich Knickerbocker's History of New York. New Edit. *Plates, 2 vols, half calf.* 8° *London,* 1821

984 IRVING (Washington) Histoire de New York (par Diedrich Knickerbocker). 2 *vols, half roan.* 8° *Paris,* 1827

985 IRVING (WASHINGTON) Het Leven en de Reizen van Christoffel Columbus. *Portrait.* 4 *vols, half green morocco, uncut.* 8° *Haarlem,* 1828

986 ISOCRATES. ORATIONES et Epistolæ, cum Latina Interpretatione Wolfii. *Calf.* *Folio, Henricus Stephanus,* 1593

987 ITALY. NIEUW VERMEERDERD EN VERBETERD GROOT STEDBOCK VAN GEHEEL ITALIE, Naauwkeurice Beschryving van alle deszelfs Steden, Paleizen, Kerken, en Voornaamste Gebouwen, enz. Naar de Origineele Aftekeningen of de Plaats en zelfs door den Heer Joan Blaeuw. *Over* 400 *finely executed Plates, many of them folded and very large.* UNCUT. 4 *vols, printed on large thick paper.* *Folio, R. C. Alberts, Graavenhaage,* 1724

That portion of this magnificent work which relates to Rome, its archæology, architecture, sculpture, and antiquities generally, is very beautiful, and of the highest historical interest. It ought to be in the library of every academy and Latin school in the country, so that he who reads Virgil or any other Latin classic author, may run to it and see authentic illustrations whereof he reads.

988 IZQUIERDO (EL P. SEBASTIAN, *de la Comp. de Jesus*) PRACTICA de los EXERCICIOS ESPIRITUALES de Nuestro Padre San Ignacio. *Title and* 81 *foliod leaves, fine copy, vellum.* 8° *Mexico, en la Impr. Nueva de la Bibliot. Mexicana,* 1756

This edition of the *Practica* is in demand by collectors in consequence of its having eleven full-paged emblematic copper-plates engraved by the distinguished Mexican artist, Antoine Moreno.

989 IZQUIERDO (EL P. SEBASTIAN) PRACTICA DE LOS EXERCICIOS ESPIRITUALES de Nuestro Padre S. Ignacio. *Fine copy, vellum.* 8° *Mexico en la Imprenta de los Heredios del Lice. D. Jos. de Jautegui,* 1782

This edition has twelve full-paged copper-plates engraved by another Mexican artist, PAVIA by name. They are the same designs as those engraved by Moreno.

990 JACKSON (Andrew) Memoirs of Andrew Jackson late Major-General and Commander in Chief of the Southern Divisions of the Army of the United States. Compiled by a Citizen of Massachusetts [Dr. J. V. C. Smith.] *Portrait, calf.* 12° *Boston,* 1828

991 JACKSON (C. T.) Second Annual Report of the Geology of the Public Lands, belonging to Massachusetts and Maine. *Uncut.* 8° *Boston,* 1838

992 JACKSON (*Major* W.) Eulogium on Gen. Washington, before the Pennsylvania Society of the Cincinnati in Philadelphia, Feby 22, 1800. *Vellum, uncut.* 8° *Philadelphia,* 1800

993 JAMAICA. Ampel en Breed Verhaal van de jongst-gewesene Aardbevinge tot Port Royal in Jamaica, op 7/17 den Jany 1692. *Fine copy, morocco.* 4° *Rotterdam,* 1692

994 JAMAICA. The truest and largest Account of the Late Earthquake in Jamaica Jan. the 7th 1692. *Half roan.* 8° *London*, 1693

995 JAMAICA. The Representation and Memorial of the Council of the Island of Jamaica. Preface by M. Wood. *Half roan.* 8° *London*, 1716

996 JAMAICA. The Laws of Jamaica, Pass'd by the Governours, Council and Assembly, and confirm'd by the Crown. *Calf.* 8° *London*, 1716

997 JAMAICA. History of Jamaica, from the earliest Accounts, to the Taking of Porto Bello by Admiral Vernon. *Maps. Calf.* 8° *London*, 1740

998 JAMAICA. *Another*, 2d Edition. 8° *London*, 1740

999 JAMAICA. Histoire de la Jamaique. Traduite de l'Anglois. 2 *vols.* 8° *London*, 1751

1000 JAMAICA. Slave Law of Jamaica; with Proceedings and Documents relative thereto. *Uncut, half blue morocco.* 8° *London*, 1828

1001 JAPAN, SIAM AND THE COREA. Wahrhaftige Beschreibungen dreyer mächtigen Königreiche, Japan, Siam, und Corea. Benebenst noch vielen andern, im Vorbericht vermeldten Sachen: So mit neuen Anmerkungen, und schönen Kupferblättern, von Christoph Arnold, vermehrt, verbessert, und geziert. Denen noch beygefüger Johann Jacob Merkleins, Ost Indienische Reise, &c. 1148 *pp. with* 12 *prel. and* 18 *sequent leaves, and many maps and plates, vellum.* 8° *Nürnberg*, 1672

This thick volume is a collection and digest by Christopher Arnold of some twenty or more of the principal authors of various countries who had written on these countries. The historical and bibliographical notes are of considerable interest.

1002 JAY (William) Prayers for the use of Families, or the domestic minister's assistant. 12° *Lewistown, Pa, Charles Bell & Sons*, 1831

1003 JAMES (*Capt.* THOMAS) THE STRANGE AND DANGEROUS VOYAGE of Capt. T. James in his intended Discovery of the Northwest Passage into the South Sea. *Fine large clean copy. No map.* 4° *Iohn Legatt, London*, 1633

1004 JAMES (W.) MILITARY OCCURRENCES OF THE LATE WAR between Great Britain and the United States of America; with an Appendix. *Maps.* 2 *vols, half calf.* 8° *London*, 1818

1005 JANEWAY (James) Memoirs of James Janeway, and of Rev. S. Peirce, by Rev. A. Fuller. *Portraits, boards, uncut.* 12° *London*, 1824

1006 JAY (James, of New York) Dissertatio Medica inauguralis, de Fluore Alba. *Half roan.* 4° *Edinburgi*, 1753

1007 JEFFERSON (Thomas) Notes on the State of Virginia. *Half Calf.* 8° *London*, 1787

1008 JEFFERSON (Thomas) NOTES on the State of Virginia. *Half blue morocco, gilt, uncut.* 8° *London*, 1787

1009 JEFFERSON (Thomas) Notes on the State of Virginia, with an Appendix. *Portrait.* 8° *New York,* 1801

1010 JEFFERSON (Thomas) Notes on the State of Virginia with an Appendix. 9th American Edition. *Portrait and Map.* 16° *H. Sprague, Boston,* 1802

M. Barbé Marbois then residing in Philadelphia as Secretary of the French Legation first suggested to Mr. Jefferson this work.

1011 JEFFERSON (THOMAS) Memoirs of, containing a concise History of the United States, from the Acknowledgment of their Independence; with a View of the Rise and Progress of French Influence and Principles, &c. 2 *vols, boards.* 8° *n. p.* 1809

1012 JEFFERSON (Thomas) A Summary View of the rights of British America. *Half calf,* SCARCE. 8° *Williamsburg, printed: Philadelphia, reprinted,* 1785

1013 JEFFERYS (THOMAS) WEST-INDIA ATLAS. 40 *Maps. Half calf.* *Folio, London,* 1775

1014 JESSY (H.) A Description and Explanation of 268 Places in Jerusalem and the Suburbs thereof as it flourished in the time of Jesus Christ. *Half calf (wanting map and frontispiece).* 4° *London,* 1654

1015 JESUITS. Travels of the Jesuits, into various parts of the World, compiled from their Letters, with Extracts from other Travellers and Notes by Mr. Lockman. *Maps and plates.* 2 *vols, calf.* 8° *London,* 1743

1016 JEWELL (*Bishop* JOHN) WORKS. *Folio, London,* 1611

1017 JEWETT (M.) Family Physician; the Latroleptic Practice of Medicine. *Cloth,* 2 *copies.* 8° *Columbus, O.* 1838

1018 JOGUES (LE R. P. ISAAC) NOVUM BELGIUM, Description de Nieuw Netherland. *Cloth, uncut.* LARGE PAPER, TIRÉ A 100 EXEMPLAIRES. *Imp.* 8° *New York,* 1862

1019 JOGUES (Le R. P. Isaac) Novum Belgium, Description de Nieuw Netherland, et Notice sur René Goupil. *Cloth, uncut,* TIRÉ A 100 EXEMPLAIRES. 8° *New York,* 1862

1020 JOHANSEN (Andrew) A Geographical and Historical Account of the Island of Bulama, with Observations on its climate, &c., with an account of the Bulam Association and of the Colony itself: To which are added authentic Documents, and a descriptive map of the Island and adjoining continent. *Map,* SCARCE. 8° *Martin & Bain, London* [1794]

The indifferent reader who is desirous of knowing the origin and progress of this Royal British *Colony of Bulama,* and where in the wide world it was or is, is respectfully referred to this scarce book, where, on the annexed map he will find that it is one of the Bisago Islands.

1021 JOHNSON (CHARLES) A general History of the Pirates. *Fine copy, calf gilt.* 8° *London,* 1724

1022 JOHNSON (Dr. Samuel) Life: to which is added Johnsonianæ, or a Selection of Dr. Johnson's Bon-Mots, etc. *Portrait, calf.* 12° *London,* 1785

1023 JONES (Charles C.) Historical Sketch of Tomo-chi-chi, Mico of the Yamacraues. *Uncut.* 8° *Munsel, Albany,* 1868

For the rare original portrait of TOMOCHICHI the celebrated Georgia Chief, see in this Catalogue under URLSPURGER.

1024 JONES (*Paul*) Life, from original Documents in the possession of J. H. Sherburne. *Boards.* 12° *London,* 1820

1025 JONES (Paul) THE LIFE, Travels, Voyages, and Daring Engagements of Paul Jones. *Half morocco, some leaves mutilated.* 12° *N. Coverley, Milk Street, Boston, n. d.*

1026 JOURNAL of the Proceedings of the Congress held at Philadelphia Sept. 5, 1774, containing the Bill of Rights, a List of Grievances, &c. To which is added (being now first printed by authority) an Authentic Copy of the PETITION TO THE KING. *Half morocco.* 8° *London,* 1775

DR. FRANKLIN, it is believed, caused this volume to be issued in London, in January, 1775. Its effect was startling, for it proclaimed to the discriminating British Public (if there was at that time such a body) that the English language had acquired new vigor and clearness in being transplanted to the Western shores. The pith, point, and force of these Public Papers, astonished the politicians and statesmen of Westminster, and delighted the friends of the Colonies. The Original Petition of the Continental Congress to the King dated Oct. 26, 1774, from which the above was printed, containing the signatures of fifty of the Delegates, after the manner of the Declaration of Independence, and second only in historical importance to that Document, is now in the possession of the writer, it having been signed in duplicate, one copy being carefully preserved by Dr. Franklin, the other sent to the King. The latter copy is still preserved in the State Paper office in London. No copy was retained by the Congress.

1027 JOURNAL of the House of Representatives and Senate of the United States 1st Congress, 3rd Session, 1790. Begun and Held at Philadelphia. 2 *vols.* *Folio, Philadelphia,* 1791

1028 JOURNAL of the Expedition to La Guira, and Porto Cavallos in the W. Indies, under Commodore Knowles. *Half mor.* 8° *London,* 1744

1029 JOURNAL d'un Voyage dans l'Interieur le l'Amerique Septentrional. [By Anbury.] *Map and plates.* 2 *vols.* 8° *London,* 1793

1030 JOURNAL of the Bishop of Montreal, during a Visit to the Church Missionary Society's North West American Mission. 12° *London, n. d.*

1031 JOURNAL of a Young Man of Massachusetts, captured at Sea by the British, May 1813, and confined at Melville Island, Halifax, Chatham in England, and at Dartmoor Prison. *Plate.* 12° *Boston,* 1816

1032 JOURNAL of a Voyage of Discovery to the Arctic Regions in H. M. Ships Hecla and Griper, 1819–20. By A. Fisher. *Map, calf gilt.* 8° *London,* 1761

1033 JOURNAL of Convention for forming a Constitution of Government for the State of Massachusetts Bay, 1799–80. 8° *Boston,* 1832

1034 JOURNALS of each Provincial Congress of Massachusetts in 1774 and 1775, with Appendix. 8° *Boston,* 1838

1035 JOURNAL OF THE VOYAGE OF THE SLOOP MARY, from Quebec, Together with an account of her Wreck off Montauk Point, L. I. Anno 1701. With Introduction and notes by E. B. O'Callaghan. "EDITION, 100 COPIES." SEWED, *uncut.* 4° *Munsell, Albany,* 1866

1036 JOUTEL (M. T.) JOURNAL HISTORIQUE du dernier Voyage que feu M. de la Sale fit dans la Golfe de Mexique, pour trouver l'Embouchure et le Cours de la Riviere de Mississippi. Redigè et mis en ordre par M^{r}. De Michel. *Fine copy, very rare in this state, calf.* 8° *Paris,* 1713

1037 JOUTEL (M. T.) Diario Historico del ultimo viaje que hizo M. de la Sale para descubrir el Desembocadero y Curso del Missicipi. Contiene la Historia tragica de su Muerte y muchas cosas curiosas del Nuevo Mundo. Escrito en idioma Frances por M. T. Joutel, uno de los compañeros de M. La Sale en el Viaje. Traducido al Español por el Coronel Jose Maria Tornel, Ministro de Mexico en los Estados Unidos. 12° *José Desnoues, Nueva York,* 1831

With a preface and some valuable notes by the translator. This edition though printed in New York was for the Mexican market.

1038 JUAN ET ULLOA. VOYAGE HISTORIQUE DE L'AMERIQUE MERIDIONALE, fait par Ordre du Roi d'Espagne. *Numerous maps and plates.* 2 *vols, calf. Fine copy.* 4° *Amsterdam et Leipzig,* 1752

1039 JUAN (Geo.) AND ULLOA (Ant.) A Voyage to South America. *Plates,* 2 *vols, calf.* 8° *Dublin,* 1758

1040 JUAN (George) and A. DE ULLOA. HISTORISCHE REISBESCHRYVING VAN GEHEEL ZUID-AMERICA. *Maps and plates.* 2 *vols, half crimson morocco, very beautiful ; uncut copy.* 4° *Te Goes, by Jacobus Huysman,* 1771

1041 JUAN (G.) AND ULLOA (Ant. de) A Voyage to South America. 3d Edit. *Maps and plates.* 2 *vols, half calf.* 8° *London,* 1772

1042 JUAN AND ULLOA. Voyage to South America. Translated from the original Spanish ; with Notes and Observations, and an Account of the Brazils by J. Adams. *Map and plates.* 2 *vols, half green mor. uncut.* 8° *London,* 1807

1043 JUAN DE LA ANUNCIACION (*del Monasteria de San Augustin de Mexico*) DOCTRINA CHRISTIANA MVY COMPLIDA, donde se contiene la exposicion de todo lo necessario para Doctrinar a los Yndios, y administralles los Sanctos Sacramentos. Compuesta en lengua Castellana y Mexicana. *Wanting the lower half of the title, and pierced by a worm, otherwise a fine large copy.* 4° *en Casa de Pedro Balli, Mexico,* 1575

Of this excessively rare early Mexican Book the text comprises 274 pages, in double columns, in Spanish and Mexican. There are six preliminary and seven sequent leaves. A copy in condition not so good as this was recently sold in London by auction for a very high price.

1044 JUAN AND ULLOA. A Voyage to South America. 5th Ed. *2 vols, half blue mor. gilt, uncut.* 8° *London,* 1807

1045 JUDICIARY. Debates in the U. S. Senate on the Judiciary. *Boards, uncut.* 8° *Philadelphia,* 1802

1046 JULIUS (N. H.) NORDAMERIKAS sittliche Zustande; nach eigenen Anschanungen in den Jahren 1834–5–6. *Plates,* 2 *vols. half green mor. uncut.* 8° *Leipzig,* 1839

1047 JULIUS (N. S.) Nord-amerikas Sittliche Zustande; nach eigenen Anshanungen 1834–6. 2 *vols, half green morocco, gilt, uncut.* 8° *Leipzig,* 1839

1048 JUNIUS. THE GENUINE LETTERS of Junius with Anecdotes of the Author. FIRST EDITION. *Calf.* 8° *London,* 1771

1049 JUNIUS; including Letters by the same writer, under other Signatures, (now first collected.) To which are added his Confidential Correspondence with Mr. Wilkes and his Private Letters addressed to Woodfall; with Preliminary Essay. Notes, Fac-similes, etc. 3 *vols, calf extra.* LARGE PAPER. Fine copy of this best Edition. *Royal* 8° *London,* 1812

1050 JUNIUS; including Letters by the same Writer, under other Signatures; his confidential Correspondence with Mr. Wilkes, and his Private Letters to Mr. Woodfall; new and enlarged Edition, by Wade. 2 *vols, cloth.* 8° *London,* 1856

1051 JUNIUS AMERICANUS. The political detection: or, the treachery and tyranny of Administration, both at Home and Abroad. *Half calf.* 8° *London,* 1770

1052 JUVENAL et Persius. Satyræ. Edidit B. Antumnus. *Half bound.* 8° *Parisiis,* 1607

1053 KALM (Peter) Travels into North America. *Map.* 3 *vols, half calf.* 8° *Warrington & London,* 1770–71

1054 KALM (Peter) Travels into North America. Translated by J. R. Forster. *Map. 2d Edition.* 2 *vols, calf.* 8° *London,* 1772

1055 KALM (Peter) Travels into North America, containing its Natural History, Account of its Plantations, etc. *Map.* 2 *vols, boards, uncut.* 8° *London,* 1772

1056 KALM (PETER) REIS DOOR NOORD AMERIKA. *Large map and plates.* 2 *vols in* 1, *half calf, uncut.* 4° *Utrecht,* 1772

Unusually fine copy; far superior to the Swedish or English Editions.

1057 KALM (PETER) REIS DOOR NOORD AMERIKA. *Map and plates.* 2 *vols in* 1, *uncut, fine copy.* 4° *Utrecht,* 1772

1058 KEMBLE (J. P.) Macbeth and King Richard the Third; an Essay, in answer to remarks in some of the Characters of Shakspeare. *Cloth.* 12° *London,* 1817

1059 KER (John) Memoirs of John Ker of Kersland, containing his Secret Transactions and Negotiations etc. 2 *vols, calf, containing much about America.* 8° *London,* 1726

1060 KEYMIS (LAWRENCE) A RELATION OF THE SECOND VOYAGE [of Sir Walter Raleigh] to GUIANA. Performed and written in the year 1596. By LAWRENCE KEYMIS. *Fine large copy, uncut, but unfortunately wanting F 4 and all after,* EXCESSIVELY RARE. 4° *Thomas Dawson, London,* 1596

1061 KINGDOM (Wm.) America and the British Colonies. Useful Information relative to the United States and the British Colonies. *Half blue morocco, uncut.* 2*d Edition.* 8° *London,* 1820

1062 KING'S CHAPEL, Liturgy of. 2*d Edition.* 8° *Boston,* 1811

1063 KIRKLAND (J. T.) DISCOURSE OCCASIONED by the Death of GEORGE WASHINGTON. Delivered December 29, 1799; to which is added Washington's Valedictory Address. *Vellum, uncut.* 8° *Boston,* 1800

1064 KIRKLAND (J. T.) Discourse &c., on Washington. *Second Edition. Vellum.* 8° *Boston,* 1800

1065 KNAPP (S. L.) Biographical Sketches of eminent Lawyers, Statesmen and Men of Letters. 8° *Boston,* 1821

1066 KNIGHT (Charles) Knowledge is Power; a view of the Productive Forces of Modern Society. *Illustrated with engravings. Cloth.* *Post* 8° *London,* 1859

1067 KOSTER (Henry) Voyages dans la Partie Septentrionale du Brésil, depuis 1809 jusqu'en 1815. Traduits de l'Anglais par M. A. Jay. *Map and colored plates. Calf.* 2 *vols.* 8° *Paris,* 1818

1068 KRUSENSTERN (A. J. VON) REIZE OM DE WERELD gedaan in de jaren 1803–6. *Plates.* 4 *vols, half calf.* 8° *Haarlem,* 1811–15

1069 L (M. DE) Histoire impartiale des Evénements Militaires et politiques dans la derniere Guerre dans les quatre parties du Monde. 3 *vols, calf.* 12° *Paris,* 1785

1070 LABAT (JEAN B.) NOUVEAU VOYAGE AUX ISLES DE L'AMERIQUE, contenant l'Histoire Naturelle de ces Pays, l'Origine, les Moeurs, la Religion et le Gouvernement des Habitans; les Guerres et les Evenements singuliers qui y sont arrivez pendant le long sejour que l'Auteur y a fait. 2 *vols. Maps and numerous plates. Half morocco, uncut, fine copy.* 4° *A la Haye,* 1724

1071 LABAT (JEAN B.) NOUVEAU VOYAGE aux Isles de l'Amerique. 6 *vols. Numerous maps and plates. Calf.* 8° *Paris,* 1722

1072 LABAT (J. B.) Another Copy. 6 vols. 12° *Paris,* 1722

1073 LABAT (J. B.) Nouveau Voyage aux Isles de l'Amerique, 6 *vols. Maps and plates. Fine copy.* 8° *Paris,* 1722

1074 LABAUME (Eugene) A circumstantial Narrative of the Campaign in Russia, embellished with Plans of the Battles of the Moswka and Malo-Jaroslavitz. 3d Edition improved. *Half calf.* 8° *London*, 1815

1075 LACKINGTON (James) Memoirs of the forty-five first Years of the Life of James Lackington. Written by Himself. *Portrait, half morocco, uncut.* 8° *London*, 1794

1076 LA CONDAMINE (M. de) Relation d'un Voyage dans l'Interieur de l'Amerique Meridionale jusqu' aux Côtes du Bresil et de la Guyane. *Frontispiece and map. Half maroon morocco, uncut.* 8° *Maestricht*, 1778

1077 LA CROIX (M. de) Review of the Constitutions of the Principal States of Europe, and of the United States of America. *2 vols, calf.* 8° *London*, 1792

1078 LAET (JOHANNES DE) NOVVS ORBIS seu Descriptionis Indiæ Occidentales Libri 18. *Maps and plates. Fine copy, old calf gilt.* *Folio, apud Elzeviros, Lug. Batav.* 1633

1079 LAET (JOANNES DE) Historie ofte Iaerlijck Verhael van de Verrichtinghen der Geoctroyeerde West-Indische Compagnie. *Black Letter, fine copy, many maps.* *Half calf.* *Folio, Elzevir, Leyden*, 1644

1080 LAET (JOANNES DE) HISTORIE ofte Iaerlijck Verhael van de Verrichtingen der Geoctroyeerde West-Indische Compagnie. *Black letter. Calf.* *Folio, Leyden*, 1644

1081 LAFITAU (JOSEPH FRANÇOIS) DE ZEDEN DER WILDEN VAN AMERIKA. *2 vols in one. Maps and numerous engravings. Calf.* *Folio, Gravenhage*, 1731

1082 LAFITAU (J. F.) Histoire des Decouvertes et Conquetes des Portugais, dans le Nouveau Monde. *2 vols. Maps and plates. Calf, fine copy.* 4° *Sangrain, Paris*, 1733

1083 LAFITAU (J. F.) Histoire des Decouvertes et Conquestes des Portugais dans le Nouveau Monde. *4 vols.* *Plates.* 8° *Paris*, 1733

1084 LAFITAU (J. F.) Histoire des Decouvertes et Conquestes des Portuguais dans le Nouveau Monde. *4 vols. Maps and plates. Fine copy.* 8° *Paris, Sangrain*, 1734

1085 LA HONTAN (*Baron* de) Nouveaux Voyages dans l'Amerique Septentrionale. *3 vols. Map and plates.* 8° *A la Haye*, 1703

1086 LA HONTAN (*Baron* de) Voyages dans l'Amerique Septentrionale. *2 vols. Maps and numerous plates* (*2 wanting*). *Old calf.* 8° *Amsterdam*, 1705

1087 LA HONTAN (*Baron* de) Voyages dans l'Amerique Septentrionale. *2 vols, calf gilt, fine copy. Maps and plates.* 8° *La Haye*, 1705.

1088 LA HONTAN (*Baron* de) NEW VOYAGES TO NORTH AMERICA, to which is added a Dictionary of the Algonkine Language. Done into English. Second Edition. *2 vols. Map and plates. Calf; very fine clean copy.* 8° *London*, 1735

1089 Lambert (Abbé) Curious Observations upon the manners &c. of Asia, Africa and America. 2 *vols, calf.* 8° *London, n. d.*

1090 Lampson (Alvan, *D. D.*) History of the First Church and Parish in Dedham, on occasion of the Completion, Nov. 18, 1838, of the Second Century since the gathering of said Church. *Uncut, sewed.* 8° *Dedham*, 1839

1091 Lancashires Valley of Achor, is Englands Doore of Hope: Set wide open, in a brief History, of the wise, good, and Powerful hand of Divine Providence, Ordering and Managing the Militia of Lancashire, etc. *Vellum, scarce.* 4° *Luke Fawne, London*, 1643

1092 LANCIEGO y EGUILAZ (*Fr.* Joseph de, Arçobispo de Mexico) Carta Pastoral, Escribe â sus amadas Hijas las Religiossas de toda su Filiacion. *Title and* 46 *leaves, fine copy.* 8° *Mexico*, 1716

1093 Lands of the U. S. General Public Acts of Congress respecting the sale and disposition of the Public Lands, with Instructions by the Secretary of the Treasury and Commission of the Land Office and Official Opinions of the Attorney General. 2 *vols, sheep.* 8° *Washington*, 1838

1094 La Pérouse (M.) Voyage de La Pérouse autour du Monde, redigée par M. L. A. Milet-Mureau. 4 *vols, calf.* 8° *Paris, An.* 6, 1798

1095 LA RIVAS (*D.* Manuel Joseph de) Grammatical construccion de los Hymnos Ecclesiasticos, dividida en siete libros, por el orden del Breviario Romano. Explicacion y medida de sus versos. 16+164 *pp.; fine copy, old calf.* Excessively scarce. 8° *En Mexico, in la Imprenta de D. Francisco Xavier Sanches*, 1738

1096 LAS CASAS (Bartolomeo de). D Bartholomæi de Las Casas, Episcopi Chiapensis, viri in omni Doctrinarum genere exercitatissimi, erudita & elegans explicatio Quæstionis: Vtrum Reges vel Principes iure aliquo vel titulo, & salva conscientia, Cives ac Subditos à Regia Corona alienare, & alterius Domini particularis ditioni subijcere possint? Ante hac nunquam abvllo Doctorum ita luculenter tractata. Edita cura & studio Wolffgangi Griesstetteri. *Fine copy, calf.* Excessively scarce. First Edition.
4° *Apud Georgium Corvinum, Francof. ad Moen.* 1571

This Piece of Las Casas was not included in his Spanish Works, first issued in 1552-3, and has never been printed in Spain.

1097 LAS CASAS (Bartolomeo de) Seer cort Verhael vande destructie van d'Indien Vergadert deur den Bischop don fray Bartolome de las Casas, oft Casaus, van sinte Dominicus orden, in Brabantsche tale getrouwelick uyte Spaensche ouergeset. 70 *leaves.* Of the highest Degree of rarity; *fine large clean copy, in vellum by Pratt,* 4° [*Brussells*] 1578

Of all the translations of this famous work of Las Casas into foreign languages this one into the dialect of Brabant is the earliest, and perhaps the most difficult to find.

1098 LAS CASAS (BARTOLOMEO DE) TYRANNIES et CRVAVTEZ des Espagnols perpetrees e's Indes Occidentales, qu'on dit Le Nouueau monde; fidelement traduictes par Iaqves de Miggrode. FIRST EDITION IN FRENCH, *fine copy, calf.* 8° *Chez F. de Ravelenghien, Anvers,* 1579

1099 LAS CASAS (B. de) SPIEGHEL DER SPAENSCHER TYRANNYE IN WEST-INDIEN, &c. *with map of the new hemisphere on the title. Fine copy in white vellum by Pratt.* 4° *Cornelis Claesz, Amst.* 1610

1100 LAS CASAS (B. de) ISTORIA O BREUISSIMA RELATIONE della Distrvttione dell' Indie Occidentali. Tradotta in Italiano dall' Ec. Sig. G. Castellani. [Printed in double columns, in Spanish and Italian.] *Matchless copy, sized paper, perfectly uncut, vellum by Pratt.* 4° *M. Ginammi, Venetia,* 1643

1101 LAS CASAS (B. de) IL SVPPLICE SCHIAVO Indiano. Tradotto in Italiano per opera di Marco Ginammi [in Spanish and Italian]. *Fine large copy, rough leaves.* 4° *Venetia,* 1657

1102 LAS CASAS (B. de) La Decouverte des Indes Occidentales, par les Espagnols. *Calf.* 8° *Paris,* 1697

1103 LAS CASAS (B. de) La Decouverte des Indes Occidentales, par les Espagnols. *Frontispiece, calf.* 8° *Paris,* 1697

1104 LAS CASAS (B. de) Relation des Voyages et des Decouvertes, que les Espagnols ont fait dans les Indes occidentales. *Calf.* 8° *Amsterdam,* 1698

1105 LAS CASAS (B. de) BREVE RELACION de la Destruccion de las Indias Occidentales. *Calf.*
16° *Filadelphia, por Juan F. Hartel, N° 126 Calle Segundo,* 1821

This very rare edition contains a preliminary Discourse of 35 pp. upon the life and character of Las Casas. Printed for the Mexican market.

1106 LASTROM (Aug. Th.) Swea och Gotha Höfdinga-Minne sedaro 1720. *Uncut.* 8° *Upsala,* 1842

1107 LAW (W.) The Way to Divine Knowledge. 8° *London,* 1752

1108 LAW (W.) An Humble, Earnest and Affectionate Address to the Clergy. 8° *London,* 1764

1109 LAWRENCE ACADEMY. Jubilee of, at Groton, Mass. July 12, 1854, with General Catalogue. 8° *New York,* 1855

1110 LAWRENCE (William) Lectures on Comparative Anatomy, Physiology, Zoölogy and Natural History of Man. 12 engravings *of heads and skulls.* 9th Ed. *Cloth.* 8° *London,* 1844

BUCKLE'S Copy, with his Bookplate, and autograph. "Henry Thomas Buckle, London, 25 Sept. 1844."

1111 LEA (*Lt.* Albert M.) Notes on Wisconsin Territory, with a map. 12° *Philadelphia,* 1836

1112 LE BEAU (S[r] C.) Voyage Curieux et Nouveau, parmi les Sauvages de l'Amerique Septentrionale. 2 *vols. Plates, half vellum.* 8° *Amsterdam,* 1738

The author in this interesting book describes the manners and customs of the Iroquois, the Hurons, the Algonquins and other tribes of Canada and south towards old Louisiana.

1113 LE CLERCQ (Le P. CHRISTIEN) NOUVELLE RELATION DE LA GASPESIE, qui contient les Mœurs et la Religion des Sauvages Gaspesiens Porte-Croix adorateurs du Soleil, et d'autres Peuples de l'Amerique Septentrionale dite la Canada. *Calf, scarce.* 8° *Paris*, 1691

This is perhaps the most important book we have on Northeastern Canada and the Province of New Brunswick.

1114 LEE (Charles) Memoirs of the late C. Lee, Aid de Camp to the King of Poland, &c, in the Service of the U. S. of America during the Revolution. *Half blue morocco, gilt, uncut.* 8° *Dublin*, 1792

1115 LEES (J.) Laws of the Customs, with the Tariff and Customs. *Cloth.* 8° *London*, 1859

1116 LE GENTIL (M.) Le Gentils Reisen in der Indischen Meeren 1761–69. *Half mor. gilt, uncut.* 8° *Hamb.* 1781

1117 LEIBNITZ (GODF. GULIEL.) NOVISSIMA SINICA Historiam temporis illustratura &c. 2da Edit. *Portrait of the Emperor of China.* 8° *n. p.* 1699

DE SUCCESSU EVANGELII APUD INDOS Occidentales. In Novâ Angliâ, Epistola. A CRESENTIO MATHERO apud Bostonienses V. D. M. *Ultrajecti*, 1699

De Successu Evangelii apud Indos Orientales Epistolæ à H. Specht & A. de May, &c.

Icon Regia Monarchæ Sinarvm nunc Regnantis. 1699

Four volumes in one, small 8vo. This piece of INCREASE MATHER is rare, especially to find it growing in the middle of this collection where it belongs. It was reprinted from the London Edition of 1688.

1118 LEIGH (Evans H.) Observations concerning all the Roman and Greek Emperors. *With engravings. Calf.* 8° *London*, 1663

1119 LEIGHTON (R.) Praelectiones Theologiæ. 4° *London*, 1693

1120 LE JEUNE (PAULE) RELATION DE CE QVI S'EST PASSÉ EN LA NOVVELLE FRANCE en l'année 1638. *Avec* Relation de ce qvi s'est passé dans le pays des Hvrons ès années 1637 & 1638, par F. J. Le Mercier. *The two parts in one volume, fine copy in white vellum, gilt edges, by F. Bedford.* EXCESSIVELY SCARCE. 8° *Chez Sebastien Cramoisy, Paris*, 1638

To form a complete collection of the *Relations* or annual reports of the Jesuit missionaries in Canada, on the Borders, and in the Great North West from about 1630 to 1680 has been the laudable ambition of many American collectors, but few if any have succeeded. Including the various editions there are nearly 50 volumes. A perfect set is the *pons asinorum* of the American collector. The historical and geographical importance of these volumes cannot well be overstated.

1121 LE JEUNE (PAULE) RELATION DE CE QUI S'EST PASSE en la NOVVELLE FRANCE sur le grand Fleuue de S. Laurens en l'année 1634. *Fine copy in old green morocco, gilt back and borders (wanting title and preliminary leaves).* 8° *Chez Sebastien Cramoisy, Paris*, 1635

1122 LELAND (J. *D. D.*) View of the Principal Deistical Writers that have appeared in England, in the last and present Century. 2 *vols, calf.* 8° *London*, 1754

1123 LENDRUM (J.) History of the American Revolution; prefixed is a Genuine History of North and South America. 2 *vols.* 8° *I. Thomas, Boston,* 1795

1124 LEON D'AFRIQUE (JEAN) HISTORIALE Description de l'Afrique, tierce Partie dv Monde. *Calf.* 8° *Anvers,* 1556

1125 LE SAGE (M.) The Adventures of Robert Chevalier, call'd De Beauchesne. Captain of a Privateer in New France. 2 *vols, calf.* 8° *London,* 1745

1126 LETTER (A) Addressed to two Great Men, on the Prospect of Peace; and the Terms necessary to be insisted upon in the Negotiation. 2d Ed. corrected. *Half morocco.* 8° *A. Miller, London,* 1760

Attributed to Junius. Relates mainly to American Affairs.

1127 LETTER (A) addressed to two Great Men on the Prospect of Peace [by Junius ?] 2d Ed. *Half roan, uncut.* 8° *London,* 1760

1128 LETTER. Remarks on the Letter Address'd to Two Great Men. In a Letter to the Author of that Piece. [On American Affairs.] *Half roan.* 8° *London,* [1759 ?]

1129 LETTERS upon Learning, wherein is shewn the Insufficiency thereof, *etc.* *Half calf.* 4° *London,* 1738

1130 LETTER (A) TO A MEMBER OF PARLIAMENT on the Regulation of the Plantation Trade [Signed J. B.] *Fine copy, in white vellum, by Pratt.* 4° *Printed in the year* 1701

An excessively rare tract. The writer J. B. complains "That several of our American Colonies, as Rhode Island, Conecticut, East and West Jersie, Pensilvania, &c., are like so many Independent Sovereignties, having the Election of Governors, either amongst themselves annually, as Rhode Island, and Conecticut; or depending on some Persons in England. . . . As the Jersies and Pensilvania," *etc.*, and are likely to divert Trade from the Mother Country, by running tobacco and other produce to Scotland, Holland, and elsewhere, contrary to the recent laws against piracy, that is illegal trade. He prays Parliament therefore to "remove all the Calamities that attend these Colonies, through their want of Unity by reassuming that part of the Grants pretended to by the Proprietors of Conecticut, Rhode Island, East and West Jersies, Pensilvania, etc., by which they claim the powers of governing, or chusing Governors, and laying them under the immediate direction of the King."

1131 LETTERS. Three Letters to the People of England on National Affairs. 6th Edition. *Calf.* 8° *London,* 1756

1132 LETTERS from a Farmer in Pennsylvania to the Inhabitants of the British Colonies, with a Preface by the Dublin Editor. *Half calf.* 8° [*Dublin*] 1768

1133 LETTERS to the Ministry from Governor Bernard, General Gage, and Commodore Hood. And also Memorials to the Lords of the Treasury, from the Commissioners of the Customs. With sundry Letters and Papers annexed to the said Memorials. SCARCE, *half roan.* 8° *Edes & Gill, Boston,* 1769

1134 LETTERS, *etc.* [By Sagittarius] "The Boston faction have professed themselves to be of a peaceable and quiet spirit. As a proof of this they pulled down the Lieut. Governor's house, broke open the Secretary's house, and demolished the

Stamp and Admiralty Offices." *p.* 1. VERY RARE, *wants title and last* 3 *leaves after p.* 120. *Half calf.* See Nuggets, N° 2425. 8° *Boston*, 1774

1135 LETTERS. A Series of Letters between Rev. J. Buckminster, D. D., Rev. Jos. Walter, and Rev. Hosea Ballou. *Board.* 18° *Windsor*, 1811

1136 LETTER (A) to Harrison Gray Otis on the present State of our National Affairs. By John Quincy Adams. *Uncut.* 8° *G. W. Nichols, Walpole, N. H.* 1808

1137 LETTERS. CHOIX DES LETTRES EDIFIANTES, ecrites des Missions Etrangères; avec des Additions des Notes Critiques, etc. Par M. * * * 8 *vols, polished calf gilt, handsome copy.* 8° *Paris*, 1808–9

1138 LETTSOM (J. C.) Memoirs of John Fothergill, M. D. Fourth Edition. *Portrait of Franklin by Heath. Calf, gilt.* 8° *London*, 1786

1139 LEWIS AND CLARKE. Travels from St. Louis to the Pacific Ocean. *Half green morocco, gilt.* 8° *London*, 1809

1140 LEWIS AND CLARKE. Travels to the Source of the Missouri River. *Half calf, gilt.* 8° *London*, 1814

1141 LEWIS & CLARKE. Reize naar de Bronnen van den Missouri in de jaren 1804–6, uit het Engelsch vertaald door N. G. van Kampen. *Maps,* 3 *vols, half brown morocco, gilt, cloth sides, uncut, fine copy.* 8° *Dordrecht*, 1816

1142 LEWIS AND CLARKE. Reize naar de Bronnen van den Missouri in de jaren 1804–5–6, Uit het Engelsch vertaald door N. G. van Kampen. *Map,* 3 *vols, half maroon morocco, fine uncut copy.* 8° *Dordrecht*, 1816

1143 LIL (Herman Van) Het Levan van William Penn. 2 *vols, half green morocco, uncut.* 8° *Amsterdam*, 1820

1144 LINDLEY (Thomas) Reise nach Brasilien und Aufenthalt daselbst in den Jahren 1802–3. Nebst einer Beschriebung der Porto-Seguro und San Salvador. *Half morocco, uncut.* 8° *Weimar*, 1806

1145 LINGARD (*Rev.* J.) Antiquities of the Anglo-Saxon Church. Second Edition. *Map, calf.* 8° *Newcastle*, 1810

1146 LINN (William, *D. D.*) Sermons, Historical and Characteristical. 12° *New York*, 1791

1147 LINN (William, *D. D.*) A Funeral Eulogy on General Washington, delivered Feb. 22, 1800, before the New York State Society of the Cincinnati. (*Wanting p.* 33 *and all after.*) 8° *New York*, 1800

1148 LINSCHOTEN (JAN HUYGHEN VAN) ITINERARIO, VOYAGE ofte Schipvaert van Jan Huygen van Linschoten naer Oost ofte Portugaels Indien. 6 *maps and* 36 *colored plates, black letter, vellum.* FIRST EDITION, *fine complete copy.* *Folio, Amstelredam*, 1596–95

For a full account and collation of this very rare first edition of Linschot, see that invaluable book entitled "Mémoire Bibliographique sur les Journaux des

Navigateurs Néerlandais réimprimés dans les Collections de DEBRY et de HULSIUS, *etc.*, en la possession de Frederick Muller a Amsterdam. Rédigé par P. A. Tiele," pp. 83–91. Few bibliographers in this country have had the opportunity to see this first edition entirely complete like the present copy.

1149 LINSCHOTEN (JOHN HUYGHEN VAN) HIS DISCOURSE OF VOYAGES INTO YE EASTE AND WEST INDIES. *Fine large, clean, and perfect copy, with a brilliant impression of the frontispiece, and with all the twelve maps, several of them the rare early impressions before the pagination was added. Old calf rebacked.* VERY SCARCE IN THIS GENUINE STATE.
Folio, John Wolfe, London, 1598

1150 LINSCHOTEN (JAN HUYGHEN VAN) HISTORIE Naturael ende Morael van de Westersche Indien: Ghecomponeert door IOSEPHUM DE ACOSTA, der Jesuitscher Oorden. Ende nu eerstinael uyt den Spaenschen in onser Nederduytsch tale ouergheset: door Ian Huyghen van Linschoten. *Very fine copy. Vellum. Black letter.*
8° *Tot Enchuysen, by Jacob Lenaertsz,* 1598

This earliest translation of ACOSTA into Dutch by LINSCHOTEN is one of the rarest books of this time pertaining to America.

1151 LISLE (Major J. G. Semple) Life of, written by Himself. *Portrait, calf.* 8° *London,* 1799

1152 LITCHFIELD COUNTY. Centennial Celebration of, August 13 and 14, 1851. 8° *Hartford,* 1851

1153 LITERARY SOUVENIR, 1832–5. Edited by Alaric A. Watts. *Plates,* 2 *vols, morocco, gilt.* 16° *London*

1154 LIVINGSTON (R. R.) Essay on Sheep. *Boards.* 12° *Concord, N. H.* 1813

1155 LIVIUS (Titus) Librorum Epitome. Lucius Florus, *in* 1 *vol. Vellum.* 8° *Aldus, Venetiis, n. d.*

1156 LIVIUS (Titus) Librorum Epitome: Lucii Flori Libri Tres; Polybii Histor. Libri Quinque in Latinam conversi in uno vol. *Calf.* 8° *Aldus, Venetiis,* 1521

1157 LIVIUS (TITUS) THE HISTORIE OF TVVO of the moste noble Captaines of the worlde, Anniball and Scipio, of their divers battailes and victories, excedyng profitable to reade, gathered and translated into English, out of Titus Livius, and other Authors, by Antonie Cope esquire. Anno M.D.LXVIII. [*should be* 1548] *Splendid copy on* LARGE PAPER, *clean and perfect, with rough leaves.* EXCESSIVELY RARE IN THIS STATE.
4° *Londini, in Aedibus Thomæ Bertheleti, typis excusum,* 1548

The title is surrounded by a copy of Holbein's beautiful wood-cut border of a procession of rollicking boys, and on the reverse are three eight-line stanzas by Thomas Berthelet the printer, on this Historie. Few books afford better specimens of English philology and orthography than this translation and compilation of Master Anthonie Cope.

1158 LLOYD (Thomas, *Stenographer*) The Trials of William S. Smith and Samuel G. Ogden for Misdemeanors, in the Circuit Court of the U. S., for the N. Y. District, July, 1806. *Calf.* 8° *New York,* 1807

7

1159 LOCCENIUS (I.) Historiæ Svecanæ, a primo Rege vsque ad Carolum XI: accedunt Antiquitatum Sveogothicarum Libri Tres eidem Auctore. *Calf.* *Thick* 4° *Lepsiæ*, 1676

1160 LOCKE, Algernon Sidney, and Lord Shaftesbury. Original Letters of, by T. Forster. *Boards.* 8° *London*, 1830

1161 LOCKE (J. L.) History of the Town of Camden, Maine; with References to the neighboring Places and adjacent Waters. *Cloth.* 12° *Hallowell*, 1859

1162 LOGARITHMS. A Treatise on the Construction of Logarithms, to which are added, Tables of Logarithms, sines and tangents. *Boards, uncut.* 4° *T. Dobson, Philadelphia*, 1802

1163 LONDON. Post Office London Directory 1854 & 1855. 2 *vols.* *Thick* 8° *London*

1164 LONDON Directory for 1855. *Thick* 8° *London*

1165 LONDON. An exact Delineation of the Cities of London and Westminster and the Suburbs thereof, with the Borough of Southwark, and all the Through-fares, Highwaies, Streets, Lanes, & Common Allies within the same, composed by a scale, and Ichnographically described by Richard Newcourt. Wm. Farthorne, sculpsit, London, 1658. Engraved from the original by G. Jarman in 1857, and Published by Stanford. London, 1863. *Size of the original,* 6 *ft* 4 *by* 3 *ft* 5 *inches, mounted on cambric and folded in blue morocco cover in* 4° *Published in this form at* £3 3*s*

1166 LONG (J.) Voyages chez differentes Nations Sauvages de l'Amerique Septentrionale. *Map, calf.* 8° *Paris*, 1794

1167 LONG (*Major* S. H.) NARRATIVE OF AN EXPEDITION to the Source of St. Peter's River, Lake Winnepeek, Lake of the Woods, *etc.*, in the year 1823. Compiled by W. H. Keating. 2 *vols, plates, half mor. uncut, fine copy.* 8° *Philadelphia*, 1824

1168 LOSA (François, *curé de l'Eglise Cathedrale de Mexico*) La Vie de Gregoire Lopez dans la Novvelle Espagne. 2d Edition. *Vellum.* 16° *Paris*, 1655

Gregory Lopez was one of the most successful of the Jesuit Missionaries among the Indians of Mexico. He is said to have been a bye-child of Philip the Second.

1169 LOOSJES (A.) Gedenkzuil ter gelegenheid der Vry-Verklaaring van Noord-Amerika. *Half brown morocco, uncut.* 8° *Amsterdam*, 1782

1170 LOSKIEL (Georg Heinrich) Geschichte der Mission der evang. Brüder unter den Indianern in Nordamerika. *Half green morocco, gilt, uncut.* 8° *Barby*, 1789

1171 LOSKIEL (G. H.) History of the Mission of the United Brethren among the Indians in North America. Translated by C. J. Latrobe. *Map, half mor. uncut.* 8° *London*, 1794

1172 LOVELAND (Samuel C. *of Reading, Vt.*) A Greek Lexicon, adapted to the New Testament with English Definitions. *Cloth.* 16° *Woodstock, Vt, by David Watson*, 1828

1173 LOWE (Joseph) An Inquiry into the State of the British West Indies. 4th Edition, *calf.* 8° *London*, 1808

1174 LUCAS (S.) A Prize Essay, read in the Sheldonian Theatre, Oxford, June 4th, 1845. 8° *London*, 1845

1175 LUCIANUS. OPERA OMNIA quæ extant, Græcé; cum Latina doctiss. Virorum Interpretatione, J. Bordelotius emendavit. *Old calf.* *Folio, Parisiis*, 1615

1176 LUCRETIUS. De Rerum Natura Libri sex: cum Paraphrastica Explanatione J. Nardii. *Calf.* 4° *Florentiæ*, 1647

1177 LUCRETIUS. De Rerum Natura Libri VI. Vita Lucretii Commentariis, *etc.* edidit Lambinus. *Calf. Folio, Lutetiæ*, 1670

1178 LUDOLPHUS (*Parochialis ecclesie in* SUCHEN RECTOR) DE TERRA SANCTA ET ITINERE jherosolomitano et de statu eius et alijs mirabilibus que in mari conspiciũtur videlicit mediterraneo. *Very fine copy, in Black letter, long lines*, 41 *to a page*, 34 *leaves*. AN EDITION OF THE HIGHEST RARITY. *Folio, without date or place, but* [*Argent. H. Eggensteyn, circa* 1475]

1179 LUNT (W. P.) Two Discourses, Sept. 29, 1839, on the Two Hundredth Anniversary of the First Congregational Church, Quincy; with an Appendix. 8° *Boston*, 1840

1180 LUSSAN (Raveneau de) Journal du Voyage fait à la Mer du Sud avec les Flibustiers de l'Amerique en 1684. 2d Edition, *calf, gilt.* 8° *Paris*, 1693

1181 LYCOPHRON. Alexandræ, sive Cassandræ uersiones duæ; una ad uerbum a G. Cantero; altera Carrmine expressa per J. Scaligerum. *Half calf.* 8° *Basileæ*, 1566

1182 LYCOPHRON. Alexandra. I. Meursius recens. et Commentario illustrav. *Calf.* 8° *Elzevir, Lugd. Batav.* 1599

1183 LYON (*Capt.* G. F.) Private Journal, during the recent Voyage of Discovery under Capt. Parry. *Map and plates, half maroon morocco, uncut.* 8° *London*, 1824

1184 LYON (G. F.) Journal. *Another copy, half maroon morocco, uncut.* 8° *London*, 1824

1185 LYTTLETON (*Lord*) Letters. First American Edition. 8° *Troy, N. Y.* 1807

1186 MABLY (Abbé de) Remarks concerning the Government and Laws of the United States, in four Letters addressed to Mr. Adams. *Half morocco.* 8° *London*, 1784

1187 MABLY (Abbé de) Remarks concerning the Government and the Laws of America, addressed to Mr. [John] Adams. *Calf.* 8° *Dublin*, 1785

It was the questions in this book which caused Mr. Adams to write his Defense of the Constitution of the United States.

1188 MACAULAY (Catharine) Address to the People of England, Scotland, and Ireland, on the Present Important Crisis of Affairs. *Half morocco.* 8° *London*, 1775

1189 McCALL (HUGH) THE HISTORY OF GEORGIA, containing brief Sketches of the most remarkable Events up to the present Day. 2 *vols.* 8° *Savannah,* 1811

1190 McCLURE (David) and PARISH (Elijah) Memoirs of the Rev. Eleazar Wheelock, D. D., Founder and President of Dartmouth College. *Portrait, calf.* 8° *Newburyport,* 1811

1191 McCOY (J.) History of Baptist Indian Missions, and the Condition of the Aboriginal Tribes. *Cloth.* 8° *Washington,* 1840

1192 McDOUGALL (Geo. J.) The Eventful voyage of H. M. Ship Resolute, in search of Sir John Franklin. *Map and engravings, half calf.* 8° *London,* 1857

1193 McKINNON (D.) Tour through the British West Indies in 1802–3. *Map, calf.* 8° *London,* 1804

1194 McKENNEY (T. L.) SKETCHES OF A TOUR TO THE LAKES, of the Character and Customs of the Chippeway Indians, and of Incidents connected with the Treaty of Fond du Lac; also, a Vocabulary of the Algic or Chippeway Language. *Illustrated with engravings, half morocco, uncut.* 8° *Baltimore,* 1827

1195 MACKENZIE (ALEXANDER) VOYAGES from Montreal, through the Continent of North America, to the Frozen and Pacific Oceans, 1789–93, with Account of the Fur Trade of that Country. *Portrait and maps, calf.* 4° *London,* 1801

This book of MacKenzie is one of the best of the kind we have, and is already of very considerable value to the American historian and topographer, but when the vast country over which he travelled shall have been developed it will become indispensable.

1196 MACKENZIE (A.) Another Copy. *Calf.* 4° *London,* 1801

1197 MACKENZIE (A.) Voyages from Montreal, through the Continent of North America. *Portrait and maps, calf, fine copy.* 4° *London,* 1801

1198 MACKENZIE (Sir Alex.) Voyages from Montreal, to the Frozen and Pacific Oceans in the Years 1789 and 1793. *Portrait and maps, 2 vols, half calf.* 8° *Philadelphia,* 1802

1199 MACKENZIE (A.) Voyages dans l'Intérieur de l'Amerique Septentrionale, faits en 1789, 92, 93. Traduits de l'Anglais par J. Castera, avec des Notes des Papiers du vice-amiral Bougainville. *3 vols, maps, half calf, uncut, fine copy.* 8° *Paris,* 1802.

This is another instance in which a translation with notes becomes even more valuable than the original, or at least greatly enhances the value of the original.

1200 MACKENZIE (Alexander) Reizen von Montreal durch Nordamerika nach dem Eismeer und der Süd-See in den Jahren 1789 und 1793. *Portrait, half brown morocco, gilt, uncut.* 8° *Hamburg,* 1802

1201 MACKENZIE (E.) View of the United States of America, and of Upper and Lower Canada. *Map and engravings, calf.* 8° *Newcastle, n. d.*

1202 MACKENZIE (Roderick) Strictures on Lt. Col. Tarleton's History of the Campaigns, in the Southern Provinces of North America, of 1780 and 1781. *Calf, fine copy.* 8° *Lond.* 1787

1203 MACKINZIE (W. L.) Lives and Opinions of Benjamin Franklin Butler and Jesse Hoyt. 8° *Boston*, 1845

1204 MACPHERSON (Charles) Memoirs of the Life and Travels of, in Asia, Africa, and America. *Calf.* 12° *Edinburg*, 1800

1205 MACRAY (*Rev.* William Dunn) Annals of the Bodleian Library, Oxford, 1598–1867. With a preliminary Notice of the earlier Library, founded in the fourteenth century. *Cloth.* 8° *London*, 1868

1206 MAFFEIUS (Ioannes Petrus) Historiarum Indicarum Libri XVI. 2 *vols, calf.* 8° *Cadomi*. 1614

1207 MAFFEI (Gio. Piet.) Le Istorie dell' Indie Orientali. Tradotte da M. F. Serdonati. 2 *vols, calf.* 4° *Bergamo*, 1749

1208 MAFFEIUS (J. P.) HISTORIARUM INDICARUM Libri XVI. *Calf.* *Folio, Jaurini*, [1752?]

1209 MAGNUS (OLAUS) DE VVONDERLIJCKE HISTORIE van de Noordersche landen beschreuen door Heere Olaus de Grote Eerstbisschop van Upsalen end Oуerste. Nu eerst ouerghestelt wten Latijn in ons Nederlantsche Duytsche sprake. FIRST LOW-DUTCH EDIT. *of exceeding rarity, fine copy, vellum.* 8° *Willem Siluius, Tantwerpen*, 1562

The quaintness and beauty of the many wood-cuts in the text of this little book make it among the most interesting of all the works on the northern regions. No doubt many of the illustrations of the Dutch voyages to Spitzbergen, Nova Zembla, Iceland, Greenland, etc., were drawn from these designs.

1210 MAJOR (RICHARD HENRY) THE LIFE OF PRINCE HENRY of Portugal, surnamed the Navigator; and its results: Comprising the discovery, within one century, of half the world. With new facts in the discovery of the Atlantic Islands; a refutation of French claims to priority in discovery; Portuguese knowledge (subsequently lost) of the Nile Lakes, and the history of the naming of America. *Portrait and maps, cloth, uncut. Published at* £1 5*s.* *Royal* 8° *London*, 1868

1211 MAKO (Abb.) Descriptio Provinciæ Moxitarum in Regno Peruano. SCARCE. 8° *Budæ*, 1791

1212 MALL (THOMAS) THE HISTORY OF THE MARTYRS Epitomised. A Cloud of Witness; or, the Sufferers mirrour made up of the Swanlike Songs and other Choice Passages of a great number of Martyrs. 2 *vols in* 1, *calf gilt.* 8° *Rogers and Fowle, Boston*, 1747

1213 MALLORY (SIR T.) Mort d'Arthure. From the Edition of 1634, with Introduction and Notes by Thomas Wright, Vols II. and III. 2 *vols, cloth.* 12° *London*, 1858

1214 MANDEVILLE. Fable of the Bees; or Private Vices, Public Benefits. *Calf.* 8° *London*, 1795

1215 MANDRILLON (Jh.) Le Voyageur Américain. *Half morocco, uncut.* 8° *Amst.* 1782

1216 MANDRILLON (Jh.) Le Spectateur Américain. Suivi de Rescherches Philosophique. *Map, half brown morocco, gilt, uncut.* 8° *Amsterdam*, 1784

1217 Mandrillon (J.) Le Spectateur Americain, ou Remarques sur l'Amerique Septentrionale, et la Republique des Treize Etats-Unis. *Calf.* 8° *Amsterdam,* 1785

1218 MANIFESTO Satisfactorio anunciado en la Gazeta de Mexico (Tom. I Num. 53) Opusculo Guadalupano Compuesto por el Doctor D. Joseph Ignacio Bartolache, natural de la Ciudad de Santa Fé, Real y Minas de Guanajuato. *Fine copy, calf.* 4° *Mexico,* 1790

This scarce volume (comprising 6 preliminary leaves, 105 pages, two copperplates, 16 supplemental pages, and a List of Subscribers' names filling 12 pages) is a bibliographical account of all the authors who have written upon the miraculous appearance in Mexico at sundry times, of the Image of Our Lady of Guadaloupe, from 1531 down. The catalogue is extensive and comprises some of the best Mexican writers, in Latin, in Spanish and even in the Indian Languages, touching incidentally on theology, law, politics, history and the education and conversion of the native tribes.

1219 Manrique (Fr. A.) Vidas de los Venerables P. Fr. Vincente Bernedo, Fr. Ivan Macias, y Fr. Martin de Porres. *Portraits.* 4° *Venecia,* 1696

1220 Mansel (H. L.) The Limits of Religious Thought, in Eight Lectures, before the University of Oxford 1858, on the Foundation of the Rev. John Bampton. Third Edition, *cloth.* 8° *London,* 1859

1221 Mansfield (*Lord*) Speech in the Cause of Campbell against Hall respecting the King's Patent for raising a Duty of 4½ per cent. on all the Exports from the Island of Grenada. *Half morocco.* 8° *London,* 1775

1222 Mant (R. *D. D.*) The Truth and Excellence of the Christian Religion, etc. in three Discourses. 12° *London,* 1819

1223 Mariner (Wm.) An Account of the Natives of the Tonga Islands. . . . . compiled by John Martin. *Frontispiece, 2 vols, half green morocco, gilt, uncut.* 8° *London,* 1818

1224 Maritime and Inland Discovery. History of. 3 *vols, cloth.* 8° *Lardner's Cab. Cyc. London,* 1830

1225 Marcellinus (Ammianus) Regnum Gestarum qui de 31 supersunt libri xviii. *Folio, Paris,* 1681

1226 Markham (Wm. *Archbishop of York*) A Sermon before the Society for the Propagation of the Gospel in Foreign Parts; Feb. 21, 1777. *Half roan.* 8° *London,* 1777

With the Charter of the Society, and an account of its proceedings 1776–7. Above 100 missionaries were scattered throughout the American Colonies at the breaking out of the Rebellion [American Revolution]. The report of their proceedings in 1776 reads strangely now. "In July last, the Congress thought proper to make an explicit declaration of independence by which all connection with Great Britain was to be broken off, and the Americans released from any alliance to our gracious Sovereign." This declaration increased the embarrassment of the clergy. To officiate publicly, and not pray for the king and royal family, according to the Liturgy, was against their duty and oath, as well as dictates of their conscience; they therefore almost all of them shut up their churches. "The venerable Mr. Beach of Newtown in Connecticut is alone to be excepted" — and upon being warned of his danger, said with the firmness and spirit of a primitive confessor "that he would do his duty, preach, and pray for the King 'till the rebels cut out his tongue."

1227 MARRYAT (Joseph) Thoughts on the Abolition of Slave Trade. 3d Edition. 1816
More Thoughts, Slaves and Slave Trade. 1816
An Examination of the Reports of the Berbice Commissioners. 1817
More Thoughts still. State of West India Colonies. 2d Ed. 1818. *Four tracts in* 1 *vol, calf, gilt.* 8° *London,* 1816–18

1228 MARSHALL (E. F.) A Spelling Book of the English Language. *Boards.* 18° *Wells River, Vt.* 1830

1229 MARSHALL (JOHN) LIFE OF GEORGE WASHINGTON, from original Papers, etc. *Portrait.* 5 *vols.* 8° *Philadelphia,* 1805

1230 MARSILLAC (J.) LA Vie de Guillaume Penn. 2 *vols, half brown morocco, uncut.* 8° *Paris,* 1791

1231 MARTENS (FED.) VIAGIO DE SPIZBERGIA, fatto l'Anno 1671. *Vellum, uncut,*
AN EXCESSIVELY RARE EDITION. 12° *Venetia,* 1680

1232 MARTINIERE (Le Sieur) Voyage des Pays Septentrionavx. *With engravings, calf.* 8° *Paris,* 1676

1233 MARTINIQUE. Voyage a la Martinique. Vues et Observations politiques sur cette Isle, avec un Aperçu de ses Productions végétales et animales. Par J. R * * * , général de brigade. *Half red morocco, uncut.* 8° *Paris,* 1804

1234 MARTYR (PETER, *ab Angleria*) PETRI MARTYRIS AB ANGLERIA Mediolanen. Oratoris clarissimi, Fernandi & Helisabeth Hispaniarum quondam regum à consilijs, DE REBUS OCEANICIS & ORBE NOVO DECADES TRES: quibus quicquid de inuentis nuper terris traditum, nouarum rerum cupidum lectorem retinere possit, copiose, fideliter, eruditeq; docetur. Ejvsdem praeterea Legationis Babylonicae libri tres.
A MATCHLESS COPY, ON LARGE PAPER, *measuring* $13\frac{1}{4}$ *by* $8\frac{3}{8}$ *inches. Vellum. Folio, Apud Ioannem Bebelium, Basileae,* 1533

Besides the first three *Decades* and the *Legatio Babylonica* this edition contains the author's *de Insulis nuper inventis*, written in 1520 from information furnished by Aliminos, Puertocarero and Montejo, Messengers from Velasquez and Cortes, and published at Basle in 1521 to supply the place of the lost *First Relation* of Cortes.

1235 MARTYR (PETER) HISTORI VON DER NEWEN WELT, UND INDIANISCHEN NIDERGAENGISCHEN KOENIGREICHS; aus dem Latein in das Teutsch gebracht durch Nicolaum Hoeniger von Koenigshofen. 2 *vols in one, in the original vellum binding.* *Folio, Sebastian Henicpetri, Basil,* 1582

1236 MARTYR (PETER, *ab Angleria*) THE DECADES OF THE NEWE WORLDE or West India, conteynyng the navigations and conquestes of the Spanyardes, &c. Wrytten in the Latine tounge, and translated into Englysshe by Rycharde Eden. *Good sound working copy, the title in admirable fac simile by Harris, the text complete but wanting the last leaf of the Contents.* BLACK LETTER. *Calf.*
4° *In Aedibus Gulielmi Powell, Londini,* 1555

See note under EDEN, No. 632, for contents of this rare work.

1237 MARTYR (PETER, *ab Angleria*) DE NOVO ORBE, OR THE HISTORIE OF THE WEST INDIES, contayning the actes and aduentures of the Spanyardes, which haue conquered and peopled those Countries &c. Comprised in eight Decades. Whereof three have been formerly translated into English by R. Eden, whereunto the other five are newly added by the Industrie, and painfull Trauaile of M. Lok, *Gent. Fine copy, red morocco, gilt edges and back.*
UNCOMMON. 4° *Thomas Adams, London,* 1612

The only edition of Peter Martyr's *eight* decades in English. This same edition was reissued with a title bearing no date, and again with one dated 1628, but beyond the title there is no other difference in the three issues.

1238 MASON (W.) Art of Short-Hand Improv'd. 12° *London, n. d.*

1239 MASSACHUSETTS. ACTS AND LAWS of His Majesty's Province of the Massachusetts-Bay in New England. *Vellum.* *Folio, Boston, N. E.* 1742

1240 MASSACHUSETTS. The true sentiments of America contained in letters sent from Massachusetts, *etc. Half roan, uncut.* 8° *London,* 1768

1241 MASSACHUSETTS. A Speech intended to have been Spoken on the Bill for altering the Charters of the Colony of Massachusetts Bay. *Half morocco, uncut.* 8° *London,* 1774

1242 MASSACHUSETTS. A Speech intended to have been Spoken on the Bill for altering the Charters of the Colony of Massachusetts Bay, by Dr. Shipley, Bishop of St. Asaph. Fourth Edition, *half morocco.* 8° *London,* 1774

1243 MASSACHUSETTS. Debates, Resolutions, and other Proceedings of the Convention of the Commonwealth of Massachusetts, convened at Boston Jan. 9, 1788. The Yeas and Nays on the decision of the Grand Question, etc. 8° *Adams & Nourse, Boston,* 1788

1244 MASSACHUSETTS. Constitution of the State of Massachusetts and of the United States, etc. *Boards, uncut.* 12° *Boston,* 1805

1245 MASSACHUSETTS. Constitution of the State of Massachusetts, and that of the U. States; with Washington's Farewell Address. *Boards.* 12° *Northampton,* 1806

1246 MASSACHUSETTS. Charters and General Laws of the Colony and Province of Massachusetts Bay; with an Appendix. *Boards, uncut.* 8° *Boston,* 1814

1247 MASSACHUSETTS. Reports of the Commissioners on the Zoölogical Survey of the State. [Reports of Dr. Emmons, Dr. Harris, and A. B. Gould.] *Uncut.* 8° *Boston,* 1838

1248 MASSACHUSETTS. Reports on the Herbaceous Plants and Quadrupeds of Massachusetts. *Uncut.* 8° *Cambridge,* 1846

1249 MASSACHUSETTS. Reports of the Commissioners on the Geological Survey of the State. *Uncut.* 8° *Boston,* 1838

1250 MASSACHUSETTS State Record 1847–51. 5 *vols, cloth.* 12° *Boston,* 1847–51

1251 MASSACHUSETTS State Record for 1847. 3 copies, and for 1850. 4 *vols.*

1252 MASSACHUSETTS. RECORDS OF THE GOVERNOR AND COMPANY of the Massachusetts Bay in New England. Edited by N. B. Shurtleff, M. D. 6 *vols*, 1628–1686. *Cloth, gilt tops.* 4° *Boston*, 1853–1854

1253 MATHER (COTTON) MAGNALIA CHRISTI AMERICANA: OR THE ECCLESIASTICAL HISTORY OF NEW ENGLAND from its First Planting in the Year 1620 unto the Year of our Lord 1698. In Seven Books, *fine large and perfect copy, with the rare original map. Old calf.* *Folio, Thomas Parkhurst, London*, 1702

1254 MATHER (INCREASE) A SERMON Wherein is shewed that the Church of God is sometimes a Subject of Great Persecution; Preached at a Publick Fast at Boston in New England; Occasion'd by the Tidings of a great Persecution Raised against the Protestants in France. *Wants title and next leaf.* 4° *Boston, for Samuel Sewall*, 1682

1255 MATHER (SAMUEL) AN APOLOGY for the Liberties of the Churches in New England; with a Discourse concerning Congregational Churches. *Half calf.* 8° *Printed by T. Fleet, Boston*, 1738

1256 MATTHEWS (J.) Voyage to the River Sierra-Leone, on the Coast of Africa; In a series of Letters during his Residence in that Country 1785 to 1787. *Plate, half green morocco, uncut.* 8° *London*, 1788

1257 MAUDUIT (Israel) Short View of the History of the Colony of Massachusetts Bay, with Respect to their Charters and Constitution. SCARCE. *Half calf.* 8° *London*, 1784

1258 MAURICE OF NASSAU. WARHAFFTIGE BESCHREIBUNG alle Victorien zu Wasser vnnd zu Land . . . durch Mavrits von Nassav. *Numerous fine plates, vellum. Folio, Leyden*, 1612

There are in this volume many important historical references to America and the West Indies.

1259 MAWE (John) Voyages dans l'intérieur du Brésil Traduits par J. B. Eyries. 2 *vols, plates, half morocco, uncut.* 8° *Paris*, 1816

1260 MAWE (John) Reizen in de Binnendeelen van Brazilië. 2 *vols, plates, half calf.* 8° *Haarlem*, 1817–18

1261 MAWE (John) Reizen in de Binnendeelen van Brazilië. 2 *vols, map and plates, half maroon morocco, uncut.* 8° *Haarlem*, 1818

1262 (MAXIMILIAN) Reise nach Brasilian in den Jahren, 1815 tot 1817. 2 *vols, plates, half maroon morocco, uncut.* 8° *Frankfurt*, 1820

1263 MAXIMILIAN (*Prins van Wied-Nieuwied*) Reize naar Brazilië in de jaren 1815–17, mit platten. 2 *vols, boards.* 8° *Groningen*, 1822

1264 MEAD (MATTHEW) The Almost Christian Discovered; or, the False Professor Tryed and Cast.
Boards. 12° *Printed by J. Draper, Boston,* 1742

1265 MEARS (John) Voyages in 1788 and 1789 from China to the N. W. Coasts of America; to which are annexed Observations on the probable existence of a North-West Passage.
2 *vols, calf, portrait.* 8° *London,* 1791

1266 MEARES (John) Voyages made in the years 1788 and 1789 from China to the N. W. Coast of America; with Narrative of a Voyage in 1786, from Bengal in the Ship Nootka, etc. 2 *vols, portrait and maps, calf gilt.* 8° *London,* 1791

1267 MEASE (James) The Picture of Philadelphia.
Frontispiece. 12° *Philadelphia,* 1811

1268 MEASE (James) Letter Transmitting a Treatise on the Rearing of Silk Worms by Mr. De Hazel of Munich.
Plates. 8° *Washington,* 1828

This rare book will recall the famous *Morus Multicalis* fever which swept over the country some years ago.

1269 MEDICAL and Agricultural Register, Vol. I.
Boards. 8° *Boston,* 1806–7

1270 MELISH (John) Travels through the United States of America, 1806–11. 2 *vols, maps.* 8° *Phil.* 1815

1271 MELLEN (John, Jr., *Pastor of the East Church in Barnstable*) Sermon at Harwich, Jan. 21, 1791, at the Funeral of Rev. Isaiah Dunster, who died Dec. 18, 1790, the 71st year of his age, and 43d of his ministry. *Hf roan.* 8° *S. Hall, Boston,* 1791

THURSDAY FORENOON.

1272 MELA (POMPONIUS) Pomponii Melæ de Orbis sitv Libri tres, accvratissime emendati unà cũ Commẽtariis Ioachimi Vadiani Helvetii castigatoribus, et multis in locis auctoribus factis: Rvrsvm, Epistola Vadiani, ab eo penè adulescente ad Rudolphum Agricolam iuniorem scripta, non indigna lectu, nec inutilis ad ea capienda, quæ aliubi in Commentarijs suis libare magis, quàm longius explicare noluit. *Fine copy, calf.*

Folio, Basiliæ, apud Andream Cratandrum, Januario, 1522

The story of this Book is too long to be told here, but it has played, and is still destined to play, a prominent part in the early geographical history of this continent. The editor's real name was Joachim Watt, born at St Gall, in Switzerland, November 29, 1484, but educated chiefly at Vienna. Although a classical scholar, theologian, and poet, he seems to have been an arduous student of geography. In fact the best books we have on the geographical effects of the discoveries of Columbus, Vespucci, the Cabots, Dias, Da Gama, Cabral, etc., came from two distinct fraternities of students; the one at St Dié, of whom Philesius was the soul, and the other at Vienna, of whom Vadianus was the moving spirit. It will not be difficult, probably, to show a connection between these two gymnasiums. Indeed, this volume helps us to many important facts. From St Dié came the suggestion to name the *Mundus Novus* of Vespucci AMERICA, and in 1512 Vadianus, in his letter to Agricola, Jr., adopts the suggestion. This letter was printed by Agricola in July, 1514, in small 4to, and dedicated to their mutual friend Caspar Velius, of Ursina, in Silicia. The same year Lucas Atlantse, an enterprising publisher of Vienna, announced as having on his anvils the works of SOLINUS, to be edited by Camers, and POMPONIUS MELA, by Vadianus. Vadianus finished his large work and it was published in 1518. In his prolegomena he speaks of the necessity, to a proper understanding of the subject, of having the prominent places pictured on a map. Young Apianus, another student at Vienna, was then at work upon his great map of the world, but this was not finished till 1520, when it appeared with the SOLINUS of Camers. This map, the first one known with the name AMERICA, was no doubt intended for both the Pomponius Mela and the Solinus. These two books are uniform in size, and after 1520 were issued together, and the map when found at all, is usually bound in the middle, between the two. Vadianus returned to St Gall, his native place, and practiced as a physician, but kept up till long after his interest in geographical studies. Having quarrelled with Camers, he reëdited his Pomponius Mela, and caused it to be reissued at Basil in 1522 (this edition), inscribing it, in an explanatory letter, dated at St Gall in April, 1521, to his friend, Dr. John Faber. This was the Faber, a native of Etaples, near Boulogne, a mathematician, an astronomer, and a geographer, who had, with others in 1499 published at Venice that superb edition of Sacrobosco, posting up cosmography and nautical astronomy to that date, and who, as Professor at Paris, in 1504, stimulated his young pupil, Mathias Ringman, to the study of cosmography. Ringman, born at Schlestadt, not far from Strasburg, having read at Paris the letter of Vespucci, translated by Giocondi, also residing in Paris, found his youthful mind fired by it to such an extent that on returning home he translated into German and printed at Strasburg, in August, 1505, Vespucci's letter. He soon after travelled into Italy, from whence he brought back a Greek MS. of Ptolemy, given him by Pico de Mirandola. This manuscript he took with him to St Dié, in Lorraine, where he was made Professor in the Gymnasium, and became, as Philesius, the moving spirit of that small circle of Professors and Canons, under the patronage of René the Second, who gave a name to the new world, renown to St Dié, and the Ptolemy of 1513 to the Press. Vadianus at Vienna, in 1512, adopted the name AMERICA. The letter to Agricola, and another tract by Vadianus, entitled *Loca aliquot, etc.*, are reprinted in both the editions of Mela, but the letter of Agricola to Vadianus is omitted. It is doubtful if Alantse's Map of 1520, by Apianus, belongs properly to this edition of 1522, printed at Basle, though it is found with it in Cranmer's copy bound with Solinus, now in the British Museum. Not the least attractive feature of this beautiful volume is the title-page, surrounded by one of HANS HOLBEIN's wood-cut borders, with his well-known signature, dated 1519.

1273 MELTON (EDWARD, *Engelsch Edelmans*) Zeldzaamie en Gedenkwaardige Zee-en Land-Reizen; door Egypten, West-Indien, Perzien, Turkeyen, Oost-Indien, en d'aangrenzende Gewesten; behelzende een zeer naauwokeurige beschrijving der genoemde Landen, benevens der zelver Inwoonderen Godsdienft, Regeering, Zeeden en Gewoonten, mitsgaders veele zeer vreemde voorvallen, ongeemene geschiedenissen, en wonderlijke wederwaringen. Aangevangen in den jaare 1660, en geëindigd in den jaare 1677. Vertaald uit d'eigene Aanteekeningen en Brieven van den gedagten Heer Melton; en met verscheidene schoone Kopere Figunren versierd.
4° *Amsterdam, by Jan ten Hoorn*, 1681

A considerable portion of this book is taken up with a description of New Netherland. There is a fine view of Cohoes Falls which has sometimes been mistaken for Niagara.

1274 MELTON (EDWARD) AENMERKENSWAARDIGE en ZELDAME WEST-INDISCHE ZEE-EN LAND-REIZEN &c. [Remarkable and Strange West-India Voyages and Travels, through the Caribbe Islands, New-Netherland Virginia and Spanish America; Containing a very curious description of the said lands, with their inhabitants, religion, government, manners and customs, strange histories and accidents, &c. Ornamented with copperplates.] *Fine large clean copy, vellum.* (*See Asher N° 16, 17 and 18.*) 4° *Amsterdam*, 1715

1275 MÉMOIRES DES COMMISSAIRES DU ROI et de ceux de sa Majesté Britannique, sur les possessions et les droits respectifs des deux Couronnes en Amerique; Avec les Actes publics & Piéces justificatives. 4 *vols, fine copy, calf.* 4° *A Paris, De l'Imprimerie Royale*, 1755–1757

These four highly important volumes contain all the discussions between the English and French Commissioners respecting their respective possessions in America, after the Peace of Aix-la-Chapelle. All geographical disputes from the time of Cabot down, are revived, and all historical and geographical books are laid under contribution. For the history of Maine or New England generally, Canada and the Eastern provinces as well as old Louisiana, the work is invaluable.

1276 MEMOIRES Geographiques, Physiques et Historiques. Sur l'Asie, l'Afrique, l'Amerique. 4 *vols, calf gilt.* 8° *Paris*, 1767

1277 MEMOIRS of an Unfortunate Young Nobleman; returned from a Thirteen Years Slavery in America where he had been sent by the wicked contrivances of his Cruel Uncle. A Story founded upon Truth and address'd equally to the Head and Heart. 2 *vols, calf gilt.* 12° *London*, 1743

1278 MEMOIRS of an Unfortunate Young Nobleman, return'd from a thirteen years Slavery in America. 2 *vols, calf gilt.* 12° *London*, 1743

1279 MEMOIRS of an Unfortunate Young Nobleman. Returned from a Thirteen Years Slavery in America. *Calf.* 8° *London*, 1743

1280 MEMOIRS of the Principal Transactions of the Last War, between the English and French in North America. From the commencement of it in 1774, to the conclusion of the Treaty at Aix-la-Chapelle. Containing an Account of . . . Nova Scotia, &c. *Half blue morocco*, SCARCE. 8° *London*, 1757

1281 Memoirs of a Life, chiefly passed in Pennsylvania, within the last sixty years. *First Edition, calf.* 8° *J. Wyeth, Harrisburg*, 1811

1282 MEMORABLE ACCIDENTS, and Unheard of Transactions, Containing an Account of Several Strange Events, Shipwrecks, Dismal Misfortunes, Stratagems, Deliverances, &c. Translated from the French; printed at Brussels 1691. Published in England by R. B. *Portrait of William III.* 16° *A. Bettsworth, London*, 1733

A considerable portion of this curious little book, somewhat resembling Mather's memorable Providences, is made up from the early voyages of the Dutch, English, and French to the North, and to the East and West Indies.

1283 MEMORABLE ACCIDENTS and Remarkable Transactions, &c. *Fine copy, boards.* 16° *Worcester, Mass.* 1795

This is a reprint or an abridgment of the above, containing only about half of the London edition.

1284 MEMORIA POLITICO-Instructiva, enviada desde Filadelfia en Agosto de 1821, a los Gefes Independientes del Anáhuac, llamada por los Españoles Nueva-España. *Fine copy, vellum.* 12° *Filadelphia, J. F. Hurtel*, 126 *Calle Secunda, Sur*, 1821

Printed for the Mexican market, during the Mexican Revolution.

1285 MEN AND MANNERS in America. By the Author of Cyril Thornton. 2 *vols, half morocco.* 8° *Edinburgh*, 1833

1286 MEN AND MANNERS in America. By the Author of Cyril Thornton, etc. 2 *vols, half calf.* 8° *Edinburgh*, 1834

1287 MENDO (ANDRES) CRISIS de los Compañia de Jesus, de su piedad, doctrina, y multiplicado fruto, que hà cogido en el universo mundo. *Fine copy, calf.* SCARCE. 8° [*Mexico*] *en la Imprenta del Colegio de S. Ildefonso*, 1765

This very earnest book (of 284 pages, with 8 preliminary and 2 sequent leaves) is substantially a defense of the Jesuits, and their conduct and usefulness in all parts of the world. The author gives a list of above 170 authors whom he quotes, many of them bearing testimony to the valuable services of the Order as missionaries among the heathen of both hemispheres. He also enumerates the Popes, and other high officials in the Church, who have testified in their favor, and declares that the movement for the suppression of the Order was instigated by the enemies of true Religion, and is headed by the Devil in person. This defense is strongly fortified by many historical allusions to services in the new world from the time of the entrance of the Dominicans into Mexico in the time of Cortes.

1288 MENDON. A Short Account of the state of Mendon Third Parish, relative to Mr. Balch's settling there in the Work of the Ministry, Sept. 14, 1768. His Conduct while with said People; and the Manner of his leaving them March 27, 1773. By an Inhabitant of the Parish. *Fine copy uncut, vellum by Pratt.* 8° *Boston*, 1773

1289 MENDOZA (Giov. Gonzales di) L'Historia del gran regno della China, fatta vulgare da F. Auanzi. *Fine copy, polished calf, by Pratt.* 16° *Venezia*, 1587

This first edition in Italian is divided into three parts, the third part being the Journal of a voyage to Mexico, and other parts of the New World. This important Journal was translated and edited by Hakluyt.

1290 MENDOZA (Gonzalez de) Historia de las Cosas mas notables, actos y costvmbres, del gran Reyno de la China &c. Con vn Itinerario del nueuo Mondo. 8° *Pedro Bellero en Anvers*, 1596

The Journal of the voyage to the New World fills pp. 295–380.

1291 MERCURIUS BRITANNICUS. Mundus alter et idem, sive Terra Australes antehac semper incognita ; accessit Thomæ Campanellae Civitas solis et Nova Atlantis Franc. Baconis. *Vellum.* 12° *Ultrajecte*, 1643

1292 MESTRE (El R. P. Miguel) Vida, y Milagros del Glorioso S. Antonia de Padua. Sol Brillante de la Iglesia, Lustre de la Religion Serafica, Gloria de Portugal, Honor de España, Tesoro de Italia, terror del Inferno, martillo perpetuo de la heregia, entre los Santos por excelencia el Milagrero. *Portrait, Vellum.* 4° *Madrid*, 1724

There is a title for you ! If San Antonia of Padua can justly be credited with half the miracles recorded here (in these 308 pp., to say nothing of the 8 prel. and 2 sequent leaves) as performed by himself, or since his departure, by his intercession, in Europe and both Indies, he was a wonderful man.

1293 METHODIST Episcopal Church. The Doctrines and Discipline. 16° *New York*, 1821

1294 METHODIST MAGAZINE. 3 *vols. Scarce.* 8° *New York*, 1818–20

Volume I. contains a Biography of John Eliot, Apostle of the Indians, and other interesting biographical and historical matter.

1295 MEXICO. COLECCION DE OBRAS y OPUSCULOS pertenecientes a la Milagrosa Aparicion de la Bellissima Imagen de Nuestra Señora de Guadalupe, que se venera en su Santuario extramuros de Mexico, reimpressas todas juntas, y unidas por un Devoto de la Señora, con el fin que con el tiempo no perezcan, ò se hagan muy raras algunas de las piezas menores. 4° *Madrid*, 1785

1296 MEXICO. LA ESTRELLA DEL NORTE DE MEXICO, aparecida al Rayar el dia de la luz Evangelica en este Nuevo Mundo, en la cumbre del cerro de Tepeyacac, orilla del mar Tezcucano, á un Natural recien convertido; pintada tres dias despues milagrosamente en su Tilma ò Capa de Lienzo delante del Obispo y de su familia, en su casa Obispal, para luz en la Fé a los Indios; *etc.* En la Historia de la Milagrosa Imagen de Nuestra Señora de Guadalupe de Mexico que se aparecio en la Manta de Juan Diego. Compusola el Padre FRANCISCO DE FLORENCIA. 4° *Madrid*, 1785

297 MEXICO. NOVENAS a la Santisima Virgen Maria Madre de Dios, para en sus Milagrosos Santuarios de los Remedios y Guadalupe de Mexico : *etc.* 4° *Madrid,* 1785

These three large and handsome volumes contain the entire history, bibliography, and theology, of the miraculous GUADALOUPANA of Mexico, from the first appearance of the Vision to Juan Diego, the Indian in 1531. This subject has become one of the Stock Institutions of Mexico, and its history and influence seem to pervade all others. No. 1295 and 1296 though distinct works, usually go together, and these two volumes are bound uniformly and lettered, Tom. I. and II. They are very fine copies, on thick paper, and bound in calf. There are five copperplate illustrations of the several appearances of the Image. No. 1297 contains the NOVENAS separately, extracted with certain alterations from No. 1295. Most of the volume is the same, but a few leaves have been changed, so as to make it a complete work by itself. The three volumes ought to go together.

298 MEXICO. BOLETIN DEL INSTITUTO NACIONAL DE GEOGRAFIA Y ESTADISTICA de la Republica Mexicana. Volumes I–X & XI (Nos. 1–7.) *Maps and plates, a complete set as far as published.* (Tom. 1 & 2, 3d Ed., 1861–64) *Mexico,* 1852–1867

Complete sets are now very difficult to make up, several of the volumes being out of print.

299 MEXICO. The History of Mexico, collected from Spanish and Mexican Historians, from Manuscripts and Ancient paintings of the Indians. By Abbé Francisco Saverio Clavigero. Translated by Charles Cullen. *3 vols, maps and plates, fine copy, old calf gilt.* 8° *T. Dobson, Phia.* 1804

300 MEXICO. Disposiciones Legales y otros Documentos relativos a la Prohibicion de Impressos por la autoridad Ecclesiastica, mandados publicar de órden del Supremo Gobierno. 138 *pp. calf gilt.* 8° *Mexico,* 1850

Relative to the prohibition of Protestant and other anti-catholic and immoral books in Mexico, 1850. The book particularly discussed, was entitled *Misterios de la Inquisicion,* though many others are named, especially some printed in New York for circulation in Mexico. The whole question of prohibition on Protestant grounds is fully discussed.

301 MEXICO. Itinerarios y Derroteros de la Republica Mexicano, publicados por los Ayudantes del Estado Mayor del Ejercito, Jose J. Alvarez y Rafael Duran. 4° *Mexico,* 1856

A most valuable book for the topography and distances throughout the several States of Mexico. Some of the routes described are very full and historical, such as those of Yucatan, Guerrero, Michoacan, Tamaulipas, Guanacuato, and Lower California.

302 MEXICO. Memoria del Secretario de Estado y del despacho de Justicia é Instruccion Publica en 1844. *Calf.* *Folio, Mexico,* 1844

303 MEYER (H. VON) ZUR FAUNA DER VORWELT. Fossile Saeugethiere, Voegel und Reptilien aus dem Molasse-Mergel von Oeningen. 12 *Plates, half morocco.* *Folio, Frankfurt,* 1845

304 MICHAUX (F. A.) Travels to the West of the Alleghany Mountains in Ohio, Kentucky, and Tennessee, *etc.* Second Edition. *Calf.* 8° *London,* 1805

305 MILET (Pierre, *de la Comp. de Jesus*) Relation de sa Captivité parmi les Onneiouts. LARGE PAPER, *very few copies printed, best white vellum gilt by F. Bedford.* 8° *Presse Cramoisy, J. M. Shea, N. York,* 1864

1306 MILBERT (J.) ITINÉRAIRE PITTORESQUE DU FLEUVE HUDSON et des Parties latérales de l'Amérique du Nord. Text 2 *vols in* 1, *large* 4° *Plates, large folio, half dark morocco.* *Folio and* 4° *Paris,* 1828

This large work upon the Hudson River and the adjacent country, with many accurate and picturesque views has become very scarce in this country. It ought to be better known, but now that most of the copies have gone to the butter-man it will soon no doubt be better appreciated. Many of the Views that could be taken in 1825 are now historical, having passed away.

1307 MILFORT (*Le General*) MEMOIRE ou Coup-d'œil Rapide sur mes differens voyages et mon Séjour dans la Nation Crëck, par le Gab. Milfort Tastanégy ou grand Chef de guerre de la nation Crëck, *etc. Calf gilt.* 8° *Paris,* 1802

1308 MILITIA. A plan for establishing a National Militia in Great Britain, and all the British Dominions of America. *Calf.* 8° *London,* 1745

1309 MILLER (E.) Medical Works, with Biographical Sketch by S. Miller. *Portrait, boards.* 8° *New York,* 1814

1310 MILLER (Samuel) A Continuation of letters concerning the Constitution and order of the Christian Ministry. *Calf.* 12° *New York,* 1809

1311 MILLER (S.) Sermon at New Haven, Conn. Sept. 12, 1822, at the Ordination of the Rev. Messrs. W. Goodell, W. Richards, and Artemas Bishop. 8° *Boston,* 1822

1312 MINADOI (J. T.) The History of the Warres betweene the Tvrkes and the Persians. Translated into English by A. Hartwell. *Calf.* 4° *Imprinted by John Wolfe, London,* 1595

1313 MINOT (G. R.) History of the Insurrections in Massachusetts in 1786. Second Edition. 8° *Boston,* 1810

1314 MINUTOLI (J. H. von) Beschreibung einir alten Stadt die in Guatimala . . entdeckt worden ist, etc. *Half calf.* 8° *Berlin,* 1832

1315 MIRÆUS (Aubert) De Statv Religionis Christianæ per Europam, Asiam, Africam et ORBEM NOVUM. *Vellum.* 8° *Col. Agrip.* 1619

1316 MIRANDA (Don F.) Expedition to effect a Revolution in South America. Second Edition. 12° *Boston,* 1810

1317 MISCELLANEA CURIOSA. Decuria I, Vols 1–10. Decuria II, Vols 1–10. Index to I and II, 1 Vol. Decuria III, Vols 1–4. 25 Vols bound in 22. *With many portraits and curious plates,* SCARCE, *and valuable. Fine copy, calf.* 4° *Jena & Frankf.* 1671-1697

A perfect garden of curious facts, buried thoughts and lost arts. Probably more modern inventions have been cribbed from this learned work than from any other. It should be in every public library.

1318 MISCELLANIES. BURNABY'S TRAVELS through the Middle Settlements in North America, 1759–60 — Short Description of the Province of South Carolina, written in 1763 — Description of the Island of Nevis — An Historical Account of the Virgin Islands. — Journal of a Voyage towards the North Pole by Com. Phipps, and Capt. Lutwidge. *Maps, boards. A valuable and scarce volume.* 8° *London*, 1775

1319 Miscellaneous. United States Almanac 1843-4, 2 vols. Rambles Farther, 2 vols. Simeon on the Liturgy, *N. Y.* 1813 Adams' Scholars' Arithmetic, *Keene, N. H.* 1823. Butler's Sketches of History, *Hartford*, 1822, etc. *Together* 12 *vols.* 8°

1320 Miscellaneous. Walker's Dictionary, *Phila.* 1818. Day's Algebra, *New Haven*, 1814. Eaton's Philosophical Instructor, *Albany*, 1824, *etc.* 11 *vols*, 8°

1321 Miscellaneous. Baptists in America, *N. Y.* 1836. Geography of New York, 1847. District School, by J. O. Taylor, *N. Y.* 1834. Pharmacopœia of the Mass. Medical Society, *Boston*, 1808. Sumner's Botany, *Hartford*, 1820, *etc.* 10 *vols*, 12°

1322 Mississippi. Vue de la Colonie Espagnole du Mississipi en l'anne 1802, par un Observateur resident. Duvallon Editeur. *Half morocco, maps.* 8° *Paris*, 1803

1323 Mississippi. View of the Valley of the Mississippi or the Emigrant's and Traveller's Guide to the West. *Map, etc. half olive morocco.* 12° *Phila.* 1832

1324 Mitchell (Rev. Elisha, *D. D.*) Memoir of; with the Tributes of Respect to his Memory, etc. *Portrait.* 8° *Chapel Hill*, 1858

1325 Mitford (Rev. J.) Sacred Specimens, selected from the Early English Poets. With Prefatory Verses. *Half calf.* 12° *London*, 1827

1326 Mnemonika, or a Tablet of Memory; a Register of Events from the earliest Period to 1829, the Matter furnished by William Darby. Revised, *etc.* 12° *Baltimore*, 1829

1327 Molina (*Abbé* J.) Essai sur l'Histoire Naturelle du Chili, Traduit avec des Notes par M. Gruvel. *Calf.* 8° *Paris*, 1789

1328 Molina (*Abbé Don* J.) Geographical and Natural History of Chili. 2 *vols, map.* 8° *Middletown, Conn.* 1808

1329 Molina (*Abbé Don* J.) Natural and Civil History of Chili; Translated, with Notes from the Spanish and French Versions, and Two Appendixes, by the English Editor. 2 *vols, map, half calf uncut.* 8° *London*, 1809

1330 Molinaeus (P.) Vates, seu de Præcognitione futurorum, et Bonis Malisque Prophetis. *Calf.* 8° *Lugd. Batav.* 1649

1331 Molinaeus (P.) Vates, seu de Præcognitione futurorum, *etc. Half calf.* 8° *Lugd. Batav.* 1640

1332 Moll (G.) Verhandeling over eenige vroegere zeetogten der Nederlanders. *Half brown morocco, uncut.* 8° *Amst.* 1825

1333 Mollien (G.) Reis door de Republik van Columbia. 2 *vols, half calf, uncut.* 8° *Dordrecht*, 1825

1334 Molucca Islands. Kort ende warachtich verhael vande heerlijcke Victorie te weghe ghebracht by de xij Schepen afghevaren wt Hollandt, onder tghebiedt vanden Generael ende Admirael der selve Schepen, Hugo Verhaghen, in de Eylanden vande Moluckes, &c. *Only two leaves, but the first announcement of an important event, in half vellum.* 4° *Jan Janssz, Rotterdam,* 1606

1335 MONROE (JAMES, *President*) Narrative of a Tour of Observation, made during the Summer of 1817, through the North-eastern and North-western Departments of the Union. *Half morocco, uncut.* 12° *Phila.* 1818

1336 MONTCALM (MARQUIS DE) Letters [in French] from the Marquis de Montcalm, Governor-General of Canada; to Messrs. De Berryer & De La Molé in the years 1757, 1758, and 1759. With an English Translation. *French and English on opposite pages, fine clean copy, in white vellum by William Pratt.* 8° *J. Almon, London,* 1777

This book seems destined to live the full age allotted to a lie. Nothing has more lives, or is harder to kill than a good political lie well told, which has once taken in statesmen, philosophers, and historians, whose reputation and interest encourage it to survive. This little book has in its day played its part on many stages, and its day seems not yet over. It has many times been pronounced spurious, yet there are some who still assert its genuineness and defend its authenticity. So it has been from its publication in March, 1777, and so it probably will be. It comprises three long letters purporting to be from the Marquis de MONTCALM, Governor-general and Commander-in-chief of Canada; the first to M. de Berryer, First Commissioner of the Marine of France, dated from Montreal, April 4, 1757; the second to the same person, dated also from Montreal, October 1, 1758; and the third to his cousin, M. de Molé, First President in the Parliament of France, dated at the Camp before Quebec, August 24, 1759, a few days only before the fall of that stronghold into the hands of the English on the 13th of September, a day forever memorable for its consequences to both England and France, and the deaths of both of the great Commanders, MONTCALM and WOLFE. The first letter occupies thirteen pages, nine of which are taken up with the copy of a letter to Montcalm, from S. J. of Boston, dated January 4, 1757, containing the cream and pith of the whole three letters, which together fill 28 pages in English, and the same number in French. This Boston Spy, whoever he was, appears to have been thoroughly well acquainted with the history, the powers, the aims, the interests, and the proclivities of the several English Colonies, both as to their relations to each other, and individually and collectively to Mother England. He proposes to Montcalm a scheme for undermining the power of Great Britain, by encouraging free trade between France and the English Colonies indirectly through Canada. He states the case philosophically, based upon well-known facts, and predicts almost precisely the course of events for the next fifteen years. Indeed, S. J. writes precisely such a letter in 1757, as a man of great intelligence could only write in 1770, or 1775, after the passage of the Stamp Act in 1765, its repeal in 1766, and the various other more or less vindictive enactments of the Parliament anent the Colonies, till the pouring out of that great vial of wrath, the BOSTON PORT BILL.

S. J. writes, page 3, "The commerce of all the other Colonies might be drawn to and fixed in Canada; for if you there introduce all kinds of manufactures, especially your Indian goods, from France, of which the middling class of our planters are so ridiculously fond; if you made considerable imports from France of your brandies, wines, and other liquors, you would find drunkards enough in the colonies to take them off your hands: thus you would soon ruin the manufactures of England, which would soon find no market here, and our money would circulate among your merchants. A double advantage would arise to you from this, since, while you were enriching yourselves, you would be impoverishing your natural enemies. It is true that England, too clearly perceiving her approaching ruin, would not fail to make heavy and loud complaints. The Parliament would immediately pass bills to suppress this commerce, so ruinous to their nation; . . . . a secret and fraudulent trade may enrich an individual, but the commerce of an extensive country must be open, free and unfettered. Let your Excellency, from hence, learn to know us." Again on page 5: "Among us, no act of Parliament, or order from the throne, has the force of a law, or can be put in execution, till after it has been agreed to and accepted in our general assemblies. Though these assemblies have not yet the power of making our own laws, yet they have at least the privilege of refusing those which are injurious and ruinous to the country; and perhaps the day is not far distant, when they will reject bills passed in England, though invested with the highest authority. Can you think that the members of these general assemblies will be such enemies to themselves and their country, as meanly to submit to the orders of England, should they take it in their heads to compel us to give them a guinea, for what we can purchase in Canada, in our own ports, for a penny?"

Speaking of the union of the Colonies, he says, "The planters of the different colonies have assembled under one standard, and thus an acquaintance, connection, and intercourse are established, and the union cemented. An important step for us, since we now shall, as it were, go hand in hand for the future. Our rights will be respected, because it would be dangerous to attack them." And on page 8, "From every circumstance I have the honor to remark to you, it is easy to foresee that England would not succeed in prohibiting our commerce with your colony; and I speak this the more confidently, as the price of the commodities which are brought us from England, begins to be offensive in the eyes of the multitude, who, even in the midst of war, cry out loudly for procuring them from some other quarter. If I am not much mistaken, all our colonies, in less than ten years, will catch fire on this occasion. Indeed, there are hardly any means of preventing it, since labour is at such an exorbitant rate in England: a necessary event in a country which has enriched itself considerably by commerce; and hence follows the consequent rise of manufactures . . . . although Canada should escape from the hands of its masters, the day will come, when the high price of English commodities will be such a weight on our colonies, as to oblige them to have recourse to a stranger; England must then be ruined. This prophetic event is the more sure, and the sooner to be expected, as the opulence of our colonies is not everywhere on an equal footing. . . . . It is unreasonable to rob them, by forcing them to buy, at a high price, what they can have almost for nothing. Common interest will unite them, and what will be the event of it? . . . . What I dare previously assure you, from a knowledge of our situation and sentiments, is, that England will fall the first victim. . . . . This who lives will see!"

In transmitting this letter, Montcalm did but little more than endorse its sentiments, but in his second letter a year later he says, "All these informations, which I every day receive, confirm me in my opinion that England will one day lose her Colonies on the Continent of America; and if Canada should then be in the hands of an able governor, who understands his business, he will have a thousand opportunities of hastening the event; this is the only advantage we can reap, for all it has cost us. As to the English Colonies, there is one essential point to be considered: they have never yet been taxed, but have always preserved that right to themselves. Were they [England] now to attempt it, I have certain assurances that the English Colonies would take fire, and the flame would spread everywhere; which, if properly fed, would embarrass England to extinguish it."

But the most pertinent predictions are in the third letter to Mr. Molé, filling nine pages. "For more than three months has Mr. Wolfe been hanging on my hands." "The enemy ruins us, but not enriches himself." "Nothing, however, is less certain: the taking of Quebec depends on one masterly stroke." "They are in a condition to give us battle, which I must not refuse, and which I cannot hope to gain. General Wolfe, indeed, if he understands his business, has only to receive our first fire, and then advancing briskly on my army, &c." "The event must decide. But of one thing be certain, that I probably shall not survive the loss of the Colony." "I shall at least console myself on my defeat, and on the loss of the Colony, by the full persuasion that this defeat will one day serve my country more than a victory, and that the conqueror, in aggrandizing himself, will find his tomb the country he gains from us." "All the English Colonies would long since have shaken off the yoke, each province would have formed itself into a little independent republic, if the fear of seeing the French at their door had not been a check upon them. Master for master, they have preferred their own countrymen to strangers, observing, however, this maxim, to obey as little as possible; but when Canada shall be conquered, and the Canadians and these Colonies become one people, on the first occasion, when England shall seem to strike at their interest, do you believe, my dear cousin, that these Colonies will obey? and what would they have to fear from a revolt?" . . . "but I doubt whether they [the English] would ever make good a landing. Add too, that in case of a general revolt, of any part of these Colonies, all the powers of Europe, secret and jealous enemies of the power of England, would at first assist them privately, and then openly, to throw off the yoke." "If the English make a conquest they are sure to change the constitution of the country, and introduce their own laws," etc. "Upon this account, Canada, once taken by the English, would, in a few years suffer much more from being forced to be English." "Farewell then to . . . obedience and fidelity; they would soon be of no use to England, and perhaps they would oppose her. I am so clear in what I now assert, that I would not give more than ten years after the conquest of Canada to see it accomplished. See then what now consoles me, as a Frenchman, for the imminent danger my country runs of losing this colony."

Such is a brief synopsis of this remarkable book. Its very prophecies in 1757–59 became the "very historical truth" of 1777, and forcibly struck home to the Ministry and the Parliament. It was published in March, '77, just in the nick of time to "go to the country" with those two vindictive Acts which drew from Burke his famous letter, of the 3d of April, to the Sheriffs of Bristol. It was announced in the *London Magazine* for April, 1777, p. 216, without comment; but the *Monthly Review* of the same month, p. 306, noticed it rather favorably and cautiously, beginning, "From these Letters, which appear to us to be genuine, although the Editor is silent," etc. The *Gentleman's Magazine* for July, p. 342, is more explicit, "That the sagacity of this accomplished General [Montcalm] was equal to his bravery, appears from the following remarkable prediction, now fatally verified, 'All the English Colonies would long since have shaken off the yoke,'" etc. . . . "The whole," says Mr. Urban, "is well worth perusal, and shows that M. de Montcalm was *tam Mercutio quam Marte.*—It is proper to add, that the authenticity of the work was lately attacked in the House of Lords by Lord Shelburne, but ably defended by Lord Mansfield." On turning to the Parliamentary Register, to the celebrated debate in the House of Lords, on the 30th of May, opened by the Earl of Chatham, and closed by Lord Abingdon, two of America's friends, in which debate Earl Gower, the Duke of Grafton, the Archbishop of York, the Bishop of Peterborough, Lord Lyttleton, the Duke of Manchester, Lord Camden, Lord Weymouth, Lord Wycombe [Earl of Shelburne], Lord Mansfield, and Lord Onslow participated, Lord Shelburne said, speaking of Montcalm's Letters, that they "had been discovered to be a forgery." But Lord Mansfield said, "He maintained his former opinions, respecting the American views of independency; but relied more upon what was argued in Montcalm's Letters, which he insisted were not spurious." The next we hear of these Letters a little further afield, is a settler from the Earl of Abingdon, printed at Oxford in June, in his *Thoughts on the Letter of Edmund Burke*, p. 56, "To get rid of these stumbling blocks of *aggressorship* [who threw the first stone] something was to be devised; and this something was, that America meant to become independent of this country. But how was this to be supported? The learned Lord [Mansfield] proved it by *innuendoes*, *by sayings* and *doings*, *à priori*, out of the American Assemblies, from Montcalm's Letters, which have been found to be forgeries," etc.

Still later, on the fifth of March, 1778, just eight years to a day after the Boston Massacre, in another great debate, in the House of Lords, on the Reconciliation Bills, Earl Temple (no great authority it is true), who had boxed the compass of opinion, said "he believed America had aimed at independency from the beginning, *etc.* . . . . . He had another strong reason to confirm him in the same way of thinking, that was, the pointed observations contained in the letters attributed to Monsieur Montcalm, which indeed bear the stamp of prediction, more than hypothetical reasoning. He observed, that the authenticity of those letters had been often disputed; but he could affirm, that he saw them in manuscript among the papers of a minister now deceased, long before they made their appearance in print, and at a time when American independency was in the contemplation of a very few persons indeed. . . . . With regard to the right of Great Britain to exact a revenue from America, I never entertained a doubt of it, nor that the colonies secretly looked forward to independency. The letters I have already alluded to prove it."

No judgment could be based on the character of the publisher, for Almon, the publisher of the *Remembrancer*, was one who printed for all parties, and for and against America. For some time the general impression remained that the Montcalm, like the Washington letters published the same year, were spurious. In 1835 Mr. Rich recorded the book with the remark — "If these letters are genuine, they show that M. de Montcalm had a very correct presentiment of what would be the consequence of attempting to tax the Colonies." In 1844, while engaged in looking up materials for a history of the old French War, the writer well recollects discussing the character of the letters with Mr. Sparks, who unhesitatingly pronounced them spurious. Mr. Bancroft was of the same opinion. The use of the word *planters* by S. J. is strong evidence that he was not a Bostonian. In 1858 appeared a volume entitled *The Plains of Abraham; Notes original and selected. By Lt. Col. Beatson, C. E.* 8° *Gibraltar, Garrison Press*, 1858, made up partly of extracts from these Montcalm letters. Col. Beatson appears to have had no suspicion that their genuineness had ever been doubted. This Gibraltar book falling into the hands of Thomas Carlyle, while achieving the Life of Frederick of Prussia, seduced the great Philosopher of Chelsea into a charming episode of eight or ten pages (Vol. V, Lond. Ed. pp. 555–563, published in March 1865) in which Montcalm shines as a great prophet. Writes Thomas, "Colonel Beatson in his recent Pamphlet, *The Plains of Abraham*, — which, especially on the military side, is distressingly ignorant and shallow, though *not* intentionally incorrect any where, — gives extracts from a Letter of Montcalm's ('Quebec, 24th August, 1759') which is highly worth reading, had we room. It predicts to a hair's breadth not only the way 'Mr. Wolfe, if he understands his trade, will take to beat and ruin me if we meet in fight;' but also, — with a sagacity singular to look at in the years 1775–77, and perhaps still more in the years 1860–63, — what will be the consequences to those unruly English, Colonial and other. 'If he beat me here, France has lost America utterly' thinks Montcalm: 'Yes; — and one's only consolation is, In ten years farther America will be in revolt against England.'" Mr. Carlyle did not succeed in finding this original edition by Almon, "which is not," wrote he, "in the British Museum Library, on applying: and seems to be a forgotten book." Mr. Carlyle will doubtless, on further inquiry, in a future edition, decide to cut out this episode, interesting as it is, as he did another on another occasion, in another book, as a sacrifice to Truth, or tapping the bottom of his tub with an explanatory note, after the manner of latter-day history, let the spirit of it drizzle away unseen.

In Sept. 1865, the writer's attention was called to this episode by Professor Newton of Cambridge, while at Fryston Hall in Yorkshire, when he at once recounted the history of the Montcalm forgery, and the whole subject was discussed by Lord Houghton (whose acquaintance with the history of literary forgeries is very extensive) Mr. William E. Forster, M. P., Prof. Newton and others. The writer then undertook to write out the story for the generous public, but on returning to London no copy of the "forgotten book" could be found in London or Oxford for many months.

Now the writer is aware that all this narrative, being mostly negative testimony, does not demonstrate that the letters are forgeries, but it seems to him to place the whole matter in such a position that hardly anything short of the actual production of the original autograph letters of the old Marquis de Montcalm will establish their authenticity. Earl Temple might have seen the letters, as he said, "in manuscript among the papers of a minister now [1778] deceased, long before they made their appearance in print" [1777]. This "long before" may have been after the passage of the Boston Port Bill in 1774, and those letters, if now produced, might not be in the handwriting of Montcalm. It was reserved for Mr. Francis Parkman, the historian, in 1869, to very nearly settle the question of the likelihood of the originals ever turning up. While at Paris in the spring of that year he had interviews with the present Marquis de Montcalm, who showed him many letters of his ancestor, and among them the letter of the 26th August to M. Molé. Mr. Parkman took a copy of it under the impression that it was in the autograph of the old Marquis, but subsequent correspondence with the present Marquis showed that the letter is *not* in the handwriting of his ancestor, thus knocking away what may perhaps be considered the last prop of the authenticity of the letters. Those who wish to pursue the subject further are referred to the admirable paper filling 17 pages in the *Proceedings of the Massachusetts Historical Society* for June, July, and August 1869, pp. 112–128, published in December, to all reasonable appearances settling the question. A good thing too that the question is now settled, for since the new life given to the fiction by Mr. Carlyle, it has found its way into Maunder and other biographical dictionaries and into encyclopædias, at the expense of the Truth of History.

1337 MONTGOMERY (G. W.) Narrative of a Journey to Guatemala in Central America in 1838. *Cloth.* 8° *New York,* 1839

1338 MOODY'S (*Lieut.* James) Narrative of his Exertions and Sufferings in the Cause of Government, since the year 1776; authenticated by proper certificates. Second edition. *Half roan.* 8° *London,* 1783

LIEUT. MOODY of New Jersey was from 1777 to 1782, five years, a Tory Spy, Ranger and Scout in the service of the British Army, chiefly between New York and Philadelphia, but sometimes up North River, and at others, about Morristown. He was attached to General Skinner's New Jersey Tory Brigade of Rangers.

1339 MOORE (FRANCIS) A VOYAGE TO GEORGIA. Begun in 1735. Containing an account of the Settling the Town of Frederica, &c.; also a Description of Savannah. *Lond.* 1744

LA CONDAMINE (M. de) A Succinct Abridgement of a Voyage from the South Sea to the Coasts of Brasil and Guiana down the River of Amazons. *Map. London,* 1747

BARTRAM (John) Observations made in his Travels from Pennsylvania to Onondago, Oswego, and the Lake Ontario in Canada. And an Account of the Cataracts of Niagara. By Peter Kalm. *Map. London,* 1751

ROBSON (Joseph) An Account of six years' residence in Hudson's Bay from 1733 to 1747. *Maps.* 8° *London,* 1752

4 *vols in one; fine large clean copies, calf.* This account of Niagara Falls, by Peter Kalm, written from Albany to a friend in Philadelphia [Bartram?] Sept. 2, 1750, is claimed by the London editor to be the "only account in our language of this stupendous object."

1340 MOORE (F.) A VOYAGE TO GEORGIA, Begun in the Year 1735. Containing an Account of the Settling the Town of Frederica, in the Southern Part of the Province; and a Description of the Soil, Air, Birds, Beasts, Trees, Rivers, Islands, *etc.* Also a description of Savannah. 8° *London,* 1744

1341 MOORE (FRANK) REBELLION RECORD; A Diary of American Events, 1860–64. *Maps, Portraits, and Engravings.* 50 *Numbers.* 8° *New York.*

Weekly Edition, Nos. 1 to 12. Monthly Illustrated Edition, Nos. 4 to 6, and Nos. 16 to 45 inclusive.

1342 MOORE (H.) Memoir of Col. Ethan Allen. 12° *Plattsburgh, N. Y.* 1834

1343 MOORE (J.) A View of Society and Manners in Italy. 2 *vols, calf.* 8° *London,* 1795

1344 MOORE (Jacob B.) Annals of the Town of Concord, N. H. from its first Settlement 1726 to 1823; with Biographical Sketches, and a Memoir of the Penacook Indians. *Uncut.* 8° *Concord,* 1824

1345 MOORE (Jacob B.) Memoirs of American Governors. *Portraits, Vol. I [All published.] Cloth.* 8° *New York,* 1846

1346 MOORE (THOMAS, *Poet, etc.*) EPISTLES, ODES, and other Poems. *Cloth.* 4° *London,* 1806

FIRST EDITION, of considerable rarity, published at three guineas, and being on paper known among the London butter-men as the *quarter-pound-pat-size,* it became popular, and the entire edition was soon *spread.* The book, read in the light of to-day in this country, is an uncommon curiosity, more provocative of smiles than frowns. A good number of the poems and poetical epistles, as well as some of the occasional pieces in prose, were written during the Poet's travels in America. His own youthful importance seems to have been dwarfed for the first time in his life by Niagara, and hence his dislike to the whole country. He was nowhere properly appreciated, not even in Washington, with its Tiber, and streets of magnificent distances, but in Canada he stood on his own soil [dirt] and threw it, and felt happier. Some of his finer poems, as, for instance, the *Canadian Boat Song*, are in this volume, but they are so mixed up with Tom Moore unrefined, that the volume as a whole is an unfortunate monument to the great Irish Poet. He wrote spitefully, and shortly after, on publishing his volume, at three times the ordinary price, wrote in his preface, respecting his productions in America, "And though prudence might have dictated gentler language, truth, I think, would have justified severer." He lived to think differently. In his last illness, on receiving from the writer a box of *Boston Crackers*, the aged Poet sent back words of thanks, adding playfully, that he never enjoyed anything with better relish, except perhaps the news that his Poems had been reprinted in America, and were read with interest on the banks of the Ohio.

1347 MOREAU (PIERRE) KLARE EN WAARACHTIGE BESCHRYVING VAN de leste Veroerten en Afval der Portuguezen in BRASIL. *Very fine copy, perfectly uncut, bound in white vellum by Pratt. With beautifully engraved map, and copperplates.* 4° *Jan Hendriksz. t'Amsterdam,* 1652

1348 MOREAU (*Gen.* Victor) The Life and Campaigns of, comprehending his trial, justification, and other events, till the period of his embarkation for the United States. *Portrait, calf.* 12° *D. Bliss, New York,* 1806

1349 MORGAN (J.) English Grammar, with Postscript, Analyses, etc. *Boards.* 12° *Hallowell,* 1814

1350 MORGAN (Jonathan, *Jr.*) Elements of English Grammar. 12° *Hallowell, Me, by Goodale and Burton,* 1814

1351 MORGAN (J.) History of Algiers; with Epitome of the General History of Barbary, from the earliest Times. *Calf.* 4° *London,* 1731

1352 MORRELL (L. A.) The American Shepherd. 12° *New York,* 1846

1353 MORRIS (Valentine) A Narrative of the Official Conduct of, the Island of St. Vincent and its Dependencies. *Half brown morocco, uncut.* 8° *London,* 1787

1354 MORSE (Jedediah) A View of the Present Situation of the United States of America. 8° *Elizabethtown, N. J.* 1789

1355 MORSE (Jed.) Tegenwoordige Staat der Verëndige Staaten van Amerika. 4 *vols, half morocco, uncut.* 8° *Amsterdam,* 1793

1356 MORSE (Jed.) New and Correct Edition of the American Geography. *Russia gilt, fine copy.* 8° *Edinb.* 1795

1357 MORSE (Jed.) Elements of Geography. Third Edition improved. *Maps.* 16° *I. Thomas, Boston,* 1798

1358 MORSE (Jed.) The American Gazeteer. *Maps.* 8° *Boston,* 1797

1359 MORSE (Jed.) The American Gazeteer. *Maps, half morocco, uncut.* 8° *London,* 1798

1360 Morse (Jed.) Prayer and Sermon delivered at Charlestown, December 31, 1799, on the Death of George Washington, with an additional Sketch of his Life. Proceedings of the Town on the melancholy Occasion, written by Jos. Bartlett, Esq. Annexed is Washington's Valedictory Address to his Fellow Citizens. *Vellum, uncut.* 8° *Charlestown,* 1800

1361 Morse (Jed.) An Appeal to the Public, on the Controversy respecting the Revolution in Harvard College, etc. *Uncut.* 8° *Charlestown,* 1814

1362 Morse (Jed.) A Report to the Secretary of War, of the United States on Indian Affairs; Comprising a Narrative of a Tour, etc. *Half green morocco.* 8° *Newhaven,* 1822

1363 Morton (D. O.) Memoir of Rev. Levi Parsons, first Missionary to Palestine, from the Western States. 12° *Burlington,* 1830

1364 Morton (Nathaniel) New England's Memorial. *The second edition, imperfect, the title and many leaves gone, but a good deal of good reading left.* *Sm.* 8° *Boston,* 1721

For an answer to Morton, see Gorton (S.) in this Catalogue, No. 813.

1365 Morton (Nathaniel) The New England's Memorial; or a brief Relation of the Planters of New England, with special reference to the first Colony thereof, called New Plymouth. 8° *Allen Danforth, Plymouth, Mass.* 1826

1366 Moule (T.) Bibliotheca Heraldica Magnæ Britanniæ. An Analytical Catalogue of Books on Genealogy, Heraldry, Nobility, Knighthood, etc., with a List of Provincial Visitations, Pedigrees, Collections of Arms and other Manuscripts; and a Supplement enumerating the principal Foreign Genealogical Works. *Frontispiece, half morocco, gilt top, uncut.* *Royal* 8° *London,* 1822

1367 Moseley (Benjamin) A Treatise on Tropical Diseases; on Military Operations, and the Climate of the West Indies. 2d edition, with considerable additions. *Russia.* 8° *London,* 1789

1368 Mounteney (Barclay) Selections from the various Authors, who have written concerning Brazil and the Gold Mines. *Map, half green morocco, uncut.* 8° *London,* 1825

1369 Mundus Alter et Idem sive Terra Australis ante hac semper incognita longis itineribus peregrini Academici nuperrime lustrata. Auth. Mercurio Britannico. [Bp. Hall.] *Beautiful copy, with the engraved frontispiece and five maps, vellum,* 8° *G. Antonium, Hannoviæ,* 1607

1370 MUÑOZ (Juan Bautista) Historia del Nuevo Mundo. Tom. I. [*all published.*] *Portrait of Columbus, half calf, uncut.* Large Paper. *Imp.* 8° *Madrid,* 1793

1371 Muñoz (Juan Bautista) Historia del Nuevo Mundo, Tom I. *Calf.* Large Paper. *Portrait of Columbus.* *Imp.* 8° *Madrid,* 1793

1372 Muñoz (J. B.) History of the New World, translated from the Spanish with notes by the Translator. Vol. I. (*No more published.*) *Portrait and map, half roan.* 8° *London,* 1797

373 MUNSTER (SEBASTIAN) LA COSMOGRAPHIE VNIVERSELLE de tovt le Monde. En laquelle, suiuant les auteurs plus dignes de foy, sont au vray descriptes toutes les parties habitables, & non habitables de la Terre, & de la Mer, etc. Auteur en partie MVNSTER, maïs beaucoup plus augmentée, ornée & enrichie, par FRANÇOIS DE BELLE-FOREST. 3 *volumes, many maps and wood-cuts, old calf,*
Folio, Chez Nicolas Chesneau, Paris, 1575

374 MURAT (Achilles) Brieven over de Zeden en Staatkunde der Vereenigde Staten van. Noord-Amerika. 2 *vols, half red morocco uncut.* 8° *Zalt-Bommel,* 1834

375 MURAT (A.) Brieven over de Zeden en Staatkunde der Vereenigde Staten, van Noord-Amerika. 2 *vols, half green morocco.* 8° *Zalt-Bommel,* 1834

376 MURRAY (James *of Newcastle*) An Impartial History of the present War in America. *Fine copy, calf, portraits and maps.* 8° *London,* [1778]

377 MURRAY (John) LETTERS and Sketches of Sermons. 3 *vols, half maroon morocco, uncut.* 8° *Boston,* 1812

378 MURRAY (L.) A new Abridgment of Murray's English Grammar, with alterations and improvements, by a gentleman of New Hampshire. 16° *Walpole, I. Thomas,* 1811

379 MURRAY (Lindley, *American Grammarian of the English Language*) English Grammar, with an appendix containing rules and observations for assisting to write with perspicuity and accuracy. 6 *copies, fine and clean as new.*
12° *Middlebury, Vt, By Samuel Swift,* 1812

380 MURRAY (Lindley) English Grammar, etc. From the 18th English edition, enlarged and improved by the author. 3 *copies, fine and clean as new.*
12° *Hallowell, Me, by Goodale & Cheever,* 1812

381 MURRAY (Lindley) English Grammar. 12° *New York,* 1832

382 MURRAY'S English Reader. 12° *Concord, N. H., H. Hill, n. d.*

383 MYSTERY REVEAL'D (The); OR TRUTH BROUGHT TO LIGHT. Being a Discovery of some Facts in Relation to the Conduct of the M——y, which, however extraordinary they may appear, are yet supported by such Testimonies of Authentic Papers and Memoirs; as neither Confidence can out-brave; nor Cunning invalidate. By a Patriot. Monstrum Horrendum. *Title and* 319 *pp. Fine copy, half roan.* 8° *London,* 1759

RARE AND IMPORTANT. The above title conveys no adequate idea of the contents of this very interesting book. The first part is a statement of affairs, and an analysis of them, from the Peace of Utrecht, till some months after Braddock's Defeat. The second part contains the Original Documents or Vouchers for the Narratives. These comprise the memorials and letters that passed between the English and French officers in Canada and Nova Scotia, and other English colonies, especially on the Ohio, from 1751 to 1755, including the chief papers that fell into the hands of the French after the surrender of Fort Necessity, and Braddock's Defeat, such as Washington's Journal and Letters, Stobo's Letter to Washington, Braddock's Letters etc., etc., some of which papers are re-translations from the French. The book is deserving of the compliment of a new edition.

1384 MYSTERIES OF ISIS; or the Science of Mathematics. Translated from the original Mythic Symbols. *Cloth,* 4 *copies,* 16° *New York,* 1858

1385 MYSTICA Ciudad de Dios, Milagro de sv Omnipotencia, y abismo de la Gracias; Historia Divina, y Vida de la Virgen Madre de Dios Reyna, y Señora Neustra Maria Santissima, Restauradora de la Culpa de Eva, y Medianera de la Gracia: Manifestada en estos vltimos siglos por la misma Señora a su Esclava Sor Maria de Jesus, Abadesa del Convento de la Villa de Agreda, de la Provincia de Burgos, etc. 3 volumes. *Fine copy, vellum.* *Folio, Madrid,* 1720

1386 MYSTICA Ciudad de Dios, Milagro de su Omnipotencia, y abysmo de la gracia: Historia divina, y Vida de la Virgen, Madre de Dios, Reyna, y Señora Nuestra, Maria Sanctissima, Restauradora de la culpa de Eva, y Medianera de la Gracia: Manifestada en estos ultimos siglos por la misma Señora à su Esclava Sor Maria de Jesus, Abadesa del Convento de la Imaculada Concepcion de la Villa de Agreda, de la Provincia de Burgos, de la Regular observancia de nuestro Serafico Padre S. Francisco. Nueva impression anadida de dos tablas. 3 volumes, *fine copy, calf.* *Folio, Ambers,* 1755

The above are two of the best editions of this most extraordinary work; a complete biography of the VIRGIN, giving the most minute and authentic details of her life, and as it is asserted, written by a special revelation. It records facts, dates, events, and divers proceedings, such for instance as the visit of the Virgin to Santiago, the fights between her body-guard of two angels and the devil, who vainly endeavored to impede her progress. One of these angels afterwards served in the guard of the Madre AGREDA. The work narrowly escaped the Index, for it was at first bitterly opposed by many of the Church, and as warmly advocated by others. At first it was condemned by the Inquisition, but afterwards was licensed. Many works have been written for and against it. Finally it triumphed over all its enemies, and is now received as thoroughly orthodox. It is a standard work in the libraries of almost all the Convents of Catholic countries. Both editions are now fortified with page after page of licenses, approvals, and recommendations.

1387 NAPIER (Lieut. Gen. Sir W.) Life and Opinions of Sir Charles James Napier, G. C. B. 4 *vols. Portraits, cloth.* 8° *London,* 1857

1388 NARRATIVE of the Expedition of Com. John Byron round the World, containing an Account of the great Distress suffered by Himself and his Companions on the Coast of Patagonia 1740–6. With a Description of St. Jago de Chili, *etc. Frontispiece, half maroon morocco, uncut.* 8° *London,* 1768

1389 NARRATIVE (A) of the Campaigns of the British Army at Washington, Baltimore, and New Orleans, 1814 and 1815. *Half morocco.* 8° *London,* 1821

1390 NATIONAL PORTRAIT GALLERY of Distinguished Americans. Conducted by J. Herring and J. B. Longacre. 4 *vols, dark blue morocco, gilt edges, many portraits, fine original complete set.* *Royal* 8° *New York,* 1834–1840

1391 NAVARRETE (*Don* M. F. DE) RELATIONS DES QUATRE VOYAGES entrepris par Christophe Colomb pour la Découverte du Nouveau Monde de 1492 a 1504; 3 *vols, map, half morocco, uncut, fine copy.* 8° *Paris,* 1828

This important work was translated into French by MM. de Verneuil and de la Roquette, who had the advantage of having their labor revised by the original Compiler, M. Navarrete. The Chief Members of the Geographical Society of Paris took an active interest in it and Messieurs Rémusat, Balbi, le baron Cuvier, Jomard, Labouderie, Letronne, de Rossel, Saint-Martin, Walckenaer, Humboldt, etc., added notes and explanations, so that, on the whole, the work is a most valuable companion for the Student of the Original Spanish, or substitute for it.

1392 NAVARRETE (PEDRO FERNANDEZ) CONCERVACION DE MONARQVIAS y Discvrsos Politicas sobre la gran Consulta que el Consejo hizo al Señor Rey Don Filipe III. al Presidente, y Consejo Supremo de Castilla. *Fine copy, vellum.* *Folio, Madrid,* 1626

This beautiful book comprises a system of Political Economy, calculated for the meridian of the Kingdom of Old Castile. It is most interesting and contains incidentally many allusions to America and its influence upon Spain. The author considers in his seventh and eighth Discourses the two great causes of the Decrease of Population of Spain, and particularly Castile. The one is the Expulsion of the Moors and the Jews, and the other is the new Discoveries and Colonies in America. The title-page designed by F. Agus. Leonardo, and engraved by Alardo de Pompa is peculiar, being an architectural design surmounted by the arms of Leon and Castile supported on either side by figures of Wisdom and Prudence, while between columns one on each side stand portraits of the two brothers of the author: Alonso Mena Navarrete the eldest brother, and Alonso Navarrete, proto-Martyr, both of the Order of Saint Domingo in Japan.

1393 NEAL (DANIEL) THE HISTORY OF NEW ENGLAND, an Impartial Account of the Civil and Ecclesiastical Affairs of the Country to 1700, with Appendix. *Map,* 2 *vols, calf, fine old copy.* 8° *London,* 1720

1394 NEAL (D.) The History of New England, with Appendix. *Map,* 2 *vols in* 1, *half calf.* 8° *London,* 1720

1395 NEAL (Daniel) The History of the Puritans from the Reformation to the Death of Q. Elizabeth. 4 *vols, calf.* 8° *Dublin,* 1759

1396 NELSON (J.) History, Topography, and Antiquities of the Parish of St Mary Islington in the County of Middlesex, including Biographical Sketches. *Illustrated by Engravings; half calf.* 4° *London,* 1811

1397 NEWELL (W.) A Discourse on the Cambridge Church Gathering in 1636. Delivered in the First Church, Cambridge, February 22, 1846. 8° *Boston,* 1846

1398 NEW ENGLAND. THE DAY-BREAKING IF NOT THE SUN-RISING of the Gospel, with the Indians in New England. *The title mended, the pagination of some leaves cropped, and the top line of D, cut off, otherwise a fair copy, half roan.* 4° *Rich. Cotes, London,* 1647

1399 NEW ENGLAND. ORIGINAL MANUSCRIPT RECORDS of the CORPORATION FOR NEW ENGLAND, IN LONDON, (*afterwards called*) THE COMPANY FOR PROPAGATION OF THE GOSPELL IN NEW ENGLAND, from the sixteenth of February 1655 to the 4th of February 1685, being the original autograph minutes of the Proceedings of the Corporation, for thirty years, by five successive Secretaries, comprising 120 leaves, or 240 folio pages, generally in good preservation and legible, but some leaves at the beginning slightly mutilated. Bound in white vellum, never printed, and never skimmed with permission by any editor or writer. *Folio*, 1655–1685

It is not easy to overestimate the historical value and literary importance of original unpublished manuscripts of this kind. When it is remembered what this Corporation of New England was in London, what good friends of New England composed it, for whom it labored, how much money it raised and remitted to Boston, how much good it accomplished; how it befriended, encouraged, and backed the Commissioners of the United Colonies; how it found out, elected, and supported Eliot, and befriended Mayhew; how it clothed, fed, physicked and educated the praying Indians; how it encouraged and paid for the printing of the Bible, and many other books, in the Indian language; how it selected and sent over Marmaduke Johnson to print at Cambridge; how it helped the College, and supported Missionaries both to the Colonists and the Savages; how it kept the Church at home alive to the wants of the Mission in New England and printed all the *Progresses of the Gospel among the Indians:* when all these memories are brought home to our business and bosoms, perhaps some other *Corporation in New England* will see enough in the Volume to secure it, and give to the world, through the press, its contents in a neat volume, and so repay an instalment of the interest on the great debt of gratitude so long over-due to that brave Old Cromwellian Corporation. This volume has long sued in vain for appreciation and a home in this country, like the Hakluyt Manuscript of 1584, the Walter Ludd of 1507, the Logbook of Capt. Luke Foxe, the Dinwiddie and Washington Papers of 1751–1758, the Private Record Book of Dieskau and Montcalm of 1755–1759, and honest old Gorton's answer to Morton in 1669. As they become lost to America they become precious and worthy of printing. It is impossible to give any adequate idea of the value of this volume by a mere description, for though it contains much that is now irrelevant to New England history, yet it all illustrates the history of the Corporation. A few extracts may interest the reader.

"14 April 1660. That it be considered by Mr. Tres^r^ and such others as hee shall thinke fitt to prepare some propositions in writing ag^t^ the next Co^rt^ to be made unto the printer for the obleidginge of him to carry on the printinge of the Bible in the Indian language in N. E. for the best advantage of the worke."

"21 of April 1660. "Mr. Tres^r^ reports that in pursuance of the Order and desire of this Court of the 14 instint hee hath treated with the printer [*Marginal note*, Marmaduke Johnson is the Printer's name] about going into N. E. to print ye Bible in the Indian Language & reportts that the printer is willing to go and bee employed in that service at the salary of £40 per Ann. besides dyett, lodginge & washinge, & a Quarter's salary in advance & his tyme to bee there for three yeares & more if the Corporation or Com^rs^ for the United Colonies please to command from the tyme of his going on shippe board & the Corporation to pay his passage thither. And the s^d^ Marmaduke Johnson is contented and willinge to give security vnto the Corporation to perform these Agreem^ts^ abovementioned. And it is ordered that Articles bee forthwith prepared accordinge to the agreement abovenamed."

"May 22, 1660. Whereas it appeares that Mr. Tho. Bell, one of the Memb^s^ of this Corporation hath pd five pounds for the passage of Marmaduke Johnson shipped on board the Prudent Mary bound for New England and more the sume of 18s for a Bed, Boulster, rugge & one Blankett for his accomodа^n^ in his voyage to N. Engl^d^ afores^d^. It is ordered that Mr. Henry Ashurst Tres^r^ of the Corporation bee desired to pay the sd Mr. Tho. Bell for sd severell sums by him disbursed accordingly." Memorandum in the margin in another hand, "Mem. Marmaduke Johnson went from Gravesend of 14 May 1660, from wch tyme his salary is to begin at £40 pr Ann."

1400 NEW ENGLAND. STRENGTH OVT OF WEAKNESSE: Or a Glorious Manifestation of the further Progresse of the Gospel among the Indians in New England, formerly set forth by Mr. Henry Whitfield. *Fine, large, clean copy, in white forrel by Pratt.* 4° *M. Simmons, London,* 1652

There were three editions at least of this tract in 1652. This one begins with STRENGTH, in large capitals, and the Preface to the Christian Reader is dated 28th Feb. 1651.

1401 NEW ENGLAND. STRENGTH OUT OF WEAKNESS. Or a Glorious Manifestation of the further Progresse of the Gospel amongst the Indians in New England, *etc,* formerly set forth by Mr. Henry Whitfield late Pastor of Gilford in New England. *The pagination of some leaves clipped, otherwise a good copy.* 4° *M. Simmons, London,* 1652

The title of this edition begins with *Strength* in Italics, and the date at the end of the Preface is 28th of April, 1651. The Epistle to the Reader is signed by 18 names.

1402 NEW ENGLAND. A DECLARATION OF THE SAD AND GREAT PERSECUTION and Martyrdom of the People of God, called Quakers, in New England for the Worshipping of God. Whereof 22 have been banished, 3 martyred, 3 had their right ears cut, 1 burned on the hand with the letter H, 31 received 650 stripes, 1 beat while his body was like a jelly, several beat with Pitched Ropes, 5 Appeals to England denied, £1044 worth of Goods taken from them, and One now lyeth in Iron-fetters, condemned to dye. Also, Some Considerations in Answer to the Petition of the Court of Boston, subscribed by J. Endicot, the Chief Persecutor, *etc. Fine large copy,* EXCESSIVELY RARE. 4° *London, for Robert Wilson,* [1660]

1403 NEW ENGLAND. PROPOSITIONS CONCERNING THE SUBJECT OF BAPTISM and Consociation of Churches; Collected and Confirmed out of the Word of God, by a Synod of Elders and Messengers of the Churches in Massachusets-Colony in New-England. Assembled at Boston, according to the Appointment of the Honoured General Court, in the Year, 1662. Whereunto is anext the Answer of the Dissenting Brethren and Messengers of the Churches of New England, *etc. Good copy in white forrel by Pratt, title-page in admirable fac-simile.* [4° *Cambridge, N. E.*] *Printed* [*by Samuel Green*] *in the year* 1662.

One of the rarest and most important books pertaining to New England History and Church Courses. It opens with an historical Preface addressed especially to the Churches of Massachusetts Colony giving a history of the *Platform of Church Discipline* agreed upon by a Synod at Cambridge in 1648, and quoting the works of many of the Lord's Worthies in New England, respecting the great subject of the baptism of infants and the infants of Church Members, and the Consociation of Churches, 12 pp. Then follows "The Answer of the Elders and other Messengers of the Churches, assembled at Boston, 1662, to the [two] Questions propounded to them by Order of the Honoured General Court," respecting Baptism and a Consociation of Churches, 18 pp. But the Synod was not unanimous. There was a Minority who made an adverse Report which fills 38 pp. and is entitled: "Anti-Synodalia Scripta Americana, Or a Proposal of the Judgment of the Dissenting Messengers of the Churches of New England, Assembled by the Appointment of the General Court, March 10, 1662, whereof there were several Sessions afterwards. This *Script* or *Treatise* falling into the hands of a Friend to the Truth [Chauncy?] and the contents thereof, &c., was published for the Churches good, although without any Commission from the Dissenting Brethren; which they are desired not to be offended with. Wherein there is an Answer to the Arguments alleadged by the Synod." The first 7 pages of this is a Preface signed *Philalethes* [President Chauncy of Harvard College] giving reasons for publishing this dissent. Then on p. 8 comes the Report addressed to Gov. ENDICOTT. It pertains only to the first question of Baptism, the two parties agreeing substantially about Consociation. The question of Baptism then a political one, exercised the Great and General Court as much as the sale of liquor has recently.

1404 NEW ENGLAND. A VINDICATION OF THE DIVINE Authority of Ruling Elders in the Churches of Christ: Asserted by the Ministers and Elders met together in a Provincial Assembly [in Cambridge] Nov. 2, 1649. Whereunto is added, An Answer to the Question, Whether are not the Brethren, and not the Elders of the Churches only, to Judge, &c. By the Rev. Increase Mather, in his Book entitled, *The Order of the Gospel.* Excessively rare. *Fine copy, vellum.* 12° *Reprinted for Public Good* [*Boston,* 1700]

1405 NEW ENGLAND. MAGNALIA CHRISTI AMERICANA: OR THE ECCLESIASTICAL HISTORY OF NEW ENGLAND, from its First Planting in 1620 to 1698. In seven Books. I. Antiquities. II. Lives of the Governors: III. Lives of Sixty famous Divines: IV. Account of Harvard College: V. Acts and Monuments of the Churches in New England: VI. A Faithful Record of Wonderful Providences: VII. *The Wars of the Lord,* with an Appendix of Remarkable Occurrences which New England had in the Wars with the Indian Salvages from 1688 to 1698. By the Learned COTTON MATHER, M. A. *Good sound perfect copy, with the map.*
Folio, Thomas Parkhurst, London, 1702

1406 NEW ENGLAND JUDGED, by the Spirit of the Lord. In Two Parts. *First,* Containing a Brief Relation of the Sufferings of the People call'd Quakers in New England, from the Time of their first Arrival there in 1656 to the Year 1660. *Second Part,* Being a further Relation of their Cruel and Bloody Sufferings from 1660 to 1665, Beginning with the Sufferings of *William Leddra* whom they put to Death. Formerly Published by George Bishop, and now somewhat Abbreviated. With an Appendix containing the Writings of several of the Sufferers; also An Answer to Cotton Mather's Abuses of said People. *Imperfect, wanting some leaves in the middle.* 8° *London,* 1703

1407 NEW ENGLAND. A Platform of Church Discipline, the Synod at Cambridge, 1808.
The Original of New England Churches. 1812
Confession of Faith of the Churches at Boston. 3 *vols in one, calf.* 12° *Boston,* 1808–12.

1408 NEW ENGLAND PATRIOT (The) being a candid Comparison of the principles and conduct of the Washington and Jeffer-

son Administrations. The whole founded upon indisputable facts and public Documents. *Uncut.*
148+12 pp. 8° *Boston,* 1810

1409 New Hampshire. Collections of the New Hampshire Historical Society. Vol. III. *Boards, uncut.* 8° *Concord,* 1832

1410 New Hampshire Festival. A Collection of Interesting Extracts relating thereto. 4° 1849

1411 New Hampshire. Transactions of the State Agricultural Society for 1850–52. *Cloth.* 8° *Concord,* 1853

1412 Newport (*Col.* Andrew) Memoirs of Col. Newport, who served as a Cavalier in the army of Gustavus Adolphus, and in that of Charles I. containing anecdotes of the principal persons in the army. New Edition, with additions. *Portrait, half calf.* 8° *London,* 1792

1413 NEWSPAPERS of Vermont. 37 *vols, half bound. Folio, viz.*

Brattleboro Eagle, Nov. 27, 1848 to Dec. 22, 1854. 7 *vols.* *Brattleboro*
Green Mountain Farmer, March 14, 1856 to Feb. 27, 1857. 1 *vol.* *Randolph*
Vergennes Independent, Dec. 8, 1854 to Dec. 27, 1856, in 1 *vol.* *Vergennes*
Star of Vermont, Oct. 21, 1854 to Oct. 20, 1855, in 1 *vol.* *Northfield*
Vermont Journal, June 24, 1853 to June 12, 1857, in 2 *vols.* *Windsor*
North Union, June 10, 1854 to Dec. 5, 1856, in 1 *vol.* *West Charleston*
Vermont Patriot, Dec. 26, 1850 to Dec. 16, 1852, in 1 *vol.* *Montpelier*
American Journal, March 10, 1855 to April 10, 1857. 1 *vol.* *Swanton*
Vergennes Citizen, May 11, 1855 to Nov. 15, 1856. 1 *vol.* *Vergennes*
Rutland Herald, June 16, 1851 to Dec. 7, 1854. 2 *vols.* *Rutland*
Northern Farmer, April 6, 1855 to March 7, 1856. 1 *vol.* *Woodstock*
Burlington Free Press, Sept. 27, 1850 to June 25, 1858, in 4 *vols.* *Burlington*
Vermont Watchman, Dec. 5, 1850, to Nov. 19, 1858, in 4 *vols.* *Montpelier*
Green Mountain Freeman, Jan. 5, 1854 to Dec. 9, 1858, in 3 *vols.* *Montpelier*
Caledonian, July 17, 1852 to June 26, 1858, in 3 *vols.* *St. Johnsbury*
North Star, June 4, 1851 to Dec. 25, 1858, in 4 *vols.* *Danville*

1414 NEWSPAPERS. The Northern Centinel, vol. I. No. 1, Dec. 13, 1810 to Dec. 25, 1829. *Bound in* 15 *vols.* Also for the years 1832 and 1833, 2 *vols. Folio, Burlington,* 1810–33
A very nearly perfect set of one of the rarest and best of the early Vermont Newspapers. For the period of the War of 1812 the collection is valuable.

1415 NEWSPAPERS. Vermont Centinel, Dec. 22, 1803 to March 18, 1808. 3 *vols.* *Folio, Burlington*
Vermont Centinel, April 2, 1806 to March 18, 1808. 1 *vol.* *Burlington*
Vermont Centinel, April 2, 1806 to March 25, 1807. 1 *vol.* *Burlington*
Burlington Gazette, vol. I. No. 1, Sept. 9, 1814 to Feb. 16, 1817, *scarce,* 1 *thick vol.*
Burlington Gazette, Sept. 16, 1814, to Feb. 13, 1817, 1 *vol.* *In all* 7 *vols, bound*

1416 NEWSPAPERS. Christian Register, May 17, 1822, to Aug. 8, 1823. 1 *vol.* *Boston*
Massachusetts Spy, Jan. 4, 1804 to May 8, 1805. 1 *vol.* *Worcester*
New England Farmer, July 15, 1854 to Jan. 17, 1857. 2 *vols.* *Boston*
Weekly Messenger, Oct. 25, 1811 to Oct. 15, 1813. 1 *vol.* *Boston*
Boston Daily Advertiser, Jan. 2, to Dec. 31, 1857, in 1 thick *vol.* *Boston*
Independent Whig, Dec. 2, 1851 to April 7, 1857. 5 *vols.* *Lancaster, Pa.*
Cotton Planter, April 24, 1852 to Aug. 4, 1853, in 1 *vol.* *Washington*
Independent, Jan. 4, 1855, to July 2, 1857. 3 *vols.* *N. York*
Daily Statesman, June 7, 1855 to June 27, 1857. 1 *vol.* *Concord, N. H.*
State of Maine, Dec. 12, 1854 to Nov. 16, 1858. 2 *vols.* *Portland*
Lancaster Times, Jan. 6, 1858 to June 1, 1859. 1 *vol.* *Lancaster, Pa.*
Patriot and Union, Jan. 6, 1857 to Aug. 26, 1858. 1 *vol.* *Harrisburg, Pa.*
New York Evangelist, Aug. 6, 1835 to Dec. 30, 1837. 6 *vols.* (*some dups*) *N. Y.*
In all 26 *vols bound*

1417 NEW TESTAMENT. THE ENGLISH HEXEPLA. Six English Translations, by Wycliffe, Tyndale, Cranmer, the Genevan, Rhemish, and the Authorized. *Very fine copy.* LARGE PAPER, *bound by Hayday, in brown morocco, gilt edges.* SCARCE. *Large* 4° *Bagster, London,* 1841

Large paper copies of this work have now become scarce.

1418 NEW TESTAMENT; an improved Version on the Basis of Archbishop Newcome's Translation, with Notes. *Half roan.* 8° *Boston,* 1809

1419 NEW WORLD. DIE NEW WELT der landschaften vnnd Insulen, so bis hie her allen Altiweltbeschrybern vnbekant, Jungst aber von den Portugalesern vnnd Hispaniern jm Nidergenglichen Meer herfunden. *Fine copy,* VERY RARE, *half vellum.* *Folio, Straszburg,* 1534

The contents of this early collection of Voyages are the same as the NOVUS ORBIS edited by Simon Grynaeus and published at Basil in 1532, this being translated and edited by Michael Herr. This is by far the rarer of the two works. For an account of the contents of the third Latin edition see No. 1456, and for the very rare Brabant edition see No. 5 of this Catalogue.

1420 NEW YORK. Acts of Assembly passed in the Province of New York from 1691 to 1718. *Calf, gilt. Folio, London,* 1719

1421 NEW YORK. Acts of Assembly, Passed in the Province of New York from 1691 to 1718. *Folio, London,* 1719

1422 NEW YORK. JOURNAL OF THE VOTES AND PROCEEDINGS of the General Assembly of the Colony of New York. 2 vols. Vol. I, April 1691 to Sept. 1743. Vol. II, from Nov. 1743 to Dec. 1765. *Half morocco. Volume* II, EXCESSIVELY SCARCE. *Folio, Hugh Gaine, New York,* 1764–1766

1423 NEW YORK. JOURNAL OF THE VOTES AND PROCEEDINGS of the General Assembly of the Colony of New York. Began the 8th Day of November, 1743, and Ended the 23d of December, 1765. Vol. II. Published by order of the General Assembly. *Folio, Hugh Gaine, New York,* 1766

This volume much rarer than the first is wanting to complete most sets.

1424 NEW YORK. LAWS OF NEW YORK from the Year 1691 to 1773 inclusive. Published according to an Act of the General Assembly. *An uncommon edition.* *Folio, Hugh Gaine, New York,* 1774

1425 NEW YORK. The Documentary History of the State of New York, arranged by E. B. O'Callaghan. 4 *volumes.* *Cloth.* 4° *Albany,* 1850–51

1426 NEW YORK. Documents relating to the Colonial History of the State of New York, procured in Holland, England and France, by J. R. Brodhead, Agent. Eleven volumes, *a complete set including the Index.* 4° *Albany,* 1850–51

1427 NEW YORK. Journal of the Votes and Proceedings of the General Assembly of the Colony of New York from 1766 to 1776 inclusive. *Fine copy, calf.* *Folio, Albany,* 1820

In March 1820, on finding that only one copy of the original Journals from 1766 to 1776 was known to exist, the General Assembly of New York voted to reprint a small edition of 50 copies only. The volume has now become excessively rare.

428 NEW YORK. Longworth's American Almanac. New York Register and City Directory for 1807. *Good clean copy.* 7° *New York*, 1807

429 NEW YORK. COLLECTIONS of the New York Historical Society. Vols I, II. 2 *vols.* 8° *New York*, 1811–14

430 NEW YORK Historical Society. Proceedings of, for the Years 1844 and 1846. 2 *vols.* 8° *New York*, 1844

431 New York Spelling, or Fourth Book. *Wood-cuts, boards, scarce.* 18° *New York*, 1813

432 NEW YORK. Census of the State of New York for 1855, Prepared by F. B. Hough. *Half morocco. Folio, Albany*, 1857

433 NEW YORK BRASIER'S and PHILADELPHIA JEWELLER'S *Engraved Cards.* 4°

1. JAMES BUVELOT, *Brasier*, At the Sign of the *Three Kettles* Hanover Square New York. Makes and Sells Copper Stills, Brewing Coppers, Copper and Brass Kettles, Fish Kettles, Tea Kettles, Kettlepots, Coffeepots, Warmingpans, Saucepans, Pyepans, Stewpans, Chafingdishes and all Sorts of Kitchen furniture & Brasiery Ware; Mends and Tins Copper and Brass after the best Manner, at Reasonable Rates; Also Sells best London Pewter; And gives Ready Money for Old Copper, Brass, Pewter, and Lead. *Engraved on copper by J. Lewes*, 1751, *within a beautiful floral border, surmounted by the* SIGN OF THE THREE KETTLES. *Size* 5 *inches by* 6. *Unique, Specimen of early New York Art.* 4°

2. EDMUND MILNE, *Goldsmith*, at the *Crown and Pearl*, near the Market, in Second-Street, Philadelphia. Makes and Sells all sorts of Gold and Silver Work, at the Lowest Prices, Likewise Jewellers Work Perform'd in the Neatest Manner, and Gives the Best Prices for Old Gold, Silver and Jewells. *Engraved by Henry Dawkins, of Philadelphia, not dated, but about* 1750, *within a beautifully designed border, highly ornamented, with various articles of silver and gold plate hung on a richly chased frame, the whole surmounted by the* CROWN AND PEARL. *Size* 6 *by* 7 *inches. A most creditable specimen of early Philadelphia art. No other copy known.*

434 NICKOLLS (Sir John) Remarks on the Advantages and Disadvantages of France and Great Britain with respect to Commerce, *etc.* Translation from the French Original [of Plumard de Dunguel]. *Calf.* 8° *London*, 1754

435 NICKOLLS (John) Remarques sur les avantages et les desavantages de la France et de la Gr. Britagne, par Rapport au Commerce, et aux autres Sources de la Puissance des Etats. Traduction de l'Anglois du Chevalier John Nickolls. Seconde Edition. *Calf, fine copy.* 8° *Leyde*, 1754

Notices the Hudson's Bay, Africa, East India, and South Sea Companies. It is not a little curious that the Original French Edition purports to be translated from the English while the First English Edition is translated from the French.

436 NICOLAUS DE CUSA. Opera Theologica, Philosophica et Juridica. *Old calf.*
Folio, Ex Officina Henriepetrina, Basileæ, 1565

437 NILES (HEZEKIAH) THE WEEKLY REGISTER: Containing Political, Historical, Geographical, Scientific, Astronomical, Statistical and Biographical Documents, essays and facts; together with notices of the Arts and Manufactures, and a record of the events of the times. Vols 1–50, from Sept. 1811 to Sept. 1836, in 50 volumes, *royal 8vo:* General Index to the first 12 vols 1811–1818, in 1 vol, and from Sept.

9

1836 to Sept. 1843 in 14 vols 4to. Together 65 vols, *an unusually good clean copy, well bound in half calf.* *Roy.* 8° *&* 4° *Baltimore,* 1811–1843

1438 Nisbet (Charles) Monody to the Memory of Rev. Dr. Charles Nisbet, late President of the College of Carlisle in Pennsylvania. *Half morocco, uncut.* 8° *Edinburgh,* 1805

1439 North (Lord) A View of the History of Great Britain during the Administration of Lord North to 1781. In two Parts, with a statement of the Public Expenditure in that period. *Title,* 2 + 412 *pp. fine copy, uncut.* 8° *London,* 1782

This volume relates almost entirely to American Affairs, and is one of very considerable importance and rarity.

1440 North America. The Present State of North America, etc. Part 1. 2d edition with emendations. *Scarce, half roan.* 4° *London,* 1755

1441 North America. The present state of Great Britain and North America Considered. *Half red morocco uncut. Scarce.* 8° *London,* 1767

1442 North America. The History of North America, with the present state of the different Colonies. *Map, calf.* 12° *London,* 1776

1443 North American Review. No. 58 (Jan. 1828), Nos. 60 to 67, 69 to 72, 74, 78 to 81, 83 to 85, 87 to 89, 105, 121, and 122, (Jan. 1844.) *Together* 27 *numbers, uncut.* 8° *Boston,* 1828–1844

1444 North American Review. Nos. 62, 64, and 67. 1829–30

1445 North Eastern Boundary (*Maine*) Considerations on the Claims of the United States. *Map, half calf.* 8° *London,* 1826

1446 Northern Tour. A Guide to Saratoga, Lake George, Niagara, *etc. Half morocco.* 16° *Phila.* 1825

1447 North Georgia Gazette (The) and Winter Chronicle. *Half brown morocco.* 4° *London,* 1821

1448 Northmore (T.) Washington, or Liberty Restored, a Poem in Ten Books. *Boards, uncut.* 12° *London,* 1809

1449 North Pole. The Possibility of Approaching the North Pole asserted. By the Hon. D. Barrington, with Appendix on a Northwest passage by Col. Beaufoy. *Map, half morocco, uncut.* 8° *New York,* 1818

1450 NOTICIA del Establecimiento y Poblacion de las Colonias Inglesas en la America Septentrional ; Religion, orden de gobierno, leyes y costumbres de sus naturales y inhabitantes ; etc. Por Don Francisco Alvares. 196 *pp. Calf.* 4° *Madrid,* 1778

Don Francisco has made a very amusing book, if not absolutely instructive. It was compiled mainly from the best English authors, with a careful examination of standard maps and charts. It was just in the time of the American Revolution, when Franklin was in Paris, Adams in Holland, and Jay in Madrid. Everybody in Spain was thirsting for reliable topographical and geographical information. This work was intended to supply just what was wanted. As a fair sample of the topography we give this brief extract from Chapter V. devoted to a description of New England, translated literally: "New England is divided into eleven Provinces and four Counties. The Provinces are as follows: Massachusets, Essex, Middlesex, Suffolck, Hampshire, Plimouth, Barnestaple, Bristol, Warwik, Connecticut, and Newaven. The Counties are: New London, Hartfort, Newhaven, and Fairfield." New York, New Jersey and Virginia are described with *similar* accuracy.

1451 NOVANGLUS and Massachusettensis; or Political Essays published in 1774 and 1775. *Boards, uncut.* 8° *Boston,* 1819

1452 NOVA SCOTIA. THE MEMORIALS of the English and French Commissioners, concerning the Limits of Nova Scotia, or Acadia. *Maps, calf.* 4° *London,* 1755

This Work, containing the various Papers drawn up by the English and French Commissioners, respecting the history and geography of Eastern Canada, Maine, New Brunswick, Nova Scotia, the Gulf of St. Lawrence, etc., is of the utmost importance to the historian of these districts. This lot should go with No. 1275 of this Catalogue.

1453 NOVA SCOTIA. The Present State of Nova Scotia; with a brief Account of Canada and the British Islands on the coast of North America. Second edition. *Half calf.* 8° *Edinburgh,* 1787

1454 NOVUS ORBIS, REGIONUM AC INSULARUM, Veteribus incognitarum (collegit J. Huttich, edidit Simon Grynæus). *Vellum, no map.* *Folio, Basileæ,* 1537

1455 NOVUS ORBIS, *etc. Another copy, very fine, pig skin, with the very rare map of the world by* SEBASTIAN MUNSTER. *Folio, Basileæ,* 1537

This large collection of Voyages, compiled by J. Huttich, and edited by Simon Grynæus, with a Geographical Preface by Sebastian Munster, all of the old University of Basle, at the expense of a Jo. Hervagius, a Basil Publisher, should find a place in every public library, inasmuch as the original editions of the Papers of which it is made up, are now almost unfindable. Considering the date of the first edition of 1532, the reader should study some of the voyages with both of his eyes open, the one to detect the mistranslations and the other the misconceptions of inland geographers, who misread the reports of the navigators. The volume contains, 1. The voyages of Cadamosto down the coast of Africa in 1454–1455; 2. The first three voyages of Columbus, 1492–1498; 3. Of Vincent Pinzon to Brazil in 1499; 4. The four voyages of Vespucci, 1497–1504; 5. Of Pedro Alvarez Cabral, 1500–1501; 6. Letter of King Emanuel to Leo X respecting the discoveries of the Portuguese in India, 1513; The Voyages of Varthema; 7. Description of the Holy Land in the 13th century, by Brocard; 8. The Relation of Joseph the Indian; 9. The three works of Marco Polo; 10. Haython's account of the Tartars; 11. Sarmatia, by Mathew Miechow; 12. Muscovie, by Paulus Jovius; 13. Peter Martyr's newly discovered Islands; 14. Stella on the Antiquities of Prussia; 15. Letter of Maximilian of Transylvania, Secretary of Charles V, to the Cardinal of Saltzburg, dated Oct. 24, 1522, giving an account of the voyages of Magellan, 1519–1522. This last piece is in none of the three previous editions of 1532 (Basil and Paris), and in German, 1534; (see No. 1419 *supra*).

1456 NOVUS ORBIS; ID EST, NAVIGATIONES primæ in Americam; quibus adjunximus Gasparis Varrerii Discvrsvm super Ophyra Regione. *Calf, gilt, scarce.* 8° *Roterodami,* 1616

1457 NUTT (David) Catalogue of Foreign Theological Books, Liturgies, Rituals, Hebrew and Syriac Literature, etc. *Half morocco.* 8° *London,* 1857

1458 BSERVATIONS on the Conduct of Great Britain with regard to the Negotiations and other Transactions Abroad. *Half roan.* 8° *London*, 1729

Relates to Admiral Hosier's, and other British Expeditions to the West Indies against the Spaniards. A very important historical volume, containing many interesting facts and statistics, not elsewhere readily found.

1459 ODESPUN (L.) CONCILIA NOVISSIMA Galliæ. *Folio, Paris*, 1646

1460 OGLE (*Sir* Chaloner) Tryal . . . before the Chief Justice of Jamaica for an assault on Gov. Trelawney, July 22, 1743. *Half morocco.* 8° *London*, 1743

1461 OEXMELIN (Alexandre-Olivier) Histoire des Avanturiers Filibusters qui se sont signalez dans les Indes. *Maps and plates.* 4 *vols in* 2 ; *vellum.* 8° *Trevoux*, 1744

1462 OLDMIXON. The British Empire in America, containing the History of the Colonies. 2d edition. 2 *vols, calf gilt, fine copy.* 8° *London*, 1741

1463 OLIVER (B. L.) The Rights of an American Citizen. *Boards, uncut.* 8° *Boston*, 1832

1464 OLIVER (B. L.) The Law Summary. 8° *Hallowell*, 1833

1465 OMAÑA y SOTOMAYOR (Dr. Gregorio) Obras de Eloquencia y Poesia premiadas por la Real Universidad de Mexico en el Certamen Literario que celebró el dia 28 de Diceimbre de 1790. Con motivo de la Exaltacion al Trono de Nuestro Católico Monarca el Sr. D. Carlos IIII, Rey de España y de las Indias. 4° *Mexico*, 1791

1466 OPPOSITION. A short history of the Opposition during the last Session of Parliament. 3d edition. *Half roan.* 8° *London*, 1779

An interesting volume relating mainly to American affairs.

1467 ORANGE. Bref recueil de l'Assasinat, commis en la personne dv tresillvstre Prince, Monseigneur le Prince d'Orange, Comte de Nassau, etc. par Jean Jauregui Espagnol. *Fine copy, half calf, scarce.* 4° *C. Plantin, Anvers*, 1582

1468 ORANGE. Discovrs svr la Blessvre de Monseignevr le Prince de' Orange. *Fine copy, half morocco.* 4° *n. p.* 1582

1469 ORBIGNY (M. ALCIDE D') Voyage pittoresque dans les Deux Ameriques. *Portraits and plates, half brown morocco, gilt.* 4° *Paris*, 1836

1470 ORIENTAL SOCIETY (American) Journal, Vol. VI, No. 1. 8° *New Haven*, 1859

1471 ORIGIN and Progress of Despotism in the Oriental and other Empires of Africa, Europe and America. *Red morocco, gilt.* 8° *Amsterdam*, 1764

1472 ORINOCO. Histoire de l'Orenoque, et des principales Rivieres qui s'y jettent. Par J. Gumilla. *Map and plates.* 3 *vols, boards.* 12° *Avignon*, 1758

1473 ORTELIUS (ABRAHAM) THEATRVM ORBIS TERRARVM. THEATRE, OFTE TOONNEL DES AERDT-BODEMS waer inne te seine sijn de Landt-tafelen van de geheele Weerelt; met een corte Verdarenge der seluer. *Fine complete copy, with all the original maps, colored, half calf.* *Folio, Antwerpen,* 1571

FIRST AND EXCESSIVELY RARE EDITION, in Dutch, almost unknown to bibliographers. Though the first Latin edition bears the date of 1570, and may have seen the light a short time before this, yet there are evidences that this Dutch edition was the one in which the work was composed. The maps are precisely the same in the two. There were several other editions in Latin between 1570 and 1600 with new maps, and retouches of the original ones, some dated, and others not, so that one feels not entirely safe in investigating the earliest geography of America till he can eye this or the Latin of 1570, or both. A thorough study of Ortelius is of the last importance to the student of the geography of the western hemisphere. He was a bibliographer, a cartographer, and an antiquarian, as well as a good mathematician and geographer, and what is of infinite importance to us now, he gave his authorities. Many of the rampant errors that disturb and puzzle us can be treed and flayed by the help of Ortelius. It was Ortelius' famous list of authorities that first gave to Humboldt the hint that Hylacomilus and Waldseemuller were one and the same person, the key to his investigations upon the St Dié fraternity, and the Vespucci voyages. When in 1862 that other valuable key, Walter Lud's *Orbis Speculum,* printed in 1507, was discovered by the writer, and found to disclose the secrets of several of the St Dié books, and when he could find no record of it elsewhere, he was delighted to find that it had not escaped Ortelius, but was recorded by him under the title, GUALTERUS LUDOVICUS. The book by Lud explained this reference, and gave us still more confidence in the List though there are still other books recorded in it of which bibliographers as yet know nothing.

1474 ORTELIUS (ABRAHAM) Epitome dv Theatre dv Monde d'Abraham Ortelivs: Auquel se represente, tant par figures que Characteres, la vraye situation, nature & proprieté de la terre vniverselle. Revue, corrigé et augmentée de plusieurs Cartes, pour la troisième fois. *Ob.* 8° *Plantin, Anvers,* 1588

1475 OSBORN (Benjamin) Truth Displayed, or a Series of Elementary Principles, with Practical Observations. 626 *pp.* 8° *Fay and Davidson, Rutland, Vt,* 1816

1476 OSBORN (B.) *Another copy.* 8° *Rutland,* 1816

1477 OSSAT (CARDINAL D') Lettres au Roy Henri le Grand, 1594–1604. *Folio, Paris,* 1624

1478 OTIS (James) The Rights of the British Colonies, Asserted and proved. The second edition. *Half morocco.* 8° *Reprinted by J. Almon, London, n. d.*

1479 OTIS (James) The Rights of the British Colonies Asserted and proved. 3d edition, corrected. *Half roan.* 8° *London,* 1766

1480 OTIS (James) A Vindication of the British Colonies. *Half roan.* 8° *Almon, London,* 1769

1481 OTIS (James) A Vindication of the British Colonies asserted and proved. 8° *London,* 1769

1482 OTTENS (REINIER en JOSUA) ATLAS VAN ZEEVAERT EN KOOPHANDEL DOOR DE GEHEELE WEERELDT. *Half morocco, uncut.* *Atlas folio, Amsterdam,* 1745

Contains numerous fine colored maps, several pertaining to America, with descriptive and historical text.

1483 OTTENS (Regner et Josue) Atlas Nouveau, contenant toutes les Parties du Monde, où sont exactement Remarquées les Empires, Monarchies, Royaumes, Etats, Republiques, *etc. etc.* 111 *large double colored maps.* *Atlas folio, Amsterdam, n. d.*

1484 OVALLE (Alonso de) Historica Relacion del Reyno de Chile, y de las missiones, y ministerios que exercita en el la Compañia de Iesvs. *Fine perfect copy, with all the maps, plates, portraits, and wood-cuts.* *Folio, En Roma, por F. Canallo,* 1646

There is even yet a doubt which is the original edition, the Italian or Spanish, both having been printed at Rome the same year, but this Spanish edition contains several more copperplates than the Italian. In this copy there is a second title, of the highest rarity, beginning "Varias, y Curiosas Noticias del Reino de Chile," etc.

1485 OVAGLIE (Alonso d') Historica Relatione del Regno di Cile, E delle missioni, e ministerij che esercita in quelle la Compagnia di Giesv. *Map & plates.* *Folio, Roma,* 1646

1486 OVIEDO (Joannes Antonio de) Succus Theologiæ Moralis pro majori pœnitentium, et confessariorum expeditione diligenter expressus. *xvi + 342 + vi pp., splendid copy in the original vellum.* 8° *Mexici, Typis Viduæ Josephi de Hogal,* 1754

1487 Owen (John *D. D.*) Two Discourses concerning the Holy Spirit and his Work [with a Preface by Nathaniel Mather.] 8° *London,* 1693

1488 P*** [*i. e.* M. de Pauw] Recherches sur les Americains [with the] Défense, *etc.* 3 *vols, calf.* 8° *Berlin,* 1770

1489 P*** [M. de Pauw] Recherches Philosophiques sur les Americains, ou Mémoires intéressants pour servir à l'Histoire de l'Espèce humaine. 3 *vols, half green morocco, gilt, uncut.* 12° *Berlin,* 1771

1490 P***. Recherches sur les Americains. 2 *vols calf, gilt.* 8° *Londres,* 1771

1491 P***. Recherches Philosophiques sur les Americains. 2 *vols, fine copy, calf.* 8° *Clive,* 1772

1492 P***. Défense des Recherches Philosophiques sur les Americains. Nouvelle Édition, corrigée et augmentée. *Fine copy, calf.* 8° *Berlin,* 1772

1493 Pagès (M. de) Voyages autour du Monde et vers les deux Poles par Terre et par Mer, 1767–76. 2 *vols, calf.* 8° *Paris,* 1782

1494 Paine (M.) Letters on the Cholera Asphyxia, as it has appeared in New York. *Half morocco.* 8° *New York,* 1832

1495 Paine (Robert Treat) Works in Verse and Prose, with Notes and Sketches of his Life and Character. *Portrait.* 8° *Boston,* 1812

1496 Paine (Thomas) A Letter to Abbé Raynal on the Affairs of North America. *Half morocco.* 8° *C. Dilly, London,* 1782

1497 PAINE (Thomas) Remarques sur les Erreurs de l'Histoire de G. T. Raynal. *Half morocco, uncut.* 8° *Amsterdam,* 1783

1498 PAINE (Thomas) Common Sense, addressed to the Inhabitants of America. *Calf.* 8° *London,* 1791

1499 PAINE (T.) Rights of Man. 5th edit. *Half calf.* 8° *London,* 1791

1500 PAINE (T.) Rights of Man, and other Tracts. *Half calf.* 8° *London,* 1792

1501 PAINE (T.) Works. *Portrait; calf.* 8° *London,* 1792

1502 PAINE (Thomas) TRACTS. *2 vols, half calf.* 8° namely,

The American Crisis,	*Lond.*	1817
Letter to Washington,	*ib.*	1817
Public Good,	*ib.*	1817
Miscellaneous Letters and Essays,	*ib.*	1819
Life. 2d Edition,	*ib.*	1821
Case of Officers of Excise,	*ib.*	1819
Letter to Abbé Raynal,	*ib.*	1819
Prospects on the Rubicon,	*ib.*	1819
Letters to the Addressers,	*London,*	1817
Letters to Citizens of the United States,	*ib.*	1819
Miscellaneous Poems,	*ib.*	1819

1503 PAINE (T.) Observations on Paine's Rights of Man by Publicola [*i. e.* John Quincy Adams.] *Calf. 5 Tracts in one vol. viz:* 8° *Edinb. n. d.*

Paine's Principles and Schemes of Government examined and his Errors Detected,	*Edinb.*	1792
A Word in Season. 6th Edition,	*ib.*	1792
Ten Minutes' Reflection,	*n. p.*	1792
Hill. The present Happiness of Great Britain,	*Edinb.*	1792

1504 PAINE (T.) Eulogy at Newbury Port, January 2, 1800, on the Life of Gen. Geo. Washington. 8° *Newburyport,* 1800

1505 PALEY (Wm.) Works. *Fine copy, calf, 7 vols,* 8° namely,

Principles of Moral Philosophy. 2 *vols,*	*Lond.*	1796
Evidences of Christianity. 5th Edition. 2 *vols,*	*ib.*	1796
Natural Theology. 1 *vol,*	*ib.*	1802
Horæ Paulinæ. 1 *vol,*	*ib.*	1794
Sermons. 1 *vol,*	*ib.*	1808

1506 PALMER (John) Journal of Travels in the United States of North America, and in Lower Canada, in 1817. *Map, half blue morocco, uncut.* 8° *London,* 1818

1507 PAMPHLETS. Innes' Present State of the British West India Colonies, 1840. Early Life and Conversion of Wm. Howe, by his Son, 1841. India and Lord Ellenborough. Fourth edition, 1844. Reply to the Same by Zeta. Second ed. 1845. Trial, Cooper *vs.* Wakley, for Libel, 1829. *In 1 vol, half calf.* 8° *London.*

1508 PANCIROLLUS (Guido) The History of many Memorable Things Lost, which were in Use among the Ancients. *2 vols in 1, calf.* 8° *London,* 1715

This work contains incidentally many interesting allusions to America, especially the early use of the term New World, Novus Orbis, etc. long before Columbus and Vespucci.

1509 PAPERS Relative to the Rupture with Spain. In French and English. *Half blue morocco, uncut.* 8° *London,* 1762

1510 PAPERS Relative to the Rupture with Spain. In French and English. *Half calf.* 8° *London*, 1762

Relates mainly to the disputes between the English and Spanish as to the West Indies.

1511 PARAGUAY. THE HISTORY OF PARAGUAY, containing a full and authentic Account of the Establishment formed there by the Jesuits from among the Savage Nations, in the very centre of Barbarism. Establishments allowed to have realized the sublime Ideas of Fenelon, Sir Thomas More, and Plato. By Father Charlevoix. 2 *vols, fine copy, old calf.* 8° *Lond.* 1769

1512 PAREDES (EL P. ANTONIO DE) CARTA EDIFICANTE, en que el P. A. Paredes de la extinguida Comp. de Jesus, refiere la Vida Exemplar de la Hermana Salvadora de los Santos, INDIA OTOMI, que reimprimen las parcialidades de San Juan y de Santiago de la Capital de Mexico. 12° *Mexico*, 1791

1513 PARKE (JOHN) THE LYRIC WORKS OF HORACE translated into English verse: to which are added a number of Original Poems. By a Native of America [Lt. Col. John Parke.] 8° *Printed by Elizabeth Oswald, Philadelphia*, 1786

This is perhaps the rarest and oddest of all the American Books of Poetry. The present copy is in fine condition in the original red morocco, gilt edges, bearing on the fly-leaf in the handwriting of Colonel Parke, the following inscription: "To the Honorable Robert Morris, Esq. Member of the General Assembly of this Commonwealth, from his very humble Servt. The Author. Philadelphia, Feb. 10, 1787." It came from the library of the late E. D. Ingraham, who wrote on another fly-leaf, "For an account of John Parke, the author of this volume, see Mr. Fisher's '*Early Poets, etc. of Pennsylvania*,' Mem. Penn. Hist. Society, Vol. 2, part 2, p. 100." The work is dedicated to General Washington, has a learned preface addressed to the subscribers whose names fill sixteen pages, and a Life of Horace inscribed to Dr. Franklin. It is adorned with an extraordinary frontispiece designed by Peter Markoe, of Philadelphia, and engraved by James P. Malcom. Parke was a Delaware poet, born about 1750, educated in the College of Philadelphia, in 1768, entered the army at the beginning of the war, and was probably attached to Washington's Division. His Odes (for they are not Horace's), are dated from 1769 to 1786, at various places, as Philadelphia, Newcastle, Head Quarters, Clove, Arundel, Camp at Middlebrook, Dover, Valley Forge, Boston, New London, Brandywine, Roxbury, New York, Brunswick, Cambridge, Baltimore, etc. etc. generally in Camp at Head Quarters, and are inscribed to almost all the officers of the army, and prominent men and women of the country, not forgetting even his personal friends the servants. Epode X, To Mævius is "addressed to His Excellency the Right Honorable JOHN EARL OF DUNMORE, late Governor of Virginia, Pirate, Kidnapper, and Negro Merchant, on his departure for England."

1514 PARKINSON (Richard) A Tour in America, in 1798-1800. 2 *vols, half calf.* 8° *London*, 1805

1515 PARKINSON (Sydney) A Journal of a Voyage to the South Seas. *Portrait, calf.* 4° *London*, 1773

1516 PARKINSON (SYDNEY) JOURNAL of a Voyage to the South Seas in H. M. Ship the Endeavour. Edited by Stanfield Parkinson. 27 *fine plates, calf.* LARGE PAPER. 4° *London*, 1773

"Parkinson was draughtsman to Sir Joseph Banks, and the engravings from his drawings have been esteemed a valuable addition to the Journal, as no other plates convey so faithful a representation of the originals."

1517 PASSARELLUS (C.) BELLUM LUSITANUM, ejusque Regni Separatio. *Boards, uncut.* *Folio, Lugduni*, 1684

1518 PATENT CASE. Argument of William Whiting, Esq., in the Case of Ross Winans *vs.* Orsamus Eaton, et al. *Cloth.* 8° *Boston*, 1853

1519 PATTIE (James, *of Kentucky*) Personal Narrative, during an Expedition from St. Louis to the Pacific Ocean, *etc.* during Journeyings of six Years Conflicts with the Indians, *etc.* Edited by T. Flint. 8° *Cincinnati*, 1833

1520 PAUL (SIMON) Commentarius de Abusu Tabaci Americanorum Veteri, et herbæ Thee Asiaticorum in Europa Novo, quæ ipsissima est Chamæleagnos Dodonæi, Myrtus Brabantica, Danicè Porsz, German. Post, Gallicè Piment Royal, Belgicé Gargel dicta; cum Figuris aneis, utensilica quadam Chinensivm eàq; pretiosissima repræsentantibus. 2 *copperplates.* 4*to Argentorati*, *Sumpt. Authoris Filij*, *S. Paulli. Biblop.* 1665

1521 PAULUS APOSTOLUS. Sanctitvdo in vtero, extra, in Solo, in Cœlo; a Claud. Davsgvio. *Calf.* 8° *Parisiis*, 1627

1522 PAUW (M. de) Recherches Philosophiques sur les Americains. 2 *vols*, *half calf*, 8° *Berlin*, 1772

1523 PENN (William) Brief Account of the Rise and Progress of the People called Quakers. Ninth edition.

1524 PENNSYLVANIA. AN ACCOUNT OF THE GREAT DIVISIONS AMONGST THE QUAKERS IN PENNSYLVANIA, &c. as appears by their own Book printed in 1692, Intituled, *The Plea of the Innocents*, *&c.* being a Vindication of George Keith and his Friends from Calumnies of Samuel Jennings, John Simcock, Thomas Lloyd, and others, in number 28. Directed to faithful Friends in Pensilvania, East and West Jersey, and elsewhere [signed at end by George Keith, and Thomas Budd.] *Fine large clean copy, with rough leaves, in white vellum, by Pratt.* 4° *London*, 1692

1525 PENNSYLVANIA. Etat présent de Pensilvanie, ou l'on trouve le Détail de ce que s'y est passe depuis la défaite du Général Braddock jusqu' à la prise d'Oswego, avec una carte. VERY RARE; *map wanting.* 12° *n. p.* 1756

1526 PENNSYLVANIA. An Historical Review of the Constitution and Government of Pennsylvania from its Origin. *Calf.* 8° *London*, 1759

1527 PENNSYLVANIA. An Historical Review of the Constitution and Government of Pennsylvania [by Dr. Franklin.] *Calf, gilt.* 8° *London*, 1759

1528 PENNSYLVANIA STATE TRIALS: containing the Impeachment, Trial and Acquittal of Francis Hopkinson and John Nicholson, Esquires, the former, Judge of the Court of Admiralty, the latter Comptroller General of the Commonwealth of Pennsylvania. Vol. I. *All published.* 8° *Philadelphia*, 1794

1529 PENNSYLVANIA. Proceedings and Debates of the Convention of Pennsylvania, to propose Amendments to the Constitution, held at Harrisburg, May, 1837. 6 *vols.* 8° *Harrisburg*, 1837–8

1530 PENNSYLVANIA. Proceedings and Debates of the Convention held at Harrisburg, commencing May 2, 1837. Vols I, II, III. 3 *vols.* 8° *Harrisburg*, 1837–8

1531 PENNSYLVANIA. Minutes of the Provincial Council of Pennsylvania, vol. I, containing the Proceedings of the Council, from March 10, 1683, to Nov. 27, 1700. 8° *Harrisburg*, 1838

With the autograph of THADDEUS STEVENS on the fly-leaf.

1532 PENNSYLVANIAN FARMER. A New Essay on the Constitutional Power of Great Britain of the Colonies in America. *Half roan.* 8° *London*, 1774

1533 PENSADOR MEXICANO [*i. e.* José Joaquin Fernandez de Lisardi] El Periquillo Sarmiento por el Pensador Mexicano 5a Edicion, corregida, aumentada, ilustrada con notas y adornada con 60 laminas finas. 4 *vols in* 2, *half morocco.* 8° *Mexico*, 1845

The author of these volumes, Don J. J. F. de Lisardi, has been styled the Cervantes of Mexico by some, while Dr. Beristain in his *Biblioteca Hispano Americana Septentrional*, calls him the American Quevedo. He has written much, and on the whole ranks perhaps as the best Mexican writer. The present work is one illustrative of Mexican character, satirizing the faults of the people, but always true to liberal and republican principles. This copy has his portrait inserted. The 60 lithographs illustrating the work are spirited and amusing. Lisardi was born in Mexico in 1771, and during the period of the Revolution wrote very much, and chiefly as the *Pensador Mexicano.*

1534 PENSADOR MEXICANO. OBSERVACIONES que el Pensador Mexicano [Senor Lisardi] hace à las Censuras que los Señores Doctores D. Ignacio Maria Lerdo, y D. Ignacio Grageda, hicieron de sus Conversaciones sexta, vigessima, y vigisema secunda, entre el payo y el sacristan. Con arreglo á los decretos del señor Provisor, de 7 de junio de 1825. 87 *pp. close type.* 4° *Mexico*, 1825

1535 PENSION ROLLS. Letter from the Secretary of War transmitting a Report of the name, rank and line of every person placed on the Pension List, Jan. 20, 1820. *Boards, uncut. Scarce.* 8° *Washington*, 1820

1536 PENSIONERS. A Census of Pensioners for Revolutionary or Military Services; with their names, ages, and places of Residence. 4° *Washington*, 1841

1537 PEREGRINACION CHRISTIANA POR EL CAMINO REAL de la Celeste Jerusalem, Dividida en nueve Jornadas, con quatro Hospicios, que son unas Estaciones devotas al modo del Via-Crucis, y Guirnaldas a la Sagrada Passion de Christo, y Dolores de su Santissima Madre, *etc.* Dispuesto todo por Fr. JOACHIN OSSUNA, Religioso Descalzo de la Santa, y Seraphico Provincia de S. Diego de Mexico. *Vellum.*
8° *Mexico, en la Imprenta de Bibliotheca Mexicana*, 1756

A kind of Mexican Pilgrim's Progress, but quite a different work from Old John Bunyan's.

1538 PERKINS (N.) Discourse at Wethersfield, April 30th 1794, at the Ordination of the Rev. Calvin Chapin. 8° *Hartford*, 1794

1539 PERKINS (N.) Discourse in Newington, January 16th 1805, at the Ordination of the Rev. Jacob Brace. *Uncut.* 8° *Hartford,* 1807

1540 PERNETTY (*Dom.*) Dissertation sur l'Amerique et les Americains. *Calf.* 8° *Berlin, n. d.*

1541 PERNETTY (Dom.) Histoire d'un Voyage aux Isles Malouines, 1763–4. Nouv. Edit. 2 *vols, half calf.* 8° *Paris,* 1770

1542 PERRY (W.) The only sure guide to the English tongue. 4th Worcester Ed. *Tow cloth.* 12° *I. Thomas, Worcester,* 1789

1543 PERSIUS (A. F.) Satyrae Sex, a Frischlino fide Paraphrasa illustratæ; Variorum Commentariis explicatæ. *Calf.* 4° *Basileae,* 1582

1544 PERU, nach seinen gegenwaertigen Zustande, dargestellt aus dem Mercurio Peruano. 2 *vols, half roan.* 8° *Weimar,* 1807

1545 PETERS (Hugh) An Historical and Critical Account of Hugh Peters. After the manner of Mr. Bayle. *Half morocco, uncut.* 8° *London,* 1751

1546 PETRONIUS ARBITER, SATYRICON, super profligatis Neroneanæ tempestatis moribus; Commentariis Notis Indicibus, etc. noviter recensente J. P. Lotichio. *Calf.* *Thick* 4° *Francofurti,* 1629

1547 PHAVORINI (V.) Lexikon (Greek.) *Fine copy.* *Folio, Basil,* 1538

1548 PHELPS (N. A.) History of Simsbury, Granby and Canton, Conn. from 1642 to 1845. 8° *Hartford,* 1845

1549 PHILOPONUS (Honorius) NOVA TYPIS transacta navigatio. Novi Orbis India Occidentalis. 19 *copperplates. Fine copy, half russia.* *Folio, n. p.* 1621

This is one of the impudentest books known. The author's real name was Caspar Plautus, a monk at Lintz in Austria. In the most fulsome style, under his assumed name of Philoponus, he inscribes the work to himself in a long and highly complimentary Dedication. He accuses the DeBrys, in their great collection of Voyages, of telling outrageous lies, forgetting apparently his own whackers. One of the plates represents a ship stranded on the back of an enormous whale. The sailors could not get her off until the monks on board descended from the ship to balæna-firma and with full ceremony performed the grand mass, whereupon the monster descended gently and all were afloat again.

1550 PHILADELPHIA DIRECTORY for 1808. Containing the Names, Trades and Residence of the Inhabitants of the City, Southwark and Northern Liberties, also a Calendar from 1st Feb. 1808 to Feb. 1, 1809. By James Robinson. 8° *Phil.* [1808]

1551 PHILADELPHIA DIRECTORY for 1811, containing the names, trades & Residences of the Inhabitants of the City, Southwark, Northern Liberties and Kensington. By James Robinson. 8° *Phil.* [1811]

1552 PHOTOGRAPHS BY ROGER FENTON, TAKEN FOR AND AT THE EXPENSE OF THE TRUSTEES OF THE BRITISH MUSEUM, from the Antique Sculptures in that National Institution, published at 7*s.* 6*d.* each, and but a few copies taken off. *Large folio in portfolio.*

For some unaccountable reason the discerning public did not purchase these art treasures, and the negatives were destroyed. They are now very scarce. To artists and libraries they are of great value, especially in this country, where we, coming late in the annals of the world, are obliged to put up with copies. Among the collection are the following, some in duplicate, and some taken in several positions: Actæon, Aelius Cæsar, Antinous as Bacchus, Antoninus Pius, Aratus, Atys, Bacchante, Barbarian Captive, Caracalla, Cupid, Diogenes, Dione, Gordianus Africanus, Greek Hero, Hercules, Hermaphrodite, Heroic Head, Hippocrates, Homeric Hero, Jupiter, Laughing Child, Laughing Satyr, Lucius Verus, Muse, Nero, Periander, Portrait of a Roman Boy, Roman Patriot, Tiberius, Venus, *etc.*

1553 PHOTOGRAPHS BY ROGER FENTON, of English Architecture and Landscapes, large size, magnificent works of art, published in London, at 15*s.* each. Few copies taken off, and the negatives destroyed. *In large portfolios.*

Among them are the following:—

Bolton Abbey, Pool below the Strid.
Salmon Pool on the Ribble.
Mill at Hurst Green.
Salmon Pool on the Ribble.
Hardwick Hall from the Park.
Apsley House, Hyde Park.
Valley of the Ribble.
View of the Hodder, Stonyhurst.
The Keeper's Rest, Ribbleside.
Old Oak, Crix Park.
Pool in the Ribble.
Magdalen College, Oxford.
The Cherwel, Oxford.
Village of Foulder.
Raglan Castle.
Bolton Abbey, Waterfall.
Park, Crix Hall.
Buckingham Palace.
Hardwick New Hall.
Hardwick Old Hall.
Paradise on the Hodder.
Achilles to Wellington.
Hack Falls, Yorkshire.
Sale Wheels Ribble.

1554 PICARD (B.) CEREMONIES ET COUTUMES RELIGIEUSES de tous les Peuples du Monde, Representées par des Figures. Avec une Explication Historique et quelques Dissertations curieuses. 4 *vols, fine copy, calf.* *Folio, Amsterdam,* 1723

This book contains much about America, with reproductions of the rare plates from DeBry and others.

1555 PICKERING (John) Collections of Words and Phrases which have been supposed to be Peculiar to the United States of America. *Boards, uncut.* 8° *Boston,* 1816

1556 PICKERING (Timothy) Review of the Correspondence between the Hon. John Adams, and Wm. Cunningham Esq. 1805–12. Second Edition. *Uncut.* 8° *Salem,* 1824

1567 PIERCE (J.) Second Century Discourse at Dorchester 17th June 1830. 8° *Boston,* 1830

1558 PIERPONT (John) The Portrait; a Poem delivered before the Washington Benevolent Society of Newburyport, Oct. 27, 1812. 8° *Boston,* 1812

1559 PIGAFETTA (ANTONIO) PRIMO VIAGGIO intorno al Globo Terracqueo ossia Ragguaglio della Navigazione, alle Indie Orientali per la via d'Occidente, 1519–22. *Maps and plates, half green morocco.* LARGE PAPER; *fine uncut copy.* 4° *Milano,* 1800

This is the fullest account we have of the Voyage round the World of Magellan in 1519–1522.

1560 PIGAFETTA (ANTONIO) PRIMO VIAGGIO intorno al Globo Terracqueo ossia Ragguaglio della Navigazione alle Indie Orientali per la via d'Occidente. *Maps and plates, fine copy, boards.* 4° *Milano,* 1800

1561 PIKE (N.) New Complete System of Arithmetic. 12° *Worcester*, 1798

1562 PIKE (*Major* ZEBULON MONTGOMERY) Voyage au Nouveau-Mexique, a la suite d'une Expédition ordonnée par le Gouvernement des États-Unis, pour reconnoître les sources des Rivières Arkansas, Kansès, La Plate et Pierre-Jaune, dans l'intérieur de la Louisiane Occidentale. Précédé d'une Excursion aux Sources du Mississippi pendant les années 1805–1807. Traduit de l'Anglais par M. Breton. 2 *vols, fine copy, half morocco, uncut.* 8° *Paris*, 1812

This book, though a translation, should be in every public library in this country. M. Breton, the translator and editor, was a geographer and well up in his subject. He at once detected the innumerable errors in the Spanish and French names of persons and places, and set himself to correct them. Meanwhile Humboldt in the *Moniteur*, complimenting the work highly, as a whole, pointed out that his own map of New Mexico, a copy of which he had left with the Secretary of State at Washington in 1804, had been appropriated with many erroneous additions, the responsibility of which additions he disclaimed. This brought out the Philadelphia editor to explain that Pike's work passed through the press in the author's absence on duty.

1563 PIKE (*Major* Z. M.) Voyage au Nouveau-Mexique pour reconnoitre les Sources des Rivières Arkansas, Kansès, *etc.* 2 *vols, half roan.* 8° *Paris*, 1812

1564 PILGRIM'S Progress. By John Bunyan. With copious notes, &c. by J. Newton, Dr. Hawker, and others. *Wood-cuts, wanting the last leaf.* 12° *Boston, by Isaiah Thomas, Jun.* 1817

1565 PILGRIM'S PROGRESS (The) In Two Parts. By John Bunyan. With original notes by Thomas Scott. *Portrait and plates, calf.* 12° *Hartford, Silas Andrus*, 1829

1566 PILGRIM'S Progress, in 2 Parts. *Plates ; a beautiful edition, calf.* 16° *Phil. R. W. Pomeroy*, 1830

1567 PISCATOR (Johannes) Ad Conradi Vorstii Parasceven Responsio Apologetica; Ejusdem ad Vorstii amicam Collationem etc. Notæ, *in* 1 *vol. calf.* 4° *Herbornœ*, 1613

1568 PISO (GULIELMUS) HISTORIA NATURALIS BRASILIÆ, *etc.* De Medecina Brasiliensi Libri quatuor; Historiæ Rerum Naturalium Libri octo. *Numerous plates.* *Folio, Amstelodami, apud Elzevirium*, 1648

1569 PISO (Gulielmus) HISTORIÆ NATURALIS ET MEDICÆ INDIÆ OCCIDENTALIS, Libri quinque. *Numerous wood-cuts, calf.* *Folio, Amst.* 1658

1570 PISTORIUS (JOANNES) RERUM GERMANICARUM veteres jam primum Publicati Scriptores VI. *Folio, Francofvrti*, 1607 GERMANICORUM SCRIPTORUM qui Rerum a Germanis per mvltas Ætates, gestarvm Historias vel Annales Posteris relinqverunt, cum Indice locuplet. *Folio, calf. Together* 2 *vols, calf.* *Folio, Hanoviæ*, 1613

1571 PITKIN (Timothy) A Statistical View of the Commerce of the U. S. of America. *Half calf.* 8° *Hartford*, 1816

1572 PITKIN (Timothy) Statistical View of the Commerce of the United States of America (with Tables illustrative of the Work.) *Half red morocco.* 8° *Hartford*, 1816

1573 PITKIN (Timothy) Statistical View of the Commerce of the United States of America. 2d ed. *Half light blue morocco, uncut.* 8° *New York*, 1817

1574 PITKIN (TIMOTHY) View of the Commerce of the United States of America. 2d edition. *Half calf.* 8° *New York*, 1817

1575 PITMAN (R. B.) On the Practicability of joining the Atlantic and Pacific Oceans by a Ship Canal across the Isthmus of America. *Map, calf.* 8° *London*, 1825

1576 PLAN OF A PROPOSED UNION between Great Britain and the Colonies, produced by one of the Delegates from Pennsylvania. *Half morocco.* 8° [*London*, 1775]

1577 PLANTATIONS. An Abridgment of the Laws in Force and Use in H. M.'s Plantations, *viz:* Of Virginia, Maryland, New England, New York, Carolina, *etc. Calf.* 8° *London*, 1704

1578 PLANTATIONS. Two Letters of the Lord Bishop of London [Edm. Gibson]: The First to the Masters and Mistresses of Families in the English Plantations abroad, exhorting to promote instruction of their Negroes. The Second to the Missionaries, instructing the same. *Fine copy, half roan.* 4° *London*, 1727

1579 PLATO. OPERA OMNIA quæ extant, Graecé et Latiné, Marsilio Ficino Interprete. *Old calf.* *Folio, apud C. Marnium, Francofurti*, 1602

1580 PLATO. OPERA OMNIA quae extant, Marsilio Ficino interprete; Graecé et Latiné. Argumentis perpetuis, Commentariis et Indice locuplet. *Calf.* *Folio, Francofurti*, 1602

1581 PLAYFAIR (W.) Commercial and Political Atlas. *Illustrated with* 40 *copperplates, half morocco. Oblong* 4° *London*, 1787

1582 PLEASURES (The) of Imagination; a Poem by Dr. Akenside. To which is added the Art of Preserving Health, a Poem, by Dr. Armstrong. *Clean copy.* 12° *New York, Wayland & Davis*, 1795

1583 PLUMIER (P. C.) NOVA PLANTARUM AMERICANARUM GENERA. *Plates, half green morocco.* 4° *Parisiis*, 1703

1584 POINTIS (M. de) RELATION de ce qui s'est fait a la prise de Cartagene sçituée aux Indes Espagnoles. *Calf.* 1*st edition, scarce.* 16° *Bruxelles*, 1698

1585 POLARI (Constant) Herinneringen eener Reize naar Nieuw York in 1831 en 1832. *Half morocco, uncut.* 8° *Leiden*, 1833

1586 POLITIANUS (ANGLIUS) OPERA omnia; quibus accessit Historia de Conjuratione Pactiana in familiam Medicam. *Vellum.* *Folio, apud Nic. Episcopium, Basiliæ*, 1553

1587 POLITICAL REGISTER, or Proceedings in the Session of Congress, Nov. 3, 1794, to March 3, 1795. With Appendix by J. T. Callender. *Vol. I, uncut.* 8° *Phila.* 1795

1588 POLITICAL TRACTS. Letter of R. Goodloe Harper to his Constituents, 1801; Giles and Bayard's Speeches on the Repeal of the Judiciary Law, 1802; Speech of Josiah Quincy in 1812 on Maritime Protection; WEBSTER'S Address before the Washington Benevolent Society at Portsmouth, July 4, 1812; *scarce.* Perpetual War the Policy of Mr. Madison, by a New England Farmer, 1812; Mr. Madison's War, a Dispassionate Inquiry, by a New England Farmer, 1812; and several others, 8°.

1589 POLITICAL (The) Writings of Joel Barlow. New Edition. 12° *New York*, 1796

1590 POLYBIUS. Ex libris selecta de Legationibus et alia, nunc primum in lucem edita. Ex bibliotheca F. Vrsini. *Calf.* 4° *Ex Offic. Plantin, Antverpiæ*, 1582

1591 POMPONIUS MELA. Jvlivs Solinvs, Itinerarium Antonini Avg., Vibibvs Seqvester. P. Victor . . . . Dionysius Afer. *In 1 vol. calf gilt edges.* 8° *Aldus, Venet.* 1518

For another edition of Pomponius Mela, see under MELA, supra, No. 1272.

1592 POMPONIUS MELA. De Sitv Orbis Libri Tres. And Schottvs recens. 8° *Ex Officina Plant, Antverpiæ*, 1582

1593 POND (Enoch) The Mather Family. *Portrait, half roan.* 16° *Boston*, 1844

1594 PONTANUS (JOHANNES J.) RERUM ET URBIS Amstelodamensium Historia. *Maps and plates, vellum.* *Folio, Amsterodami*, 1611

FIRST EDITION of considerable rarity, and great importance to the geographer and to the historian of the East and West Indies. As a part of the history of Amsterdam Pontanus gives an account of all the early voyages to the North and elsewhere fitted out from that port, among others naming Henry Hudson.

1595 PONTANUS (Johan. J.) HISTORISCHE BESCHRYVINGHE der seer wyt beroemde Coop-Stadt Amsterdam. Ende nuert des Autheurs laetste Copije in Nederduyts overgheset, door Pet. Montanum. *Maps, and fine engravings, black letter, calf.* FIRST EDITION in Dutch. *Folio, Amsterdam*, 1614

1596 POOR RICHARD Revived; Or, Barber & Southwick's Almanack: for the year 1799. Calculated for the meridian of Albany. By Old Father Richard. 8° *Albany*, 1799

1597 POPE (Alex.) An Essay on Man: To which is added the Universal Prayer, Messiah, &c. 12° *Windsor, Vt, Farnsworth & Churchill*, 1810

1598 POPHAM (*Sir* Home) A Description of Prince of Wales' Island, in the Straights of Malaca. 8° *London*, 1805

1599 POPPLE (HENRY) A MAP OF THE BRITISH EMPIRE IN AMERICA, with the French and Spanish Settlements. Engraved by Wm. Henry Toms *on 20 sheets, bound in one volume, half red basil.* *Folio, London*, 1733

The largest and best map of America, at this date, 1733. This copy contains the rare Index map, on the 21st sheet. On the 1st sheet is a large view of the Falls of Niagara, nearly 20 years before Kalm's accurate description, claimed as the first. See No. 1339 of this Catalogue. On sheet iv are views of New York and Quebec. On plate 12 are charts on a large scale of the harbors of New York and Charleston, while on plate 8 is perhaps the earliest known complete survey of BOSTON HARBOR, with the Islands, ship channel, depth of the water, etc.

1600 PORCACCHI (THOMASO) L'ISOLE PIV FAMOSE del Mondo descritto da, et intagliate da Girolamo Porro. *With many copperplate maps, fine copy, vellum.*
First Edition. *Folio, Venetia,* 1576

1601 PORCACCHI (Th.) L'ISOLE PIV FAMOSE del Mondo descritto da, et intagliate da Girol. Porro. *Numerous maps, vellum,* *Folio, Venetia,* 1576

1602 PORCACCHI (Th.) L'ISOLE piu Famose del Mondo. *Numerous finely engraved maps and views by Gir. Porro.*
Vellum. *Folio, Venetia,* 1580

1603 PORCACCHI (Th.) L'Isole piv famose del Mondo, etc. *Folio, Venetia,* 1580

1604 PORCACCHI (Th.) L'Isole piv famose del Mondo, etc. *Splendid copy on* LARGE THICK PAPER, *measuring* 14 *by* 10 *inches, excessively rare in this state, vellum.*
Folio, Padova, 1620

1605 PORCACCHI (Tomaso) L'Isole piu famose del Mondo. *Maps not inserted in the text, but separate. A scarce edition; half green morocco.* 4° *Venetia,* 1686

1606 PORCUPINE (Peter, *i. e. Wm. Cobbet*) Works [comprising six tracts] 4th Edition. *Fine copy, calf.* 8° *Philad.* 1796

1607 PORCUPINE (Peter, *i. e. Wm. Cobbet*) The Rush-Light, 15th Feb.-Aug. 30, 1800. *Scarce, half calf.* 8° *W. Cobbet, New York* [1800]

This highly spiced and Cobbety publication comprising six numbers, begun in Philadelphia and finished in London, fills 309 pages, and is perhaps the most difficult of all Cobbet's many personal squibs to find complete. It grew out of a lawsuit with Dr. Benj. Rush "the noted bleeding Physician," of Philadelphia, in which Cobbet was mulcted $5,000 damages for slander. He took it out in spice.

1608 PORTER (ELIPHALET, *of Roxbury*) AN EULOGY ON GENERAL WASHINGTON, delivered Jan. 14, 1800, before the Inhabitants of the Town of Roxbury. *Fine clean copy, sized paper, white forrel by Pratt.* 8° *Manning & Loring, Boston,* 1800

1609 PORTER (Jacob) Topographical Description and Historical Sketch of Plainfield, in Hampshire County, Massachusetts, May 1834. (*Portrait of the Author inserted.*)
Uncut. 8° *Prince & Rogers, Greenfield,* 1834

THURSDAY AFTERNOON.

1614 PORTEUS (B.) A Letter to the Governors, Legislatures, in the British West India Islands. *Half mor.* 8° *London*, 1808

1615 PORTLOCK (NAT. EN GEO. DIXON) REIS naar de Noord-West Kust van Amerika in de jaren 1785–6, 7, 8. *Map and plates, half green morocco.* 4° *Amsterdam*, 1795

1616 PORTRAITS. Eighty-four small oval portraits of poets, historians, dramatists, statesmen, etc. by various engravers, published by Harrison & Co. of London, in 1794, and 1795, printed uniformly on octavo sheets, with brief biographies, printed underneath. *Loose in a cover.* 8° *London*, 1794–5

1617 PORTUGUESE INQUISITION. Authentic Memoirs concerning; with Remarks on the infamous Character given of the British Nation by a late Apologist for that horrid Tribunal. *Calf.* 8° *London*, 1769

1618 PORTUS (Simon) Dictionarum Latinum Græco-Barbarum et Litterale. 4° *Paris*, 1635

1619 POSTLETHWAYT (Malachy) Britain's Commercial Interest, Explained and Improved. 2 *vols, calf.* 8° *London*, 1757

1620 POSTILLE MAIORES IN EPISTOLAS & EUANGELIA: tam dominicaliũ feriatorumq; dierum: q; festoR sanctorumq; omniũ per totius anni decursum: vna cũ passione Jesu christi e qttuor euangelistis cõcinnata. In his oĩbus preclara plurimorũ doctorum enucleatio. *Very fine large clean copy, with rough leaves:* 364 *leaves.* 4° *Basiliæ*, 1514

If these well-known POSTILLS OF GUILLERMUS are growing a little out of date among theologians, this edition is becoming much sought for by lovers of ancient art in consequence of its being adorned with a beautiful title-page, one large cut, and 156 small wood-cuts, nearly all of them bearing the signature of the celebrated wood engraver URSE GRAFF. These small cuts, measuring about 1½ by 1⅝ inches, are very spirited, and clever. They represent chiefly the events in the life of our Saviour and his Apostles. Some few of the cuts are not signed and some of them are repeated, but on the whole, this book is a mine of beauty of design. Few artists of his day surpassed in fertility of genius Urse Graff. He sprang up on a sudden about ten years before Holbein.

1621 POTTER (C. E.) HISTORY OF MANCHESTER, N. H. formerly Derryfield, including that of ancient Amoskeag of the Middle Merrimack Valley; with the Proceedings of the Centennial Celebration Oct. 22, 1851. *Portraits and Engravings.* 8° *Manchester, N. H.* 1856

1622 POTTER (Israel R.) Life and Remarkable Adventures of, *Boards.* 16° *Providence*, 1824

1623 POWNALL (Thomas) The Administration of the Colonies. Third Edition, revised and enlarged. *Calf.* 8° *London*, 1766

1624 POWNALL (T.) The Administration of the Colonies (The Fourth Edition), wherein their Rights and Constitution are discussed and stated. *Calf.* 8° *London*, 1768

1625 Pownall (T.) The Administration of the British Colonies (4th Edition). *Calf.* 8° *London*, 1768

1626 Pownall (T.) The Administration of the Colonies. 4th Edition. *Half calf, gilt.* 8° *London*, 1768

1627 POWNALL (T.) The Administration of the British Colonies. Fifth Edition, wherein their Rights and Constitution are discussed and stated. 2 *vols, half morocco, uncut.* 8° *London*, 1784

Best Edition. The various editions of this excellent work are a good index of the progress of knowledge in England of the affairs of the Colonies. Gov. Pownall's experience in America, and his position after his return, enabled him to speak with authority.

1628 POWNALL (THOMAS) A TOPOGRAPHICAL DESCRIPTION of such Parts of North America as are contained in the (annexed) Map of the Middle British Colonies, etc. in North America. *Fine copy on* LARGE PAPER, 17 *by* $10\frac{3}{4}$ *inches, with the map colored.* VERY RARE IN THIS STATE. *Half calf.* *Folio, London*, 1776

1629 POYNTZ (JOHN) THE PRESENT PROSPECT of the Famous and Fertile Island of Tobago; with a Description of its Situation, Growth, Fertility, *etc.* Second Edition. *Half roan.* 4° *London*, 1695

1630 PRADT (M. de) Les trois derniers mois de l'Amerique Meridionale et du Bresil. *Half morocco, uncut.* 8° *Paris*, 1817

1631 PRADT (*M. L'Abbé* de) Lettres a M. L'Abbé de Pradt par un Indigène de L'Amerique du Sud. *Half blue morocco, uncut.* 8° *Paris*, 1818

1632 PRATT (*Rev.* E.) History of Eastham, Wellfleet and Orleans, County of Barnstable, Mass. from 1644 to 1844. *Cloth.* 8° *Yarmouth*, 1844

1633 PRATT (Phinehas) A Declaration of the Affairs of the English People that first inhabited New England. Edited with notes by Richard Frothingham, Jr. 8° *Boston*, 1858

100 copies printed for private distribution. Pratt arrived in New England in May 1622, and died at Charlestown, 19 April, 1680.

1634 PREACHER. The American Preacher; Or a Collection of Sermons from some of the most eminent Preachers now living in the United States of different denominations. Vols III and IV. *Sheep.* 8° *New Haven, by Abel Morse*, 1793

1635 PRENTISS (S. W.) Narrative of a Shipwreck on the Island of Cape Breton, in a Voyage from Quebec 1780. Fourth Edition. *Calf.* 12° *London*, 1783

1636 Prescott (James) Report of his Trial by Impeachment. *Boards, uncut.* 8° *Boston,* 1821

1637 Present (The) State of Great Britain and North America. *Half calf.* 8° *London,* 1767

1638 President's Messages, 1812. 8° *Washington,* 1812

1639 Price (Richard) Essays. 5 *vols in* 1, *calf.* 8° *London,* 1773–80 *viz:*

Preface to the Third Edition of a Treatise on Reversionary Payments. 1773
Price (R.) Observations on Civil Liberty. 6th Edition. 1776
Price (R.) Additional Observations. 2d Edition. 1777
Eden. Four Letters to the Earl of Carlisle. 1779
Price (R.) Essay on Population. 2d Edition. 1780

1640 Price (R.) Observations on the Nature of Civil Liberty, the Principles of Government, and the Justice and Policy of the War with America. *Half morocco.* 8° *London,* 1776

1641 Price (R.) Another copy. *Half mor.* 8° *London,* 1776

1642 Price (R.) Observations on the Nature of Civil Liberty. 3d Edition. *Half roan.* 8° *London,* 1776

1643 Price (R.) Additional Observations on the Nature of Civil Liberty and the War with America. 2d Edition. *Half morocco.* 8° *London,* 1777

1644 Price (R.) Three Letters to Dr. Price, containing Remarks on his Observations on the Nature of Civil Liberty, the Justice and Policy of the War with America, *etc.* *Half morocco.* 8° *London,* 1776

1645 Price (R.) Remarks on a Pamphlet lately published by Dr. Price, entitled Observations, *etc.* *Half roan.* 8° *London,* 1776

1646 Price (R.) Remarks on Dr. Price's Observations on the Nature of Liberty, *etc.* *Half roan.* 8° *London,* 1776

1647 Price (R.) Additional Observations on the Nature and Value of Civil Liberty and the War with America, *etc.* Second Edition. *Half morocco.* 8° *London,* 1777

1648 Price (R.) Observations on the Importance of the American Revolution, and the Means of making it a Benefit to the World. *Half calf.* 8° *Reprinted, Boston,* 1784

1649 Price (R.) Two Tracts on Civil Liberty; The War with America and the Debts and Finances of the Kingdom. *Calf.* 8° *London,* 1788

1650 Price (R.) Sermon at Hackney 10th Feb. 1779, on the General Fast. 3d Edition. *Half roan.* 8° *London,* 1779

1651 Prideaux (J.) Lectiones decem de totidem Religionis Capitibus, praecipue hoc tempore Controversis prout publice habebantur Oxoniæ in Vesperijs. *Half bound.* 4° *Oxoniæ,* 1626

1652 Prideaux (J.) Lectiones. *Another, Vellum.* 4° *Oxoniæ,* 1626

1653 Prideaux (J.) Viginti-duae Lectiones, Oxoniae in Vesperiis quibus accessurint Tredecim Orationes Inaugurales; Subnectuntur Lex Conciones pro More habitae, *etc.* *Calf.* *Folio, Oxoniæ,* 1648

1654 PRIESTLEY (Joseph) A General History of the Christian Church. 2 *vols, half green morocco.* 8° *Northumberland, Pa.* 1803–4

1655 PRIOR (M.) MISCELLANEOUS WORKS. *Portrait,* 2 *vols, calf.* 8° *London,* 1760

1656 PROCLUS. IN PLATONIS TIMÆON, COMMENTATIORUM, Libri quinque, Graecé. *Very fine copy, calf.* *Folio, Froben, Basiliæ,* 1534

1657 PROCEEDINGS OF A BOARD OF GENERAL OFFICERS. Held by Order of His Excellency Gen. Washington, Commander-in-Chief of the Army of the United States of America, respecting MAJOR JOHN ANDRÉ, Adjutant General of the British Army, September 29, 1780. To which are appended, The Several Letters which passed to and from New York on the Occasion. Published by Order of Congress. *Fine copy, perfectly uncut.* 8° *Providence : Printed and sold by John Carter* [1780]

1658 PROPOSAL (A) for humbling Spain. Written in 1711 [relating to the West Indies.] *Half roan.* 8° *London,* [1739]

1659 PROSPECT (The) before us. Vol. I. "But, Sir! it has an awful Squinting! It squints at Monarchy." *Uncut.* 8° *Richmond, Virginia,* 1800

1660 PROUD (ROBERT) HISTORY OF PENNSYLVANIA, in North America, from its original Settlement under William Penn in 1681, till after the Year 1742. *Portrait and maps.* 2 *vols, half calf.* 8° *Philadelphia,* 1797

1661 PSALTERIUM, HEBRÆUM, GRÆCUM, ARABICUM, & CHALDÆUM cu tribus latinis interpretationibus & glossis. [*At end*] *Impressit miro ingenio, Petrus Paulus Porrus, genuæ in ædibus Nicolai Iustiniani Pauli, anno* 1516 *mense VIIIIbri. Very fine large clean copy. Vellum.* *Folio, Genoa,* 1516

JAMES THE ANTIQUARY of Milan, in April 1506, suggested to the Dominican monk Giustiniani of Genoa, then 36 years of age, to occupy his leisure (otium cum negotio) in collecting, collating, and publishing in one volume the Psalms of David, in Hebrew, Greek, Arabic, and Chaldean, together with three of the best Latin versions extant, and with comments of his own. Ten years were devoted to this great work, and the present volume, the first Polyglot of the Psalms, was the result. It is inscribed to Leo X by Giustiniani from Genoa in August 1516. In the notes there are several historical and geographical references to contemporary events of considerable interest, such as that to Ps. 29, v. 6, where he interprets the *unicorn* to be a *rhinoceros,* and says that he had seen a picture of one lately brought to the King of Portugal from India. But the most interesting of all the notes is the very long one on the 4th verse of the xix Psalm, wherein Giustiniani gives an account of the life and voyages of his fellow-townsman Columbus. There are several points in this notice which we do not find elsewhere printed so early, especially respecting the second voyage, and the Survey of the south side of Cuba, as far as Evangelista in May and June, 1494. Almost all other accounts of the Second Voyage, except that of Bernaldez, end before this Cuba exploring expedition. Ferdinand Columbus accuses Giustiniani of telling fourteen lies in this paper, but they are small ones.

1662 PSALMES. THE WHOLE BOOKE OF PSALMES. Collected into English meter by Thomas Sternhold, John Hopkins and others, conferred with the Hebrue, with apt Notes to sing them withall. *Black Letter, polished calf, extra, by W. Pratt.* *Folio, Printed by the assignes of Richard Day, London,* 1585

A beautiful edition of excessive rarity, not more than three or four copies being known.

1663 PSALMS. A New Version, fitted to the Tunes used in Churches with Hymns collected chiefly from Dr. Watts. By Brady and Tate. 12° *Boston, by S. Hall.* 1791

1664 PSALMS. A New Version, by Brady & Tate, First Worcester Edition. *Good copy.* 12° *Worcester, Mass. by Isaiah Thomas,* 1788

1665 PSALMS. A New Version of the Psalms of David, *etc.* By N. Brady and N. Tate. First Worcester Edition. With Hymns. 12° *Worcester, Mass. by Isaiah Thomas,* 1788

1666 PSALMS. A New Version of the Psalms of David fitted to the Tunes used in Churches. By N. Brady and N. Tate. *Fine copy. Scarce.* 12° *Boston, by John Perkins,* 1773

1667 PSALMS. A new version by Tate & Brady. With a Collection of Hymns from Dr. Watts (*wants title and next leaf.*) *A very rare edition.* 12° *Boston, McAlpine & Fleming,* 1765

1668 PSALMS. A new version of the Psalms of David. Fitted to the Tunes in Churches. By N. Brady and N. Tate. [With Appendix containing a number of Hymns taken chiefly from Dr. Watts.] *Old calf.* VERY RARE. 8° *Boston, by Edes & Gill,* 1755.

1669 PSALMS of David Imitated *etc.* by Isaac Watts, corrected and accommodated to the use of the Church of Christ in America, with Hymns and Spiritual Songs. 2 *volumes in* 1. *Very fine clean copy.* 16° *Newburyport, by John Mycall, n. d.* [1795 ?]

1670 PSALMS (The) of David Imitated in the Language of the New Testament. By Isaac Watts. Hymns and Spiritual Songs. In three books. By Isaac Watts. 2 *vols in* 1. *Fine clean copy; scarce.* 16° *Walpole, by Isaiah Thomas & Co. J. G. Watts, printer,* 1812

1671 PSALMS. Sacred Poetry: Consisting of Psalms and Hymns adapted to Christian Devotion, in public and private, selected from the best authors, with variations and additions. By Jeremy Belknap, D. D. A new edition, with additional Hymns. 12° *Boston, by Th. Wells,* 1820

1672 PSALMS OF DAVID IMITATED BY DR. WATTS. New edition, in which the Psalms omitted by Dr. Watts are versified, local passages are altered, and a number of Psalms are versified anew, in proper metres. By Timothy Dwight, *D. D.* President of Yale College. At the request of the General Association of Connecticut. To the Psalms is added a selection of Hymns. *Fine copy, sheep.* 16° *Hudson & Goodwin, Hartford,* 1801

On the principle embodied in the advice of the old Translators, to be ever watchful to keep our candlesticks polished, the General Association of Connecticut, after the American Revolution, in burnishing up their Psalmody among other works, discovered on it many specks and defects. Accordingly, in June, 1795, Dr. Dwight was requested to revise, improve, complete and adapt Dr. Watts' Psalms, and add thereto a collection of Hymns, from Watts, Doddridge, and others. In 1798, the General Assembly of the Presbyterian Church of the United States initiated steps to accomplish the same object; but subsequently learning what was in progress in Connecticut, postponed the matter. Dr. Dwight having completed his great work by the middle of 1799, it was referred to a Joint Committee appointed by both the Association and the General Assembly to examine and report upon. This Joint Committee met at Stamford, in Connecticut, 10th of June, 1800, and approved and recommended this new version for the use of the Churches in the United States.

1673 PSALMS. By Dr. Watts. New edition by Dr. Dwight. With Hymns. 16° *Hartford, by Hudson & Goodwin*, 1803

1674 PSALMS. By Dr. Watts. New edition by Dr. Dwight. With Hymns. 16° *Hartford, Hudson & Goodwin*, 1808

1675 PSALMS. By Dr. Watts. New edition by Dr. Dwight. With Hymns. *Fine copy, sheep.* 16° *Hartford, Hudson & Goodwin*, 1811

1676 PSALMS. By Dr. Watts. New edition, by Dr. Dwight. With Hymns. 16° *Hartford, Hudson & Goodwin*, 1814

1677 PSALMS. By Dr. Watts. New edition, by Dr. Dwight. With Hymns. 24° *New York, McDermot & Arden*, 1816

1678 PSALMS. By Dr. Watts. New edition, by Dr. Dwight. 24° *Hartford*, 1817

1679 PSALMS. By Dr. Watts. New edition, by Dwight. 24° *Hartford, by Silas Andrus*. 1817

1680 PSALMS. By Dr. Watts. New edition, altered, *etc.* by Timothy Dwight. 24° *New York*, 1822

1681 PSALMS. By Dr. Watts. New edition, by Dr. Dwight. With Hymns, etc. 24° *New Haven*, 1827

1682 PUBLIC LANDS. Laws of the United States and the Documents respecting the Public Lands. 8° *Washington*, 1828

1683 PUBLIC LANDS. Laws, Instructions, and Opinions. 2 *vols.* 8° *Washington*, 1838

1684 PUEBLA (*Mexico*) CONSTITUCION POLITICA del Estado libre y soberano de Puebla, sancionada por su Congreso Constituyente en 7 de Diciembre de 1825. Con las reformas que le dió la Ley de 1° de Junio de 1831. 46 *pp.* 16° *Puebla*, 1848

In the same volume are the following scarce *books, viz:*

ARANCEL de los honorarios y derechos judiciales que se han de cobrar en el departamento de Puebla por los Secretarios y empleados de su Tribunal superior, Jueces de primera instancia, Alcaldes, Jueces de Paz, Escribanos, etc. Mandado observar por la Suprema Corte de Justicia de la Republica Megicana, conforme a lo prevenido, en el Articulo 55 de la ley de 23 de Mayo de 1837. 40 *pp.* 16° *Puebla*, 1841

NOTICIA del editor sobre el establecimiento del oficio de escribano, *etc.* pp. 15–34.

ELEMENTS of the English and Spanish Grammar, with a Vocabulary of the words most used in both languages. 80 *pp.* 16° *Puebla, by John Valle*, 1848

1685 PUFFENDORF (S.) Introduction to the History of the Principal States of Europe. *Portrait, calf.* 8° *London*, 1700

1686 PULLEIN (*Rev.* Samuel) The Culture of Silk, or an Essay on its rational Practice and improvement. In four parts. *Calf, gilt.* 8° *London*, 1758

1687 PULTENEY (Richard) Historical and Biographical Sketches of the Progress of Botany in England from its origin to the Introduction of the Linnæan System. 2 *vols, calf.* 8° *London*, 1790

This copy is from the library of James Kennedy, who has added many manuscript notes, giving bibliographical and biographical notices of many of the botanists, considerably enhancing the value of this particular copy.

1688 PULTENEY (William) Thoughts on the Present State of Affairs with America, and the Means of Conciliation. *Half morocco.* 8° *London*, 1778

1689 PULTENEY (W.) Thoughts on the Present State of Affairs with America, and the Means of Conciliation. 3*d edition, half morocco.* 8° *London*, 1778

1690 PULTENEY (W.) Thoughts on the Present State of Affairs with America. 4*th edition, half roan.* 8° *Dodsley, London*, 1778

1691 PULTENEY (W.) Thoughts on the Present State of Affairs with America. 4*th edition, half roan.* 8° *London*, 1778

1692 QUAKERS. Newe Schwarmgeister-Bruit, oder Historische Erzhlung. I. Von den Quakern. II. Der Ranter. III. Dess Robins Sect. IV. Der Wieder einnehmung der Juden in Engeland. V. DER INDIANER IN NEW-ENGELAND. *Half crimson morocco.* 12° *in Jahr*, 1661

1693 QUAKERS. A Collection of Memorials concerning . . Quakers in Pennsylvania, New Jersey, *etc.* 1787. *Calf.* 8° *Lond.* 1798

1694 QUARITCH (Bernard) A General Catalogue of Books, arranged in Classes. *Half red mor.* 8° *Lond.* 1868

No public library, or well-posted collector, should be without this portly catalogue, the best one of the kind issued during the present decade.

1695 QUINCE DIAS EN LONDRES, o sea corto viage de un Frances a Inglaterra a fines de 1815. Traducido al Castellano. *Calf.* [*As good as a play.*] 12° *Mexico*, 1826

Chapter XIV. El muséo británico. Other chapters are headed: El café, el domingo, la taberna, *los jerifes*, goddam, los periodicos, caricaturas, la Torre de Londres, el suicido, etc.

1696 QUINCTILIANUS. De Institutione Oratoria. Emend. atque Lectiones varant. adjecit E. Gibson. *Calf.* 4° *Oxoniæ*, 1693

1697 QUINCY (Josiah) Observations on the Boston Port Bill. *Half roan.* 8° *Lond.* 1774

1698 QUINCY (J.) Address to the Board of Aldermen, City of Boston, Jan. 3, 1829, on taking final Leave of the Office of Mayor. *Uncut.* 8° *Boston*, 1829

1699 QUINCY (J.) Centennial Address to the Citizens of Boston, Sept. 17, 1830. *Uncut.* 8° *Boston*, 1830

1700 RALEIGH (*Sir* Walter) Judicious and Select Essays and Observations. Upon the first Invention of Shipping, The Misery of Invasive Warre, The Navy Royal and Sea-Service. With his Apologie for his Voyage to Guiana. *Portrait by Vaughan, fine copy.* 16° *Lond. for Humphrey Moseley,* 1650

1701 RALEIGH (*Sir* Walter) The Prerogative of Parliaments in England, [also, Maxims of State — Instructions to his Son and to Posteritie, corrected and enlarged — A dutiful Advice of a loving Son to his Father — The Skeptic — On the Opulence of Cities — On the Seat of Government — Letters on his VOYAGE TO GUIANA — Poems — Dying Speech.] *Portrait by Vaughan.* 16° *Lond. W. Sheares,* 1661

1702 RALEIGH (*Sir* Walter) Judicious and Select Essayes and Observations, etc. with his Apologie for his Voyage to Guiana. *Portrait by Vaughan, fine impression, calf, very fine copy.* 12° *London, for A. M.* 1667

1703 RALEIGH (Sir W.) Remains. *Portrait, calf.* 16° *Lond.* 1675

1704 RALEIGH (Sir Walter) An Abridgement of . . History of the World, by Philip Raleigh, his Grandson. *Calf.* 8° *London,* 1700

1705 RALEIGH (Sir W.) Remains; with the Addition of some Letters never Printed before. *Portrait, calf.* *Small* 8° *London,* 1702

1706 RALEIGH (Sir W.) Remains . . . With the addition of some Letters never before Printed. *Fine copy, calf.* 12° *Lond.* 1702

1707 RALEIGH (SIR WALTER) Works . . . together with Letters, Poems, and Life. By Thos. Birch. *Portrait, 2 vols, calf, fine copy.* 8° *Lond.* 1751

1708 RAMIREZ (*D.* Jose Fernando) Proceso de Residencia contra Pedro de Alvarado. Ilustrado con estampas sacadas de los antiguos codices Mexicanos, y Notas y Noticias biograficas, criticas y arquelogicas. Lo publica paleografiado del MS. original el Lic. Ignacio L. Rayon. *Portrait of Alvarado, and plates of Mexican picture writings, colored, half calf.* 8° *Mexico,* 1847

Pedro de Alvarado was Cortes' right-hand man, not only in the conquest of Mexico, but in his subsequent career, as explorer and governor of provinces. Hence, this book supplying original, authentic material of history, is of importance.

1709 RAMSAY (DAVID) HISTORY OF THE REVOLUTION OF SOUTH CAROLINA, from a British Province to an Independent State. 2 *vols, calf.* 8° *Trenton,* 1785

1710 RAMSAY (David) History of the Revolution of South Carolina. 2 *vols, fine copy, sheep.* 8° *Trenton,* 1785

1711 RAMSAY (David) The History of the American Revolution. 2 *vols, half calf gilt, very fine copy.* 8° *Philad.* 1789

1712 Ramsay (David) Geschiedenis van de Noord Amerikaansche Staats-Omwenteling. *4 vols, half green morocco, fine uncut copy.* 8° *Campen.* 1792–94

1713 Ramsay (David) Geschiedenis van de Noord Amerikaansche Staats-Omwenteling. *2 vols, half brown morocco, uncut.* 8° *Campen.* 1792

1714 Ramsay (D.) History of the American Revolution. *2 vols, marbled calf.* 8° *London,* 1793

1714* Ramsay (D.) Another. *2 vols, calf.* 8° *Lond.* 1793

1715 Ramsay (David) The History of the American Revolution. New Edition. *2 vols, fine copy, half brown levant morocco, uncut.* 8° *Lond.* 1793

1716 Ramsay (David) The Life of George Washington. *Calf.* 8° *Lond.* 1807

1717 Ramsay (James) An Essay on the Treatment and Conversion of African Slaves, in the British Sugar Colonies. *Russia.* 8° *London,* 1784

1718 Ramsay (James) An Essay on the Treatment and Conversion of African Slaves in the British Sugar Colonies. *Calf.* 12° *Dublin,* 1784

1719 Raumer (F. von) De Vereenigde Staten van Noord-Amerika. *2 vols, half maroon morocco, uncut.* 8° *Deventer,* 1849

1720 Rawlinson (R.) The Deed of Trust and Will, containing his Benefactions to the University of Oxford. 8° *London,* 1755

1721 Raymond (R. W.) Mineral Resources of the States and Territories west of the Rocky Mountains. *Cloth.* 8° *Washington,* 1869

1722 RAYNAL (*Abbé* Guilaume Thomas) A Philosophical History of the British Settlements in North America. *2 vols, calf.* 12° *Edinb.* 1776

1723 Raynal (*Abbé* G. T.) History of the British Settlements and Trade in North America. *Map. 2 vols in 1, half calf.* 12° *Edinb.* 1776

1724 Raynal (*Abbé* G. T.) Révolution de l'Amérique. *Fine portrait of the author, half morocco.* 8° *Londres,* 1781

1725 Raynal (*Abbé* G. T.) Révolution de l'Amerique. *Calf.* 8° *Lond.* 1781

1726 Raynal (*Abbé* G. T.) The Revolution of Amerika; a New Translation. *Half roan.* 12° *Lond.* 1781

1727 Raynal (*Abbé* G. T.) The Revolution of America. 8° *Lond.* 1781

Josephus (F.) A Short Abridgement of the History of. *2 vols in 1, calf.* 8° *Lond.* 1806

1728 Raynal (Abbé G. T.) Staatsomwenteling van America. *Half red morocco, uncut.* 8° *Amst.* 1781

1729 Raynal (Abbé G. T.) Staatsomwenteling van Amerika. *Half morocco, uncut.* 8° *Amst.* 1781

1730 Raynal (*Abbé* G. T.) The Revolution of America. *Half calf.* 12° *Edinb.* 1782

1731 RAYNAL (Abbé G. T.) HISTOIRE PHILOSOPHIQUE ET POLITIQUE des Etablissemens et du Commerce des Europeens dans les deux Indes. *Portrait and plates.* 10 *vols, calf.* 8° *Geneve,* 1780

1732 RAYNAL (Abbé G. T.) History of the Settlements and Trade of the Europeans in the East and West Indies. *Portrait.* 6 *vols, calf.* 12° *Edinburgh,* 1782

1733 READ (*Gen.* J. Meredith) Historical Inquiry concerning Henry Hudson, his Friends, Relatives, and early Life; his Connection with the Muscovy Company, and Discovery of Delaware Bay. *Uncut.* 8° *Munsell, Albany,* 1866

1734 READY. Federal Ready Reckoner. 12° *Worcester,* 1795

1735 REAL COMPANIA GUIPUZCOANA DE CARACAS: Noticias Historiales Practicas de los sucessos, y adelantimientos de esta Compañia, desde su fundacion año de 1728, hasta el de 1764, por todos los Ramos, que comprehende su Negociacion. Unense en este libro los Anteriores impressos, que andaban divididos, como Piezas instructivas, y defensivas de la Compañia, *etc.* Dispuesto todo por la Direccion de la misma Real Compañia Año de 1765. 183 *pp. fine copy, vellum,* 4°

1736 RECOLLECTIONS of Samuel Rogers. Second Edition. *Cloth.* 12° *London,* 1859

1737 RECUEIL DE VOYAGES AU NORD, contenant divers Mémoires très utiles au Commerce et à la Navigation. Nouvelle Edition, corregée et mise en meilleur ordre. 10 *vols, fine copy, half blue morocco, yellow edges, maps and plates.* 8° *Amsterdam, J. F. Bernard,* 1731–1738

THE BEST AND RAREST EDITION of this important Collection of Voyages to the North. To the first volume is prefixed an historical Introduction by J. F. Bernard, of 186 pages, in which is traced in a masterly manner, the progress of Geography, with a chronological account of voyages, from Columbus to the early part of the 18th century. This Introduction is not in the earlier editions.

1738 REEVES (John) History of the Government of the Island of Newfoundland. *Half blue morocco, uncut.* 8° *Lond.* 1793

1739 REFLEXIONES SOBRE EL BANDO de 25 de Junio ultimo contraidas a lo que dispone para con los Eclesiasticos Rebeldes, y al recurso que en solicitud de su revocacion dirigieron, en 6 de Julio á este Illmo. Cabildo, varios clérigos y cinco religiosos de Mexico. Escribialas D. PEDRO DE LA PUENTE, Oidor de esta Audiencia y Superintendente de Policia. 243 *pp. with* 4 *prelim. and* 2 *sequent leaves, fine copy, calf.* 4° *Mexico,* 1812

A Book of the highest interest for the modern history of Mexico. By the celebrated BANDO, of the 25th June, 1812, the clergy who joined the Rebellion were ordered to be punished like other chiefs of the Army of Independence. On the 6th of July following the insurgent clergy claim their old immunity. It is the object of this book to combat that claim. All history, sacred and profane, is ransacked for precedents. Every rebellion, from that successful one of Lucifer down, is laid under contribution for authorities and examples. The Bible, the councils, the fathers, the doctors, and the bishops, in tremendous bibliographical array, are quoted and referred to. As a bibliography of the subject alone the volume is of considerable value.

1740 REGLAMENTO para el Ejercicio y Maniobras de la Infanteria. 12° *Mexico,* 1840

1741 REGULATIONS lately Made concerning the Colonies, and the Taxes Imposed upon them, considered. *Half morocco.* 8° *London,* 1765

1742 RELATION DE CE QVI S'EST PASSÉ EN LA NOVVELLE FRANCE de plvs Remarquable aux Missions de la Compagnie de Jesus ès annés 1656 et 1657 (*pp.* 21–33 *in MS.*) SCARCE. 8° *Paris, Seb. Cramoisy & Gabriel Cramoisy,* 1658

This RELATION comprises Letters of P. PAUL LE JEUNE, P. LE MERCIER, and P. PAUL RAGUENEAU. See No. 1120, *supra.*

1743 RELATION d'un Voyage du Pole Arctique au Pole Antarctique par le Centre du Monde. Avec la Description de ce perilleux Passage, et des choses marveilleuses et étonnantes qu'on a découvertes sous le Pole Antarctique. Avec Figures. *Fine copy, calf.* 8° *Paris,* 1723

1744 RELATION abrégée d'un Voyage fait dans l'interieur de l'Amérique Meridionale. Depuis la Côte de la Mer du Sud, jusqu' aux Côtes du Brésil et de la Guiane, en descendant la Riviere des Amazones. Par M. de la Condamine. *Map.* 8° *Paris,* 1745. Lettre a Madame . . . . sur l'emeute populaire excitée en la Ville de Cuença au Perou le 29 d'Août, 1739. 2 *vols in* 1, *calf.* 8° [*Paris*] 1746

1745 RELATION du Voyage de la Mer du Sud aux Cotes du Chili, du Perou et du Bresil 1712–14. Par M. de Fresier. *Maps and plates.* 2 *vols in* 1, *vellum, fine copy.* 8° *Amst.* 1717

1746 RELIGIOUS Courtship. 12° *Montpelier, Vt.* 1810

1747 REMARKS on the Review of the Controversy between G[t] Britain and her Colonies. *Half roan.* 8° *Lond.* 1769

1748 REMARKS on the Rescript of the Court of Madrid, and on the Manifesto of the Court of Versailles; with Appendix containing the Rescript, the Manifesto, and a Memorial of Dr. Franklin to the Court of Versailles. *Half morocco.* 8° *Lond.* 1779

1749 RENGGER et Longchamp. Essai Historique sur la Révolution du Paraguay. *Half brown morocco, uncut.* 8° *Paris,* 1827

1750 REPORT on Indian Affairs, comprising Narrative of a Tour in the Summer of 1820. By Rev. J. Morse. 8° *New Haven,* 1822

1751 REPUBLIC of the United States; embracing also a Review of the late War between the United States and Mexico. *Cloth.* 12° *New York,* 1848

1752 RERUM GERMANICARUM, Cum Indicibus copiosissimis Omnia recensuit et edidit H. Mebomius, 3 *vols in* 2. *Portrait, vellum.* *Folio, Helmæstadii,* 1688

A book of great historical value, now become scarce.

1753 RESOLUTIONS (The) of the House of Commons on the great and Constitutional Questions between the Privileges of the House of Commons and the Prerogative of the Crown, 1783–84. *Half roan.* 8° *London,* 1784

1754 REVIEW (A) of the Military Operations in North-America from the Commencement of the French Hostilities on the Frontiers of Virginia in 1753 to the Surrender of Oswego, on the 14th of August, 1756. Interspersed with various Observations, &c. on the American Transactions in general, and more especially on the Political Management of Affairs in New York. [By Wm. Livingston of New Jersey & Wm. Smith of New York.] *Fine large clean copy.* 4° *J. Dodsley, London,* 1757

1755 Revolution de l'Amerique. Par l'Abbé Raynal. *Calf, gilt.* 8° *London,* 1781

1756 Revolution de l'Amerique. Par l'Abbé Raynal. *Half brown morocco, uncut.* 8° *London,* 1781

1757 Rhoads (Asa) New Instructor, or American Spelling-Book. *Boards.* 12° *Stanford,* 1804

1758 Rich (Jeremiah) Rich Redivivus, Or Short Hand Improved. In a More Briefe and Easie Method than hath been set forth. Now made publique by Nathaniel Stringer, a quondam Scholar. *Portrait, fine copy, engraved throughout.* 8° *London,* [1686 ?]

1759 Rich (J.) The Pen's Dexterity, or the Ingenious and useful Art of writing Short-Hand, containing Twenty Copperplates. 16° *Leeds,* 1792

1760 Richardson (John) Account of his Life, and Services in the Work of the Ministry in England, Ireland, America, *etc. Calf.* 8° *London,* 1757

Treats chiefly of his first and second visits to America.

1761 Richardson (John) An Account of the Life of that Ancient servant of Jesus Christ, John Richardson, his trials and services in England, Ireland and America. 3d Edition. *Calf.* 8° *London,* 1774

Richardson sailed from London for Maryland in 1700, and spent two or three years in travelling through Virginia, Carolina, Pennsylvania, New Jersey, New York, New England, etc.

1762 Richardson (W. H.) The New Hampshire Town Officer. 12° *Concord,* 1829

1763 Ridgely (David) Annals of Annapolis, from its first Settlement in 1649 until the War of 1812: with various Incidents in the History of Maryland. *Cloth.* 12° *Baltimore,* 1841

1764 Ridgely (David) Annals of Annapolis. *Another copy. Cloth.* 12° *Baltimore,* 1841

1765 Rights (The) of the British Colonies asserted and proved. 3d edition corrected. *Half roan. Scarce.* 8° *London,* 1766

1766 Rights (The) of Great Britain asserted against the Claims of America. Being an Answer to the Declaration of the General Congress. 3d Edition, with additions. *Half roan.* 8° *London,* 1776

1767 Rios (Epitacio de los) Compendio de la Historia de Mexico desde antes de la Conquista hasta los tiempos presentes.

Adornada con 16 estampas lithográficos que representan los hechos mas interesantes de la historia. Publicala Simon Blanquel. *Half calf.* 12° *Mexico,* 1852

In the Appendix is a convenient list of all the Viceroys and Governors of Mexico from the Conquest by Cortes in 1520 to 1812.

1768 Rippon (John) A Selection of Hymns from the best authors intended to be an appendix to Watts' Psalms and Hymns. *Good copy.*
Scarce. 16° *Elizabethtown, N. J. by Shepard Kollock,* 1792

1769 Rippon (John, *D. D.*) A Selection of Hymns from the best authors, intended to be an appendix to Dr. Watts' Psalms and Hymns. *Half morocco, fine copy, uncut.* 12° *For the Author. London, and sold by the Baptist Ministers at Philadelphia, Boston and New York, n. d.* [1800?]

This is one of the author's own copies, carefully revised by himself, and corrected with a pen in very many places, in his own handwriting. Some of the alterations and corrections are interesting if not amusing, as *f. i.* in the 41st Hymn, verse 6, "Again the spirits lifts his sword" is altered to "Again the Spirit lifts his sword.'

1770 Rippon (John) A Selection of Hymns from the best authors. Second Edition. 12° *London, n. d.*

The author's own copy, with many Manuscript notes preparing this for a new edition.

1771 Rippon (John) A Selection of Hymns. A new edition, with eleven original hymns not inserted in any other Selection.
Calf. 16° *London,* [1800]

1772 Ripperda (Dude de) Memoirs of, with Account of the most remarkable Events between 1715 and 1736. 8° *London,* 1740

1773 Ritter (A.) History of the Moravian Church in Philadelphia, from its Foundation in 1742. *Portraits and Engravings. Cloth.* 8° *Philadelphia,* 1857

1774 Rimius (Henry) History of the Moravians. Vol. I. *London,* 1759
Narrative of the Herrnbinters, &c. 2d Edition. 2 *vols, half calf.* 8° *London,* 1753

1775 RIVERO (E. de) and Tschudi (J. D. de) Antiquidades Peruanas. 58 *colored plates,* 2 *vols,*
Text 4°, *Plates, oblong folio, Vienna,* 1851

This large and costly work is perhaps the most elaborate and valuable one that has hitherto appeared on the archæology and antiquities of Peru, prior to the Conquest by the Spaniards.

1776 Roberts (George) The four years voyages of Captain G. Roberts. Written by himself. *Map, calf.* 8° *London,* 1726

1777 Robertson (William) The History of America. First Edition. 2 *vols, calf.* 4° *London,* 1777

The list of authorities used by Robertson in this great work, constitutes one of the best Catalogues of Books relating to America, made up to the time of the American Revolution.

1777* Robertson (W.) The History of America. 3 *vols, Portrait, Boards, uncut.* 8° *London,* 1778

1778 ROBERTSON (W.) The History of America, Books IX and X, containing the History of Virginia to the Year 1688; and of New England to the Year 1652. *Boards, uncut.* 8° *Philadelphia,* 1799

1779 ROBERTSON (W.) Geschiedenis van Amerika. 5 *vols, vellum.* 8° *Amst.* 1778–1801

1780 ROBERTSON (W.) Histoire de l'Amerique. 4 *vols, maps, half calf.* 8° *Amsterdam,* 1779

1781 ROBIN (Abbé) Nieuwe Reize door Noord-America, in . . . 1781. *Half calf, uncut.* 8° *Amst.* 1782

1782 ROBISON (J.) Proofs of a Conspiracy against all the Religions and Governments of Europe, carried on in the Secret Meetings of Free Masons, Illuminate, etc. Fourth Edition. 8° *New York,* 1798

1783 ROBISON (J.) Proofs of a Conspiracy against all the Religions and Governments of Europe, carried on in the Secret Societies of Free Masons, Illuminate, *etc.* Third Edition. *Russia.* 8° *London,* 1798

1784 ROBINSON (Wm. Davis) Gedenkschriften der Omwenteling in het Rijk van Mexico. *Half morocco.* 8° *Haarlem,* 1823

1785 ROBINSON (W. D.) Gedenkschriften der Omwenteling in het rijk van Mexico. *Portrait, half brown morocco, uncut.* 8° *Haarlem,* 1823

1786 ROBSON (J.) Account of Six Years' Residence in Hudson's Bay, from 1733 to 1736, and 1744 to 1747. *Boards.* 8° *London,* 1752

1787 ROCHEFORT (CÆSAR DE) HISTOIRE NATURELLE et Morale des Antilles de l'Amerique. Avec un VOCABULAIRE CARAIBE. *Plates.* 4° *Rotterdam,* 1658

FIRST EDITION, of very considerable historical value, though Le Père DU TERTRE asserts, in the preface of his larger work in 1667, that M. de Rochefort, a minister of the gospel at Rotterdam, stole his manuscript in 1654, from the printers, and published it as his own.

1788 ROCHEFORT (C. de) Naturlyke en zedelyke Historie van d'Eylanden de Voor-Eylanden van Amerika. *Plates. Calf, gilt edges.* 4° *Rotterdam,* 1662

1789 ROCHEFORT (C. de) Histoire Natvrelle des Iles Antilles de l'Amerique. *Vignette and plates,* 2 *vols, calf.* 16° *Lyon,* 1667

1790 ROCHEFORT (C. de) Histoire Naturelle des Iles Antilles de l'Amerique. 2 *vols, many copperplates in the text, calf.* 16° *Lyon, chez C. Fovrmy,* 1667

1791 ROCHEFOUCAULD-LIANCOURT (Duc de la) VOYAGE DANS LES ETATS-UNIS de l'Amerique, fait en 1795–6–7. 8 *vols in* 4, *half crimson morocco.* 8° *Paris,* 1799

1792 RODRIGUEZ (*El P. F.* MANUEL, *of Portugal*) Explicacion de la Bvlla de la SANCTA CRVZADA y de las clausulas de los Iubileos y Confessionarios que ordinariamente fue le conceder su sanctidad, muy prouechosa para Predicandores, Curas, y Confessores, aun en los Reynos donde no ay Bulla.

Diuidese este libro en tres partes. En la primera se trata de la Explicacion de la Bulla concedida à los viuos. En la secunda la de los defunctos. En la tercera de la Composicion: y a la postre se declara el Motu proprio de Pio V. en el qual se prohibe la entrada de las mugeres en lo interior de los Monasterios de Frayles, *etc.* *Old calf.* 4° *Salamanca,* 1594

If any Protestant desires really to get back to first principles and to know precisely whereof he charges the Catholics of Rome, a careful perusal of this book will help him, as it is intended for the guidance of the priests rather than the instruction of the people.

793 RODRIGUEZ de Arispe (D. Pedro Joseph) Colosso Eloquente, que en la solemne aclamacion del D. Fernando VI. erigió sobre brillantes columnas la reconocida lealtad, y fidelissima gratitud de la Imperial, y pontificia Universidad Mexicana, Athenas del Nuevo Mundo; Dedicalo a sus reales plantas, *etc.* el Dr. y Mrò. D. Thomas de 'Cuevas, Garzez de los Fallos, Colegial, *etc.* 20 *prel. leaves; Text xcviii and* 174 *pp. Vellum, fine copy, but some leaves wormed.* 4° *Mexico,* 1748

Probably no monarch ever had erected to him in honor of his accession to the throne such a tower of brilliants as this volume contains in honor of Ferdinand the VI of Spain. The whole University of Mexico, the Athens of the new world, as they delight to call it, seems to have conspired to outdo and overleap itself by ingenious trifling in prose and verse, and prosy verse. The volume is filled with epigrams, polygrams, roundrobins, romances, gratulations, distiches, octaves, tentaves, puns, jokes, redondillas, anagrams, programs, chronograms, puzzles, catches, drolls, boustrophedons, sonnets, odes, acrostics, double acrostics, treble acrostics, stanzas, suns (v. pp. 40–41), saphics, acrostics of letters, acrostics of syllables, acrostics of words, poems of whole lines, half lines, first halves, last halves, up-readings, down-readings, to be read to the left of us, and to the right of us, in Latin and Spanish, in sense, in nonsense, indeed, in everything but common sense. The university of Mexico seems on that occasion to have thrown its entire Faculty into wit, with a solemn determination to express *all* the wit it had, even if compelled to live witless ever after.

794 Rodriguez de San Miguel (Juan) La Republica Mexicana en 1846, ó sea Directorio-general de los Supremos Poderes, y de las Principales Autoridades, Corporaciones y Oficinas de la Nacion. 198 *and* 123 *pp.* 8° *Mexico,* 1845

An excellent book of reference, with important statistics and historical events. There is also considerable bibliographical information, not easily found elsewhere.

795 Rogers (Ammi) Memoirs of the Rev. Ammi Rogers, A. M. a clergyman of the Episcopal Church, educated at Yale College, ordained in New York, persecuted in the State of Connecticut for twenty years, and finally falsely accused and imprisoned in Norwich Jail for two years. Also an Index to the Holy Bible. 3d Edit. with additions, omissions, and alterations. 8° *J. W. Copeland, Middlebury, Vt,* 1830

796 Rogers (N.) The Wild Vine: or an Exposition on Isaiah's Parabolical Song of the Beloved. 4° *London,* 1632

797 Rogers (*Major* Robert) A Concise Account of North America. *Calf.* 12° *Dublin,* 1769

798 Rogers (*Capt.* Woodes) Voyage autour du Monde en 1708–11. Traduit de l'Anglois. 2 *vols, map and engravings, fine copy. Calf.* 8° *Amsterdam,* 1716

1799 ROGERS (*Capt.* Woodes) A Cruising Voyage round the World; First to the South Seas, thence to the East Indies, and homeward by the Cape of Good Hope. *Maps.* *Calf.* 8° *London*, 1718

1800 ROSA (Santa) Kurtze Erzehlung desz Wunderlichen Lebens, vnd viel werthen Tods der Gottseeligen Schwester Rosæ de S. Maria von Lima gebürtig, aus der dritten Regel desz Heyligen Vatters Dominici. *Scarce.* 16° *Prag*, 1668

1801 ROSA (Santa) Admirabilis Vita, Virtus, gloria S. Rosæ à S. Maria Virginis Limanæ Ordinis Prædicatorum primi ex Occidus Indiis Amœnæ sanctitalis Fructus, &c. *Fine copy.* 8° *S. Uzschneider, Augustæ Vindel*, [1672]

American female saints are so rare that this Life of SANTA ROSA OF LIMA has passed through more editions probably than that of any other saint in the same time.

1802 ROSCIO (J. G. *Citizen of Venezuela*) El Triunfo de la Libertad sobre el Despotismo, en la Confesion de un pecador arrepentido de sus errores politicos, *etc.* *Half calf.* 4° *Oajaca, en Mexico*, 1828

1803 ROSS (Alexander) View of all Religions in the World (including America.) *Calf.* 12° *London*, 1653

1804 ROSS (Alexander) 's Weerelds Gods-Diensten, of Vertorg van alle de Religien en Ketteryen in Asia, Africa, America en Europa. *2d edition.* *Copperplates, vellum.* 8° *Dordricht*, 1692

1805 ROSS (Arthur A. of Newport) A Discourse, embracing the Civil and Religious History of Rhode Island: delivered April 4th, 1838, at the Close of the second century for the first Settlement of the Island. *Cloth.* 12° *Providence*, 1838

1806 ROSS. The Speeches of Mr. Ross and Mr. Morris, 16th of February, 1803, in the Senate of the United States, on the right of free navigation of the Mississippi River. 48 *pp.* *Scarce.* 8° *n. p.* 1803

1807 ROTHELIN (ABBÉ) Catalogue des Livres de feu M. l'Abbé D'Orleans de Rothelin, par G. Martin. *Priced.* *Calf.* *Thick* 8° *Paris*, 1746

THE ABBÉ ROTHELIN was the first bibliographer of distinction who collected and collated the Voyages of the DeBrys. His famous set was sold in this sale, and produced about as many cents then as it would bring dollars now. This Catalogue contains many voyages and travels. The prices of many of the lots are given. Few catalogues of this period are so difficult to meet with as this.

1808 ROZIERE (E. de) Formules Inedites publiées d'apres un Manuscrit de la Bibliotheque de Saint Gall. *Uncut.* 8° *Paris*, 1853

1809 RUBALCAVA (JOSEPH GUTIERREZ DE) Tratado historico, politico, y legal de el Comercio de las Indias Occidentales, pertenecientes a los Reyes Catholicos, conforme al tiempo de Paz, y Guerra, en interpretacion de las Leyes de la Nueva Recopilacion â ellas. Prima Parte. Compendio Historico del Comercio de las Indias, desde su principio hasta su actual estado. *Cadiz* [1750.] 54 *and* 351 *pages*: [*followed by a Second Part.*] PROYECTO para Galeones, y Flotas de el Perù, y Nueva España, y para Navios de Registro, y Avisas que Navegaren a ambos Reynos. Año 1720. 2 *vols in one, fine copy, vellum.* 8° *Cadiz*, [1750]

This is one of the rarest and most important volumes of this collection. One has but to glance at the table of contents of the 19 chapters of the first part, and the 8 chapters of the *Proyecto*, to convince himself of its high historical value.

1810 RUFAHL (Ludwig) Die Geschichte der Vereinigten Staaten von Nordamerika. 3 *vols, boards.* 8° *Berlin*, 1832

1811 RURAL MAGAZINE, or Vermont Repository. Vol. 2. 8° *Rutland, Vt*, 1796

The second volume only, fine copy, extremely rare, by Williams, Author of the History of Vermont.

1812 RUSH (Benjamin) Essays, literary, moral and philosophical. *Calf.* 8° *Philadelphia*, 1798

1813 RUSH (B.) Three Lectures upon Animal Life, delivered in the University of Pennsylvania. *Calf* 8° *Philadelphia*, 1799

1814 RUSSELL (W. S.) Guide to Plymouth, and Recollections of the Pilgrims. *With engraving. Cloth.* 12° *Boston*, 1846

1815 S (I.) A BRIEF AND PERFECT JOURNAL of the late Proceedings and Success of the English Army in the West Indies, continued until June the 24th, 1655; together with some queries inserted and answered. By I. S. an Eye-witness. *Half roan.* 4° *London*, 1655

The result of this grand Cromwellian expedition of 10,000 men under Gen. Venables and Admiral Penn (the father of our William), was the acquisition of Jamaica to the English Commonwealth. The Glory of God, the Propagation of the Gospel, and the discomfiture of the wicked of a False Church, were the high-sounding rallying cries, while private gains, wholesale thievings, unchristian selfish cruelties, out-Spanishing the Spanish iniquities of the previous century, were the mainsprings of action. They aimed at Hispaniola and Cuba, and barely secured Jamaica. This tract fills an important gap in the history of English possession in the West Indies.

1816 SACRA NEMESIS, the Levites Scourge, or Mercurius (Britan. Civicus) Disciplin'd. *Calf.* 4° *Oxford*, 1644

1817 SADEUR (Jacques) Les Avantures de Jacques Sadeur dans la Decouverte et le Voyage de la Terre Australe, etc. *Very fine large copy, calf gilt.* 12° *Mortier, Amst.* 1732

1818 SAGEAN (Mathieu) Extrait de la Relation des Avantures et Voyage. *Large paper, bound in white vellum, by F. Bedford.* 8° *A la Presse Cramoisy de J. M. Shea, N. York*, 1863

1819 ST JOHN (J. H.) LETTERS from an American Farmer: describing certain Provincial Situations etc. of the British Colonies in N. America. New Edition, with an accurate Index. *Map, half morocco, uncut.* 8° *London*, 1783

1820 ST JOHN (J. H.) Letters from an American Farmer to a Friend in England. 12° *M. Carey, Philadelphia*, 1793

1821 SALAZAR Y OLARTE (Ignacio de) Historia de la Conquista de Mexico, Secunda Parte [De Solis' History being the first part.] *Vellum, some leaves mutilated.* *Folio, Cordova,* 1743

1822 SALLUST. La Conjuracion de Catilina y la Guerra de Jugerta (in Spanish and Latin.) *Fine copy, old calf.* *Folio, Ibarra, Madrid,* 1772

The best specimen of fine printing ever executed in Spain. What Baskerville did at Birmingham, Didot in Paris, Bordone in Italy, Ibarra did in Spain, with this difference, that Ibarra rested his abilities on this one book.

1823 SANCTIUS (Franc) Minerva, sivè de Causis Latinæ Linguæ, Commentarius. 8° *Amstelod.* 1664

1824 SANDERUS (N.) Origine ac Progressu Schismatis Anglicani. *Calf.* 8° *Colon. Agrip.* 1585

1825 SAN FERMIN (El P. Fr. Antonio de) Defensa del Homo Attritus. Compuesta por el P. Fr. A. de San Fermin, Carmelita Descalzo. *Fine copy, calf.*
4° *Guadalaxara por D. Mariano Valdés Telles Giron,* 1802

A very pretty quarrel between the Carmelites and Dominicans, in which a large number of Mexican books and authorities are referred to, and no little Mexican biography and bibliography are incidentally brought out. The book is dedicated to Dr. J. M. BERESTAIN, the distinguished author of the *Bibliotheca Hispano-Americana Septentrional.* *3 vols, 4to, Mexico,* 1816–19.

1826 SAN JOSEPH BETANCUR (*P. Fr.* PEDRO) REGLA, Y CONSTITUTIONES DE LA SAGRADA RELIGION BETHLEMITICA, FUNDADA EN LAS INDIAS OCCIDENTALES. 4 *prel. leaves (the first blank) and* 90 *pp. Fine copy, calf.*
4° *En Mexico, por la Viuda de D. J. Bernarda de Hogal,* 1751

A book of very great rarity, as well as of considerable importance in the Church History of New Spain. Father San Joseph Betancur died at Guatemala the 25th of April, 1667, in the 41st year of his age. Following the title is a full-page, well-executed copperplate engraving by TRONCOSO, an artist of Mexico, dated 1748, representing Father Betancur on his knees before the Infant Saviour, in the lap of his mother, in the stable at Bethlehem, with Saint Joseph in attendance.

1827 SANSON (Joseph) Travels in Lower Canada. *View of Quebec. London,* 1820.—MOLLIEN (G.) Travels in Africa, to the Sources of the Senegal and Gambia. 2 *vols in* 1, *uncut.* 8° *London,* 1820

1828 SANSON (LE SIEUR, *Geographe du Roy*) ATLAS. 120 *large folded maps, colored, half morocco.*
Thick atlas Folio, Paris, 1691

1829 SANTAGNELLO (M.) Dictionary of the Peculiarities of the Italian Language. *Cloth.* 8° *London,* 1820

1830 SANTA TERESA (FR. MANUEL DE, *de los Conventos de Zelaya y Toluca, Mexico*) INSTRUCTORIO Espiritual de los Terceros, Terceras, y Beatas de Nuestra Señora del Carmen. *xiv* + 226 *pp. followed by* Novena de la Soberana Emperatriz de Cielo y Tierra Maria Santisima del Carmen. 24 *leaves, fine copy, vellum.* SCARCE. 8° *En Mexico, Jose Jauregui,* 1787

Following the title is a well-executed engraving of the Queen of Heaven, by M. Villavicencia, a Mexican artist.

1831 SANTO DOMINGO. Vida de J. J. Dessalines, Gefe de los Negros de Santo Domingo; con notas muy circunstanciadas sobre el origen, caracter y atrocidades de los principales Gefes de aquillos Rebeldes desde el principio de la Insurreccion en 1791. Traducida del Frances por D. M. G. C. Año de 1805. Reimprimese por Don Juan Lopez Cancelada, Editor de la Gazeta de esta N[ueva] E[spaña.] *Fine copy.*
4° *Mexico, Oficina de Mariano de Zuñiga y Ontiveros,* 1806

This extraordinary book to be appreciated must be seen. It is adorned with ten elaborate and highly-finished copperplate line engravings, four of them large oval portraits of BIASON, LOUVERTURE, CRISTOBAL and DESALINES the first Emperor of Hayti, exceedingly well engraved by Rea of Mexico. The remaining six are historical prints, designed and engraved by Manuel Lopez, artist of Mexico. Though intended for serious high art, there is a grotesque absurdity about some of the scenes truly laughable. Witness the murder of the young mother in the field in the foreground, and a landscape of trees and mountains in the background (p. 33), and the coronation scene (p. 73) where Desalines is represented 'high on a throne' with his loyal supporters of sable hue on either side, so dark that nothing but the whites of their eyes relieve the picture.

1832 SANTO THOMAS (*Fray* DIEGO DE, *Padre de la Provincia de San Diego en Nueva España, y Guardian del Convento de Santa Maria de los Angeles de Ocholopozco*) CEREMONIAL Y MANUAL Sacado del Missal Romano de Pio V. Reformado por la Santidad de Clemente VIII y Vrbano VIII, Ajustado al estilo estrecho, y reformado de los Religiosos de Descalços de N. P. S. Francisco de la Provincia de San Diego desta Nueua España. *viii* + 272 + *vi pp. Fine copy, morocco, gilt sides.*
4° *Impresso in Mexico: En la Imprenta de Iuan Ruyz,* 1660

This fine book from the library of the Convent of Santa Barbara de Peubla, of the highest degree of rarity, is of great importance in the Ecclesiastical History of Mexico.

1833 SARDO (*Fr.* JOAQUIN) RELACION HISTORICA y moral de la Portentosa Imagen de N. Sr. Jesuchristo crucificado aparecida en una de las Cuevas de S. Miguel de Chalma, hoy Real Convento y sanctuario de esta nombre, de religiosos Ermitanos de N. G. P. y Doctor S. Agustin, en esta Nueva España, y en esta Provincia del Santisimo nombre de Jesus de Mexico. Con los Compendios de las Vidas de los dos Venerables Religiosos legos y primaros Anacoretas de este santo desierto, F. Bartolme de Jesus Maria, y F. Juan de San Josef. Nuevamente escrita por el R. P. Predicador Jubilado y Prior actual de este Real Convento, F. Joaquin Sardo. *Fine copy, calf.* 4° *Mexico,* 1810

A book of considerable historical interest outside of the particular religious subject treated. It fills 8 prelim. leaves and 386 pp. The Apparition of the SANTO CRISTO DE CHALMA, representing which there is a copperplate frontispiece prefixed to this volume, occurred in Mexico in 1539, and from that day to this its history has been interwoven with the ecclesiastical, and is sometimes inseparable from the political, history of Mexico, especially so far as the management and education of the Indians intrusted to the missionaries of the Order of St Augustin are concerned. The large number of the earliest and rarest books relating to New Spain, referred to and quoted in this work, renders it indispensable to the historian. It is furthermore replete with biographical notes and references, not easily found elsewhere.

1834 SARMIENTO DE GAMBOA (PEDRO) Viage al Estrecho de Magallanes, en los Annos de 1579 y 1580. *Plates, calf.* 4° *Madrid,* 1768

1835 SARMIENTO DE GAMBOA (Pedro) Viage al Estrecho de Magallanes. *Plates, half calf, gilt.* 4° *Madrid,* 1768

1836 SARTINE (M. de) The Green Box of Monsieur de Sartine, found at Melle de Thé's Lodgings. Fifth Edit. *Lond.* 1779
An English Green Box: Or the Green Box of the R—t H—e E—d L—d Churdlow, given by Mrs. Harvey to Roger O'Tickle Valet de Chambre to ——— ——— Esq., M. P. 2d Ed. corrected. 2 *vols in* 1, *half calf.* 8° *London,* 1779

These two political squibs both pertain incidentally to American affairs. In the former Franklin plays a prominent part. The latter is a feeble imitation applicable to English affairs, printed with the usual dashes of the printers who had not the courage at that time to print the names of English Statesmen in full. In this copy several of these blanks are filled up in MS. by W. Cole.

1837 SAUVIUS (A.) STAATE-BUCH. Verfasst und fortgesetst durch Hermann Adolph Authes. *Vellum.* *Thick* 4° *Franckfurt,* 1656

1838 SAVAGE (J.) Our Living Representative Men. *Cloth.* 12° *Philadelphia,* 1860

1839 SAXIUS (S.) Onomastici Literarii Epitome. *Boards, uncut.* 8° *Traj. ad Rhenum,* 1792

1840 SAY (Thomas) A Short Compilation of the Extraordinary Life and Writings of Thomas Say, in which is faithfully copied from the Original Manuscript the Uncommon Vision which he had when a young man. *Calf.* 12° *Budd & Bartram, Philadelphia,* 1796

1841 SCHAEFFER (Den Ridder von) BRASILIË als onafhankelijk Rijk. 2 *vols, half olive morocco, uncut.* 8° *Amsterdam,* 1825

1842 SCHMIDTMEYER (Peter) Travels to Chili over the Andes, in the Years 1820 and 1821. *Map and plates, calf.* 4° *Lond.* 1822

1843 SCHMITZ (L.) History of Rome to the Death of Commodus, A. D. 192. 8° *London,* 1849

1844 SCHOOLCRAFT (Henry R.) Narrative of an Expedition through the Upper Mississippi to Itasca Lake. *Map, cloth.* 8° *New York,* 1834

1845 SCHOTT (ANDREAS) HISPANIÆ ILLUSTRATÆ, seu Rerum, Urbiumque Hispaniæ, Lusitaniæ, Aethiopiæ et Indiæ Scriptores. *Maps, complete in 4 vols, fine copy, scarce, calf.* *Folio, Francofurti,* 1603–8

" Cet ouvrage est tres estimé, et l'on s'en procure difficilement des exemplaires complets; il faut avoir, soin de verifier si, dans le tome IV. se trouvent les dix derniers livres de l'Histoire, de Mariana en latin: ces dix livres qui forment une partie separée, avec un titre particulier daté de 1606 manquent souvent, ce qui diminue alors le prix des exemplaires." — *Brunet.*

This is a fine complete copy with the rare fourth volume (the last ten books of Mariana) bound at the beginning of the third volume. This rare and important Body of Spanish History is frequently referred to by Spanish writers, especially Muños and Navarrete, under the name of ESCOTO. Besides other papers referring to the New World, Columbus' Letter to Raphal Sanxis, translated by de Cosco, is reprinted in full.

1846 SCOTT (Job) A Journal of his Life, Travels and Gospel Labours. 12° *London*, 1797

1847 SCOTT (Job) The Same, with Corrections and Additions. *Half bound.* 8° *London*, 1815

1848 SCOTT (J.) The Christian Life. *Calf.* 8° *London*, 1685

1849 SCULTERIUS (A.) Annalium Evangelii per Europam Decas prima ab anno 1516 ad an. 1526. *Calf.* 8° *Heidelbergæ*, 1618

1850 SEAMAN (E. C.) Essays on the Progress of Nations. *Cloth.* 12° *New York*, 1846

1851 SEEBOHM (F.) The Oxford Reformers of 1498; a History of the Fellow-work of John Colet, Erasmus and Thomas More. *Cloth.* 8° *London*, 1867

1852 SELDEN (ALMIRA) EFFUSIONS OF THE HEART, contained in a number of Original Poetical Pieces, on various subjects. 152 *pp. fine copy*, SCARCE. 12° *Bennington, Darius Clark*, 1820

1853 SELDEN (JOHANNES) FLETA; seu Commentarius Juris Anglicani, sic nuncupatus, sub Edwardo Rege etc; subjungitur, etiam ad Fletam Dissertatio Historica. *Calf.* 4° *Londini*, 1647

FIRST EDITION. "This methodical and learned work derives it name from the circumstance of having been composed, when its author was a prisoner in the Fleet." — *Lowndes.*

1854 SEMI-CENTENNIAL Anniversary of the University of Vermont. A Historical Discourse by Rev. John Wheeler, an address by J. R. Spalding, a Poem by Rev. O. G. Wheeler, with an Account of the Proceedings. 8° *Burlington*, 1854

1855 SEMLER (J. S.) Algemeine Geschichte der Ost und Westindischen Handlungsgesellschaften in Europa. *Numerous maps and plates, 2 vols, calf.* 4° *Halle*, 1764

1856 SENATORS. Sketches of United States Senators, of the Session of 1837–38. *Cloth.* 12° *Washington*, 1839

1857 SEPP (Antony) Reiss-Beschreibung, wie selbe auss Hespanien in Paraquariam kommen, etc. *Boards.* 16° *Bressau*, 1699

1858 SETTLEMENTS IN AMERICA. An Account of the European Settlements in America. 2d Edition. 2 *vols, calf.* 8° *London*, 1758

1859 SETTLEMENTS, *etc.* 2d Edition, with improvements. 2 *vols, calf.* 8° *London*, 1758

1860 SETTLEMENTS, *etc.* 3d Ed. 2 *vols, calf.* 8° *Lond.* 1760

1861 SETTLEMENTS, *etc.* 5th Ed. 2 *vols, calf.* 8° *Lond.* 1770

1862 SETTLEMENTS, *etc.* 5th Ed. 2 *vols, calf.* 8° *Lond.* 1770

1863 SEWALL (SAMUEL) PHÆNOMENA QUÆDAM APOCALYPTICA ad aspectum Novi orbis configurata. Or some few Lines towards a description of the New Heaven as it makes to those who stand upon the New Earth. *The top outer corner fatigued and rotten, but none of the text gone. 2d Edition.* 4° *B. Green, Boston*, 1727

1864 SEYBERT (Andrew) STATISTICAL ANNALS of the United States of America; founded on Official Documents. *Half red morocco.* 4° *Philadelphia*, 1818

1865 SEYBERT (A.) Statistical Annals of the United States of America; founded on Official Documents. 4° *Phila.* 1818

1866 SHAIK MANSUR. History of Seyd Said, Sultan of Muscat; with an Account of the Countries and People on the Shores of the Persian Gulf, particularly of the Wahabees. *Map, half calf.* 8° *London*, 1810

1867 SHAM PATRIOT (The) Unmasked: Or an exposition of the fatally successful Arts of Demagogues who exalt themselves by flattering and swindling the people, etc. Being a series of Essays by *Historicus* and first published in "The Balance." [By Ezra Sampson.] 16° *Sampson, Chittenden & Croswell, Hudson, N. Y.* 1802

1868 SHARP (Bartholomew) The Voyages and Adventures of, and others in the South Sea. Published by P. A., Esq. *Calf.* 8° *London*, 1684

1869 SHEA'S PUBLICATIONS. RARE TRACTS ON CANADA AND OLD LOUISIANA. 8 *vols, half red morocco, gilt tops, uncut,* 100 COPIES ONLY OF EACH PRINTED. 8° *Cramoisy Press, Nouvelle York*, 1855–59

RELATION de ce qui s'est passé de plvs remarqvable dans la Mission des Abnaquis a l'Acadie, l'Année 1701 par le Pere Vincent Bigot de la Comp. de Jesus.
RELATION du Voyage, par feu M. Robert Cavalier, Sieur de la Salle pour decouvrir dans la golfe du Mexique l'embouchure de Missisipy.
RELATION du Voyage des premieres Ursulines a la Nouvelle Orleans et de leur etablissement en cette ville, par la Rev. Mère St. Augustine de Tranchepain.
JOURNAL de la Guerre du Micissipi, contre les Chichachas, en 1730 et finie en 1740. Par un Officier de l'Armée de M. de Nouaille.
JOURNAL du Voyage du R. P. Jacques Gravier de la Comp. de Jesus en 1700, depuis les pays des Illinois jusqu'a l'embouchure du Mississipi.
REGISTRES des Baptesmes et Sepultures, qui se sont faits au Fort Duquesne pendant les annees 1753–54–55 et 56.
LA VIE du R. P. Pierre Joseph Marie Chaumont de la Comp. de Jesus, Missionaire dans la Nouvelle France. Ecrite par lui-meme l'an 1688.
SUITE de la Vie du P. Pierre Joseph Marie Chaumont, par un Pere de la meme Compagnie.

1870 SHEBBEARE (J.) Le Peuple Instruit; ou Alliances de la Grande Bretagne, etc. depuis le commencement des troubles sur l'Ohio. *Half morocco.* 12° 1756

1871 SHEBBEARE (J.) An Essay on the Origin of National Society. *Half roan.* 8° *London*, 1776

1872 SHEFFIELD (John, *Lord*) Observations on the Commerce of the American States, with Appendix. *Half calf.* 8° *London*, 1787

1873 SHEFFIELD (John, *Lord*) Observations on the Commerce of the American States; with an Appendix. Sixth Edition enlarged. *Half morocco, uncut.* 8° *London*, 1784

1874 SHEFFIELD (John, *Lord*) Observations on the Manufactures, Trade and present State of Ireland. *Calf.* LARGE PAPER. 8° *London*, 1785

1875 SHEIL (J.) Plain and Rational Account of the Catholic Faith: First American Edition. 8° *Albany*, 1814

1876 Shelvocke (Geo.) Voyage round the world, by way of the Great South Sea, in 1719–1722. 2d Edit. *Map and plates, fine copy, calf gilt.* 8° *London*, 1757

1877 Shepard (C. W.) Report on the Geological Survey of Connecticut. 8° *New Haven*, 1837

1878 Shepard (Thomas *Late Pastor of the Church of Christ at Cambridge in New England.*) The Parable of the Ten Virgins. *Calf.* *Folio, London*, 1695

1879 Shepard (Thomas) The Parable of the Ten Virgins. *Half calf.* *Folio, Reprinted* [*London*] 1695

1880 Shepard (Thomas) The Sound Beleever, a Treatise of Evangelical Conversion. *Calf.* 8° *London*, 1670

1881 Shepard (Thomas) The Sincere Convert. Newly corrected. 12° *Gideon Lithgow, Edinburgh*, 1647

An edition of uncommon rarity.

1882 Shepard (Thomas, *Preacher of God's Word in New England*) The Sincere Convert; Discovering the small number of true Beleevers, *etc.* The Fifth Edition, corrected and much amended by the author. 8° *London, M. Simmons*, 1650
The Sound Beleever, a Treatise of Evangelicall Conversion, *etc.* 2 *vols in one.* 8° *London, R. Dawlman*, 1649

1883 Shepard (Thomas) The Sincere Convert discovering the small Number of true Beleevers, &c. corrected and much amended by the Author. 8° *London, E. Cotes*, 1655

1884 Shepard (Thomas) The Sincere Convert discovering the small Number of True Beleevers. Corrected Ed. *Calf.* 8° *London*, 1664

1885 Shepard (Thomas) The Sincere Convert, Discovering the small Number of Beleevers and the great difficulty of Saving conversion; whereto is now added the Saint's Jewel. 8° *London*, 1659

1886 Shepard (Thomas) Another Edition. *Calf.* 8° *London*, 1672

1887 Shipley (*Dr. Bishop of St Asaph*) Speech intended to have been spoken on the Bill for altering the Charter of the Colony of Massachusetts Bay. *Half morocco.* 8° *Boston*, 1774

1888 SHIRLEY (James) The Maids Revenge. A Tragedy, as it hath been acted with good applause at the private house in Drury Lane, by her Majesty's Servants. *Vellum.* 4° *London*, 1639

1889 Shirley (William, *Governor of Massachusetts Bay*) Letter to the Duke of Newcastle; with a Journal of the Siege of Louisbourg, and other Operations of the Forces, during the Expedition against the French Settlements on Cape Breton. *Imperfect, wanting after* D 2. 4° *Boston, Printed by J. Draper for D. Henchman*, [1746]

1890 SHORT (A) Introduction to the Latin Tongue; being the Accidence, abridged and compiled in that most easy and accurate method, wherein the famous MR. EZEKIEL CHEEVER taught, and which he found the most advantageous, by 70 years experience. 18th Edit. *Fine copy.*
16° *John Mycall, Newburyport,* 1785

1891 SICILY. A Tour through Sicily and Malta. In a Series of Letters to Wm. Beckford, from P. Brydone, 2 *vols. in one, 3 copies fiue and clean as new.*
12° *Thomas Dickman, Greenfield, Mass.* 1798

1892 SIDONS (C.) De Vereenigde Staaten van Noord-Amerika. *Half blue morocco, uncut.* 8° *Leeuwarden,* 1828

1893 SILVA (J. M. P. da) Parnaso Brazileiro ou Selecção de Poesias dos melhores Poetas Brazileiros desde o descobrimento do Brasil precedida de uma Introducção Historica e Biographica sobra a Literatura Brazileira. 2 *vols, half maroon morocco, uncut.* 12° *Rio de Janeiro, E. & H. Laemmert,* 1843

The Historical and bibliographical Introduction (pp. 7–45) tracing the literary history of Brazil from the year 1500 to 1800 is a curious and interesting record. At the end of vol. 2, is bound an interesting catalogue of 64 pages, comprising the books published by E. & H. Laemmert, Rua da Quitanda 77 Rio de Janeiro.

1894 SKETCH of the Internal Condition of the U. States of America and of their Political Relations. By a Russian. *Uncut.* 8° *Baltimore,* 1826

1895 SKINNER (J. S.) Journal of Agriculture July 1847 to July 1848. *With Illustrations, cloth.* 8° *New York*

1896 SLADE (William) Vermont State Papers; a Collection of Records and Documents connected with the assumption and establishment of government by the People of Vermont, with the Journal of the Council of Safety, the First Constitution, &c. *Sheep.* 8° *Middlebury,* 1823

FRIDAY FORENOON.

1897 SIMPLE COBLER (THE) OF AGGAWAM IN AMERICA. Willing to help 'mend his Native Countrey, lamentably tattered, both in the upper-Leather, and sole, with all the honest stitches he can take. BY THEODORE DE LA GUARD [NATHANIEL WARD of Ipswich.] The Third Edition, with some Additions.
4° *Printed by J. D. & R. I. for Stephen Bowtell, Lond.* 1647

There were five distinct editions, with considerable alterations and additions, of this witty work issued in the year 1647, the first two without the edition being indicated, followed by the 2d, 3d and 4th. This *third* edition, as far as the experience of the writer goes, is the most difficult of the five to find.

"No King can King it right,
Nor rightly sway his Rod;
Who truely loves not Christ,
And truly fears not God." — Page 73.

"So farewell England old,
If evill times ensue,
Let good men come to us,
Wee'l welcome them to New." — Page 79.

(*Specimen bricks.*)

1898 SIMPLE COBLER of Aggawam in America. *Cloth.* 12° *Boston,* 1843

1899 SLAVERY. An Essay on the Slavery and Commerce of the Human Species, particularly the African. With additions. *Half brown morocco, uncut.* 8° *Dublin,* 1786

1900 SMITH (C.) Classical Atlas containing Distinct Maps of the Countries described in Ancient History, both sacred and profane. 4° *London,* 1809

1901 SMITH (J.) Chronicon Rusticum Commerciale; or Memoirs of Wool, etc. 2 *vols, calf.* 8° *London,* 1747

1902 SMITH (J.) Another Copy. 2 *vols, calf.* 8° *London,* 1747

1903 SMITH (CAPTAIN JOHN, *sometymes Governour of Virginia, and Admirall of New England*) THE GENERALL HISTORIE OF VIRGINIA, NEW-ENGLAND AND THE SUMMER ISLES: with the names of the Adventurers, Planters, and Governours, from the first beginning, An° 1584 to this present 1626. *A fine large clean tall copy (measuring* 11 *by* 7½ *inches) with a brilliant impression of the beautiful title-page engraved by John Berrá, and the four maps, mounted on the finest muslin; bound in the best French gros grained red morocco, by Pratt, in every respect a desirable copy, with none of the usual defects, except a little restoration by*

Harris, hardly to be seen, in the centre of the title, and in the margins of the large Map of Virginia.
Fol. Printed by I. D. & I. H. for Michael Sparkes, Lond. 1627

Of the *three* impressions of the large map of Virginia, first published in 1612, this is the second, and the right one for this edition, before *Sparkes Point* was put in. Of the *nine* editions of the map of New England, with the portrait of Capt. Smith this is the *third*, before the portrait was retouched, before Charles River was extended, and before Salem and Boston were put in. Very few copies of the editions of 1624, 1626, and 1627 have all the right maps. The plate of the map of New England was much altered after 1627, and names of places added which were not given till 1628, 1630, or later. It is very important to have the right maps, corresponding to the date of the edition.

1904 SMITH (M.) A Geographical View of the Province of Upper Canada, with a Description of Niagara Falls, and remarks relative to the situation of the inhabitants respecting the War. 12° *For the Author, Hartford,* 1813

1905 SMITH (S. S.) Essay on the Causes of the Variety of Complexion and Figure in the Human Species. 2d edition. 8° *New Brunswick,* 1810

1906 SMITH (S. S.) An Essay on the causes of the Variety of Complexion and Figure in the Human Species. Second Edition. *Calf.* 8° *New Brunswick,* 1810

1907 SMITH (William *of Philadelphia*) Discourses . . . during the War in America. *Calf.* 8° *London,* 1759

1908 SMITH (W.) Discourses on Public Occasions in America. 2d edition. 8° *London,* 1762

1909 SMITH (W.) Discourses on Public Occasions in America. With an Appendix. 2d edition. 8° *London,* 1762

1910 SMITH (William) The History of the Province of New York. *Half calf.* 8° *London,* 1776

1911 SMITHSONIAN CONTRIBUTIONS TO KNOWLEDGE. Vols I and III to VI. *Illustrated with numerous engravings.* *5 vols.* 4° *Washington,* 1848–54

Vol. I. Ancient Monuments of the Mississippi Valley. By Squier and Davis. *Out of print and* SCARCE.
Vol. III. Observations on Terrestrial Magnetism by J. Locke, M. D. Monograph of the Fresh Water Cottoids of North America, by C. Girard. Nereis Boreali-Americana, by W. H. Harvey, M. D. Part I. Melanospermæ, Plantæ Wrightianæ Texano-Neo-Mexicanæ, by Asa Gray, M. D. Part I. Occultations visible in the United States, 1852, by John Downes.
Vol. IV. Grammar and Dictionary of the Dakota Language. Edited by Rev. S. R. Riggs.
Vol. V. A Flora within Animals, by J. Leidy, M. D. Memoir on the Extinct Species of American Ox, by J. Leidy, M. D. Anatomy of the Nervous System of Rana Pipiens, by Jeffries Wyman, M. D. Nereis Boreali-Americana, by W. H. Harvey, M. D. Part II. Rhodospermæ Plantæ Wrightianæ Texano-Neo-Mexicanæ, by Asa Gray, M. D. Part II.
Vol. VI. Plantæ Fremontianæ, by J. Torrey. Marine Invertebrata of Grand Manan, by W. Stimpson. Winds of the Northern Hemisphere, by J. H. Coffin. Ancient Fauna of Nebraska, by J. Leidy, M. D.

1912 SMYTH (J. F. D.) A Tour in the United States of America. *2 vols, calf.* 12° *Dublin,* 1784

1913 SMYTH (*Capt.* William Henry) Life and Services of Capt. Philip Beaver, late of H. M. Ship Nisus. *Half calf, uncut.* 8° *London,* 1829

1914 Snellius (Willebrordus) Descriptio Cometæ, 1618. 4° *Lug. Bat.* 1619

1915 Snowden (Richard) History of North and South America, to the Death of Washington. *Maps.* 2 *vols in* 1. 12° *Philadelphia,* 1806

1916 SOCIETAS JESU. Litteræ Apostolicæ quibus Institutio, Confirmatio et varia Privilegia continentur. *And many other works in* 11 *vols, half bound.* Scarce and valuable. 8° *Antuerpiæ,* 1635

Besides the above title these eleven volumes contain many other books and tracts, printed separately, relating to the Jesuits, forming altogether a collection of great value.

1917 Solazzi (D. Juan Antonio) Avisos de Santa Maria Magdalina de Pazzis, a varias Religiosas, y Reglas de perfeccion, que ella receviò de Jesu-Christo. Dadas à luz en lengua Toscana por Don Juan Antonio Solazzi. Traducidas en España, por vn Religioso de la Compañia de Iesvs. *Stained.* 12° *Mexico,* 1721

1918 Solinus. In Solini Polyhistorem Emendationes. Mart. Ant. Delrio. Solini Vita per I. Camertem. Solini Polyhistor; *in uno vol. vellum.* 4° *Plantin, Antverpiæ,* 1572

1919 Solinus. Another copy, with Manuscript Index and Notes. *Calf.* 4° *Antverpiæ,* 1572

1920 Solis (Don Antonio de) Historia de la Conqvista de Mexico. Poblacion, y Progressos de la America Septentrional. *Vellum.* *Folio, Madrid,* 1704

1921 Solis (Ant. de) Historia de la Conquista de Mexico. 2 *vols.* 8° *Barcelona,* 1771

1922 Solis (Ant. de) Historia de la Conquista de Mexico. 2 *vols.* 8° *Barcelona,* 1771

1923 Solis (Ant. de) Historia de la Conquista de Mexico. 3 *vols, calf gilt.* 12° *Madrid,* 1791

1924 Solis (Ant. de) Historia de la Conquista de Mexico. 3 *vols, half brown morocco, uncut.* 12° *Madrid,* 1791

1925 Solis (Ant. de) Historia de la Conquista de Mexico. 3 *vols, paper.* 12° *Madrid,* 1819

1926 Solis (Ant. de) Histoire de la Conquête du Mexique, ou de la Nouvelle Espagne. *Plates, calf.* 4° *Paris,* 1691

This first edition in French of De Solis is seldom met with.

1927 Solis (Ant. de) Histoire de la Conquête du Mexique. 2 *vols, plates, calf gilt, fine copy.* 8° *La Haye,* 1692

1928 Solis (Ant. de) Histoire de la Conquête du Mexique. 2 *vols, plates, calf.* 8° *Paris,* 1704

1929 Solis (Ant. de) Histoire de la Conquête du Mexique. 4e Edit. 2 *vols, calf.* 8° *Paris,* 1714

1930 Solis (Ant. de) Histoire de la Conquête du Mexique. 5e Edit. 2 *vols, map and plates, calf.* 8° *Paris,* 1730

1931 Solis (Ant. de) Histoire de la Conquête du Mexique. 6e Edit. 2 *vols, map and plates, calf,* 8° *Paris,* 1759

1932 Solis (Ant. de) Histoire de la Conquête du Mexique, ou de la Nouvelle Espagne par Fernand Cortez. 6e Edition. 2 *vols, calf gilt.* 8° *Paris*, 1777

1933 Solis (Ant. de) Histoire de la Conquête du Mexique. 6e Edition. 2 *vols, maps and plates, calf gilt.* 8° *Paris*, 1774

1934 Solis (Ant. de) Histoire de la Conquête du Mexique, par Fernand Cortez. 6e Edition. 2 *vols, calf.* 8° *Paris*, 1774

1935 Solis (Ant. de) The History of the Conquest of Mexico. 2 *vols, calf.* 8° *Dublin*, 1727

1936 Solis (Ant. de) The History of the Conquest of Mexico. 2 *vols, maps and plates, calf.* 8° *London*, 1738

1937 Solis (Ant. de) History of the Conquest of Mexico. 2 *vols, map and plates, calf.* 8° *London*, 1738

1938 SOLORZANO PEREYRA (Juan de) Obras Varias. *Fine copy.* Scarce. *Folio, Madrid*, [1676]

Dr. Solorzano, a member of the Council of the Indies, was a voluminous legal writer of distinction, in Spain. His great work was the *Politica Indiana* in two volumes folio, but his various minor productions collected in this large volume, nearly all relate more or less to American affairs.

1939 Somers (Lord) The Judgment of whole Kingdoms and Nations concerning the Rights, Power, and Prerogative of Kings and the Rights of the People. 12th Edition, corrected. *Half calf.* 8° *Solomon Southwick, Newport, R. I.* 1774

1940 Sommer (J. G.) Beschrijving der Nieuwe Staten van America. 2 *vols, frontispiece, half brown morocco, uncut.* 8° *Amsterdam*, 1828

1941 Sophocles. Tragoediæ, cum omnibus Graecis Scholiis, et cum Latinis J. Camerarii. *Calf.* *Folio, H. Stephani*, 1568

1942 South Carolina. Reports of Judicial Decisions of the Constitutional Court of S. C. 1817, 1818. 2 *vols, half calf.* 8° *Charleston*, 1819

1943 South Carolina. An Historical Account of the Rise and Progress of the Colonies of South Carolina and Georgia. [By Mr. Hewitt.] 2 *vols, half maroon morocco, uncut.* 8° *London*, 1779

1944 Southey (Robert) Lives of the British Admirals, with the Naval History of England. Vols 1, 2, and 5, *and duplicate of vol* 2. 4 *vols, cloth.* *London*, 1833–40

1945 Souza (Pero Lopes de) Diario da Navegaçao da Armada que foi à terra do Brasil, en 1530, soba Capitania-Mor de Martim Alfonso de Souza, escripto por seu irmâo Pero Lopez de Souza. Publicado por Francisco Adolfo de Varnhagen. *Portrait, fine copy, uncut.* 8° *Lisbon*, 1839

1946 Spafford (Horatio Gates) Gazetteer of the State of New York. 8° *Albany*, 1813

1947 Spain. Historia der Konigreich Hispanien, Portugal und Aphrica. *Curious plate of a naval Engagement. Vellum.* *Folio, Muñchen*, 1589

1948 Spain. A proposal for humbling Spain [by robbing her of the West Indies.] 2d Edition. *Half roan.* 8° *London* [1739]

1949 Spain. Papers relative to the rupture with Spain. In French and English [about the West Indies.] *Half calf, gilt.* 8° *London*, 1762

1950 Spanhemius. Dissertationum Historici Argumenti Quaternio. *Calf.* 8° *Lugd. Batav.* 1679

1951 Spanish America. A concise History of, containing a succinct Relation of the Discovery and Settlement of its several Colonies, etc. *Fine copy, calf.* 8° *London*, 1741

1952 Spanish America. Outline of the Revolutions in Spanish America; or, an Account of the Origin, Progress, and actual state of the War carried on between Spain and Spanish America. By a South American. *Half green morocco.* 12° *New York*, 1817

1953 Spanish America. Outline of the Revolution in Spanish America, *etc.* 12° *New York*, 1817

1954 Spofford (J.) Gazetteer of Massachusetts. *Map.* 12° *Newburyport*, 1828

1955 Sprague (William B.) Sermon on the Twenty-fifth Anniversary of his Installation at Albany. 8° *Albany*, 1854

1956 Sprengel und Forster. Newe Beitrage zur balker und Landerkunde, 12 vols in 6. 8° *Leipzig*, 1790

1957 Spring (G.) Sermon, Preached in the North Church, Hartford, Dec. 1, 1824, at the Ordination and Installation of Rev. C. Wilcox. 8° *Hartford*, 1825

1958 Stamp Act. A short history of the conduct of the present Ministry with regard to the American Stamp Act. *Half roan, uncut.* 8° *London*, 1766

1959 Stamp Act. Protest against the Bill to repeal the American Stamp Act of Last Session. *Half roan.* 8° *Paris*, 1766

1960 Stark (Caleb) History of Dunbarton, N. H. from the Grant by Mason's Assigns 1751 to 1860. *Cloth.* 8° *Concord*, 1860

1961 Stark (Caleb) Memoir and Correspondence of Gen. John Stark; with Notices of several other Officers of the Revolution; also a Biography of Capt. Phinehas Stevens and Col. Robert Rogers. *Cloth.* 8° *Concord*, 1860

1962 State. The Present State of Great Britain and North America. *xvi and* 263 *pp. Half calf.* 8° *London*, 1767

1963 State of the Protestants of Ireland, under the late King James's Government, in which Their Carriage towards him is Justified, etc. With Appendix. *Calf.* 4° *London*, 1691

1964 Stedman (C.) History of the Origin, Progress, and Termination of the American War. 2 *vols, maps, calf.* 4° *London*, 1794

1965 STEDMAN (C.) HISTORY. Another copy. 2 *vols, maps, half russia.* 4° *London,* 1794

1966 STEDMAN (C.) THE HISTORY OF THE ORIGIN, PROGRESS, AND TERMINATION OF THE AMERICAN WAR. By C. Stedman, who served under Sir William Howe, Sir H. Clinton, and the Marquis Cornwallis. A MATCHLESS COPY, *sized paper, pure and clean, perfect,* UNCUT EDGES, *gilt tops; bound by F. Bedford in best gros grained green morocco, gilt backs; with all the maps complete. The sizing and binding alone cost* $35. EXCESSIVELY RARE IN THIS CONDITION.
4° *J. Murray, For the Author, London,* 1794

1967 STEDMAN (*Capt.* J. G.) NARRATIVE OF A FIVE YEARS' EXPEDITION AGAINST THE REVOLTED NEGROES OF SURINAM, from the Year 1772 to 1777, elucidating the History of that country, and describing its Productions, Natural History, etc. with an Account of the Indians of Guiana. 2 *vols. Illustrated with* 80 *fine Engravings. Calf.* 4° *London,* 1796

1968 STEDMAN (CAPT. J. G.) NARRATIVE of a five years' Expedition against the Revolted Negroes of Surinam in Guiana, from 1772 to 1777, describing its Productions, Natural History. 2 *vols, maps and plates, calf.* 4° *London,* 1796

1969 STEEL'S COMPLETE MARINE ATLAS. An extensive Collection of Charts, made from Observations and Surveys of the most experienced Navigators, both British and Foreign. 60 *large folded charts,* 2 *vols, half calf.* PUBLISHED AT £16 16*s. Fine copy.* *Atlas Folio, London,* 1812

Complete sets of these charts published under the authority of the Admiralty have become very rare.

1970 STEELE (Sir R.) Epistolary Correspondence; now first printed from the Originals, with Literary and Historical Anecdotes by Nichols. 2 *vols, calf.* 8° *London,* 1787

1971 STENOGRAPHY. An Improved System of Stenography: containing analogous abbreviations, adapted to the convenience of Instructors and Practitioners. 3d Edition, enlarged and improved. By Phinehas Baily.
Stitched. 12° *Poultney,* (*Vt,*) *Smith & Shute,* 1822

1972 STEPHEN (J.) Speech in the House of Commons March 6, 1809, on Mr. Whitbread's Motion relative to the late Overtures of the American Government. *Half morocco.* 8° *London,* 1809

1973 STEPHENS (WILLIAM, *First Secretary and Historian of the Colony of Georgia, and Keeper of its Black Book*) The Castle-Builders; or the History of William Stephens of the Isle of Wight, Esq. lately deceased. A Political Novel, never before published in any language. *Scarce.*
Calf. 8° *For the Author, London,* 1759

Stephens resided sixteen years in Georgia where he died. See No. 352 of this Catalogue.

1974 STEVENS (HENRY, G M B) HISTORICAL NUGGETS. Bibliotheca Americana or a Descriptive Account of my Collection of rare Books relating to America. — "I will buy with you, sell with you." *Shakspeare.* *2 vols, cloth, gilt tops, edges uncut, new.* *Post* 8° *Whittingham, London,* 1862

This work printed in the best style of the Chiswick Press, regardless of time, comprises 3000 Titles given in full, with the collation and price of each work. It was intended as far as it went to be a manual for collectors of this expensive class of books. But it did not go very far, containing as it does not a selection, but only such books as the author happened to possess at that time. It was intended to supply the deficiences by additional volumes, but these have never appeared, and probably never will in this form.

1975 STEVENS (Henry, G M B F S A) Catalogue of my English Library collected and described by Henry Stevens. I will buy with you, sell with you, *Shakspeare.* PRINTED FOR PRIVATE DISTRIBUTION. 12° *Cloth. C. Whittingham, Nov.* 1853

1976 STEVENS (Henry, G M B, etc.) Historical and Geographical Notes on the earliest Discoveries in America, 1453–1530. With comments on the earliest Charts and Maps; the mistakes of the early Navigators, and the blunders of the Geographers; the Asiatic Origin of the Atlantic coast line of North America, how it crept in and how it crept out of the Maps. The whole illustrated by the Tehuantepec Railway Company's Map of the world on Mercator's projection, and photo-lithographic fac-similes of many of the earliest maps and charts of America. *With frontispiece and six large sheets of maps, cloth, uncut, gilt top.* 8° *New Haven: Office of the American Journal of Science. London: Office of the Author,* 4 *Trafalgar Square,* 1869

Only 75 copies printed for sale, all alike, on Whatman's best thick hand-made paper, illustrated with one new map of the world, and fac-similes of 16 of the very earliest known maps of America, arranged on five large sheets of bond paper. Net published price $10.

1977 STEVENS (SIMON) THE TEHUANTEPEC RAILWAY, its Location and Advantages under the LaSere Grant of 1869. *Cloth, price* $3.50. 8° *D. Appleton & Co. New York,* 1869

Of this book one may read in the last Aug. N° of the *Historical Magazine,* p. 106: "This curiously-constructed volume opens with an Introduction [by Simon Stevens, President of the Tehuantepec Railway Company] in which the character of the LaSere Grant [of 1869] for a right of way, from ocean to ocean, is carefully described; with copies of the Charters granted by Mexico and Vermont; and specifications of the proposed work. Then follow, what possess most interest to us, — *Historical and Geographical Notes,* 1453–1869, the former by Henry Stevens, the widely-known Bibliopole of London; the latter by some unknown hand. The whole is elaborately illustrated with Maps and Engravings; and, typographically considered, it is a volume of great beauty. In his *Historical Notes,* Mr. Henry Stevens has briefly glanced on the Old World as it was four hundred years ago" — and traced the progress of discovery and exploration down to 1530, especially so far as it pertained to the New World and its development and gradual recognition as an independent hemisphere. He treats of the earliest maps, the mistakes of the navigators, the blunders of the geographers, etc. etc. and endeavors to show for the first time on record, that the coast lines originally laid down as the north-eastern coast of Asia was afterwards adopted as the eastern coast of North America. The effect of this discovery, if maintained, must considerably modify our previously-conceived notions as to our early geography, chronology, and history. The above-named article concludes with: — "Such a paper, sandwiched in a prospectus for a new railway, is as unusual as it is judicious. The volume which contains it will be sought for and perused by hundreds who would not otherwise have cared for it;

and it will be advertised and talked of, within Massachusetts and without, as no other similar production has hitherto been. For that reason let us advise our readers who are interested in such inquiries to seek to obtain a copy." Only a limited number was printed, chiefly as presents to capitalists known to be interested in the great project of Interoceanic Communication by means of the Tehuantepec Railway. Not fifty copies have been offered for sale.

1977* STEVENS (W.) Memoirs of. *Boards.* 8° *London,* 1812

1978 STEVENSON (W. B.) RELATION HISTORIQUE et Descriptive d'un Séjour de vingt ans dans l'Amerique de Sud ou Voyage, en Aracaunie au Peroue, et dans la Colombie. 3 *vols, half green morocco.* 8° *Paris,* 1826

1979 STEVENSON (W. B.) Reisen in Arauco, Chile, Peru, und Columbia, 1804–23. 2 *vols, boards.* 8° *Weimar,* 1826

1980 STEWART. A Coole Conference between the Scottish Commissioners Cleared. Reformation, and the Holland Ministers Apologeticall Narration, brought together by a well-willer to both. *Half morocco.* 4° *London,* 1644

1981 STEWART (John, "*Walking Stewart*") The Revelation of Nature with the Prophesy of Reason. *Calf.* 12° *Printed by Mott and Lyon for the Author. New York,* 4800

1982 STEWART (J.) Past and Present State of Jamaica; with Remarks on the Moral and Physical Condition of the Slaves, *etc. Half maroon morocco, uncut.* 8° *Edinburgh,* 1823

1983 STILES (Ezra, *President of Yale College*) Life of Ezra Stiles, D. D. By Abiel Holmes. *Portrait.* 8° *Thomas & Andrews, Boston,* 1798

1984 STILLMAN (S.) Sermon, occasioned by the Death of George Washington, Delivered Dec. 29th, 1799. *Uncut.* 8° *Boston,* 1800

1985 STIMPSON (W.) A Revision of the Synonomy of the Testaceous Mollusks of New England. *Plates.* 8° *Boston,* 1851

1986 STOECKLEIN (JOSEPHUS) DER NEWE WELT-BOTT, mit allerhand nachrichten dem Missionarum Societatis Jesu, *etc.* 32 Theile, bound in 4 thick volumes. *Very fine copy, in old pig skin. Maps and plates. Folio, Augsburg,* 1726–1755

This rare and highly important collection of Letters from the Jesuit Missionaries in all parts of the World, deserves to be better known to the American historians. It is the great repertory of these valuable Letters. Not only are all the celebrated *Lettres Edifiantes* translated and incorporated into this German Compilation, but very many more are added, so that it becomes the great storehouse of topography, history and geography of India, China, Japan, Borneo, Persia, Turkey, and the whole of the Western hemisphere. There are letters from every part of North and South America, and especially the more remote provinces of Mexico, of California, Brazil, Peru, Quito, and Paraguay; nor do we fail to find letters from Canada and the Eastern Provinces; Maine, New York, the Great West and the Valley of the Mississippi. The historical mouser who has waded through Stöcklein, must necessarily have accumulated details which cannot be found elsewhere.

1987 STOECKLEIN (JOSEPHUS) DER NEWE WELT–BOTT, mit allerhand nachrichten dem Missionarum Soc. Jesu. 24 *parts, bound in* 3 *volumes. Maps and plates. Folio, Augsburg & Wein,* 1726–1732

1988 STODDARD (*Major* A.) Sketches, Historical and Descriptive, of Louisiana. *Scarce and valuable.* 8° *Philadelphia,* 1812

1989 STOKES (ANTHONY) View of the Constitution of the British Colonies, in North America and the West Indies, at the time the Civil War broke out on the Continent of America. *Half calf.* 8° *London,* 1783

1990 STOKES (Anthony) A View of the Constitution of the British Colonies in North America, etc. *Calf.* 8° *London,* 1783

1991 STONE (E.) New Mathematical Dictionary. *Calf.* 8° *London,* 1726

1992 STONE (E.) Half Century Sermon, delivered at Reading, North Parish, May 19th, 1811. 8° *Salem,* 1811

1993 STORY (Joseph) Discourse at the Request of the Essex Historical Society, September 18th, 1828, in Commemoration of the First Settlement of Salem, Massachusetts. *Uncut.* 8° *Boston,* 1828

1994 STORY (Joseph) Discourse at the Request of the Essex Historical Society, 18th September, 1828, in Commemoration of the First Settlement of Salem. *Uncut.* 8° *Boston,* 1828

1995 STORY (THOMAS) A Journal of the Life of Thomas Story: Containing an account of his Remarkable Convincement of, and Embracing the Principles of Truth, as held by the People called Quakers; And also, of his Travels and Labours in the Service of the Gospel: With many other Occurrences and Observations. *Fine copy, large paper, old calf.* *Folio, Isaac Thompson, Newcastle upon Tyne,* 1747

The above title gives no indication of the value of this book for American history and biography. The author was a shrewd, sharp-witted Quaker, born in the north of England; had his eye-teeth cut while in the Church of England before he seceded and joined the Quakers. After travelling in Scotland and round about, he drifted towards London in 1697, where he had the good fortune to make the acquaintance of William Penn. Their intimacy soon ripened into friendship, and in the autumn of 1698, Story embarked at London for Pennsylvania. The next year he made a progress through New Jersey, New York City, Long Island, Connecticut, Rhode Island, to Boston and vicinity, and even into New Hampshire, spreading everywhere the true light of Truth and confounding the Priests. He interviewed Rollon-God Cotton of Sandwich, and spiced him well. He is particularly racy about the laws of Connecticut and Massachusetts. "Such is the great Bondage and Slavery that People are in to their hired Preachers, who had noosed them into a Law of their own making, destructive of the Liberty of their Consciences and Civil Rights," etc. He found himself again in Philadelphia at the beginning of the year 1700, ready to return to England; but William Penn, appreciating his abilities, offered many inducements to him to remain. He became a member of the Governor's Council, the Keeper of the Great Seal, the Master of the Rolls, the Recorder of Deeds, and one of the Commissioners of Property. On the granting of a Charter about this time to the inhabitants of Philadelphia, erecting it into a City, Story was appointed the First Recorder. Soon after he again travelled to New England and elsewhere at the North, and into Virginia and Carolina at the South. In 1706 he married a daughter of Edward Shippen, of Philadelphia, formerly of Boston. He remained in the Government of Pennsylvania till 1708, when he went to the West Indies and thence to England. Altogether nearly 300 pages of this work are occupied by the author's travels and labors, political and pious, in America. Indeed, it is the largest book of Travels in what is now the United States up to this time, 1708.

1996 STRANGWAYES (George) The Vnhappy Marksman. Or a Perfect and Impartial Discovery of that late Barbarous and Unparallel'd Murther Committed by Mr. George Strangwayes, Formerly a Major in the King's Army on his Brother-in-law Mr. John Fussel an Attorney, on Friday the Eleventh of February. Together with a full Discovery of the Fatal Cause of those unhappy Differences which first occasioned the Suits in Law betwixt them. Also the behavior of Mr. Strangways at his Tryal. The dreadful Sentence pronounced against him. His Letter to his Brother-in-law, a Member of Parliament. The words by him delivered at his death; and his stout, but Christian-like manner of dying. Published by a Faithful Hand. Ovid. Trist. lib. 5. *Strangulat inclusus dolor, atque cor æstuet intus.* Excessively rare. *Fine copy, vellum, 32 pp.* 4° *London, T. N. for R. Clavell,* 1659

Victor Hugo, in his recent novel, "*L'homme qui rit,*" describing the horrors of the *Press-house of Newgate*, has brought the subject of this little book into terrible prominence. That author, so far as the scenes are laid in England, professes that he has not exceeded the reality, and that he has not gone beyond the letter of the law or the not unfrequent practice of the courts. Yet he has portrayed scenes of torture in Protestant England that were rarely or never exceeded by the Inquisition of Spain. The London *Times* of the 14th of last October, in reviewing M. Hugo's book, asserts that the author has disregarded history, and introduced scenes which it is impossible to believe could have ever taken place in England. A week later, in the London *Telegraph*, of the 22d October, Mr. Swinburne, the poet, comes out in an able and perfectly convincing defense of his French friend, and shows that it was the common practice, when a prisoner of a certain class refused to plead, to condemn him to the torture of the *press* till death, or till he consented to plead. Mr. Swinburne alludes to this case of Major Strangwayes as the last case of one dying under this torture, about the middle of the 18th century. He was herein mistaken one century, as to Major Strangwayes, but there was a case in 1720, of Spiggott who submitted to the press with much courage for some time, but finally yielded, plead, lived awhile, and died a wretch in body and soul, two or three years later. Several papers have appeared in England on this subject within the last few years, but this original account seems to be little known, while at the same time it gives important details, and far exceeds in official horrors anything written by M. Hugo or Mr. Swinburne. The high social position of the murderer and the murdered, and the whole chain of circumstantial evidence, are given in full in this contemporary account. For reasons which he deemed sufficient, Major Strangwayes refused to plead when brought before the court, and "persisting in his first resolution not to plead, hears from the offended court this dreadful sentence :—

"*That the Prisoner be sent to the place from whence he came; and that he be put into a mean House stopped from any Light: and that he be laid upon his Back, with his Body bare, saving something to cover his Privy parts; That his Arms shall be stretched forth with a Cord, the one to one side of the Prison, the other to the other side of the Prison; and in like manner shall his Legs be used: And that upon his Body shall be laid as much Iron and Stone as he can bear, and more; And the first day shall he have Three Morsels of Barley Bread, and the next day shall he drink thrice of the Water in the next Channel to the Prison Door, but no Spring or Fountain Water: And this shall be his punishment till he die*"

Thus in the *Press-house* in London, in February, 1658, because he would not plead, the prisoner died, his *friends* looking on, and some of them even mounting the press among the iron and the stones in kindness to hasten his horrid death. Can Victor Hugo over color these simple facts?

An age later, in 1692, Giles Corey of Salem Farms, paid a like penalty. In Massachusetts a witch's soul was snaked out of his body by an old law, while a

Stoughton was the Chief Justice and acting Governor. Giles Corey was not extinguished, but his story has become long after, one of the much talked-of "*New England Tragedies.*" Well might the poet muffle the scene of the New England "*press-house,*" and leave it to the passing-bell to announce the horrid death. And well might young Cotton Mather exclaim: —

"O sight most horrible! In a land like this,
Spangled with Churches Evangelical,
Inwrapped in our salvations, must we seek
In mouldering statute-books of English Courts
Some old forgotten Law, to do such deeds?
Those who lie buried in the Potter's Field
Will rise again, as surely as ourselves
That sleep in honored graves with epitaphs;
And this poor man, whom we have made a victim,
Hereafter will be counted as a martyr!" — *Longfellow.*

1997 STRATEN-PONTHORZ (Auguste Van der) LE BUDGET DU BRÉSIL, ou Recherches sur les Resources de cet Empire dans leur Rapports avec les Interets Europeens du Commerce et de la Navigation. *Portrait; 3 vols, half green morocco.* LARGE PAPER, *fine uncut copy.* *Royal* 8° *Bruxelles,* 1854

1998 STRONG (Nathan) The Doctrine of Eternal Misery Reconcileable with the Infinite Benevolence of God. 8° *Hartford,* 1796

1999 STRONG (NATHAN) Discourse on the Death of George Washington, in the North Presbyterian Church, Hartford, Dec. 27, 1799. *Uncut.* 8° *Hartford,* 1800

2000 STRUYS (J.) ROMEO EN JULIETTE. OP DE REGHEL: Naer een se booghen vaert, en vlucht te seer verbolghen, Plach diekmael in't ghemeeen een haeste volte volghen. Ghespeelt op de Amsterdamsche Camer, op Kermis, A° 1634. *Fine clean copy, vellum.* 4° *D. C. Houthaeck, Amsterdam,* 1634

THIS EXCESSIVELY RARE PLAY by Struys, founded on Shakespeare's "Romeo and Juliet," usually sells for £5 to £10 in London. The impression in this copy of the spirited vignette, on the title, representing Juliette at the tomb of the Capulets, killing herself with the dead Romeo's sword, is most brilliant.

2001 STUART (James) Drie Jaren in Noord Amerika. *3 vols, half maroon morocco, uncut.* 8° *Gorinchem,* 1835–36

2002 STUART (James) Drie Jaren in Noord Amerika. *3 vols, frontispieces, half morocco, uncut, fine copy.* 8° *Gorinchem,* 1835–36

2003 STUART (Moses) Sermon at Salem, Nov. 5, 1818, at the Ordination of Pliny Fisk, Levi Spaulding, Miron Winslow and Henry Woodward, Missionaries. *Uncut.* 8° *Andover,* 1818

2004 STUART (M.) Rules of Greek Accent and Quantity. 12° *Andover,* 1829

2005 SUBSTANCE of Gen. BURGOYNE's Speeches, on Mr. Vyner's Motion, May 26th, and on Mr. Hartley's Motion, May 28, 1778; with Appendix containing Gen. WASHINGTON's Letter to Gen. Burgoyne. 8° *London,* 1778

2006 SUGAR TRADE. Candid and Impartial Considerations on the Nature of the Sugar Trade. [By Dr. John Campbell.] *Maps, calf.* 8° *London,* 1763

2007 SUGAR TRADE. Candid Considerations on the Nature of the Sugar Trade. *Maps, calf.* 8° *London,* 1763

2008 Sugar Trade. Candid and Impartial Considerations on the Nature of the Sugar Trade; the comparative Importance of the British and French Islands in the West Indies, etc. *Maps, half morocco, uncut.* 8° *London*, 1763

2009 Sullivan (J.) History of Land Titles in Massachusetts. 8° *Boston*, 1801

2010 SUPPLEMENTVM Supplementi Chronicarum ab ipso Mundi Exordio usq; ad redemptionis Nostræ Annum. M.ccccc.x. editum. Et nouissime recognitũ. Et castigatum a Jacobo Philippo Bergomãte [Foresti] ordinis Heremitarũ. *Half calf.* *Folio, Venetiis*, 1513

See *supra*, Notes under Numbers 175 and 176 of this Catalogue.

2011 Sylburgius (F.) Saracenica, siue Moamethica, Graece et Latine. *Calf.* 8° *H. Commelinus*, 1595

2012 Tacitus. Commentaria in Taciti de Moribus et Populis Germanorum And. Althameri, Brentii. *August. Vindelic*, 1580. Commentarii in Taciti Germaniam, Melancthonis, Penceri, Glateani Bircameri, 1579. *In uno vol.* 8°

2013 Tactics. Infantry Tactics for the U. States Militia. 12° *Boston*, 1830

2014 Tailor (Thomas, *D. D.*) Christ Revealed. *Calf.* 4° *London*, 1635

2015 Talbot (E. A.) Cinq Années de Sejour au Canada, suivres d'un Extrait du Voyage de M. J. M. Duncan en 1818–19. Traduit par M. Eyries. *Map and plates.* *3 vols, half crimson morocco, uncut.* 8° *Paris*, 1825

2016 Talvj. Geschichte der Colonisation von New England. *Half green morocco.* 8° *Leipzig*, 1847

2017 TANNER (*R. P.* Mathas) Die Gesellschaft Jesu bisz zur vergiess ung ihres Blutes wider den Gotzendienst, Unglauben, und laster, für Gott, den wahren Glauben, und Tugendten in allen vier Theilen der Welt streitend: Das ist: Lebens-Wandel, und Todtes-Begebenheit der jenigen, die ausz der Gesellschafft Jesu umb verthätigung Gottes, des wahren Glaubens, und der Tugenden, gewaltthätiger Weisz hingerichtel worden. *With frontispiece and many copperplate engravings.* *Thick folio, Gedruckt zu Prag*, 1683

A rare and very important historical work. It contains the lives and martyrdoms of the Jesuit missionaries in the four parts of the Globe. Some of those who perished in Asia and Africa had previously labored in America. Part IV is devoted entirely to America, comprising pages 563 to 738, and contains biographies, some of them very full, of fifty-eight missionaries, all of whom were put to death by the savages in some horrid form or other. These terrible deaths are illustrated by thirty-nine copperplates in the text, representing all sorts of tortures, each more horrid than the last, equal in refinement of cruelty, almost to that of the Spanish savages who first explored and devastated the New World. Nine perished in Florida, viz: Peter Martinez, Sept. 28, 1566 ; Louis de Quiros, Gabriel de Solis, and Jean Mendez, the 4th of Feb. 1571; and John Baptiste de Segura, Gabriel Gomez, Peter de Limarez, Sanctius Savallius and Christopher Rotundus, the 8th Feb. 1571. Several in Peru, Brasil, Paraguay

Quito, Mexico, and California. But perhaps the most interesting part of the volume to us is pp. 647–694, containing the lives of the French Jesuits among the Hurons, the Iroquois, and other nations of Canada, New York, and the West, comprising the biographies of Fathers Isaac Jogues, Antoine Daniel, Jean de Brebeuf, Gabriel Lallemant, Charles Garnier, Natalis Chabanel, Cornelius Beudin, Jacob Basil, and Jacob Vhuteux. The Life of Father Jogues filling 27 pages, is the fullest in the volume. He is represented as being tortured to death by the Iroquois on the 18th of October, 1646, first by three Indians pulling out the nails of his fingers and toes with pincers.

2018 TAPIA ZENTENO (CARLOS DE) ARTE NOVISSIMA de Lengua Mexicana. *Fine large copy, vellum.*
4° *En Mexico, por la Viuda de D. Joseph Bernardo de Hogal,* 1753

At the head of the dedication are the arms of the Archbishop of Mexico, engraved by ANTONIO MORENO, *Mexici sculpsit.* The volume contains eleven preliminary leaves, and 58 pages. Aside from the intrinsic value of the work as one of the principal ones upon the languages of Mexico, there is on the tenth leaf a piece of elaborately ingenious trifling worth mentioning. It is an *Elogio* of sixteen lines, by Dr. Miguel Joseph Moche, upon the Author, so arranged in concentric circles, like a wheel of sixteen spokes, that each line terminates in A, placed at the hub. The middle letter of each line is a capital. Then reading first round the tire, then the middle circle, ending at the hub with A, we have these 33 letters: *D.* TAPIA DE SENTENO MUI FELIZ VIVA.

2019 TARAPHA (Franciscus) Francisci Taraphæ Barcinonen. De origine, ac rebus gestis Regum Hispaniae liber, multarum cognitione refertus. *Portrait on title, fine copy, scarce, calf gilt.* 8° *In Aedibus Joannis Steelsij, Antverpiae,* 1553

See on p. 182 for an account of the early voyages down the coast of Africa, and the new Islands of the Atlantic. On p. 196 is an account of the discovery of America by Columbus.

2020 TAXATION no Tyranny; an Answer to the Resolutions and Address of the American Congress [By Dr. Johnson.] Third Edition. *Half morocco, uncut.* 8° *London,* 1775

2021 TAYLOR (Isaac) Memoirs of the late Jane Taylor. *Boards.* 18° *Lowell,* 1829

2022 TAYLOR (J. B.) Lives of Virginia Baptist Ministers. *Cloth.* 12° *Richmond,* 1837

2023 TELLIAMED; or the World Explain'd; containing Discourses between an Indian Philosopher and a Missionary on the Diminution of the Sea, the formation of the Earth, &c. *Fine copy, calf.* 8° *W. Pechin, Baltimore,* 1797

2024 TENNENT (Gilbert) Three Sermons on Rev. III. 3. Preached at New York, April 1742, with Appendix.
12° *Printed by S. Kneeland, Boston,* 1743

2025 TIMPERLEY (C. H.) THE PRINTER'S MANUAL; containing Instructions to Learners, with Scales of Impositions, etc. *Half calf.* *Royal* 8° *London,* 1838

2026 TERENTIUS. Comædiae sex, cum Donati commentariis. *Calf.* 8° *Basiliæ,* 1616

2027 TERENTIUS. Comædiæ, studio P. Victorii editæ.
8° *Heidelbergæ,* 1687

2028 TESTAMENT. THE FIRST NEW TESTAMENT PRINTED IN THE ENGLISH LANGUAGE (1525 or 1526.) Translated from the Greek by WILLIAM TYNDALE. Reproduced in fac-simile, with an Introduction by FRANCIS FRY, F. S. A. *Cloth, uncut.* PUBLISHED AT £7 7*s.* 8° *Bristol, Printed for the Editor,* 1862

This exact fac-simile, in lithography, of above 700 closely printed pages, in black letter, taken from the unique copy preserved in the Baptist College Library at Bristol, of the first edition of TYNDALE'S NEW TESTAMENT, is a monument of the industry and pious zeal of Francis Fry. For all practical purposes in philology, theology, and history, it is every way as good and useful as the original, which would to-day probably produce a thousand guineas were it unfortunately put up to auction. This edition, very limited, was issued in this style at seven guineas, and a few copies on vellum at £42.

2029 TESTAMENT. 'Η Καινὴ Διαθήκη. Novum Testamentum, juxta exemplar Joannis Millii accuratissime impressum. EDITIO PRIMA AMERICANA. *Fine copy, sheep ; a scarce edition.* 12° *Wigorniæ, Massachusettensi, Isaias Thomas, Jr. April,* 1800

2030 TESTAMENT. 'Η Καινὴ Διαθήκη. Novum Testamentum Grece ex recensione J. J. Griesbachi cum selecta lectionum varietate. *Calf.* 8° *Cantab. Nov.-Angl.* 1809

2031 TESTAMENT. 'Η Καινὴ Διαθήκη. Novum Testamentum, juxta exemplar Joannis Millii accuratissime impressum 12° *Bostoniæ, Esias Thomas, Jun.* 1814

2032 TESTAMENT. 'Η Καινὴ Διαθήκη. Novum Testamentum, cum versione Latina Ariæ Montani. Auctore Joanne Leusden. *Calf, good copy.* 12° *G. Long, Novi-Eboraci,* 1821

2033 TESTAMENT. 'Η Καινὴ Διαθήκη. Novum Testamentum Graece ex recensione Jo. Jac. Griesbachii omissa selecta lectionum varietate ejus. *Lipsiæ,* 1805. *Cantab. Nov.-Ang.* 1809 *Fine copy, calf.* 12° *Philad. cura & impensis Abneri Kneeland edita.* *Typis, W. Fry,* 1822

2034 TESTAMENT. 'Η Καινὴ Διαθήκη. Novum Testamentum Graecum, ad exemplar Roberti Stephani editum. Cura P. Wilson. 12° *Hartfordiæ,* 1827

2035 TESTAMENT. 'Η Καινὴ Διαθήκη. Ad exemplar Roberti Stephani. Cura P. Wilson. 12° *Phil.* 1831

2036 TESTAMENT. 'Η Καινὴ Διαθήκη. Ad exemplar Roberti Stephani accuratissime editum. Cura P. Wilson, Coll. Columb. Neo-Ebor. Prof. Emer. *Clean.* 8° *Phil. Haswell,* 1838

2037 TESTAMENT. Das Neue Testament, *etc.* nach der Deutschen Uebersetzung D. Martin Luthers. 7e Auflage. *Fine copy, sheep.* [See O'Callaghan, p. 127.] 12° *Phil. bey G. & D. Billmeyer,* 1815

2038 TESTAMENT. Das Neue Testament unsers Herrn und Heilandes Jesu Christi, nach der deutschen Uebersetzung D. Martin Luthers. 8e Auflage. SCARCE, *very fine copy, calf. with clasps.* 8° *Germantown, Pa. bey M. Billmeyer,* 1819

2039 TESTAMENT (Das Neue), nach der Uebersetzung Martin Luthers. 12° *Phil. Kimber & Sharpless,* 1838

2040 TESTAMENT. Le Nouveau Testament de Notre Seigneur Jesus-Christ. Imprimé sur l'Édition de Paris de Varmée 1805. *Fine copy, uncut.* 8° *Philadelphie, par J. Bouvier,* 1814

2041 TESTAMENT. Le Nouveau Testament, *etc.* imprimé sur l'edition de Paris, de 1805. 12° *New York, par A. Paul,* 1826

2041* TESTAMENT. Ἡ Καινὴ Διαθήκη. Novum Testamentum, juxta exemplar Joannis Millii accuratissime impressum. Editio prima Americana. *Very fine copy. Calf.*
8° *Wigorniæ, Massachusettensis : Excudebat Isaias Thomas, Jun. Singulatim et numerose eo vendita officinæ suæ, April*–1800.
This first Worcester Edition, in fine order, has become very rare. Prefixed is a Chronological Table of the Books of the New Testament, by Caleb Alexander.

2042* TESTAMENT. Ἡ Καινὴ Διαθήκη. Novum Testamentum, cum versione Latine Ariæ Montani, in quo tum selecti versiculi 1900, quibus omnes novi Testamenti voces continentur, asteriscis notantur; tum omnes & singulæ voces, semel vel sæpius occurrentes, peculiari nota distinguuntur. Auctore Johanne Leusden, Professore. Editio prima Americana: qua plurima Londiniensis errata, diligentissime animadversa, corriguntur: Cura Johannis Watts.
8° *Philadelphiæ, S. F. Bradford*, 1806

2043* Testament. Ἡ Καινὴ Διαθήκη. Novum Testamentum juxta exemplar Joannis Millii accuratissime impressum.
8° *Bostoniæ, Esaias Thomas, Jun.* 1814

2044* Testament. Ἡ Καινὴ Δαιθήκη. Novum Testamentum Græcum. Ad exemplar Roberti Stephani accuratissime editum. Cura P. Wilson. Stereotypis Hammondi Wallis, Novi Eboraci. 8° *Hartfordiæ, O. D. Cooke & filios*, 1827

2045* Testament. Das Neue Testament unsers Herrn und Heilandes Jesu Christi nach der Deutschen Uebersetzung D. Martin Luthers. Mit Kurtzem inhalt eines jeden Capitels, vnd vollständiger Answeisung gleicher Schriftstellen, *etc.* Drette Auflage. *Fine copy in old calf, with clasps.*
8° *Germantown (Pa.) bey Michael Billmeyer*, 1803
At the end, on the inside of the cover, is pasted a rare copper-plate, representing the Christian Library, wherein one man is reading the Scriptures to eight others, all in knee-breeches and buckles. It is a worthy piece of Pennsylvania art, designed and engraved by James Poupard probably long before 1803.

2046* Testament. Das Neue Testament unsers Herrn und Heilandes Jesu Christi, nach der Deutschen Uebersetzung Dr. Martin Luthers, *etc.* Die erste Auflage. *Very fine copy. Calf.*
8° *Somerset (Pa.) by Friedrich Goeb*, 1814

2047* Testament. Il Nuovo Testamente del Nostro Signore e Salvatore Gesu Cristo; tradotto in lingua Italiana da Giovanni Diodati. *Morocco.* 32° *Londra, Bagster*, 1833

2048* Testament (The New) *Corners of K* 6 *and L* 1 *torn off.*
8° *Newbury-Port, by John Mycall*, [1791]

2049* Testament (The New) Appointed to be read in Churches. 12° *Worcester, by Isaiah Thomas, Jr. Sept.* 1802

2050* Testament (The New) 8° *Brooklyn, T. Kirk*, 1805

2051* Testament (The New)
8° *Hartford, Hudson & Goodwin*, 1814

2052* Testament (The New)
8° *Concord, N. H. by Daniel Coolidge*, 1814

2053* TESTAMENT (The New) Stereotyped by B. & J. Collins. 8° *Hartford, Conn. by Oliver D. Cooke,* 1820

2054* TESTAMENT (The New) 12° *Hartford, by G. Goodwin & Sons,* 1822

2042 Testament (The New) *Poor copy.* 12° *Newburyport, Parker & Robinson,* [1801]

2043 TESTAMENT. The New Testament, *etc.* appointed to be read in churches. *Imperfect, wanting several leaves, but has beginning and end, an uncommon imprint.* 12° *Brookfield, Mass. by E. Merriam & Co.* 1808

2044 TESTAMENT. The New Testament, *etc. Fine copy, sheep, not noted by O'Callaghan.* 8° *New York, by G. Long,* 1811

2045 TESTAMENT (The New) *etc.* 8° *New York, S. A. Burtus,* 1811

2046 TESTAMENT (The New) *etc.* Appointed to be read in Churches. *Poor copy.* 12° *New York, Evert Duyckinck,* 1813

2047 TESTAMENT (The New) 12° *Hartford, by Hudson & Goodwin,* 1813

2048 TESTAMENT (The New) *etc.* Russell's fifth Stereotyped Edition. 12° *Hartford, Russell,* 1819

2049 TESTAMENT (The New) 12° *Providence, R. I. by Miller & Hutchins,* 1821

2050 TESTAMENT (The New) 12° *Hartford, O. D. Cooke,* 1821

2051 TESTAMENT (The New) 19th Edition. 12° *Hartford, for the Booksellers,* 1822

2052 TESTAMENT (The New) *etc.* 16° *Bennington, Vt, by D. Clark,* 1824

2053 TESTAMENT (The New) *Plates, morocco.* 12° *Hartford, Silas Andrus,* 1824

2054 TESTAMENT (The New) *Calf.* 24° *Phil. Am. S. S. Union,* 1829

2055 TESTAMENT (The New) *etc.* 8° *Boston, Lilly, Wait & Co.* 1833

2056 TESTAMENT (The New) 12° *Windsor, Vt, Ide & Goddard,* 1834

2057 TESTAMENT (The New) 16° *Roby, Kimball & Merrill, Concord, N. H.* 1839

2058 TESTAMENT. The New Testament, with the Marginal Readings, compendious annotations, and copious references to parallel and illustrative passages. *Half roan.* 12° *Keene, N. H. J. & J. W. Prentiss,* 1840

2059 TESTAMENT. The New Testament, *etc. Clean copy, sheep, not in O'Callaghan.* 12° *B. Olds, Newark, N. J.* 1842

2060 TESTAMENT (The New) 12° *Claremont, N. H. n. d.*

2061 TESTAMENT. The Four Gospels in Greek from the text of Griesbach, with a Lexicon in English. 8° *Boston,* 1825

2062 TESTAMENT. The Gospel of St. John in Greek and English, interlined and literally translated, with a transposition of the words into their due order of construction. And a Dictionary. By E. Friederici. 12° *New York, for the Author,* 1830

2063 THACHER (J.) Essay on Demonology, Ghosts, etc.; also an Account of the Witchcraft Delusion at Salem in 1692. *Uncut.* 12° *Boston,* 1831

2064 THACHER (PETER) SERMON, occasioned by the Death of George Washington, Feb. 22, 1800, before the Governor and Legislature of Massachusetts. *Uncut.* 8° *Boston,* 1800

2065 THAYER (JOHN, *of Boston*) RELACION DE LA CONVERSION DEL JUAN THAYER, antes Ministro Protestante en Boston en la America Septentrional, y convertido a la Religion Catolica en Roma el dia 25 de Mayo de 1783. Escrita por el mismo. SCARCE. *Calf.* 8° *Valencia,* 1788

2066 THESAURUS GEOGRAPHICUS: or, the Compleat Geographer, being the Chorography, Topography, and History of Asia, Africa, and America. Third Edition, enlarged, *with maps by Moll. Calf.* *Folio, London,* 1709

Includes ample accounts of every part of America and Africa, with a Catalogue of Books relating to the countries. The title-page to the first part is wanting.

2067 THESPIAN Dictionary; or, Dramatic Biography of the Eighteenth Century. *Portraits, calf, rare.* 12° *London,* 1802

2068 THEVENOT (MELCHISEDEC) RECUEIL DE VOYAGES DE M. THEVENOT. [AVEC DÉCOUVERTE DE QUELQUES PAYS ET NATIONS DE L'AMÉRIQUE Septentrionale par LE P. MARQUETTE, *with* Carte de la découverte faite l'an 1663 dans l'Amérique Septentrionale, *i. e.* the MISSISSIPPI RIVER] *Other maps and plates, vellum.* 8° *Chez Estienne Michallet, Paris,* 1681

This map of the Mississippi River, accompanying Father MARQUETTE'S Voyage, is believed to be the earliest printed map of that River.

2069 THEVET (ANDRÉ) HISTORIA DELL' INDIA AMERICA DETTA ALTRAMENTE FRANCIA ANTARTICA, di M. Andrea Tevet; Tradotta di Francese in Lingva Italiana, da M. Givseppe Horologgi. *Fine, clean, perfect copy, half calf.* 8° *In Venezia appresso Gabriel Giolito di Ferrari,* 1561

André Thevet was a good, honest, credulous writer, who knew personally all the contemporary French navigators to Canada and Brazil, and believed everything they told him. His book therefore has great value as an honest record, but must be read with care and caution. This edition has become very rare.

2070 THEVET (André) Historia dell' India America, etc. *Another copy, vellum.* 8° *Venezia,* 1561

2071 THIERRY (A.) Conquest of England by the Normans. Translated by Hazlitt. *2 vols. Port. cloth.* 8° *London,* 1847

2072 THOMAS (DALBY) AN HISTORICAL ACCOUNT OF THE RISE AND GROWTH OF THE WEST-INDIA COLLONIES, and of the great Advantages they are to England in respect to Trade. *Fine copy, perfectly uncut, except the top, which is short.* 4° *London,* 1690

2073 THOMAS (Gabriel) An Historical and Geographical Account of the Province and Country of Pensilvania and of West-New-Jersey in America. *With a map of both Countries. Cloth.* 12° *London,* 1698. *Lithographed N. York,* 1848

Annexed is an autograph letter to S. G. Drake from Henry Austin Brady, Esq., of N. York, who published this fac-simile reprint, 'and who was lost in the *Arctic.*

2074 THOMAS (Pascoe) JOURNAL of a Voyage to the South-Seas, and round the Globe in H. M. Ship the Centurion, under the command of Commodore Anson. *Calf.* 8° *London,* 1745

2075 THOMAS (Pascoe) A true Journal of a Voyage to the South Seas. *Calf, gilt.* 8° *London,* 1745

2076 THOMPSON (James) A Complete Treatise on the Mensuration of Timber, etc. With a description of the sliding rule and Gunter's scale, etc. 12° *Troy (N. Y.), Wright, Wilbur & Stockwell,* 1805

2077 THOMPSON (George) Narrative of the Arrest, Trial, Conviction, and Imprisonment of Work, Burr, and Thompson in Missouri Penitentiary for attempting to Aid some Slaves to Liberty. *Cloth.* 12° *Hartford,* 1855

2078 THOMPSON (THOMAS) A SALUTATION OF LOVE and tender Invitation unto all People but more especially to the Inhabitants of New England, Rhode Island and Long Island, *etc.* *Fine copy, in blue morocco, uncut.* SCARCE. 8° *London,* 1713

2079 THOMPSON (Zadok) Gazetteer of the State of Vermont. *Map.* 12° *Montpelier,* 1824

2079* THOMPSON (Zadok) Another Copy. 12° *ib.* 1824

2080 THOMPSON (Zadok) The Green Mountain Repository. *A complete set in* 1 *vol. Scarce.* 12° *Burlington,* 1832

2081 THOMPSON (Zadok) Geography and Geology of Vermont. *With Engravings.* 12° *Burlington,* 1848

2082 THOMPSON (Zadok) History of the State of Vermont, from its earliest Settlement to the close of the year 1832. 12° *Burlington,* 1833

2082* THOMPSON (Z.) The same. 4 *copies.* 12° *ib.* 1833

This is one of the best and most conscientious abridged histories we have of any of the States. The Story of the Green Mountain Boys is told with great earnestness and simplicity.

2083 THORNTON (J. Wingate) The Landing at Cape Anne; or the Charter of the first permanent Colony of the Territory of the Massachusetts Company, now discovered and first published from the original MS. with a History of the Colony, 1624–1628. Roger Conant, Governor. *With fac-simile of the Charter. Half morocco.* 8° *Boston,* 1854

2084 THOROWGOOD (THOMAS) IEWES IN AMERICA, or, PROBABILITIES THAT THE AMERICANS ARE OF THAT RACE. With the removall of some contrary reasonings, and earnest desires for effectuall endeavours to make them Christians. *Green morocco by Hayday. A fair but short copy.* EXCESSIVELY RARE. 4° *London,* 1650

2085 THOUGHTS on the late Transactions respecting Falkland's Islands. 2d Ed. [by Dr. Johnson.] *Half roan.* 8° *London,* 1771

2086 THUMB (Thomas) The History of England. *Wood-cuts.* 12° *London,* 1749.

2087 THURSDAY LECTURES. A Course of Sermons on Early Piety. By the eight Ministers who carry on the Thursday Lecture in Boston: with a Preface by Dr. INCREASE MATHER. 12° *S. Kneeland, Boston, N. E.* 1721

2088 TJASSENS (Johan) Zee Politie der Vereenichde Nederlanden. *Black letter, vellum.* 4° *Graven-Hage,* 1652

A rare and important book pertaining to the Naval Affairs of Holland, in which there is contained incidentally very much respecting America and the West Indies.

2089 TODD (*Rev.* H. J.) Some Account of the Life and Writings of John Milton. Second Edition with Additions, and a VERBAL INDEX TO THE WHOLE OF MILTON'S POETRY. *Portrait. half calf, uncut.* 8° *London,* 1809

2089* TOKEN (The) or Affection's Gift, a Christmas and New Year's present. Edited by S. G. Goodrich. *Morocco.* 8° *New York, n. d.*

2090 TRACTATE (A) ON CHURCH MUSIC; being an Extract from the reverend and learned Mr. Peirce's vindication of the Dissenters. The Christian Religion shines brightest in its own dress; and to paint it, is but to deform it. Dr. Nichol's Defence of the Church of England. *Fine copy, uncut, half roan.* 8° *London,* 1786

On the back of the title is, "This Tractate on Church Music is inscribed to the reverend Doctor Chauncy and the reverend Mr. John Clark, the Ministers; and to the several members of the FIRST CONGREGATIONAL DISSENTING CHURCH IN BOSTON IN AMERICA." The interest of this tract is considerably enhanced by a knowledge of the circumstances which called it forth. This copy belonged to Mr. S. Toms, the antiquary of London, who in 1786 wrote his autograph on the title, and an account of the origin of the book on the reverse of it. It is well known that Mr. THO. BRANDE HOLLIS, one of the benefactors of Harvard College, had acquired a wide-spread reputation, like the late George Peabody, for wealth and liberality, and like him was not unfrequently subjected to calls for considerable sums of money for objects in which he had either no sympathy, or did not feel that *he* should be bled. Among these applications was one from Dr. Charles Chauncy and the pillars of the First Congregational Church of Boston for £500, to buy an Organ. Instead of granting this extraordinary request from a well-to-do Society, Mr. Brande Hollis caused, it is said, 500 copies of this TRACTATE to be printed and sent over to the Members of the Society, endeavoring thereby to inculcate in them that modesty and simplicity in their public worship, which they seemed for the moment to be outgrowing. Feeling somewhat diffident about the ability of his compilation to effect its object, Mr. Brande Hollis submitted it to two friends "because he knows the deserved esteem with which their names are regarded in America." These two gentlemen, Dr. Price and Dr. Kippis, in a Postscript, add their testimony against the use of instrumental music in Churches. Finally on a small slip at the end is pasted this quotation from Monsieur le Chevalier de Chastellux, a French officer, who served with LaFayette in the American War. "A judgment may, generally, be formed of a people, by their mode of worship: If it be simple and modest, then they are active, and industrious; if it be full of solemnity and pomp, then they are vain and frivolous; if it be melancholy and austere, then they are fierce, violent, and obstinate." Never before probably was so much pious sarcasm concealed in so small a book.

2091 TRACTS. 7 *vols bound in* 1, *calf.* 8° *London,* 1710–15

1. Burnet (Thos.) The necessity of impeaching the late Ministry. 3d Edition *London,* 1715
2. The Whigs Vindicated. J. Withers. " 1715
3. A New Method for discovering the longitude by Whiston & Ditton. " 1714

4. The Assiento Contract consider'd, Trade of Jamaica. *London*, 1714
5. The Political State of Great Britain. " 1713
6. A List of both Houses of Parliament. " *n. d.*
7. The Modern Fanatick. . By W. Bissett. " 1710

2092 TRACTS. 10 *in* 1 *vol, half russia.* 8° *viz:—*

1. Considerations, on the imposition of 4½ p. cent. *Lond.* 1774
2. Protest against the Bill to repeal the American Stamp Act. *Paris*, 1766
3. Conduct of the Administration in the prosecution of Wilkes. *Lond.* 1764
4. Robinson. Peace the best Policy. 2d edit. " 1777
5. Sketch of the Controversy respecting Tangour. *n. p. n. d.*
6. Account of particulars relative to the demise of the Crown. *Lond.* 1760
7. Letters from a Member of Parliament in London. " 1763
8. Conduct of the Ministry. " 1760
9. Considerations on the Present Peace. " 1763
10. Examination of the Rights of the Colonies. " 1766

2093 TRACTS, 21 *bound in* 6 *vols, calf.* 8° *viz:—*

1. Letter to Dr. Lowth. 3d edit. *Newcastle*, 1766
2. Letter from the Bishop of London on occasion of late earthquake, *Lond.* 1750
3. Dodd, Rev. W. Sermon . . . September 26, 1759. 2d edit. *ib.* [1759]
4. Hard Case of a Country Vicar. *Wants title.* *n. p. n. d.*
5. An Address to Persons of Fashion, etc. 2d edit. *Lond.* 1761
6. Substance of Gen. Burgoyne's Speeches, May, 1778. 3d edit. *ib.* 1778
7. Letter to the Author of the Divine Legation. 4th edit. *ib.* 1766
8. Patten. The sufficiency of the external evidence of the gospel. *Oxford*, 1757
9. State of the British and French Colonies in North America. *London*, 1755
10. Price. A discourse on the love of our Country. *ib.* 1790
11. Priestley. Letter to Rt. Hon. W. Pitt. 2d edit. *ib.* 1787
12. Bealey. Observations on Mr. Owen's Sermon. *Warrington*, 1790
13. The Danger of repealing the Test Act. *Lond.* [1789]
14. Episcopal Opinions on the Test and Corporation Acts. *ib.* 1790
15. The Enthusiasm of Methodists and Papists compared. 2d edit. 2 parts. *ib.* 1749
16. A Charge to the Clergy of the Diocese of Lichfield and Coventry. *ib.* 1744
17. Proceeding of a Court Martial . . upon Lord George Sackville. *ib.* 1760
18. Fownes. An Enquiry into the Principles of Toleration. 3d edit. *Shrewsb.* 1790
19. The Evidence of the Resurrection cleared. *Lond.* 1744
20. The Nature of Patronage and the Duty of Patrons. *ib.* 1735
21. Waterland. Discourse of Fundamentals. *Cambr.* 1735

2094 TRACTS. A COLLECTION, *in one volume.* 8° 1764–70, *viz:*

1. Thoughts on the Origin and Nature of Government, occasioned by the late dispute between Great Britain and her American Colonies, written 1766. *Lond.* 1769
2. The Rights of the British Colonies asserted and proved. By James Otis. *ib. n. d.*
3. The Justice and Necessity of Taxing the American Colonies demonstrated. *ib.* 1766
4. The Grievances of the American Colonies candidly examined. *ib.* 1766
5. The Objections to the Taxation of Our American Colonies by the Legislature of Great Britain briefly considered. *ib.* 1765
6. Some Thoughts on the Method of improving and securing the advantages which accrue to Great Britain from the Northern Colonies, *imperfect.* *ib.* 1765
7. An Examination of the Rights of the Colonies. By a Gentleman of the Bar. *ib.* 1766
8. A Succinct View of the Origin of Our Colonies, with their Civil State. *ib.* 1766
9. The necessity of Repealing the American Stamp Act demonstrated. *ib.* 1766
10. Plain and Seasonable Address to the Freeholders of Great Britain on the Present Posture of Affairs in America. *ib.* 1766
11. Considerations which may tend to promote the Settlement of our new West India Colonies. *ib.* 1764
12. Letters from a Farmer in Pennsylvania to the Inhabitants of the British Colonies. *ib.* 1768

13. Observations on Several Acts of Parliament. Published by the Merchants of Boston. *Lond.* 1770
14. The Regulations lately made Concerning the Colonies and the Taxes imposed upon them. *ib.* 1765

Together, 14 *important tracts in one volume, half morocco, lettered contents, from the library of the late Joseph Parkes.*

2095 TRACTS, 7 *in one volume, half calf*, 8° *viz:* —

1. Candid and impartial narrative of the transactions of the Fleet under Lord Howe. *Lond.* 1779
2. Pulteney. Considerations on present state of Public Affairs. " 1779
3. Letter from Gen. Burgoyne to his Constituents. " 1779
4. Opposition mornings with Betty's Remarks. " 1779
5. A Short history of the Administration during the Summer recess. " 1789
6. Eden. Four letters to the Earl of Carlisle. " 1779
7. Facts addressed to the Landholders, etc. of Gt. Britain. 2d edit. " [1779]

2096 TRACTS, 26 *in* 3 *volumes, half calf.* 8° *viz:* —

1. Price. Observations on Civil Liberty. 5th ed. *Lond.* 1776
2. Wollstonecraft. Vindication of the Rights of Man. 2d edit. " 1790
3. Thelwall. The Rights of Nature. 3d edit. " 1796
4. Morgan. An Appeal to the People of G. B. " 1796
5. Adair. Letter to C. J. Fox. 3d edit. " 1802
6. Dyer. Address . . on the doctrine of Libels. " 1799
7. Mackintosh. Discourse on the Law of Nature, etc. 3d edit. " 1800
8. Anti-Jacobin Review, Oct. 1798. " 1798
9. Curtis. Sequel to the Printed Paper. " 1792
10. Louvet. Narrative of Dangers. " 1795
11. Gieyes. Life of. " 1795
12. Fox. Speech, March 24, 1795. " 1795
13. Erskine. View of the . . War with France. 5th edit. " 1797
14. Boissy d'Anglas. Speech on policy of the French Republic. " 1795
15. Battle of Lodi. [Historical Picture.] " 1803
16. Wakefield. Reply to Bp. . . of Landaff. 2d edit. " 1798
17. Letter to the Ld. Mayor. " 1799
18. Observations on a pamphlet, — "Why do we go to War?" " 1803
19. Horne Tooke. Letter to the Times. " 1807
20. Trial of Joseph Gerrald. *Edinb.* [1794]
21. Holcroft. Narrative of facts relating to a prosecution for High Treason. *Lond.* 1795
22. Holcroft. Letter to the Rt. Hon. W. Windham. " 1795
23. O'Connor. State of Ireland. *n. p.* 1798
24. Life of Rev. Jas. Coigly. " 1798
25. Fenwick. Observations on the Trial of Jas. Coigly. *Lond.* 1798
26. Letter to William Pitt. " 1799

2097 TRACTS. Facts and their Consequences, by the Earl of Stair, 1782. Origin and Narrative of the Marratta and Rohilla Wars in 1773 and 4–1781. Interest of Great Britain with regard to her American Colonies, with Appendix, by James Anderson, 1782. *In* 1 *vol, half calf.* 8° *London*

2098 TRADE. A New Discourse of Trade. By Sir Josiah Child. 4th edition. *Calf gilt.* 8° *London,* [1690]

2098* Transactions of the Fifth Annual Meeting of the Western Literary Institute and College of Professional Teachers, held at Cincinnati, Oct. 1835. *Cloth.* 8° *Cincinnati,* 1836

2099 TREATY of Amity, Commerce and Navigation, between his Britannic Majesty and the United States of America. 2d edition. 8° *Philadelphia,* 1795

2100 TREGELLES (S. P.) The Jansenists: Their Rise, Persecutions by the Jesuits, and Existing Remnant. *Half calf.* 12° *London,* 1851

2101 TREWEN (El. CONSTANT) Fasti Romanorum Liviani; hoc est juxta Historiam et Calculum T. Livii Patavini. *Calf.* 4° *Gedani, n. d.*

2102 TRIAL of Thomas O. Selfridge, for Killing Charles Austin, August 4, 1806. 8° *Boston,* [1806]

2103 TRIAL. By Special Commission. The Trial of Antichrist, otherwise the Man of Sin, for High Treason against the Son of God, Tried at the Sessions House of Truth, before the Rt. Hon. Divine Revelation, Lord Chief Justice, the Hon. Justice Reason, the Hon. Justice History, etc. Taken in short-hand by a Friend to St. Peter. *First American edition.* 12° *Boston,* 1810

2104 TRIAL of Jonathan Syntax, for the Murder of the King's English. 8° *Scatter and Squabble, New York,* 1835

2105 TRIAL of Prof. John Webster, for the Murder of Dr. Geo. Parkman in the Medical College, Nov. 23, 1849. 8° *Boston,* 1850

2105* TRIOMPHE (Le) du Nouveau Monde; Réponses Académiques, formant un nouveau Systême de Confédération, fondé sur les besoins actuels des Nations Chrétienns-commerçantes, & adapté à leurs diverses formes de Gouvernement. Par l'Ami du Corps Social [Jean Brun.] 2 *vols in* 1, *calf.* 8° *Paris,* 1785

A very funny production, and one that even now some of the hide-bound political economists of the old world might study with profit. The aim and general scope of the author may be seen in his earnest replies to the three questions proposed in 1783 by the Academy of Lyons, namely,—1. Has the Discovery of America been an advantage or a disadvantage to the Human Family? If the results have been favorable, what means should be employed to secure and transmit them to our successors? Or if they are bad what means ought to be adopted to remedy them? These and similar questions, proposed to or by the Academies of Berlin, Besançon, Metz, Liège, Chalons, Angers, Manheim, Madrid, Arras, Bordeaux, Mentone and Toulouse, are all so discussed and handled by our Author, Jean Brun, as to render the answers a perfect Triumph to the New World. Indeed, from these learned answers one can see that the Americans, native and foreign, are indeed useful to the Human Family, if in fact they are not a part even of that family.

2106 TROTTER (John Bernard) Memoirs of the latter years of Charles James Fox. *Cloth.* 8° *London,* 1811

From the library, with book-plate, of the late H. T. BUCKLE, who has written on the fly-leaf, "An ill work by a weak man. H. T. B." The author was private Secretary to Mr. Fox.

2107 TRUMBULL (Benjamin) A Discourse Delivered at the Anniversary Meeting of the Freemen of the Town of New-Haven, April 12, 1773. 8° *New Haven,* 1773

2108 TRUMBULL (*Col.* Jonathan) Memoir of. *Portrait.* 8° 1841

2109 TRUMBULL (John) M'Fingal: a Modern Epic Poem. *First complete Edition.* 12° *Hudson & Goodwin, Hartford,* 1782

2110 TRUMBULL (John) McFingall, a Modern Epic Poem. Fifth edition, with explanatory Notes. *Half morocco.* 8° *London,* 1792

2111 TRUMBULL (John) McFingall, a Modern Epic Poem; with Notes. 18° *Boston,* 1799

2112 TRUMBULL (John) POETICAL WORKS, containing McFingal with Notes; Progress of Dullness; and a Collection of Poems on various Subjects. *2 vols in 1, half russia.* 8° *Hartford,* 1820

2113 TRUTH DISPLAYED: in a Series of Elementary Principles, by Benjamin Osborn. 626 *pp.* *Sheep.* 8° *Rutland, Vt, by Fay & Davidson,* 1816

2114 TUCKER (John, *of the First Church in Newbury*) Remarks on a Sermon of Rev. Aaron Hutchinson, of Grafton, *Valour for the Truth,* preached at Newbury Port, April 23, 1767. *Half roan, uncut.* 8° *T. & J. Fleet, Boston,* [1767]

2115 TUCKER (John) Two Discourses, occasioned by the Death of the Rev. Mr. John Lowell, Pastor of the Congregational Church in Newburyport. Delivered June 7th, 1766. *Half morocco, uncut.* 8° *Printed by Thos. & John Fleet, Boston,* 1767

2116 TUCKER (Josiah) Four Tracts, together with two Sermons [partly on American affairs.] *Calf gilt.* 8° *Gloucester,* 1774

2117 TUCKER (Josiah) An Humble Address and Earnest Appeal, *etc.* Whether a connection with or separation from the Continental Colonies of America be most to the National Advantage of these Kingdoms. *Half roan.* 8° *Gloucester,* 1775

2118 TUCKER (Josiah) An Humble Address to Personages in Great Britain and Ireland. Connection with or Separation from the Colonies of America. *Half roan.* 8° *Gloucester,* 1775

2119 TUDOR (H.) Narrative of a Tour in North America, comprising Mexico; with an Excursion to Cuba. *2 vols.* *Cloth.* 8° *London,* 1834

2120 TUOMEY (M.) First Biennial Report of the Geology of Alabama. 8° *Tuscaloosa,* 1850

2121 TUPPER (Ferdinand Brock) Family Records, containing Memoirs of Major-General Sir Isaac Brock, K. B., Lieut. C. W. Tupper, and Col. W. De Vic Tupper, *etc.* and Life of Te-Cum-Seh, *etc.* *2 plates, half brown morocco, uncut.* 8° *Guernsey,* 1835

2122 TURELL'S (Mr.) Brief and Plain Exhortation to his People on the late Fast, Jan. 28, 1747–8, *title mended. Half roan.* 8° *Rogers & Fowle, Boston,* 1748

2123 TURKS. DE THURCIE DESTRUCTIO SUBUERSIONESQ; ac euulsione libellus fatidicus mirabilisq; ac admirandus Sumptus & excerptus ex quodũ mirabili tractatu quẽ quidam doctissimus virorũ ac theologie doctor & edidit atq; composuit. 4° *Cum mira arte per Johannem Froschouer in ciuitate Auguste impress.* 1498

With illuminated letters, heightened with gold, and with a miniature of the Infant Christ, colored and gilt.

2124 TURNER (Sharon) History of the Anglo-Saxons, from their first Appearance above the Elbe, to the Death of Egbert. *Map, half calf, uncut.* 8° *London,* 1799

2125 TUSTIN (Josiah P.) A [Historical] Discourse delivered at the Dedication of the New Church Edifice of the Baptist

Church and Society in Warren, R. I. May 8, 1845 [with an historical Appendix], 193 *pp. and* The History of Warren, R. I. from the Earliest Times; with particular notices of Massasoit and his Family. By G. M. Fessenden. 125 *pp.* 2 *vols, in* 1, *cloth.* 12° *Providence*, 1845

2126 Twiss (T.) The Oregon Question Examined, in respect to Facts and the Law of Nations. *Map, cloth.* 8° *Lond.* 1846

2127 TWIST (Johannem van) Beschrijving van Guseratte. . . . anders genaemt den grooten Mogoll. *Very fine copy, uncut, white vellum, by Pratt.* Scarce. 4° *Hendrick Doncker, Amsterdam*, 1647

This valuable work contains an account of the early voyages to India generally, and a full description of the kingdom of Guseratta in particular.

2128 Tyler (Royal, *Chief Justice of Vermont*) The Algerine Captive, or Adventures of Dr. Updike Underhill. 2 *vols, in* 1. 16° *Hartford*, 1816

2129 UCHTERITZ. Kurtze Reise Hr. Heinrich von Uchteritz, Worinnen vermeldet, was er auf derselben für Unglück und Glück gehabt, sonderlichwieer gefangen nach West Indien geführet, zur Sclaverey verkaufft, und auff der Insel Barbados, etc. [*See* Nuggets, No. 2719.] Scarce. 4° *Schleszwig*, 1666

2130 Ulloa (Ant. de) Noticias Americanas: Entretenimientos Phisicos-Historicos sobre la America Meridional, y la Septentrional Oriental. *Half blue morocco, uncut.* 4° *Madrid*, 1772

2131 Ulloa (Ant. de and Geo. Juan) A Voyage to South America. 5th Edition. *Maps and plans*, 2 *vols, half blue morocco.* 8° *London*, 1807

2132 Ulloa (*Don*) Memoires Philosophiques, Historiques Physiques, concernant la Decouverte de l'Amerique, ses anciens Habitans, etc. 2 *vols, half calf.* 8° *Paris*, 1787

2133 Ulloa (*Don*) Memoires Philosophiques, Historiques Physiques, concernant la Decouverte de l'Amerique, ses anciens Habitans, leurs Moeurs, Usages, *etc.* 2 *vols.* 8° *Paris*, 1787

2134 Umfreville (Edward) The present state of Hudson's Bay, containing a description of the Fur Trade. *Half morocco, uncut.* 8° *London*, 1790

2135 United States of America. The Constitutions, *etc. Calf.* 8° *Philadelphia, printed: London, reprinted*, 1782

2135* United States. The Constitutions of the several Independent States of America, the Declaration of Independence, &c. &c. *Portrait of Washington, calf.* 8° *London*, 1783

2136 United States. A Collection of the Constitutions of the Thirteen United States. *Calf.* 8° *Glasgow reprinted*, 1783

2137 United States. Constitutions des treize États-Unis de l'Amerique. *Half calf.* 8° *Philadelphia*, [*Paris*] 1783

2138 UNITED STATES. The Constitutions of the United States; the Declaration of Independence; and the Federal Constitution, with the Amendments thereto. This edition contains the Constitution of Vermont, not in any former one.
Calf, fine copy. 12° *Philadelphia, Carey, Stewart & Co.* 1791

2139 UNITED STATES. Return of the whole number of Persons within the United States, 1800. SCARCE, *half morocco, uncut.* 8° *Washington,* 1802

2140 UNITED STATES. MESSAGE from the President of the United States accompanying a Statement of Expenditures from the 1st of January, 1797, by the Quarter-Master General and the Navy Agents for the Contingencies of the Naval and Military Establishments, and the Navy Contracts. 23d December 1802 ordered to lie on the Table. *Half calf,* VERY RARE. *Folio, Washington,* 1803

2141 UNITED STATES. The Constitutions, Declaration of Independence, etc. *Calf.* 8° *Philadelphia,* 1806

2142 UNITED STATES. Rules and Regulations of the Field Exercise, etc. of Infantry, in 1814. *Calf.* 8° *New York,* 1815

2143 UNITED STATES. Commercial Regulations of the Foreign Countries with which the United States have Commercial Intercourse. *Sheep.* 8° *Washington,* 1819

2144 UNITED STATES. History of, by a Citizen of Massachusetts. 12° *Keene, N. H.* 1823

2145 UNITED STATES. A General Outline of the United States of North America, her Resources and Prospects. *Half red morocco.* 8° *Philadelphia,* 1824

2146 UNITED STATES. History of the United States from their first Settlement as Colonies to 1812. *Half calf.* 8° *London,* 1826

2147 UNITED STATES. Abstract of the Fifth Census, 1832. *Half morocco, uncut.* 8° *Washington,* 1832

2148 UNITED STATES. Fifth Census; or Enumeration of the Inhabitants of the United States, 1830. To which is prefixed a Schedule, etc. taken according to the Acts of 1790, 1800, 1810, 1820. *Folio, Washington,* 1832

2149 UNITED STATES. Sixth Census, or Enumeration of the Inhabitants in 1840. *Half sheep.* *Folio, Washington,* 1841

2150 UNITED STATES. Sixth Census, *another copy.* *Folio, Washington,* 1841

2151 UNITED STATES. OFFICIAL REGISTER 1822, 1830, 1832, 1833, 1835, 1838, 1839, 1841, 1843. 9 *vols.* 8° *Washington.*

2152 UNITED STATES. The same for 1832, 1833, 1839, 1841. 4 *vols.* 8°

2153 UNITED STATES Official Register. 8° *Washington,* 1839

2154 UNITED STATES BONDS and Securities; by Belding, Keith, & Co. *Cloth.* 8° *London,* 1867

2155 UNITED STATES (THE) MAGAZINE: A Repository of History, Politics and Literature. For the Year 1779. Vol I. (*All published ?*) *Fine clean copy,* UNCUT, *half red morocco.* 8° *Francis Bailey, Philadelphia,* 1779

2156 UPHAM (C. W.) Lectures on Witchcraft, comprising a History of the Delusion in Salem in 1692. *Cloth. First Edition.* 12° *Boston,* 1831

2157 Upham (T. C.) American Sketches. *Boards, uncut.* 12° *New York,* 1819

2157* UPPER CANADA. A Short Topographical Description of his Majesty's Province of Upper Canada. To which is annexed a Provincial Gazetteer. *Half blue morocco, uncut.* 8° *London,* 1799

2158 URLSPERGER (SAMUEL) AUSFÜHRLICHE NACHRICHT von den Saltzburgischen Emigranten, die sich in America niedergelassen haben, [*with the*] Continuations 1 to 5. 2 *vols, vellum.* 4° *Halle,* 1735–40

Volume I. has a fine impression of the rare portrait of Tomo Chachi Mico, or King of Yamacrau, engraved by John Jacob Kleinschmidt, from a painting by C. Verelst.

2159 USSELINX (WILLEM) NAEDER BEDENCKINGEN, OVER DE ZEE–VAERDT, Coophandel ende Neeringhe, als mede de versekeringhe vanden Staet deser vereenichde Landen, inde teghenwoordighe Vrede-handelinghe met den Coninck van Spangnien ende de Aerts-hertoghen. EXCESSIVELY RARE. 4° *Ghedruckt in het Jaerons Heeron,* 1608

This is one of the earliest and most important publications of Wm. Usselinx, that clear-headed, far-seeing political economist, to whom Holland is perhaps more indebted than to any other one man, for her rapid growth and prosperity, between 1600 and 1635, through the encouragement of her East and West India Trade.

2160 USSELINCX (WILLEM) VERTOOGH, hoe nootwendich, nut ende profijtlick het sy voor de vereenighde Nederlanden te behouden de Vryheyt van te handelen op West-Indien, Inden vrede metten Coninck van Spaignen. [An Essay showing how necessary and profitable it is for the United Netherlands to preserve freedom of trade to the West Indies, in the peace with the K[s] of Spain.] 4° [*Amst.* 1608]

For an account of the rarity, historical importance, and intrinsic value of the writings of Usselincx, see Asher's Bibliographical Essay, pp. 73–97, No. 99 of this Catalogue.

2179 VADIANUS (Joachimus) Epitome trivm Terræ Partivm, Asiæ, Africæ et Europæ compendiariam locorum descriptionem Continens, *etc. Very fine large clean copy, calf.* 8° *Tigvri, apud Ch. Froschouerum,* 1534

The general opinion among the German Geographers of this date was that whatever parts of the world did not properly pertain to Europe and Africa somehow belonged to Asia. Up to 1533, Vadian, Schoner, Fine, and many others placed the discoveries of Cortes, and all before him, in Asia. This book, therefore, becomes important to the student of American History, not so much to trace out actual geographical information, as to see how befogged the learned were even twenty years after Columbus was in his grave.

2180 VAENUS (OTHO) AMORVM EMBLEMATA, figvris æneis incisa stvdio Othonis Væni Batavo-Luddunensis. *Oblong* 8° *Antverpiæ*, *Venalia apud Auctorem*, 1608

Contains 124 Copperplate Emblems, illustrative of the freaks and fancies of Master Dan Cupid, with descriptive letter-press in Latin, Dutch, and French.

2181 VAILLANT (J.) Scripture compared with itself in proof of the Doctrine of the Holy Trinity. 8° *London*, 1819

2182 VALLE (Juan N. del) El Viagero en Mexico ó sea capital de la Republica encerrada en un libro. *Plates and large map of the City of Mexico. Half calf.* 12° *Mexico*, 1859

2183 VALLETTE (ELIE) The Deputy Commissary's Guide within the Province of Maryland. *Calf.* 8° *Annapolis*, 1765

VERY RARE. The title-page of the present copy is mutilated, the lower outer corner being torn off.

2184 VALVERDE (*Don* ANTONIO SANCHEZ) Idea del Valor de la Isla Española, y utilidades, que de ella puede sacar su Monarquia. 4° *Madrid*, 1785

VALVERDE (A. S.) La America vindicada de la calumnia de haber sido Madre del Mal Venerio: Por el autor de la Idea del Valor de la Isla Española. 2 *vols in* 1. *Fine copies. Vellum.* 4° *Madrid*, 1785

In this latter book many authors are quoted with early references to America, most of whose books are referred to by no writer on American bibliography.

2185 VALVERDE (D. Antonio Sanchez) Idea del Valor de la Isla Española *and* La America Vindicada. 2 *vols in* 1. *Another copy, vellum.* 4° *Madrid*, 1785

2186 VANDER LINDEN (J. A.) De Scriptis Medicis Libri Duo. 8° *Amstelaed.* 1662

2187 VAN SCHAACK (Henry C.) The Life of Peter Van Schaack, embracing selections from his Correspondence during the Revolution, and his Exile in England. *Portrait. Cloth.* 8° *New York*, 1842

2188 VAUX (Roberts) Memoirs of the Life of Anthony Benezet. *Half green morocco, gilt.* 12° *York*, 1817

2189 VARGAS (D. Ignacio) Elogio Historico de Maria Santissima de Guadelupe de Mexico. En tercetos endecasilabos. Con notas instructivas y curiosas de lo escrito de la Maravillosa Aparicion y Milagros obrados hasta el dia en beneficio del Reyno. 26 *pp. with* 2 *prelim. and* 2 *sequent leaves, uncut.* 4° *Mexico*, 1794

2190 VARGAS (D. Ignacio) Elogio Historico, *etc. Another edition.* Corregido y añadido por el mismo. 2 *prelim. leaves, and* 28 *pages.* 4° *Mexico*, 1798

This production consists of a poem of 10 pages in honor of Our Lady of Guadalupe, preceded by a finely engraved copperplate representation of the vision, followed by 16 or 18 pages of valuable historical notes. The edition of 1798 contains considerably more than that of 1794.

2191 VASQUEZ (GABRIEL) COMMENTARIORUM AC DISPUTATIONUM in S. Thomam, *etc.* 8 *vols in* 4. *Very fine copy, of the* HIGHEST RARITY. *Folio*, *Lugdvni*, 1631

With the exceedingly beautiful frontispiece representing the Veil of the Temple through the rent of which the reader is invited to a glimpse of the learned and wonderful contents of this book. The usual price in London is £20.

2191* VECHNERUS (D.) Hellenolexia, sive Parallelismus Graeco-Latinus. *Vellum.* 8° *Lipsiæ*, 1680

2192 VEGA (El YNCA GARCILASSO DE LA) Prima Parte de los Commentarios Reales que tratan del origen de los Yncas, Reyes que fueron del Peru, *etc.* Secunda Impresion, emendada; y añadida la Vida de Inti Cusi Titu Jupanqui, penultimo Inca. *Fine copy.* *Folio, Madrid, Officina Real*, 1723

With the above are the following works, viz:

HISTORIA general del Peru, trata el descubrimiento de el, y como lo ganaron los Españoles. *Folio, Madrid*, 1722

LA FLORIDA del Inca. Historia del Adelantado Hernando de Soto, governador y Capitan General del reino de la Florida. Y de otros heroicos caballeros Españoles e Indios. *Folio, Madrid*, 1723

CARDENA (Gabriel, *i. e.* ANTONIO GONZALES BARCIA) Ensayo Chronologico para la historia general de la Florida. Contiene los descubrimientos y principales sucesos, acaecidos en esta Gran Reino, á los Españoles, Franceses, Suecos, Dinamarqueses, Ingleses, y otras naciones entre si y con los Indios, etc. Y los Viages de algunos Capitanes, y pilotos para el mar de el Norte, a buscar Paso á Oriente, ó union de aquella tierra, con Asia, desde el año de 1512, que descubrio la Florida, Juan Ponce de Leon, hasta el año de 1722. *Folio, Madrid*, 1723

Together 4 volumes, folio, bound in 2, in calf, good copy. Complete sets of these works from the editorship and revision of Barcia have become scarce.

2192* VEGA (*Ynca* Garcilasso de la) Histoire des Yncas Roys du Perou; contenant leur origine, depuis le premier Ynca Manco Capac, *etc.* Traduite par J. Baudoin. *2 vols, maps and plates, fine copy, calf.* 8° *Amst.* 1704

2193 VEGA (*Don* PEDRO DE LA) La Rosa de Alexandria, entre flores de humanas, y divinas letras, Sta. Catalina Virgen regia, virtudes de sv vida, trivnfos de sv Mverte. Dedicala la Parochia de sv titvlo de esta Ciudad de Mexico, el Dr. Alonso Alberto de Velasco, Avogado de la Real Audiencia de esta Nueva España, y el Doct. Antonio de la Torre, al Capitan Don Christoval de la Mota Ossorio, *etc.* *Fine copy, calf gilt.* 4° *Sevilla*, [1727]

This work though printed in Spain is essentially Mexican, being intended, no doubt, for the Mexican market. The author, the editors, and the dedicatee are all Mexicans, as appear by the several official papers in the prolegomena.

2194 VELASCO (*El Dr. D.* ALFONSO ALBERTO DE) Exaltacion de la divina Miseracordia en la milagrosa renovacion de la Soberana Imagen de Christo Señor Nuestro Crucificado, que se venera en la Iglesia del Convento de Señor San Joseph de Religiosas Carmelitas Descalzas de la Antigua Fundacion de esta Ciudad de Mexico. *Vellum.* 4° *Mexico*, 1790

Important and interesting for the Ecclesiastical History of Mexico.

2195 VELASQUEZ DE CARDENAS (CARLOS CALEDONIO) BREVE PRACTICA, y REGIMEN DEL CONFESSIONARIO de Indios, en Mexicano y Castellano para Instruccion del Confessor principiante, &c. *Sheep.* 16° *Mexico*, 1761

2196 VENEGAS (MIGUEL) NOTICIA E LA CALIFORNIA. *Maps, 3 vols, fine copy, vellum.* 4° *Madrid*, 1757

2197 VENEGAS (Miguel) A Natural and Civil History of California. 2 *vols, calf, gilt, fine copy.* 8° *London,* 1759

2198 VENEGAS (Miguel) A Natural and Civil History of California. 2 *vols, red calf, fine copy.* 8° *London,* 1759

2199 VENEGAS (Miguel) History of California. *Map and Plates.* 2 *vols, calf.* 8° *London,* 1759

2200 VENEGAS (MIGUEL) NATURAL AND CIVIL HISTORY OF CALIFORNIA. Translated from the Spanish. *Maps and Plates.* 2 *vols, calf.* 8° *London,* 1759

2201 VENEGAS (Miguel) Natuurlyke en Burgerlyke Historie van California. *Map and Engraving.* 2 *vols, half calf, uncut.* 8° *Haarlem,* 1761

2202 VENEGAS (MIGUEL) Natuurlyke en Burgerlyke Historie van California. 2 *vols, maps and plates, calf, fine copy.* 8° *Amsterdam,* 1777

2203 VESPUCCI (ALBERICO) NEWE VNBEKANTHE LANDTE UND EIN NEWE WELDTE IN KURTZ VERGANGER ZEYTHE ERFUNDEN. [*At end*] Also hat ein endte dieses Büchlein welches auss wellischer sprach in die dewtschen gebracht vnd gemachte ist worden, durch den wirdigẽ vnd hochgelarthen herrẽ JOBSTEN RUCHAMER. Vnd durch mich *Georgen Stüchszen zu Nüreinbergk, Gedrückte der* 20° *tage des Monadts Septembris,* 1508. *Folio.*

Fine large copy, measuring 11⅛ by 7⅞ inches, in half russia binding, with many rough leaves. Small holes by a worm and a nail (easily mended) slightly disfigure the volume, but not so as to obscure the text. Will make a splendid copy when cleaned, sized, and bound. This, one of the earliest and most important books relating to the Great Discoveries of the East and West, is a translation of the *Paesi novamente retrovati of* 1507, and, like that book (which has lately sold as high as £75), contains the voyages of Cadamosto, 1454–55, of de Cintra in 1462, of Vasco da Gama, 1497–1500, of Cabral in 1500–1501, of Columbus, 1492–1498, of Alonso Negro and the Penzons, of Vespucci, third voyage, 1501–1502, of Cortereal, 1500–1501, etc.

2204 VESPUCCI (ALBERICO) Americus Vespucci, eines florenzischen Edelmannes, Leben, und nachgelassene Briefe, worinnendessen Entdeckungen der newen Welt und die Merkwürdigkeiten seiner Reisen historich und geographisch beschrieben werden. Aus dem Italienischen des Herrn Abts ANGELUS MARIA BANDINI übersetzet, und mit Anmerkungen erläutert. *Portraits of Vespucci and Dante.* 8° *Hamburg,* 1748

This German edition of *Bandini* is much rarer than the original Italian, and is particularly valuable for new views expressed by the German editor. The able article on Vespucci in the North American Review, by Caleb Cushing, in 18—, was based on this translation, he then not being able to procure the original.

2205 VESPUCCI (Amerigo) Elogio d'Amerigo Vespucci che ha riportato il premio dalla nobile Accademia Etrusca di Cortona Nel di 15. Ottobre dell' anno 1788. Con una dissertazione giustificativa di questa celebre Navigatore del P. STANISLAO CANOVAI delle Scuole Pie pubblico Professore di Fisica-Mathematica. Terza Edizione Con illustrazioni ed Aggiunte, e con una Seconda Dissertazione sulla Vicende delle Longitudini Geografiche. *Fine copy, uncut, half morocco.* 4° *Firenze,* 1790

2206 VESPUCCI (Amerigo) Elogio di, con una Dissertazione Giustificativa di questo celebre Navigatore del P. Stan. CANOVAI. *Boards. Quarza Edizione.* 4° *Firenze,* 1798

2207 VERMONT. A List of Arrearages of Taxes, due from the several Towns in the State of Vermont, Sept. 15, 1795. *Uncut, clean copy. Scarce*; 200 *copies only printed.* [1795] 4° *Western District: Vt, Rutland: for the use of the Members.*

2208 VERMONT. DESCRIPTIVE Sketch of the Present State of Vermont. By John A. Graham. *Portrait. Calf.* 8° *London,* 1797

2209 VERMONT. Official Papers; Containing the Governor's [Isaac Tichenor] Speech to the Legislature of Vermont; their Answer, with the Proposed Amendment; and the Protest of the Minority on the Acceptance of the Answer, by the House. *Uncut.* 8° *Montpelier, by Samuel Goss,* 1808

These important papers relate chiefly to the Embargo.

2210 VERMONT. Natural and Civil History of Vermont, by Samuel Williams. *Second Edition.* 2 *vols.* (*Wanting the map.*) 8° *Burlington, Vt,* 1809

2211 VERMONT. Committee's Report, on the Vermont State Bank. 8° *Montpelier,* 1812

2212 VERMONT. H. C. Denison's Resolutions calling on the Governor for copies of any Correspondence he may have had with Military Officers, relative to detaching the Militia; &c. *Half calf.* 8° *Montpelier, Walton and Goss,* 1814

This important tract has now become very rare. The correspondence reflects the highest credit upon the Green Mountain Boys, who flocked over to Plattsburg, and joined the small force under the Command of General Macomb. The British fleet soon struck to the gallant Macdonough, and the "Noble Lads of Canada" soon changed their song to —

"We are too far from Canada, run for life, boys, run."

2213 VERMONT. History of the State of Vermont, from its Discovery and Settlement to the Year 1830. By N. Hoskins. 12° *Vergennes,* 1831

2214 VERMONT STATE PAPERS, from 1779 to 1786 inclusive: with the Proceedings of the First and Second Councils of Censors. Edited by William Slade. 8° *Middlebury,* 1823

2215 VERMONT. History of the State of Vermont from its earliest settlement to the close of the year 1832. By Zadok Thompson. 12° *Burlington,* 1833

2216 VERMONT. *The same,* 3 *copies.* 12° 1833

2217 VERMONT. Journal of the Council of Censors, held at Montpelier June and Oct. 1841, and at Burlington in 1842. 8° *Burlington,* 1842

2218 VERMONT. The Revised Statutes of the State of Vermont passed Nov. 1839. To which are added several Public Acts now in force, and to which are prefixed the Constitutions of the U. S. and Vt. *Calf.* 8° *Burlington*, 1840

2219 VERMONT Quarterly Gazetteer; a historical Magazine, a Digest of the history of each Town. Edited by Abby Maria Hemmenway. Nos. 1 to 6.
8° *Ludlow, Vt, July*, 1860, *to Aug.* 1863

2220 VERMONT Quarterly Gazetteer. *Another copy. Nos.* 1–3, 5 *and* 6. 5 *Nos.* 8° 1860–63

2221 VICARIO (El) de Wakefield, Novella escrita en Ingles por Oliverio Goldsmith. *Half morocco.* 8° *Mexico*, 1852

In the same volume is the following: —
EL AMOR de Una Niña. Novela Original de T. A. Garcia de Quevido. 8° *Mexico*, 1852

2222 VIDA de la Extatica Viuda, y humilde Princesa SANTA BRIGITTA (vulgo Brigida) de Suecia, Fundadora del Orden del Salvador. Su Autor: El Lic. D. Josef Antonio de Travesedo y Peredo, Presbytero, *etc.* Añadese al fin un compendio de la Vida de la Venerable Doña Marina de Escobar, Fundadora de esta Religion mitigada en España. Por el mismo Autor. *Vellum, very rare.* 4° *Pamplona*, 1783

2223 VIEW of the Constitution of the British Colonies in North America and the West Indies at the time the Civil War broke out on the Continent of America. By Anthony Stokes. *Half brown morocco, gilt, uncut.* 8° *London*, 1783

2224 VIEW of the Constitution of the British Colonies at the Time the Civil War broke out on the Continent of America. By A. Stokes. *Half brown morocco, uncut.* 8° *London*, 1783

2225 VIGNOLES (Charles) Observations upon the Floridas. *Half crimson morocco, uncut.* 8° *New York*, 1823

2226 VIGNOLES (Charles) Observations on the Floridas. *Half green morocco.* 8° *N. York*, 1823

2226* VIGNOLES (Charles) Observations upon the Floridas. *Half green morocco, uncut.* 8° *N. York*, 1823

2227 VILAPLANA (P. Fr. HERMENEGILDO, *del Colegio de la Santa Cruz de Queretaro*) HISTORICO, y SAGRADO NOVENARIO de la Milagroso Imagen, del Pueblito, de la Santa Provincia de Religiosos Observantes de San Pedro y San Pablo de MICHOACAN. 16 *prel. leaves, and* 192 *pp. fine copy, vellum.*
8° *Mexico, en la Imprenta de la Bibliotheca Mexicana*, 1765

2228 VILLAGRA (GASPARDE) HISTORIA DE LA NVEVA MEXICO. *Vellum.* EXCESSIVELY SCARCE. *Sm.* 8° *Alcala*, 1610

2229 VILLALPANDÆUS (G. C.) Apologia Indictionis Concilii Tridentini adversus J. F. Montanum.
Boards. 4° *Ingolstadii*, 1563

2230 VILLEGAS (ALONSO DE) LIBRO DE LA VIDA y Milagros de N. S. Iesu Christo en dos Lenguas, AYMARA y Romance, traducido de el que recopilo el Licenciado Alonso de Villegas, quitadas, y añadidas algunas cosas, y acomodado a la capacidad de los Indios. Por el Padre LVDOVICO BERTONIO. 4° *Impreso en el Pueblo de Iuli, de la Prouincia de Chucuyto, con la emprẽta de Francisco del Canto,* 1612

AN EXCESSIVELY RARE BOOK in the AYMARA, or one of the great languages of Peru. A perfect copy, comprises 8 prelim. and 3 sequent leaves, with 666 pp. of text. This copy unfortunately wants 23 leaves, viz. all before p. 9 (A5) also pp. 11 to 22, 29–30, 659–660, and the sequent leaves.

2231 VILLEGAS (D. FRANCISCO DE QUEVEDO) POESIAS, que publicò D. Francisco de Quevedo Villegas, Cavallero del Orden de Santiago, Señor de la Torre de Juan Abad, con el nombre del Bachellèr Francisco de la Torre. Añadese en esta Secunda edicion un Discurso, en que se descubre ser el verdadero Autor el mismo Don Francisco de Quevedo: Por Don Luis Joseph Vilazquez, Cavallero del Orden de Santiago, de la Academia Real de la Historia. *Fine copy, vellum.* 4° *Madrid,* 1753

2232 VIMONT (P. BARTHELEMY) RELATION DE CE QVI S'EST PASSÉ EN LA NOVVELLE FRANCE en l'annee 1640 [with an extra chapter (13th) in continuation, by Paul Le Jeune.]

RELATION de ce qvi s'est passé dans le pays des Hvrons Pays de la Novvelle France [Par Hierosme Lalemant] Juin 1639–Juin 1640. 2 *vols in* 1, *excessively scarce. Fine copy in vellum.* 8° *S. Cramoisy, Paris,* 1641

For others of these Relations see Nos. 1120 and 1121 of this Catalogue.

2233 VINDICATION of the Result of the late Council at Ipswich; by all the Members of the Council. 8° *Newburyport,* 1805

2234 VIRGINIA. Case of the Planters of Tobacco in Virginia, as represented by Themselves; with a Vindication of the said Representation. *Half morocco.* 8° *London,* 1733

2235 VIRGINIA. The Case of the Planters of Tobacco in Virginia, as represented by themselves. *Half morocco.* 8° *J. Roberts, London,* 1733

2236 VIRGINIA. Abridgement of all the Public Acts of the Assembly of Virginia. By John Mercer. *Half calf, uncut.* 8° *Glasgow,* 1759

2237 VIRGINIA. JOURNAL OF THE HOUSE OF BURGESSES from 10 Feb. to 11th April 1772. *Fine copy,* OF THE HIGHEST RARITY AND HISTORICAL IMPORTANCE. *Folio, Williamsburgh: Printed by William Rind, Printer to the Colony,* 1772

2238 VIRGINIA. Proceedings and Debates of the Virginia State Convention of 1829–30; to which are subjoined the New Constitution of Virginia and the Votes of the People. *Polished calf.* *Royal* 8° *Richmond,* 1830

2239 VIRGINIA. List of Non-Commissioned Officers and Soldiers of the Virginia State Line, and Non-Commissioned Officers, Seamen and Marines of the State Navy. *Uncut.* 4° *Richmond,* 1835

2240 VIRGINIA. Report of the Revisors of the Code of Virginia, made to the General Assembly Dec. 1847. 8° *Richmond*, 1848 — Report of the Revisors, etc. made Jan. 1849 — Report of the Revisors, etc. made in July 1849, being their final Report, and relating to the Criminal Code. *Richmond*, 1849 — Amendments made by the Joint Committee of Revision, etc. *Together 4 vols, sewed, excessively rare.* 8° *Richmond*, 1848-50

2241 VIRGINIA Military Institute, Regulations of. *Half roan.* 12° *Richmond*, 1854

2242 VIRGILIUS. OPERA OMNIA, Bucolica, Georgica, Aeneis, Civis et Culex: cum Commentario F. Taubmanni, edento C. Taubmanno. *Calf.* 4° *Apud C. Schvrervm*, 1618

2243 VIVES (Juan Luis) Dialogos de J. L. Vives, traducidos en Lengua Castellana por el Dr. Cristobal Coret y Peris. *Calf.* 16° *Mexico*, 1827

2244 VOCABULARY. Nuevo Vocabulario Filosofico Democratico. Indispensable para todos los que deseen entender la Nueva Lengua Revolucionaria. 2 *vols in* 1. *Calf.* 12° *Mexico*, 1834

The dry sarcasm of this book is something delightful, when applied to the Mexicans just after their great struggles for independence. These are some of the new words taught and explained to the new-fledged Republicans just emerged from the ignorance and barbarism of the Old Empire into the broad light of the Revolution: Aristocracy, Citizen, Constitution, Democracy, popular elections, emigration, education, farmer, frugality, governor, honor, humanity, Jacobin, liberty, law, literature, public opinion, pacto social, patria, patriot, politics, republic, religion, reason, rents, sans-culottes, truth, virtue, etc. all explained in a Pickwickian or Noviomagian manner.

2245 VOLTAIRE. Letter to several of his Friends. Translated by Rev. Dr. Francklin. 12° *Dublin*, 1770

2246 VOS (JAN) ARAN EN TITUS, of Wraak en Weerwraak; Den vijfden Druk. *Fine copy, with copperplate frontispiece, vellum.* 4° *Jacob Lescaille, Amsterdam*, 1656

A VERY RARE Play, based upon Shakespeare's TITUS ANDRONICUS. The first edition was printed in 1641.

2247 VOSSIUS (J.) De Septuaginta Interpretibus, eorumque Tralatione et Chronologia Dissertationes. *Calf.* 4° *Hag. Comitum*, 1661

2248 VOYAGES. Recueil de divers Voyages faits en Afrique et en l'Amerique. *Calf.* 4° *Paris*, 1674

2249 VOYAGES. Recueil de divers Voyages faits en Afrique et en l'Amerique, qui n'ont point esté encore publiez; Contenant l'Origine, les Mœurs, les Coûtumes & les Commerce des Habitans de ces deux Parties du Monde. *Maps and plates. Calf.* 4° *Paris*, 1684

The volume contains a translation of Ligon's History of Barbadoes with the map laying down the estates and names of the different planters; also, De la Borde's Account of the Manners and Customs of the Caribs, an Account of Guiana and what can be done there (anonymous), the Description of Jamaica with the Observations of Governor Thomas, Account of the Island of Barbadoes (anonymous), and a Description of St. Christopher's (anonymous).

2250 VOYAGES. A Collection of Voyages undertaken by the Dutch East-India Company, to find out the North-East Passage, *etc. Maps, calf. Scarce and valuable.* 8° *London*, 1703

2251 VOYAGE. A new Voyage to the North: Containing a full Account of Norway, *etc. Calf.* 8° *London*, 1706

2252 VOYAGE. Relation du Voyage de la Mer du Sud aux Cotes de Chili, etc. par M. de Fresier. *Plates.* 2 *vols in* 1, *calf.* 8° *Amst.* 1717

2253 VOYAGES. Recueil des Voiages qui ont servi à l'établissement, &c. aux progrès de la Compagnie des Indes Orientales, formée dans la Provinces-Unies des Pais-Bas. Seconde Edition, reveué, & augmentée. *Maps and plates.* 5 *vols.* 8° *Amsterdam*, 1725

The Dedication is signed De Constantin.

The 1st volume contains a brief history of the rise and progress of the East-India Company.

2254 VOYAGE de la Baye de Hudson. Fait en 1746–7. Par H. Ellis. *Map and plates*, 2 *vols, calf.* 8° *Paris*, 1749

2255 VOYAGE HISTORIQUE de l'Amerique Meridionale. Par M. Juan et M. Ulloa. *Maps and plates*, 2 *vols, calf, gilt. Very fine copy.* 4° *Amsterdam et Leipzig*, 1752

2256 VOYAGE d'un Philosophe [M. Poivre] ou Observations sur les moeurs & les arts des peuples de l'Afrique, de l'Asie et de l'Amerique. *Calf.* 8° *Yverdon*, 1768

2257 VOYAGEUR AMERICAIN, ou Observations sur l'Etat, la Cuture, la Commerce des Colonies Britanniques en Amerique. Traduit et augmenté par M. J. M. *Boards.* 8° *Amsterdam*, 1782

2258 VOYAGEUR AMERICAIN, ou Observations sur les Colonies Britanniques en Amerique. *Map, calf.* 8° *Amsterdam*, 1783

2259 VOYAGE to South America, describing at large the Spanish Cities, Towns, Provinces, *etc.* on that extensive Continent. By Juan and Ulloa. Translated with Notes, *etc.* by J. Adams. *Maps and plates.* 2 *vols, half blue morocco, fine uncut copy.* 8° *London*, 1807

2260 VRIES (SIMON DE) CURIEUSE AENMERCKINGEN der bysonderste Oost en West-Indische berwonderens-waerdige-Dingen; Nevens die van China, Africa en andere Gewesten des Werelds. *Maps and numerous plates.* 4 *vols, calf.* 4° *Utrecht*, 1682

2261 WADDINGTON (John) John Penry, the Pilgrim Martyr, 1559–1593. *Frontispiece, cloth.* 12° *London*, 1854

2262 WAFER (Lionel) New Voyage, and Description of the Isthmus of America, giving an Account of the Author's Abode there, the Indian Inhabitants, etc. *Map and plates, calf.* 8° *London*, 1699

2263 WAFER (Lionel) NEW VOYAGE and Description of the Isthmus of America, giving an Account of the Author's Abode there, etc. *Plates, calf.* 8° *London*, 1704

2264 WAFER (Lionel) Les Voyages, contenant une Description de l'Isthme de l'Amerique et de toute la Nouvelle Espagne. Traduits par M. de Montirat. *Map.* 8° *Paris*, 1706

2265 WAKEFIELD. Correspondence of, with the Right Hon. Charles James Fox, 1796–1801. *Half calf.* 8° *London*, 1813

2266 WALKER (J.) Rhetorical Grammar. First American Edition. *Boards, uncut.* 8° *Boston*, 1814

2267 WALSH (Robert) Appeal from the Judgments of Great Britain, respecting the United States of America. 8° *Philadelphia*, 1819

2268 WALSH (Vicomte) Lettres Vendéennes. 2 *vols, calf, gilt.* 12° *Paris*, 1829

2269 WALTER (Nehemiah, *of Roxbury*) A DISCOURSE concerning the Wonderfulness of Christ. Delivered in several Sermons. [With an Introduction by Increase Mather.] *Wants pp.* 83–94. *Boston, B. Green, for Eleazer Phillips*, 1713

2270 WALTER (REV. NEHEMIAH, *Pastor of the First Church in Roxbury*) DISCOURSES on the whole LVth Chapter of Isaiah, preparatory to Communion at the Lord's Table. To which is added the Author's last Sermon. *Calf.* 8° *Printed by D. Fowle, in Ann Street, Boston, N. E.* 1755

2271 WALTER (R.) Voyage round the World, 1740–4, under Commodore George Anson, compiled from his Papers and Materials, by R. Walter. Sixth Edition. *Half calf.* 8° *London*, 1749

2272 Wansey (Henry) An Excursion to the United States of North America, in the Summer of 1794. 2d Edition. *Portrait of Washington, calf.* 12° *Salisbury*, 1798

2273 WANSEY (Henry) An Excursion to the United States of North America in 1794. 2d Edit. *Portrait of Washington, calf.* 12° *Salisbury*, 1798

2274 WAR. A Complete History of the late War, to the Peace, 1763. 2 *vols, calf, gilt, fine copy.* 8° *London*, 1764

2275 WAR OF 1812. Exposition of the Causes and Character of the late War between the U. States and Great Britain. [Attributed to Mr. Secretary Dallas.] *Uncut.* 8° *Middlebury*, 1815

2276 WAR in Disguise, or the Frauds of Neutral Flags. *Boards.* 8° *London*, 1806

2277 WARD (J.) Dissertations upon several Passages of the Sacred Scriptures. *Calf.* 8° *London*, 1761

2278 WARD (EDWARD) The London-Spy. Complete in Eighteen Parts. The third edition. 2 *vols, calf.* 8° *London*, 1706

This Compilation contains Ned Ward's famous Voyage to New England, and description and character of Boston about 1690.

2279 WARDEN (D. B.) DESCRIPTION Statistique, Historique et Politique des Etats-Unis, des premiers Etablissemens jusqu'a nos jours. *Maps. 5 vols, half maroon morocco, uncut, fine copy.* 8° *Paris*, 1820

2280 WARDEN (D. B.) Statistical, Political, and Historical Account of the United States of N. America, from the Period of their first Colonization to the present Day. *Map. 3 vols, half crimson morocco, uncut.* 8° *Edinburgh*, 1819

2281 WARDEN (D. B.) A Statistical, Political, and Historical Account of the United States. *Map. 3 vols, fine copy, half maroon morocco, uncut.* 8° *Edinburgh*, 1819

2282 WARE (HENRY, *Pastor, First Church in Hingham*) Sermon on the Death of George Washington, Supreme Commander of the American Forces during the Revolutionary War, &c. died Dec. 14, 1799, delivered at Hingham, Jan. 6, 1800. *Uncut, sized paper, vellum, by Pratt.* 8° *S. Hall, Boston*, 1800

2283 WARREN (John) An Eulogy on the Hon. Thomas Russell, late President of the Society for Propagating the Gospel among the Indians and others in North America, etc. 4° *Boston*, 1796
FISKE (Oliver) An Oration pronounced at Worcester on the Anniversary of American Independence July 4, 1797. *2 vols in 1, half calf.* 4° *Isaiah Thomas, Worcester*, 1797

2284 WARREN (*Mrs.* Mercy) History of the Rise, Progress and Termination of the American Revolution. *3 vols, calf, fine copy.* 8° *Boston*, 1805

FRIDAY AFTERNOON.

2285 ASHINGTON (GEORGE) Letters from George Washington to several of his Friends, in June and July, 1776, in which is set forth an interesting view of American Politics at that all important Period. *Fine copy, uncut. Sized paper, white vellum by Pratt.* 8° *Republished at the Federal Press, Philadelphia,* 1795

2286 WASHINGTON (GEORGE) Official Letters to the American Congress, written during the War between the United Colonies and Great Britain. 2 *vols.* 8° *London,* 1795

2287 WASHINGTON (George) Epistles Domestic, Confidential, and Official, written about the Commencement of the American Contest, when he entered in Command of the Army. *Boards.* 8° *New York,* 1796

2288 WASHINGTON (George) *Another copy. Boards.* 8° *New York,* 1796

2289 Washington (George) Epistles Domestic, Confidential and Official. *Half morocco, fine uncut copy.* 8° *New York,* 1796

2290 WASHINGTON (GEORGE) The President's Address to the People of the U. States, 17th Sept. 1796. *Fine copy, uncut, vellum.* FIRST EDITION, 16 pp. 8° *n. p. n. d.* 1796

2291 WASHINGTON (George) An Address to the People of the United States. *White vellum by Pratt.* 8° *S. & J. Adams, New-Castle, Del.* 1796

2292 WASHINGTON (G.) Collection of Speeches to both Houses of Congress at the Opening of every Session, with their Answers. Also the Addresses to the President and his Answers; with Appendix. 12° *Boston,* 1796

2293 WASHINGTON (G.) The Last Will and Testament. *Vellum. Fine, clean, uncut copy.* 8° *Boston,* 1800

2294 WASHINGTON (G.) The Address to the People of the United States, on declining being considered a Candidate for their future Suffrages. *Fine copy, sized paper, white vellum by Pratt.* 8° *J. Cushing, Salem,* 1800

2296 WASHINGTON (G.) An Address in Latin by Joseph Willard, President, and a Discourse in English by David Tappan, in Cambridge, Feb. 21, 1800, in Commemoration of George Washington. *Fine copy, uncut, bound in white vellum.* 8° *S. Etheridge, n. p.* 1800

2297 WASHINGTON (George) A Poem. Sacred to the Memory of George Washington, adapted to the 22d of February, 1800. 8° *Hartford,* 1800

2298 WASHINGTON (G.) Political Legacies, with Appendix, containing an Account of his Illness, Death, and the National Tributes of Respect paid to his Memory, with a Biographical outline of his Life and Character. *Neat calf.* 8° *Boston,* 1800

2299 WASHINGTON (G.) Letters to Arthur Young, Esq., and Sir John Sinclair. *Boards, uncut.* 8° *Alexandria,* 1803

2300 WASHINGTON (G.) The Conduct of Washington compared with that of the present Administration, in a series of Letters, *etc.* By a Friend of Truth. *Vellum.* 8° *Boston,* 1813

2301 WASHINGTON (G.) Constitucion Federal de los Estados Unidos de America, con dos Discursos del General Washington. *Sewed.* 12° *Mexico,* 1823

2302 WASHINGTON (G.) Life of, with Cuts. 12° *Phila.* 1838

2303 WASHINGTON (G.) Diary of, from 1789 to 1791, embracing the Opening of the First Congress; with his Journal of a Tour to the Ohio in 1753. Edited by B. J. Lossing. *Cloth.* 12° *N. York,* 1860

2304 WATSON (J. F.) Annals of Philadelphia, being a Collection of Memoirs, Anecdotes, and Incidents of the City and its Inhabitants, from the Days of the Pilgrim Founders. *Boards.* 8° *Philadelphia,* 1830

2305 WATTERSTON (George) New Guide to Washington. *Map and many plates, cloth.* 12° *Washington,* [1847–48]

2306 WATTERSTON (George) New Guide to Washington, with 17 Engravings and a Map. 12° *Washington,* 1847–8

2307 WATTS (Isaac) Appendix containing a Number of his Hymns. *Half calf.* 12° *Boston,* 1765

2308 WATTS (I.) Hymns and Spiritual Songs. First Worcester Edition. 8° *I. Thomas, Worcester,* 1786

2309 WATTS (I.) Another Copy. *I. Thomas, Worcester,* 1786

2310 WATTS (I.) Hymns and Spiritual Songs. First Worcester Edition. 8° *Worcester, I. Thomas,* 1786

2311 Watts (I.) The Rational Foundation of a Christian Church. *Calf.* 8° *London,* 1747

2312 WATTS (Isaac) The PSALMS of David. Imitated in the Language of the New Testament and apply'd to the Christian State and Worship. The Third Edition with the Preface and Notes. SCARCE. *Morocco.* 8° *London, for John Clark,* 1722

2313 WATTS (I.) Psalms. 14th Ed. 12° *London, J. Oswald,* 1747

To this copy are added 8 pages of "Tunes in the Tenor Part fitted to the Several Metres. Engraved by Francis Hoffman."

2314 WATTS (I.) The Psalms of David. Imitated, *etc.* 12° *Hartford, by Patten & Webster,* 1780

2315 WATTS (I.) PSALMS OF DAVID imitated, *etc.* The fortieth edition, corrected, and accommodated to the use of the Church of Christ in America. *Fine clean copy, scarce.* 12° *Newbury-Port, by John Mycall,* 1781

At the end of this copy is bound a rare little book of 16 pages, engraved on copper. "A Select number of plain Tunes adapted to Congregational Worship. By Andrew Law, A. B. Joel Allen, Sculpsit."

2316 WATTS (I.) Psalms. 40th Edition, corrected, *etc.* 12° *Newbury-Port, by John Mycall,* 1781

2317 WATTS (I.) Psalms and Hymns. 12° *Boston, J. Bumstead, for J. Boyle & D. West,* 1792

2318 WATTS (I.) Psalms and Hymns. 16° *Exeter (N. H.) by John Lampson,* 1794

2319 WATTS (Isaac) The Psalms of David imitated, *etc.* Together with Hymns and Spiritual Songs. With Tables Complete. 8° *Northampton Mass. by Wm. Butler,* 1799

2320 WATTS (Isaac) The Psalms of David, *etc.* Corrected and accommodated to the use of the Church of Christ in America. *With* HYMNS and Spiritual Songs, *etc.* 2 vols in one, *good copy.* 16° *Brookfield, by E. Merriam & Co. Oct.* 1802

2321 WATTS (I.) Psalms and Hymns. Corrected and accommodated to the use of the Church of Christ in America. 16° *Brookfield, Mass. by E. Merriam & Co. Oct.* 1802

2322 WATTS (Isaac) The Psalms of David Imitated, *etc. and* HYMNS and Spiritual Songs. 2 *vols in one, large type, a scarce edition, calf.* 12° *Boston, by Manning & Loring,* 1803

2324 WATTS (I.) Psalms and Hymns. 12° *Boston, Manning & Loring,* 1806

2325 WATTS (I.) Psalms and Hymns. *Fine clean copy, sheep.* 16° *Sutton (Mass.) by Sewall Goodridge, for Caleb Burbank,* 1808

2326 WATTS (I.) Psalms and Hymns. 12° *Boston, by Manning & Loring,* 1808

2327 WATTS (Isaac) The Psalms of David, imitated in the language of the New Testament and applied to the Christian State and Worship. *Fine clean copy.* 16° *Isaiah Thomas & Co. Walpole, N. H.* 1812

2328 WATTS (Isaac) The Psalms of David imitated in the language of the New Testament, *etc.* *Fine clean copy.* 16° *Isaiah Thomas & Co. Walpole, N. H.* 1812

2329 WATTS (I.) Psalms and Hymns. 12° *Boston, N. Willis,* 1813

2330 WATTS (I.) Psalms and Hymns, *etc.* Corrected and accommodated to the use of the Church of Christ in America. 16° *Cambridge-Port, by Thomas Parker,* 1816

2331 WATTS (I.) Psalms and Hymns. Carefully revised, with directions for Musical Expression. 12° *Boston, by S. T. Armstrong,* 1819

2332 WATTS (I.) Psalms and Hymns. 24° *Exeter, N. H., J. I. Williams,* 1819

2333 WEBB (D.) An Inquiry into the Beauties of Painting; and into the Merits of the most celebrated Painters. Fourth Edition. *Calf.* 8° *London,* 1777

2334 WEBSTER (Noah) A Collection of Essays and Fugitive Writings. 8° *Boston*, 1790

2335 WEBSTER (NOAH) Grammatical Institute of the English Language. Third Con. Ed. 12° *Hartford*, 1792

2336 WEBSTER (NOAH) Grammatical Institute of the English Language; Thomas and Andrews' third Edition. 12° *Boston*, 1794

2337 WEBSTER (Noah) An American Selection of Lessons in Reading and Speaking. 8th Connecticut Edition. *Calf.* 12° *Hudson and Goodwin, Hartford*, 1793

2338 WEBSTER (Noah) Grammar of the English Language. *Boards.* 12° *New York*, 1798

2339 WEBSTER (Noah) American Lessons in Reading and Speaking. Cushing and Appleton's Edition. *Boards.* 12° *Salem*, 1801

2340 WEDGWOOD (H.) A Dictionary of English Etymology. Vol. I. (A. D.) *Cloth.* 8° *London*, 1859

2341 WEIR (R. W.) Picture of the Embarkation of the Pilgrims from Delft-Haven. 8° *New York*, 1843

2342 WELD (Isaac, *Jun.*) Travels through the States of North America, and the Provinces of Upper and Lower Canada. 2d edition. 2 *vols, calf, gilt.* 8° *London*, 1799

2343 WELD (Isaac, *Jun.*) Travels through the States of North America, and Upper and Lower Canada, 1795–7. Third Edition. *Maps and plates.* 2 *vols, calf gilt.* 8° *London*, 1800

2344 WELD (Isaäc, *Jun.*) Reizen door die Staaten van Noord-Amerika, en de Provintiën van Opper-en Neder Canada. *Maps and plates.* 3 *vols, half brown morocco, uncut.* 8° *In den Haage*, 1801

2345 WELD (Isaäc, *Jun.*) Reizen door de Staaten van Noord-Amerika en de Provintiën van Opper-en Nedder-Canada, 1795–7, uit het Engelsch door S. van Hoek. *Plates.* 3 *vols, half roan.* 8° *Den Haage*, 1801

2346 WELD (I. Jr.) Reizen door de Staaten van Noord-Amerika, en de Provintiën van Opper-en Nedder-Canada, 1795–7. 3 *vols, half yellow morocco, uncut.* 8° *Den Haage*, 1801–2

2347 WELD (I.) Statistical Survey of the County of Roscommon. *Map, cloth, uncut.* 8° *Dublin*, 1832

2348 WELWOOD (Andrew) Meditations representing a glimpse of Glory, or a Gospel-Discovery of Emmanuel's Land. *Impt. in index. Calf.* 12° *Rogers & Fowle, Boston*, 1744

2349 WELWOOD (J.) Memoirs of the most Material Transactions in England, for the last Hundred Years preceding the Revolution in 1688. Second Edition. *Calf.* 8° *London*, 1700

2350 WESLEY (John) A Calm Address to our American Colonies. *Half morocco.* 8° *London*, 1775

2351 WESLEY (John) A Calm Address to the Inhabitants of England [on American Affairs.] *Half roan.* 12° *Lond.* 1777

2352 WESLEY (J. and C.) Hymns and Spiritual Songs. Twenty-fourth edition. 12° *London*, 1786

2353 WEST (H.) Bidrag til Beskrivelse over St. Croix, med en over St. Thomas, St. Jean, Tortola, Spanishtown, og Crabeneiland. 8° *Kiöbenhaven*, 1793

2354 WEST (Stephen) An Essay on Moral Agency, containing Remarks on Edward's Freedom of the Will. 2d edition. *Calf.* 8° *Thos. Cushing: Salem*, 1794

2355 WEST (Stephen) *Another copy. Calf.* 8° *Salem*, 1794

2356 WEST INDIES. A BRIEF AND PERFECT JOURNAL of the late Proceedings and Successe of the English Army in the West-Indies. *Fine copy, calf.* 4° *London*, 1655

See note under S. (I.) No. 1815.

2357 WEST INDIES. Extracts from Parliamentary Papers, relative to the West Indies. *Cloth.* 8° *London*, 1846

2358 WEST INDIA COMPANY (Dutch) Anderde Discovrs by forma van Missive [in which is concisely shown the necessity of the East and West India navigation, and the importance of the wealthy inhabitants contributing largely to the newly chartered West India Company, &c.] *Very fine copy, uncut, in polished calf, by Bedford (see Asher, No.* 95.) 4° *n. p.* 1622

2359 WEST INDIA COMPANY (Dutch) Consideratien ende Redenen [Considerations and Reasons of the Directors of the chartered West India Company, on the Present Truce with Spain.] *Asher, No.* 130. *Fine copy, polished calf, by Bedford.* 4° *Haerlem*, 1629

2360 WEST INDIA PLANTERS. Substance of the Evidence on their Petition. *Half roan.* 8° *Lond.* 1775

2361 WETMORE (A.) Gazetteer of the State of Missouri. *Boards.* 8° *St. Louis*, 1837

2362 WHEELOCK (ELEAZAR, *Founder of the Indian Charity School, or Dartmouth College*) A sermon at North-Haven, Dec. 25, 1760, at the Ordination of Benjamin Trumbull [Historian of Connecticut] to the Pastoral Office there. *Half morocco, uncut.* 8° *S. Kneeland, Boston*, 1761

2363 WHEELOCK (*Rev.* Eleazar) Memoirs of Rev. Eleazar Wheelock, D. D. Founder and President of Dartmouth College. By David McClure and Elijah Parish. *Portrait.* 8° *Newburyport*, 1811

2364 WHISPERER (The) Containing the most spirited papers ever yet published: By an Enemy to Oppression and Tyranny. [In 25 numbers, from February to July, 1770.] *Calf, scarce.* 8° *Lond.* [1770]

Two of Junius' Letters appear in this bold publication, and many more by other authors in a similar spirit.

2365 WHISTON (Wm.) Primitive Christianity Reviv'd. 4 *vols, calf.* 8° *London*, 1711

2366 WHITE (G. S.) Memoir of S. Slater; and History of the Cotton Manufacture in England and America. Second Edition. *Cloth.* 8° *Philadelphia,* 1836

2367 WHITE (REV. NATHANIEL, *Pastor of a Congregation at Summer Islands*) THE PASTORS CHARGE AND CURE, or a sermon at first preached in Latin at Oxford, afterwards translated by the Author. The preaching of which created the Author much trouble, and in the winding-up of all, suspension from the Ministry, and thereupon inforcement to leave his native country. *Maroon morocco.*
VERY RARE. 4° *M. Simmons, London,* 1645

Dr. Belknap says that this Mr. White was one of the earliest graduates of Harvard College, Class of 1646, but the preface of this book shows that the Doctor was mistaken.

2368 WHITEFIELD (George) Journal of a Voyage from London to Savannah. in Georgia. 5th Edition. *London,* 1739
Continuation from his arrival at Savannah. 2d Edition. *Lond.* 1739
Continuation from his arrival at London. 3d Edition. *ib.* 1739
Continuation during the time he was in England. 2d Edition. *ib.* 1739
4 *tracts in* 1 *volume. Calf.* 8°

2369 WHITEFIELD (George) The two first Parts of his Life, with his Journals. *Calf, gilt.* 12° *Lond.* 1756

2370 WHITEFIELD (G.) The Two first Parts of his Life, with his Journals. *Calf.* 8° *London,* 1756

2371 WHITING (JOHN) A CATALOGUE OF FRIENDS' BOOKS; written by many of the People, called Quakers, from the Beginning or First Appearance of the said People. *Very fine clean copy, perfectly uncut, sized paper, polished calf extra, by F. Bedford.* UNIQUE *in this condition.* 8° *J. Sowle, London,* 1708

A large portion of the titles recorded in this volume relate to America. Few bibliographical works exist, on any subject, more exhaustive, or more honestly done. It has been incorporated, after the manner of latter-day bibliography, entire (but with reverent hands) in Joseph Smith's great work on Quaker Literature, but it is refreshing to consult old Whiting, in his truthful simplicity, in his own volume.

2372 WHITING (John) Persecution exposed in some memoirs relating to his sufferings. 2d Edit. *Calf.* 8° *Lond.* 1791

Contains much respecting the Quakers, and their happiness and sufferings in New England, Pennsylvania, New Jersey, Rhode Island, &c.

2373 WHITMAN (B.) Index to the Laws of Massachusetts; from the Adoption of the Constitution to 1796.
12° *Thomas, Worcester,* 1797

2373* WHITMAN (Benjamin) An Index to the Laws of Massachusetts; from the Adoption of the Constitution to 1796. *Sheep.* 12° *Worcester: Thomas & Co.* 1797

2374 WHITWORTH (Sir Charles) State of Trade of Great Britain, from 1697. *Half brown morocco. Folio, London,* 1776

2375 WILBERFORCE (William) A Letter on the Abolition of the Slave Trade. *Calf.* 8° *London,* 1807

2376 WILKINSON (Sir J. G.) On Color, and a general Diffusion of Taste among all Classes. *Illustrated by Colored Plates and wood-cuts, cloth.* 8° *London,* 1858

2377 WILLARD AND TAPPAN. Latin and English Addresses, before the University in Cambridge, Feb. 21, 1800, in Commemoration of Gen. George Washington.
Vellum. 4° *Boston, S. Etheridge,* 1800

2378 Willard (D.) History of Greenfield.
Cloth. 16° *Greenfield,* 1838

2379 WILLARD (Emma) History of the United States. Third Edition. 8° *New York,* 1830

2380 WILLDENOW (C. L.) Historia Amaranthorum. *Colored plates, scarce.* *Folio, Turici,* 1790

2381 WILLIAMS (*Rev.* J.) Two Essays on the Geography of Ancient Asia. *Map, boards.* 8° *London,* 1829

2382 WILLIAMS (Samuel) The Natural and Civil History of Vermont. *First Edition. Map.* 8° *Walpole, N. H.* 1794

2383 WILLIAMS (Samuel) The Natural and Civil History of Vermont. *Map.* 8° *Walpole, N. H.* 1794

2384 WILLIAMS (Samuel) The Natural and Civil History of Vermont. *Map, 2 vols. 2d Edition.* 8° *Burlington,* 1809

2385 WILLETS (Jacob) An easy Grammar of Geography. 2d ed. corrected and enlarged. 12° *Poughkeepsie, by P. Potter,* 1815

2386 WILLIS & SOUTHERAN. Catalogue of upwards of 50,000 volumes of ancient and modern Books. *Good.* 8° *Lond.* 1862

2387 WILSON AND MCKEAN. Commentaries on the Constitution of the U. States of America, in which are unfolded the Principles of Free Government, and the superior Advantages of Republicanism Demonstrated. *Half morocco, uncut.* 8° *London,* 1792

2388 WINCHESTER (Elhanan) A Plain Political Catechism. Wherein the great principles of Liberty, and of the Federal Government are laid down. *Fine copy.*
16° *Greenfield (Mass.) T. Dickman,* 1796

2389 WINCHESTER (E.) The Universal Restoration, in Four Dialogues. 8° *London,* 1792

2390 WINGFIELD (Edward Maria) "A Discourse of Virginia." By E. M. Wingfield the first President of the Colonie. Now first printed from the Original Manuscript in the Lambeth Library. Edited with notes and an Introduction by CHARLES DEANE. 100 COPIES PRIVATELY PRINTED. *Cloth, gilt edges.* 8° *Boston,* 1859

2391 WINTERBOTHAM (W.) Historical View of the American United States, and of the European Settlements in America and the West Indies. *Portrait and Maps. 4 vols, calf.* 8° *Lond.* 1795

2392 WINTERBOTHAM (W.) View of the United States of America, and of the European Settlements in America and the West Indies. First American Edition with Additions and Corrections. *Portrait of Washington. 4 vols, calf.* 8° *New York,* 1796

2393 WINTERBOTHAM (W.) View of the American United States, and of the European Settlements in America and the West Indies. *Portrait and Maps. 4 vols, half morocco, fine uncut copy.* 8° *London*, 1799

2394 WINTHROP (John, *Professor of Math. in Harvard College*) Relation of a Voyage from Boston to Newfoundland for the Observation of the Transit of Venus, June 6, 1761. *Wanting all after p.* 22, *uncut.* 8° *Edes & Gill, Boston*, 1761

2395 WINTHROP (John) Arrangement of several Scripture Prophecies relative to Antichrist; with their Application to the Course of History. *Uncut.* 8° *Boston*, 1795

2396 WINTHROP (John) An Attempt to arrange in the Order of Time those Scripture Prophecies, yet remaining to be fulfilled. *Uncut.* 8° *Cambridge*, 1803

2397 WINTHROP (Robert C.) Fourth of July Oration, on laying the Corner-stone of the National Monument to the Memory of Washington. 8° *Washington*, 1848

2398 WISCONSIN. Observations on the Wisconsin Territory. *Map. Cloth.* 12° *Philadelphia*, 1838

2399 WISCONSIN GAZETTEER, Alphabetically arranged by J. W. Hunt. 8° *Madison*, 1853

2400 WISE (J.) A VINDICATION OF THE GOVERNMENT OF THE NEW ENGLAND CHURCHES. *Small* 8° *Boston*, 1772

2401 WISNER (B.) History of the Old South Church in Boston, in Four Sermons, Delivered May 9 and 16th, 1830. *Uncut.* 8° *Boston*, 1830

2402 WITCHCRAFT. Lectures on Witchcraft, Comprising a History of the Delusion in Salem, in 1692. By Charles W. Upham. FIRST EDITION. *Calf, gilt.* 12° *Boston*, 1831

2403 WITHER (Geo.) Hymns and Songs of the Church; with an Introduction by Ed. Farr. *Frontispiece. Cloth.* 12° *London*, 1856

2404 WITSIUS (HERMANN) Hermanni Witsii Exercitationum Academicarum Maxima ex parte historico- & critico-theologicarum, duodecas. *Vellum.* 8° *Ultrajecti*, 1695

This learned book seems to have escaped the notice of American Bibliographers. Of the twelve Dissertations in it, the first two, filling 118 pp. pertain to America, the subject being: I. Qua disputatur Evangelium per Apostolos Americanis olim prædicatum fuisse. II. Qua ostenditur probari non posse quod Euangelium per Apostolos Americanis prædicatum sit.

2405 WOLCOTT (Oliver) Address to the People of the U. States on the Subject of the Report of a Committee of the House of Representatives, presented 29th April, 1802. *Uncut.* 8° *Hartford*, 1802

2406 WOOLMAN (J.) Journal of his Life, Gospel Labors, and Christian Experiences; with his Works containing his last Epistle and other Writings. *Calf.* 8° *Dublin*, 1794

2407 WOLLASTON (William) The Religion of Nature Delineated *Portrait inserted. Calf.* 4° *London*, 1726

2408 WOLLASTON (WILLIAM) The Religion of Nature Delineated. *Calf, gilt, by Bedford.* 4° *London*, 1726

This is the Book upon which Franklin, in his Autobiography, says he worked when first in London with Palmer, at the age of 18. From Wollaston he imbibed those ideas which the same year he gave to the *Press* in his *Liberty and Necessity*, and soon after in most of the copies of that little book to the *fire*.

2409 WOLLSTONECRAFT (Mary, *Mistress of Imlay of Kentucky*) Vindication of the Rights of Woman. 12° *Philadelphia*, 1794

2410 WORD (A) to Federalists, and to those who loved the Memory of Washington. *Vellum.* 8° *n. d.*

2411 WORLD in Miniature, or Entertaining Traveller. *Map and plates. Third Edition. 2 vols, calf, gilt.* 8° *London*, 1752

2412 WRIGHT (J.) The American Negotiator, or the Currencies of the British Colonies in America, etc. *Calf.* 8° *London*, 1761

2413 WRIGHT (J.) The American Negotiator, or the Various Currencies of the British Colonies in America. *Calf.* 8° *London*, 1761

2414 WRIGHT (J.) The American Negotiator, or the Currencies of the Colonies. *Third Edition. Calf.* 8° *London*, 1765

2415 WRIGHT (J.) American Negotiator, or the Various Currencies of the British Colonies. *Third Edition. Calf.* 8° *London*, 1765

2416 WRIGHT (*Miss* Fanny) Voyage aux Etats-Unis de Amerique, ou Observations sur la Société, les Mœurs, *etc.* en 1818–19–20. Traduit par J. T. Paresot. 2 *vols, half maroon morocco, uncut.* 8° *Paris*, 1822

2417 WRIGHT (Miss F.) *Another copy.* 2 *vols, half calf.* 8° *Paris*, 1822

2418 WRIGHT (Miss F.) Tafereelen van Noord Amerika, of Reize door de Vereenidge Staten. *Frontispiece.* 2 *vols, half maroon morocco, uncut.* 8° *Amsterdam*, 1822

2419 WYLIE (*Rev.* J. A.) The Papacy, its History, Dogmas, Genius, and Prospects. *Cloth.* 8° *Edinburgh*, 1851

2420 WYNNE (J. H.) History of the British Empire in America, including all the Countries in North-America, and the West Indies, ceded by the Peace of Paris. 2 *vols, map, calf.* 8° *London*, 1770

2421 WYNNE (J. H.) General History of the British Empire in America. *Map*, 2 *vols, calf, fine copy.* 8° *London*, 1770

2422 YORICK (Mr. *i. e. L. Sterne*) A Sentimental Journey through France and Italy. First Worcester Edition with engraved frontispiece. 2 *vols in* 1. 8° *Worcester, Isaiah Thomas*, 1793

2423 YORK (Thomas) Practical Treatise of Arithmetick. *Old calf.* 12° *London*, 1687

2424 YOUNG (A.) Preliminary Report on the Natural History of the State of Vermont. 8° *Burlington*, 1856

2425 ZALIKOGLOS (Greg.) Lexikon tes Gallikes Glosses (Greek and French Dictionary.) *Half bound.* *Royal* 8° *En Benetia*, 1815

2426 ZARATE (AUGUSTIN) LE HISTORIE DELLO SCOPRIMENTO ET CONQUISTA DEL PERV. *Fine copy, vellum, of very great rarity and historical merit.* 8° *Venegia*, 1563

2427 ZARATE (Augustin de) Histoire de la Decouverte et de la Conquête du Perou. Traduite . . par S. D. C. *Plates and maps. 2 vols, old calf.* 8° *Paris*, 1716

2428 ZARATE (Augustin de) Histoire de la Decouverte et de la Conquête du Perou. Traduite par S. D. C. 2 *vols. Maps and plates. Fine copy, calf.* 8° *Paris*, 1716

2429 ZARATE (Augustin de) Histoire de la Découverte et de la Conquête du Perou. *Maps and plates.* 2 *vols, calf.* 8° *Paris*, 1774

2430 ZARZA (*D.* JUAN ANTONIO GONZALES DE LA, *Br. en Sagrada Theologia, Cura y Juez Ecclesiastico, de los Partidos de Yztapalapam, y Xalatlaco ; y actual de Huitzuco, y Tlaxmalae*) SIESTAS DOGMATICAS, en las que con estylo dulce, claro y llano, por un Niño, es cabalmente instruido un Ranchero en los quatro partes principales de la Doctrina Christiana. 12 *prelim. leaves and* 507 + 10 *pp. vellum.* SCARCE. 4° *Mexico*, 1765

This dogmatical religion in after-dinner naps is an extraordinary book.

2431 ZAVALA (*D.* Lorenzo de) Ensayo Historico de las Revoluciones de Mexico desde 1808 hasta 1830. 2 *vols, uncut, stained.* 8° *Paris* [*for the Mexican Market*], 1831

This is said to be a well-written and impartial history of Mexican independence. After having freed itself from the despotism of the princes of Old Spain, this author, after recapitulating the struggles for independence, advocates the bold doctrine that even worse tyrants are to be overthrown in Mexico before she will be a free country. He pronounces the power of the clergy even more intolerable than the despotism of princes, and hence the work could not have been printed in Mexico.

ADDENDA.

2432 GUIRRE (*Don* Manuel Benito) Los Niños Pintados por ellos mismos, obra arreglada al Español por D. M. B. Aguirre, Vice-Director de la Academia de Instruccion Primaria. Publicala en Mexico Vicente Garcia Torres. *With 20 large lithographs of boyish life in Mexico.* 8° *Mexico*, 1843

LAS NIÑAS Pintadas por ellas mismas; sus tripos, caractéres y retratos. Obra escrita en Frances por A. Saillet, y traducida al Español por algunos Mexicanos afectos á la tierna niñez. Publicada por V. G. Torres. *With 18 large lithographs representing girlish life.* 2 *vols in* 1, *half mor.* 8° *Mexico*, 1844

2433 ALCOZER (*El R. P. Fr.* Joseph Antonio, *del Colegio de Propaganda Fide de Nuestra Señora de Guadalupe de Zacatecas*) CARTA APOLOGÉTICA a favor del Titulo de Madre Santisima de la Luz, que goza la Reyna del Cielo Maria Purisima Señora nuestra, y de la Imagen que con el mismo Titulo se venera en algunos Lugares de esta América. *Fine copy, calf.* 4° *Mexico*, 1790

Facing the Dedication is a fine copperplate engraving by Tomas Suria, Mexico, 1790, representing the Queen of Heaven, surrounded by her attendant angels, rescuing a young man from the jaws of Hell.

2434 ALEXANDER (Caleb) A Grammatical System of the English Language. 12° *Rutland, Vt, by Fay & Burt*, 1819

2435 APOLOGIA DE LOS ASNOS, compuesta en Renglones asi como versos por un Asnólogo aprandiz de poeta. *Fine copy, half morocco.* 16° *Asnopolis*, 18349

Elogio del Rebuzno, ó sea Apendice a la Apologia de los Asnos. 2 *vols in* 1. 16° *Rebusnopolis*, 18349

There is a good laugh on every page of this little book. The take-off of Spanish dedications, licenses, censuras, etc. is sufficiently amusing. The list of authors quoted and referred to fills 9 pages, many of whose names appear nowhere else. The poem itself fills about 80 pages, while the notes, built up in the truly asinine order, fill about 175 pages, and almost take away the breath of the reader with their learning and profound scholarship. Asses, and their bouts and whereabouts, are traced in every part of the world, but how, not being indigenous, they come to occupy the New World so extensively is a puzzle which the author has given his mind to most successfully. Lege—

¿A quien debe la America la dicha
De hallarse ya poblada de jumentos?
A la España lo debe, si, á la España:
Es gloria nuestra que en el hemisferio,
Nuevo-Mondo llamado, ya se encuentren
Asnos, que el descubrirse bien sabemos
No haberse conocido. ¡Americanos,
Semejante favor agradecednos!
Si los nombres de Franklin y de Jenner
Tanta fama y tal gloria se adquirieron;

Si el de Cortés y Américo han dejado
A la posteridad recuerdo eterno,
¿Porque el nombre de un fraile Franciscano,
Del Padre Cordovés, que al Mundo-Nuevo
Acia el Sur el primero fue con Asnos,
En bronces esculpido no le vemos? *etc.* — Page 17.

2436 ARIOSTO. Orlando Furioso.
CHATEAUBRIAND. Los Natchez, trad. por Flamant.
CHATEAUBRIAND. Los Martires, trad. por Flamant.
FERNANDEZ y Gonzales (M.) El Condestalle Don Alvaro de Luna, novela histórica.
4 *vols in* 1, *illustrated edition.* *Imp.* 8° *Madrid*, 1851

2437 AUBERTEUIL (M. Hilliard d') Essais Historiques et Politiques sur les Anglo-Américains. 4 *vols in* 2, *fine paper, calf. Plates and colored maps.* 4° *Bruxelles*, 1782

2438 BARLOW (James) Una Nueva Gramatica del Idioma Ingleses. *Calf.* 4° *Mexico*, 1842

2439 BERGAÑO y VILLEGAS (D. SIMON) LA VACUNA, canto dirigido á los Jóvenes por D. Simon Bergaño y Villegas. Co una Silva de Economia Politica, del mismo autor. *Fine clean copy.* 16° *Nueva Guatemala, por D. Ignacio Beteta*, 1808

It seems to have been reserved for this poet of Guatemala to first commit the praises of *cowpox* or vaccination, and Dr. Jenner to immortal verse. He had not only to overcome the prejudices of the people, but the dogged [dogma'd) conservatism of the Church. If we may judge of his services by the beautiful frontispiece to the volume, engraved by Francisco Cabrera of Guatemala, it must have been complete. This engraving is $3\frac{1}{2}$ by $2\frac{1}{2}$ inches square. In the foreground on the right stands the friendly cow tied to a tree in the open pasture, and by her the Doctor; on the left, seated on a bank, with fingers on the musical strings is the poet doing his pastoral, while the children, all naked and bare, come rushing over the hills,

Asi corren los niños, por librarse
De la peste feroz, à Vacunarse.

The two poems fill 70 pages, besides 4 prelim. leaves.
Bound in the same volume are the following scarce works: —
PLAN de la Constitucion Politica de la Nacion Mexicana, 86 pp. 16° *Mexico*, 1823
CATICISMO de la Independencia en siete Declaraciones, por Ludovico de Lato-Monte, 71 pp. 16° *Mexico*, 1821
MAXIMAS y Reglas de Educacion y Urbanidad, con un tratado de Ortographia Castellana para el uso de las Escuelas de primeras Letras, 68 pp. 16° *Guadalaxara*, 1822
Not a bad idea this to teach spelling along with good manners.

2440 BIBLE. Authorized Version. *Fine copy, calf.*
8° *Boston, W. Greenough, Printer, for Lincoln & Edmands*, 1817

2441 BIBLE. Authorized Version. *Good copy. Sheep.* 8° *Hartford, for H. Hudson*, 1827

2442 BOTURINI BENADUCI (Lorenzo) Idea de una Nueva Historia General de la America Septentrional. Fundada sobre material copioso de Figuras, Symbolos, Caractères y Geroglificos, Cantares, y Manuscritos de Autores Indios, ultimamente descubriertos [*with* Catalago del Museo Historico Indiano del L. B. B. quien llegò a la Nueva España por Feb. del año 1736, *etc.*] *Fine copy, portrait, calf.* 4° *Madrid*, 1746

2443 BOTURINI BENADUCI (Lorenzo) Idea de una Nueva Historia, *etc.* *Another copy, fine and complete, with the catalogue of manuscripts, maps, and printed books. Vellum.* 4° *Madrid*, 1746

2444 BOWDITCH (Nath'l) The New American Practical Navigator. 12th new stereot. edition. 8° *N. York*, 1841

2445 BOYLE (*Capt.* Robert) The Voyages and Adventures of, intermix'd with the story of Mrs. Villars, an English Lady with whom he made his surprising Escape from Barbary; The history of an Indian Captive, etc. With the Voyage of Richard Castleman and a Description of the City of Philadelphia in Pennsylvania [in 1710.] 2d Edition. *Frontispiece, calf.* 8° *London*, 1728

2446 BRACKENRIDGE (H. M.) Voyage to South America performed by Order of the American Government in 1817 and 1818, in the Frigate Congress. 2 *vols, half calf* [*Vol. I wants sheet* X.] 8° *London*, 1820

2447 BULFINCH (Thomas, A. M. *Nov-Anglicanus*) Dissertatio Medico Inauguralis de Crisibus. Quam ax auct. D. J. Gowdie, Acad. Edinb. Praef. etc, Pro Gradu Doctoratus, etc. Ad diem 6 Oct. 8° *Edinburgh*, 1757

2448 BYRON (*Com.* John) The Narrative of in a late Expedition round the World. *Half calf.* 8° *London*, 1768

2449 CALATAYUD (*El P.* Pedro de) METHODO PRACTICO, y Doctrinal, dispuesto en forma de Cathecismo por preguntas y respuestas, para la Instruccion de las Religiosas en las obligaciones de su Estado, y en el camino de la perfeccion, y para que sus Confessores puedan con mas expedicion, practica, y alivio entendèr, y governar sus conciencias. *Fine clean copy, vellum.* 4° *Valladolid*, 1749

2450 CALVILLO (*El P. D.* Juan Bautista Diaz) Discurso sóbre los males que puede causar la Desunion entre Españoles ultramarinos y Americanos, aprobado por el ilustre Claustro de esta real y pontificia Universidad en el que se juntó la tarde del 4 de Octubre de 1810. 16 *pp. sewed.* 4° *Mexico*, 1810

2451 CALVILLO (*El P. Dr. Don* Juan Bautista Diaz) Sermon que en el aniversario solemne de gracias a Maria Santissima de los Remedios, celebrado en esta santa iglesia catedral el dia 3° de Octubre de 1811 por la victoria del Monte de las Cruces. 60 pp. 4° *Mexico*, 1811

NOTICIAS para la Historia de Nuestra Señora de los Remedios desde el año de 1808 hasta el corriente de 1812. Ordenabalas el Autor del Sermon antecedente. pp. 61–269. 2 *vols in* 1, *fine copy.* 4° *Mexico*, 1812

An extraordinary volume, of considerable historical interest. According to this pious author Our Lady of Mexico, between 1808 and 1812, seems not only to have taken an active interest in the spiritual welfare of the faithful, but seems to have done her best to thwart the schemes of the rebels and republicans in the various provinces of Mexico. She set her face firmly against the spirit of Mexican Independency, and became quite a politician, but always attached to the royal party. The pious political frauds contained in this volume must ever give it a prominent place among the books relating to the History of the Mexican Revolution.

2452 CAMPILLO Y COSIA (Joseph del) Nuevo Sistema de Gobierno Económico para la América. Con los males y daños que le causa el que hoy tiene, de los que participa copiosamente España; y remedios universales para que la primera tenga considerables ventajas, y la segunda mayores intereses. 32 *and* 297 *pp. Very uncommon, fine copy. Vellum.* 12° *Madrid,* 1789

2453 CAYET (PIERRE VICTOR) Histoire de la Guerre sovs le Regne dv tres Chrestien Roy de France et de Navarre Henry IIII. — CHRONOLOGIE NOVENAIRE, *etc.* 4 *vols. Calf.* 8° *Paris, Iean Richer,* 1608–1612

A rare and important work. To the title-page of the 4th volume is added, "avec le succez de plusieurs navigations faictes aux Indes Orientales, Occidentales & Septentrionales, depuis le commencement de l'an 1598, iusques à la fin de l'an 1604." The most important of the voyages here referred to is that recorded on pp. 416–425 of the Expedition of Du Pont to Canada in 1603, as described by Champlain. There are many other references to America.

2454 CERVANTES SAAVEDRA (MIGUEL DE) VIDA y HECHOS del Ingenioso Cavallero Don QVIXOTE DE LA MANCHA. Nueva Edicion, coregida y ilustrada con differentes Estampas muy donosas, y apropriadas á la materia. 2 *vols. Plates. Very fine large copy, in the original calf gilt.* VERY RARE IN THIS CONDITION. 8° *En Bruselas, a costa de Pedro de la Calle,* 1671

2455 CHAVES (HIERONYMO DE, *Astrologo y Cosmographo*) CHRONOGRAPHIA o Reportorio de los tiempos, el mas copioso y preciso que hasta ahora ha salido á luz. *Very fine copy, of an* EXCESSIVELY RARE *book. Calf.* 4° *Sevilla, en casa de Alonso Escrivano,* 1572

This excessively rare book, comprising 272 foliod leaves, is one of the handsomest books ever printed in Spain. There is a good wood-cut portrait of the author on the title, and many geographical, astronomical, and scientific wood-cuts throughout the volume, one of the most interesting of which is a delineation of the New Hemisphere on the reverse of folio 95. The volume is of very considerable interest to the student of early American geography, chronology, and history. It contains the latitudes and longitudes of most of the chief places in the new world, and in the Calendar a very full list of the Spanish and Portuguese saints and saint-days. As many places were named by the discoverers from the saint's day on which the discovery was made, hence from the name we can sometimes arrive at the date. This book is full of such suggestive material, and therefore must hereafter become a hand-book for the student of early American history. For instance if the *Rio de San Antonio* described by Oviedo in 1537 as laid down by ALONZO DE CHAVES in his famous map of 1536, on the authority of Gomez' voyage, be identified as the Hudson River, then Gomez must have been there on the 13th of June, 1525, and as several other places between Narraganset and Chesapeake Bays were named by Gomez after saints it will not probably be difficult to solve the historical puzzle as to whether Gomez coasted north or south. We find nothing in this book to connect our Jerome de Chaves with the celebrated geographer, Alonzo de Chaves, but as they were both of Seville, it is not unlikely that they will turn out to be father and son.

2456 CHRONOLOGIE Septenaire de l'Histoire de la Paix entre les Roys de France et d'Espagne . . . . . . avec nauigations faictes aux Indes Orientales, Occidentales & Septentrionales, 1598–1604. *Fine copy, calf,* 8° *Paris, Iean Richer,* 1612

On page 416 begins Champlain's account of the Expedition of Du Pont to Canada in 1603, — a very important document sandwiched here out of sight.

2457 CLAVIGERO (FRANCISCO JAVIER) Historia de la California, Obra postuma del Padre Francisco Javier Clavigero, de la Compañia de Jesus. Traducida del Italiano por el presbitero don Nicolas Garcia de San Vicente [*In the same volume*] Relacion Historica de la Vida del Venerable Padre Fray Junipero Serra Por Padre F. Francisco Palou. 2 *vols in* 1, *small type. double columns.* SCARCE. *Imp.* 8° *Mexico*, 1852

2458 CONCEPTIO IMMACVLATA DEIPARÆ MARIÆ Virginis celebrantvr V. Acrostichidibus continentibus tria millia Anagrammata numeralia deducta exoratione Angelica. Ex eius Litania. Ex antiphona Salue Regina, & Ex hymnio Aue Maris Stella. Ex Alphabeti literis. Et aliqua Anagrammata sunt ad examen redacta, vt Lector facilius videat vtrvm pura sint nec ne. A Francisco de Santo Ioanne, & Bernedo Presbytero Hispano Capellano Cappellæ Paulinæ vbi colitur SS. Imago B. Mariæ Virginis à S. Lucâ depincta in Sacro Sancta Basilica Liberiana S. Mariæ Maioris Romæ.
Fine copy, vellum. 8° *Romæ, F. Tizzoni*, 1686

EXCESSIVELY RARE AND PIOUS.

A book crammed full of pious and ingenious trifling, licensed as *opusculum istud esse valde pium, elaboratum operosè.* Besides the five acrostics and 3000 numeral anagrams, the volume contains at the end a few literal labyrinths and puzzles that must have taken some devout monk months to work up. It is a little difficult at once to recognize the holy mystery that is said to pervade the numeral anagram, but one can readily see the holy impudence when this engine of conversion is turned on the enemies of the church. The 22 letters of the alphabet receive each a numeral value, A to I being the units 1–9; K to S the tens, 10–90; and T, V, X, and Z the hundreds, 100–400. These values, therefore, when applied to epithets of the Virgin, foot up thus:—

Nivea Maria 376
Mater Deipara 376
Veneranda 376
Porta manes 376
Admirabilis Maria 376 (Page 50.)

This same mysterious numbering, applied to the enemies of the church, it is said will reverse the mirror of holiness and show the naked truth. This is proved by a single instance in the Latin name *Martinus Luther* let down into the vulgar German pronunciation *Martin Lauter*. If the corresponding numbers of these 12 letters be added together they will produce the mysterious trinity of sixes, 666, the very number of the Beast. The Œcumenical Council itself cannot make any truth appear plainer.

2458* CONNECTICUT Register and United States Calendar for the years 1821, 1822, 1825, and 1826, 4 *vols, good copies.* 16° *Hartford*, 1821–26

See No. 484 of this Catalogue for other numbers of this Register.

2459 CONSTITUTIONS of the several Independent States of America; the Declaration of Independence: the Articles of Confederation, the Treaties, &c. With an Advertisement by the Editor. FIRST ENGLISH EDITION. *Half calf.* 8° *London, for J. Stockdale*, 1782

2460 CONSTITUCIONES de las Religiosas perpetuas del divino sacramento del altar, bajo la proteccion de Maria Santissima de los Dolores.

REGLAMENTO y Declaraciones de la regla sobre el ejercicio de lo que debe practicarse en nuestro venerable Monasterio de la perpetua adoracion del divino Sacramento del Altar.
2 *vols in* 1, *half morocco, plates.* 8° *Mexico*, 1850

2461 CORNWALLIS (Earl) An Answer to that part of the Narrative of Lieut. Gen. Sir Henry Clinton, K. B. which relates to the Conduct of Lieut. General Earl Cornwallis during the Campaign in North America, in 1781. *Sewed, uncut.* 8° *London, for Debrett*, 1783

2462 CREVECŒUR (Hector St. John de) Voyage dans la Haute Pensylvanie et dans l'État de New-York, par un Membre adoptif de la Nation Onéida. Traduit et publié par l'auteur des Lettres d'un Cultivateur Américain. 3 *vols, calf. Maps and plates.* 8° *Paris*, 1801

Though called a translation, this is believed to be an original work by M. de Crevecœur, whose initials only appear at the end of the very neat dedication to Washington. The author spent nearly a quarter of a century in America; saw Washington in 1774 come to the first Congress fresh from his farm, witnessed his extraordinary career, and in 1797 saw him retire to the private life of an agriculturist. His experience, therefore, enables him to give much information and personal gossip not readily found elsewhere. The portrait of Washington in the first volume is an interesting one, "Gravé d'après le Camée peint par Madame Bréhan à Newyork en 1789." There is also a fine portrait of KÉSKÈTOMAH, an Onondaga Sachem, and of KOOHASSEN, an Oneida Warrior.

2463 DARBY (William) The Emigrant's Guide to the Western and Southwestern States and Territories: Comprising a Geographical and Statistical Description of the States of Louisiana, Mississippi, Kentucky, and Ohio; The Territories of Alabama, Missouri, Illinois, and Michigan; and the Western parts of Virginia, Pennsylvania, and New York. 3 *maps, calf.* 8° *New York*, 1818

2464 DEL RIO (*Don* ANDRÉAS MANUEL) Elementos de Orictoynosia, ó del conocimiento de los Fósiles, dispuestos, segun los princípios de A. G. Wérner, para el uso del real Seminario de Minería de Mexico. Primera Parte, que comprehende las Terras, Piedras y Sales. *A scarce and important scientific work.* 4° *Mexico*, 1795

2465 DICTIONARY. A New English Dictionary: or a complete collection of the most proper and significant Words and terms of Art, *etc.* The Seventh Edition, carefully revised, with many important additions. By J. K. *Calf.* 8° *Lond.* 1759

2466 EATON (Amos) Philosophical Instructor, or Webster's Elements of Natural Philosophy. 8° *Albany*, 1824

2466* EATON (Amos) Philosophical Instructor. 8° *Albany*, 1824

2467 EATON (Amos) Chemical Instructor: presenting the familiar method of teaching the Chemical Principles and Operations. *2d Edition, considerably altered. Half calf.* 12° *Albany*, 1826

2468 EDDES (William) Letters from America, historical and descriptive; comprising occurrences from 1769 to 1777, inclusive. By W. Eddes, late Surveyor of Customs, &c. at Annapolis in Maryland. *Half calf.* 8° *Lond.* 1792

2469 EGUIA (*Don* José Joaquin) Memoria sobre la Utilidad é Influjo de la Minera en el Reino: Necesidad de su formento, y arbitrios de verificarlo. *Fine copy. Spanish morocco.* 4° *Mexico,* 1819

A highly important work upon the regulations of the mines and development of the precious metals in the various provinces of Mexico.

2470 EMBLEMS. DECLARACION MAGISTRAL sobre las Emblemas de ANDRES ALCIATO: Con todas las Historias, antiqvedades, moraledad, y doctrina, tocante a las bvenas costvmbres. 716 *pp. with* 4 *prel. and* 8 *sequent leaves, with above* 200 *wood-cuts, vellum.* 4° *Valencia,* 1684

2471 EMBLEMS. BENEDICTI Haefteni Scholia Cordis, sive adversi a Deo Cordis ad eumden reductio et instructio. *Fine copy. Vellum.* 12° *Antverpiæ apud H. & C. Verdvssen,* 1699

The trials and vicissitudes of the poor human heart are pictured herein in fifty-five emblems engraved on copper. Perhaps the most strongly poetical one is that of the three prowling dogs from hell, that had eaten a rotten, neglected human heart, and had been made sick thereby.

2472 ENSAYO. Imparcial sobre el gobierno del rey D. Fernando VII; escrito en Madrid por un Español en Mayo del presente año, y dado a luz en Versalles por un amigo del autor. *Calf.* 8° *Paris,* 1824

2473 EPINOY (*Don* ESTEBAN DEL) Compendio de la Esfera y uso del Globo, despuesto en doce Dialogos entre Maestro y Discipulo. 38 *pp. Fine copy, vellum.* 4° *Madrid,* 1768

Bound up with this scarce tract, and apparently by the same author, is an original unpublished manuscript, closely written, of nearly 400 pages, entitled "Tratado de la Esfera. Proposiciones, Problemas y Notas para la mejor inteligencia."

2474 ERCILLA y ZUNIGA (Alonso de) La Araucana. Poema.
BALBUENA (Bernardo de) El Bernardo. Poema heroico.
ESPRONCEDA (José de) El Diablo Mundo.
3 *vols in one, illustrated editions.* *Imp.* 8° *Madrid,* 1852

2475 FEDERALIST (The) A Collection of Essays written in favor of the New Constitution, as agreed upon by the Federal Convention Sept. 17, 1787. 2 *vols.* 12° *New York,* 1788–1799

2476 FISHER (Alexander) A Journal of a Voyage of Discovery to the Arctic Regions in H. M. Ships Hecla and Griper in 1819 and 1820. Fourth Edition, corrected. *Maps, half calf, uncut.* 8° *Lond.* 1821

2477 FLOREZ (*El P. Mro. Fr.* Plácido) La mas noble Montañesa Nuestra Señora del Brezo, su prodigiosa Aparicion, y algunos de los innumerables milagros que ha obrado y abra el Señor por la piados y continuado intercesion de su Santisima Madre en este divino Simulacio, en beneficio y consuelo de todo los fieles, sus devotos. *Vellum.* 126 *pages with* 6 *prel. and* 3 *sequent leaves.* 16° *Mexico,* 1807

An interesting volume, a sort of *Memorable Providences* of New England, calculated for the latitude and priestcraft of Mexico. Preceding the text is a very fine copper-plate engraving of the "Aparicion" of Our Lady of Brezo, by Francisco Gordillo, Mexico, 1806.

2478 FORSTER (John Reinhold) History of Voyages and Discoveries made in the North. *Map, half calf.* 8° *Dublin,* 1786

2479 FRANKLIN (Benjamin) Political, Miscellaneous, and Philosophical Pieces. Now first collected, with explanatory plates, notes, and an Index to the whole. *Fine copy, calf.* 8° *London, for J. Johnson,* 1779

This copy has the autograph of P. Knight on the title-page, and under the portrait of Franklin, facing the title, there is written in the same hand, but at different times in different ink, the following: —

Eripuit cœlo fulmen, sceptrumq; Tyrannis.
Eripuitq; Jovi fulmen, *sceptrumq;* Teranti
Viresque
Manilius |Lucretius|

2480 FRANKLIN (Benj.) Political, Miscellaneous, and Philosophical Pieces. *Portraits and plates, fine copy, calf.* LARGE PAPER. 4° *Lond.* 1779

2481 FRANKLIN (Benj.) Experiments and Observations on Electricity, made at Philadelphia. To which are added Letters and Papers on Philosophical Subjects. The whole corrected, methodized, improved, and now collected into one volume, and illustrated with Copper-plates. Fifth Edition. *Fine copy, half calf.* 4° *London,* 1774

2481* GEORGIA. A State of the Province of Georgia, attested upon oath in the Court of Savannah, November 10, 1740. *Fine copy, half roan.* 8° *London,* 1742

2482 GONZALEZ DE LA REQUERA (*Dr. Don* Juan Domingo) FAMA POSTUMA del Excelentisimo é ilust. Señor Dr. D. J. D. Gonzalez de la Requera: del Consejo de su Majestad: caballero gran cruz de la real y distinguida orden Española de Carlos III. Dignisimo XVI. Arzobispo de Los Reyes. Por el mismo Autor de la Oracion Funebre [Dr. D. Joseph Manuel Bermudez.] *Portrait.*
4° *Lima, en la Imprenta Real de los Huérfanos,* 1805

Besides the above, this volume contains the *Carmen Funebrum, Traduccion del Epitafio, Oracion Funebre, Testimonios de Gratitud, Assertum Vespertina,* &c.

2483 GOSPEL SONNETS: or Spiritual Songs. In 6 Parts. Second American Edition from the 24th English. To which is now prefixed an Account of the Author's Life and Writings. By Ralph Erskine. 2 *copies, fine and clean as new.*
12° *Isaiah Thomas, Jun. Worcester, Feb.* 1798

2484 HALSALL (James C.) Sequel to the Law of Human Progress. *Cloth.* 12° *Richmond, Va. Colin & Nowlan,* 1854

2485 HANDBOOK for farmers, mechanics, &c. Containing a Lumber-Dealer's Guide for timber measure: Scantling of timber measure: Board measure: Wood table: &c.
12° *Bellows Falls, Vt,* 1847

2486 HENRY (Alexander) Travels and Adventures in Canada and the Indian Territories between 1760 and 1776. *Fine copy. Calf.* 8° *New York,* 1809

2487 HARIOT (THOMAS) A BRIEFE AND TRUE REPORT OF THE NEW FOUND LAND OF VIRGINIA, of the commodities and of the nature and manners of the naturall inhabitants. Discouered by the English Colony there seated by Sir Richard Greinuile Knight In the yeere 1585. Which remained Vnder the gouernement of twelve monethes, At the speciall charge and direction of the Honourable SIR WALTER RALEIGH Knight lord Warden of the stanneries Who therein hath beene fauoured and authorised by her Maiestie and her letters patents: This fore booke Is made in English By Thomas Hariot seruant to the abouenamed Sir Walter, a member of the Colony, and there imployed in discouering. Cvm gratia et privilegio Cæs. Ma^tis^ specia^li^ *Francoforti ad Mœnvm Typis Ioannis Wecheli, svmtibvs vero Theodori DeBry Anno* CIↃ IↃXC. *Venales reperivntvr in officina Sigismvndi Feirabendii* [*Colophon*] *At Franckfort, Inprinted by Ihon Wechel, at Theodore DeBry, owne coast and chardges.* MDXC. *Folio, Franckfort,* 1590.

A FINE, LARGE, BROAD, CLEAN, AND EVERY WAY PERFECT AND DESIRABLE COPY of the rarest and most precious book relating to English North America. Including this, the writer does not know of the existence of more than half a dozen perfect copies. These are the copies in the British Museum and Bodleian Libraries, and in the private collections of Mr. Lenox, Mr. Brown, and Mr. Christie-Miller. There is a very imperfect one in the library of Harvard College, and one wanting two leaves, belonging to Sir Thomas Phillipps. No copy complete in England is known to have been sold for less than £100 for the past hundred years, and one has been understood to have changed hands at double that sum, and probably will again if the opportunity occurs.

It has become the fashion within the last few years for bibliographers, especially those who have got beyond their depth, to depreciate and decry the great collection of voyages of the DeBrys. They charge that these famous engravers had not a due regard for historic truth, and drew upon their imaginations for most of their fine pictures of men, animals, and things in foreign countries. The accounts of Virginia and Florida, being parts one and two of the American Collection, are said to be overdrawn, mere fancy sketches, and therefore calculated only to mislead the truth-loving historian. These charges are based solely on negative testimony, that is, they say, that none of the original paintings used by the DeBrys are known to exist, and the engravings have the appearance of German manufacture.

Now it has been the good fortune of the writer, in his bibliographical mousings up and down the world, to light upon the original paintings which DeBry used for his Virginia, and part of his Florida, and to turn up other facts which, all put together, not only clear the DeBrys of the charge of disregard of truth, but go far toward establishing their great Collections as trustworthy, and as honestly put forth by them. If the Voyagers exaggerated their own accounts, it was not the fault of the DeBrys. A synopsis of the story may perhaps as well be recorded here as anywhere, and may be brought back to the anvil, re-hammered, and worked up with authorities hereafter.

It is well known that, after the failure of the Huguenot attempts to make settlements in Florida under Ribault and Laudonnièr in 1562–1566, the artist of the latter expedition — one of the very few who escaped the terrible massacre by Menendez — Le Moine by name, retired to London, resided in the Blackfriars, and subsequently became a "servaunt to Sir Walter Raleigh." Raleigh had known Hakluyt and his studies in Cosmography, while student at Oxford, and subsequently in London, while interested in the expeditions of Frobisher, Gilbert, and others, had intercourse with the author of *Diverse Voyages.* Again, somewhat later, after finishing his little matters in Flanders, Raleigh found himself in Paris, and there was Hakluyt again, nominally Chaplain to the English Embassy under Sir E. Stafford, but really hunting historical and geographical material for a greater work on the voyages of his countrymen among the outside barbarians. Here in 1584 Hakluyt finished for Raleigh an elaborate geographical treatise, designed to induce Elizabeth to grant to Raleigh and his friends a liberal charter for discovery and plantation in a more southern latitude than had before been attempted by the English. They pitched upon the territory just north of that which they found described in Laudonnièr's Journal, which Hakluyt had secured, and which was pictured in the maps and drawings of Le Moine. A reconnoitring expedition had been sent out by Raleigh in 1584 under the command of Amidas and Barlow, which returned in September. The results of this voyage, and Hakluyt's Paper (63 closely-written large folio pages), entitled, "A particular discourse concerning the greate necessitie and manifold comodyties that are like to grow to this Realme of Englande by the westerne discoveries lately attempted, written in the yere 1584, by Richarde Hakluyt . . . at the requeste of Mr. Walter Raleigh before the coming home of his two Barkes" [from the north of Florida] *etc.* secured from the Queen the desired Charter for *six years and no more*, that is, to make discoveries and found plantations up to 1590, when the Charter expired by limitation. This manuscript of Hakluyt fell into the hands of the writer some fifteen years ago, and he tried for a year or two to place it in America, but without success. It was afterwards sold to Sir Thomas Phillipps. It is soon to be printed for the first time by the Maine Historical Society. In the autumn of 1867 the writer had the honor of calling the learned Dr. Woods' attention to it, and suggesting its publication by the Maine Historical Society.

While in Paris, Hakluyt induced his friend Basanier to edit Laudonnièr's Journal, and publish it under the patronage of Raleigh, while he himself, under the same patronage, brought out his excellent edition of Peter Martyr's Eight Decades, with the best map by F. G. of the new hemisphere that had been compiled up to that time. Basanier's book appeared in 1586, and Hakluyt's in 1587. Laudonnièr's Journal fell into the hands of Theodore DeBry, an enterprising engraver at Frankfort, formerly of Liège. One of the ten or a dozen who escaped the massacre in Florida was a young man named DeBry, probably a relative of the engraver. At all events the engraver took a deep interest in the work, and in 1587 went to London to see Le Moine in the Blackfriars, with a view of obtaining some of his paintings, to enable him to reproduce Laudonnièr's Journal with illustrations. But being at the time in Raleigh's service, Le Moine was either unable or unwilling to give DeBry all he wanted. But Le Moine dying the next year, DeBry returned to London in 1588, and succeeded in buying of the widow the rest of the Florida collection. But while there he fell in with Hakluyt, who was then engaged in bringing out his first folio Collection of Voyages. Hakluyt informed DeBry of the recent Virginia Expeditions under Raleigh's Charter, and suggested that, instead of bringing out his Florida as a separate book, he had better take the new book of Master Thomas Hariot, just out of the press, and illustrate it from the portfolio of John White, the artist sent out by Queen Elizabeth as chief Draughtsman in the expedition of 1585, who had recently returned, dedicate the work to Raleigh, and so begin a grand illustrated collection of voyages, the Virginia being the first part, the Florida to be held back to form the second part. Hariot, White, Raleigh, and DeBry all fell into this arrangement, and Hakluyt agreed to write the descriptions of White's maps and pictures. DeBry thus having filled his portfolios with copies of White's works and the originals of the late Le Moine's paintings, returned to Frankfort, and, with incredible enterprise and perseverance, brought out his *Virginia* in 1590, and the *Florida* in 1591, the latter as the Second Part of a Collection of Voyages. The Florida by this arrangement had been enlarged by additional pieces and plates. From this brief statement it will be perceived that thus far DeBry's Collection is perfectly authentic, and in its origin is essentially English. In another place we think it will not be difficult to show that he was alike painstaking and straightforward in the materials of all the other parts of both his *America* and *India*, and hence it must follow that the Collections are as deserving of confidence as the original Voyages from which they are reprinted, translated, and edited.

But in reprinting Hariot's report, and illustrating it with White's pictures, did not DeBry exaggerate and embellish? The answer is No, for the following reasons: In the year 1865 John White's original paintings in Water Colors, made for Sir Walter Raleigh in 1585, fell by purchase into the hands of the writer, and in March 1866 fell into the right place in the Grenville Library in the British Museum, at the moderate cost to the Trustees of £236 5*s.* 0*d.* They now are a prominent part of the world-renowned "Grenville DeBry." A glance at the drawings will show that they are the works of an artist, and portraits whether of men, women, animals, fish, fowls, fruits, or plants. They are highly finished. DeBry's copies are very close, but not embellished. The following extracts from the writer's report on the collection, dated 22d March, 1866, when offering it to the Trustees of the British Museum, are given with the hope of removing some of the aspersions that have been of late cast upon this famous collection, and encouraging collectors to repose confidence in the honesty of the great Frankfort family of engravers. The drawings are beautifully bound in two volumes in red morocco.

"To A. Panizzi, Esq. etc. etc. British Museum. . . . . The two volumes, with some aids from the Grenville Library, will speak for themselves, but the following notes may facilitate your researches. They are chiefly drawn out of Hakluyt, Purchas, DeBry, Hariot, Captain John Smith, and others.

"The larger volume contains 76 Original Drawings in colors, done for Sir Walter Raleigh by John White, the English Painter who was sent by Queen Elizabeth in 1585 to Virginia, as principal draughtsman in Raleigh's famous Second Expedition for exploring the country and planting his 'First Colonie.' This Expedition of seven ships was under the command of Admiral Sir Richard Grenville, the ancestor, I believe, of the founder of the Grenville Library. Thomas Candish, or Cavendish, was also of the fleet, and Master Ralph Lane was the Governor of the Colonie. This 'First Colonie,' consisting of 109 men, remained in Virginia one whole year, and then returned to England in July, 1586, in Sir Francis Drake's fleet returning victorious from the West Indies, because the long expected supplies and reinforcements from England had not arrived. Fourteen days after their departure Sir Richard Grenville arrived with new stores and new planters, to find the Old Colonie deserted.

"To Thomas Hariot and John White, two of these 109, we owe nearly all we know of that grand and most unfortunate expedition, and it is not too much to say, I think, that to them alone we may fairly ascribe nearly all the accurate knowledge we have of the Indians, and the natural history of that country for a full century later.

"Nothing is recorded of John White in Modern Dictionaries of art or biography, yet from DeBry and Hakluyt we learn that he was both an eminent artist, and an influential man in his day. He made no less than four voyages to Virginia; was an 'adventurer' in the 'First Colonie;' the Governor of the 'Second Colonie' in 1587; and the grandfather of Virginia Dare, the first English child born in North America; the friend and agent of Raleigh, and the associate of Hariot. Many of Governor White's Letters and Journals are preserved by his friend Hakluyt. His last voyage to Virginia was in 1590, as chief of Raleigh's 'Fifth Expedition,' to aid and reinforce the Colonie of 1587. He returned unsuccessful the same year, and retired to Ireland, whence he dated a letter, long and important, to his friend Hakluyt, 'from my house at Newtowne in Kylmore the 4th of February, 1593.'

"Theodore DeBry in his second visit to London in 1588, was introduced to White by Hakluyt, who suggested to that eminent engraver, then projecting his Grand Collection of Voyages, to reprint Hariot's 'Report of Virginia,' then just issued, and illustrate it with the pictures of John White. Hakluyt also persuaded DeBry to delay his *Florida* and make the *Virginia* his First Part. White's pictures were copied, and the artist returning to Frankfort, with incredible enterprise completed the engravings in a masterly manner, and issued the work in 1590, in folio, four editions, in four languages, English, French, German, and Latin, a monument of Beauty and Art to himself, to Hariot, and to John White. Not more than five or six copies of the English edition are now known in England, and for the last century have never sold complete for less than 100 guineas, and would now bring probably 200 guineas. The copy in the Grenville Library is the finest I have seen.

"These drawings now offered to the Trustees are no doubt the identical paintings that were copied by DeBry and published in 1590. Beautiful as DeBry's work is, it seems tame in the presence of these original drawings. DeBry copied only about one third of the drawings. The rest have never been engraved, though some of them were used in the *Florida*, and in the third and sixth Parts. There is a volume of White's [perhaps partly Le Moine's] drawings in the Sloane Collection (N° 5270) but they are not duplicates of these. A few of them are similar designs. The price of this volume is 200 guineas (£210.) The price of the smaller volume, if the other be taken, is 25 guineas (£26 5*s.* 0*d.*; together £236 5*s.* 0*d.*) The story of the smaller volume is very curious. At the fire at Sotheby's in June, 1865, the drawings were saturated with water, and remained so for three weeks under heavy pressure, which produced these remarkable 'off-tracts.' I have had them carefully preserved, reversed in the binding and sized, at no little cost of time and money.

"I am, Dear Sir, Yours faithfully, HENRY STEVENS."

Such is the brief history of this remarkable book, the only copy of which it is believed that has ever been offered by auction in this country. Its authenticity cannot be doubted. It contains nearly all we know of Raleigh's Old Colonie, which he himself never saw, and which resulted in an entire failure, probably owing to the unfortunate limitation of the enterprise to six years. No such expensive efforts were ever after made by any expedition or Colony to collect such vivid and picturesque material of the New World, its inhabitants, and natural products.

2488 HERCKMANS (ELIAS) DER ZEE-VAERT LOF Handelende van de gedenckwaerdighste Zee-vaerden met de daeraenklevende op en onderganghen der Voornaems te Heerschappeijen der gantscher Wereld. In VI Boecken Beschreven. *Fine copy, vellum.*

Folio, Amsterdam, bij Jacob Pieterss Wachter, 1634

The author of this excessively curious and rare work was Vice-Admiral of the celebrated expedition of the Dutch in 1643, under Admiral Hendrick Brouwer, against the Spaniards of Chili; first printed at Amsterdam in 1646, and three years later forming the 25th Part of the Collection of Hulsius. Brouwer dying on the passage out, the command fell upon HERCKMANS, who was probably the amateur compiler and editor of the various Journals. This *Zee Vaert Lof* is an elaborate historical poem in six books in honor of Navigation. All the celebrated voyages of the world from Noah to 1632 are recorded in chronological order. The voyages of discovery, leading up to the discovery of America, are mentioned with considerable detail, and after Columbus are recorded most of the voyages both to the east and the west, especially the expeditions of the Dutch navigators. The voyages to the north are all mentioned in the text and notes. The volume is beautifully illustrated by an engraved title and eighteen exquisite etchings in the text. The one at the beginning of the third book bears the mark of Rembrandt, with the date 1633.

2489 HERNANDES (FRANCISCUS) Francisci Hernandi, Medici atque Historici Philippi II. Hisp. et Indiar. Regis, et totius Novi Orbis Archiatri, Opera, cum edita, tum inedita, ad autographi fidem et integritatem expressa, impensa et jussu regio, 3 *vols, calf.* SCARCE. 4° *Madrid, Ibarræ Heredum*, 1790

See No. 891 of this Catalogue. Hernandes, or the Third Pliny, spent seven years by order of Philip the Second, in active research into the natural history of the plants and animals of New Spain. Shortly after his death his MSS. and Collections were placed in the hands of Dr. Nardo Antonio Ricci, who abridged the MSS. and printed at Rome before 1628, a large folio volume in Latin, with many wood-cuts. But a copy of a part of his abridgment had somehow found its way back to Mexico in time to be reabridged and translated into Spanish by Francisco de Ximenes and printed there in 1615. A part of the original collection was burnt with the library of the Escurial in 1671. This edition is not to be compared with the work of Dr. Ricci. This is more of Hernandes without his editors, more correct, with many additions, but without any illustrations. Had Hernandes lived to edit and publish his own work, as Humboldt and Bonpland did theirs two hundred years later, it is not likely that these two friends would have then laid before the public so much that was entirely new to the philosophers of the old world.

2490 HERSCHEL (SIR JOHN, F. H.) Outlines of Astronomy. 4th Edition, *half calf.* 8° *Lond.* 1851

From the Library of H. T. Buckle, author of the "History of Civilization," with his book-plate and MS. notes. On a separate sheet Mr. Buckle has written four pages of notes, a kind of analysis of the work, and on the top of the 4th page has made this memorandum relating to an American Book, "For a very clear account of Parallax, see 'Comstock's Natural Philosophy,' pp. 324–326."

2491 HIDALGO (*El M. R. P. Mrô. Fr.* Miguel, *Fundador de las quatro Missiones en la Provincia de Californias, etc.*) GLORIAS DOMINICANAS en su esclarecido, é ilustre Militar tercer Orden. Tomo 1°. Contiene el Origen de este Venerable Instituto, su antiqüedad, y precedencia á todas las Ordenes Terceras de la Militante Iglesia: &c. 2 *Copper-plates, fine copy, calf.* [*No more printed?*] 4° *Mexico,* 1795

2492 HIDALGO (Miguel) y ALLENDE (Ignacio) Pública Vindicacion del illustre Ayuntamiento de Santa Fé de Guanaxuato justificando su conducta moral y politica en la entrada y crimenes que cometieron en aquella Ciudad las huestes insurgentes agabilladas por sus corifeos M. Hidalgo, Ignacio Allende. *Fine copy, calf.* 4° *Mexico,* 1811

2493 HOLMES (Isaac) An Account of the United States of America, derived from actual observation, during a residence of four years in that Republic. *Colored map, much behind time. Half calf.* 8° *Lond.* 1823

2494 HOMERI ILIAS. FRANCISCI XAVERII ALEGRE MEXICANI VERACRUCENSIS Homeri Ilias Latino carmine expressa. Editio Romana Venustior, et emendatior. *Vellum, wormed in the back.* 8° *Apud Salvionem, tipographicum Vaticanum,* 1788

This revised Roman edition of Alegre's Homer's Iliad differs considerably from the first edition of 1776. See No. 927 of this Catalogue. On the title-page of this edition are medallion portraits of Homer and Alegre, and on the next leaf is a copper-plate engraving representing the Mexican Arms over a preface headed MEXICANA CIVITAS, and signed by Joannes à Malo de Villavicencio.

2495 HOPKINS (Bp. J. H.) Christianity Vindicated in 7 Discourses on the external Evidence of the New Testament. *Bds.* 12° *Burlington,* 1833

2496 HUBBARD (*Hon.* John) The American Reader; containing a selection of narrations, harangues, addresses, etc. Fifth Edition. 12° *Walpole, N. H. by Isaiah Thomas,* 1811

2497 HUBBARD (John) The Rudiments of Geography, being a concise description of the various Kingdoms, States, Empires, and Islands in the World, *etc.* 6th Edition, revised and corrected. *Fine copy.* 12° *Barnard (Vt,) by Joseph Dix,* 1814

2498 HUNTER (John D.) Memoirs of a Captivity among the Indians of North America. *Half calf.* 8° *Lond.* 1823

2499 IXTLILXUCHITL (*Don* Fernando de Alva) Horribles Crueldades de los Conquistadores de Mexico, y de los Indios que los auxiliaron para subjugarlo a la corona de Castilla. Publicala por suplemento a la historia del Padre Sahagun, Carlos Maria de Bustamante. 12 + 118 *pp. Uncut, stained.* SCARCE. 4° *Mexico,* 1829

2500 JAMAICA. A Description of the Island of Jamaica. 2 *vols, fine copy, calf.* 8° *Lond.* 1790

2501 KALM (Peter) Travels into North America, containing its Natural History, *etc.* Translated by J. R. Forster. Second edition. 2 *vols, clean copy, calf.* 8° *Lond.* 1772

2502 KEMPIS (THOMAS à) Tractat de la Imitaciò de Christo, y menysprev del Mon. del V. Thomas de Kempis, Canonge Regular del Orde de S. Augusti. Dividit en quatre Llibres. Tradvhit en Llengva CATHALANA de son original Llati, per lo Rev. Pere Bonavra, Prevere, &c. y a la Fi Trobarà la Anima fervorosa algunas Oracions devotas per acostarse dignament al Sagrament de la Penitencia, y rebrer devotament la Eucharistia Santa Anyadit en esta ultima impressò ab 27 estampas apropriadas à la materia. Dedicat a Jesu-Chirist Deu, Pare, y Redemptor nostre. *Fine copy, vellum.* 16° *Barcelona, Ioan Piferrer,* 1740

This little edition of à Kempis in the Catalan dialect, with 27 wood-cuts, has now become very rare. The inducements offered by the Archbishop and the Bishops to read this work are curious, and if still in force, may still do good in this latitude. "Los Illustrissims, y Reverendissims Senyors Arquebisbe, y Bisbes de Cathalunya han concedit 320. dias de perdò, à tots los qui llegiràn, ò ohiràn llegir ab atenciò un Capital del present Llibre."

2503 KEMPIS (Thomas à) De la Imitacion de Christo, y Menos precio del Mundo. En 4 Libros, traducidos nuevamente en Español por el P. Juan Eusibio Nieremberg. Van añadidos los Avisos, &c. sacados de las Obras del mismo Padre Juan Eusibio. *Copper-plates, calf.* 16° *Madrid,* 1788

2504 KEMPIS (Thomas à) De la Imitacion de Christo y Menosprecio del Mundo. Trad. por J. E. Nieremberg. Van añadidos los Avisos. *Copper-plates, fine copy.* 16° *Madrid,* 1790

2505 LA HONTAN (*Baron*) DES BERUHUTEN Herrn Baron De La Hontan Neueste Reisen nach Nord-Indien, oder dem Mitternächtischen America, mit vielen besondern und bey keinem Scribenten befindlichen Curiositæten. Aus dem Frantzösischen übersetzet von M. Vischer. *A scarce edition, with Preface by M. Vischer.* 16° *Hamburg und Leipzig,* 1709

2506 LA HONTAN (*Baron*) REIZEN van den Baron van La Hontan in het Noordelyk Amerika. *Many maps and plates. Fine uncut copy, in morocco, 2 vols.* 12° *In's Gravenhage, by Isaac Beauregard,* 1739

This Dutch edition, which is rare, contains many historical and geographical notes, and is in many respects better than either the English or French editions.

2507 LEBEAU (Sr C.) AVANTURES du Sr C. LeBeau, avocat en Parlement, ou Voyage curieux et nouveau, parmi les Sauvages de l'Amérique Septentrionale. Dans le quel ou trouvera une Description du Canada, etc. 2 *vols, maps and plates. Calf, fine copy.* 8° *Amst. chez H. Uytwerf.* 1738

2508 LUMBIER (*El Rev. P. M. Fr.* Raymundo) Noticia de las sesenta y cinco Proposiciones, nvevamente condenadas por N. SS. P. Inocencio XI. mediante su Decreto de 2 de Mayo del Año 1679. Sexta Impression, añadidas, *etc.* *Vellum.* 4° *Madrid,* 1682

2509 LYON (*Capt.* G. F.) The Private Journal of, during the recent voyage of discovery under Captain Parry. *Map and plates, half morocco, uncut.* 8° *Lond.* 1825

2510 MASSACHUSETTS REGISTER and United States Calendar for 1806, 1807, 1809, 1810, 1811, 1812, 1814, 1815, 1816, 1817, 1818, 1819, 1821. *Good copies*, 13 *vols.* 16° *Boston*, 1806–21

2511 MACKAY (Alexander) Western India. Reports addressed to the Chambers of Commerce of Manchester, Liverpool, Blackburn and Glasgow by their Commissioner the late A. Mackay. Edited by James Robertson with preface by Thomas Bazley. *Maps, cloth.* 8° *Lond.* 1853,

2512 MEXICANS. LOS MEXICANOS PINTADOS por si mismos, por varios Autores. *With more than* 30 *fine large lithographs, representing the Mexicans in various characters and employments.* Edition de M. Murguia. *Half morocco. Imp.* 8° [*Mexico*, 1855]

2513 MEXICO. REALES ORDENANZAS para la direccion, régimen y gobierno del importante cuerpo de la Mineria de Nueva-España, y de su real Tribunal General. De Orden de su Magestad. *xlvi and* 214 *pp. Frontispiece. Folio. Madrid*, 1783

A volume indispensable to the mineral history of Mexico, as it contains the standard ordinances, rules, and regulations respecting the mines and miners of Mexico, California, etc. This copy, printed in large type, has many MS. notes.

2514 MEXICO. Memorias, etc. 5 *vols in* 2, *half calf, viz.:* *Imp.* 8° *Mexico*, 1845

MEMORIA del Secretario de Estado y del dispacho de Guerra y Marina, el dia 11 de Marzo de 1845.

MEMORIA del Ministro de Relaciones Exteriores y gobernacion, el 12 de Marzo de 1845.

MEMORIA del Ministro de Justicia è Instruccion publica presentada por el Secretario, Año de 1845.

MEMORIA de la Direccion general de la Industria Nacional.

2515 MEXICO. United Mexican Mining Association. Report of the Court of Directors. Dated 13th June, 1827. *Boards, uncut, maps.* 8° *Lond.* 1827

A former possessor, whose opinion is entitled to respect, has written in this copy, "Curious, as showing the style of early English investment in Mexican mines, and the rascality and stupidity of their Managers."

2516 NEW HAMPSHIRE REGISTER AND UNITED STATES CALENDAR for the years 1813 to 1815, 1820 (impt.) 1821 to 1836, 1838 to 1858; *in all* 41 *Volumes; an unusually fine and full set of this scarce Register* [*see in* 1824 *an account of the previous Registers*]. 16° *Concord*, 1813

2516* NEW HAMPSHIRE REGISTERS, another set for the years 1815 (impt.), 1821 to 1825, 1828, 1829, 1831, 1834, 1836, 1839, 1841 to 1845, 1849, 1851, 1853 to 1855, and 1858; *in all* 24 *vols.* 16° *Concord*, 1815–1858

2517 NEWSPAPERS. THE BOSTON DAILY ADVERTISER from 1832 to 1843; 2 volumes a year, very nearly if not quite complete. 26 volumes unbound. *Folio, Boston*, 1834–43

2518 NEWSPAPERS. THE NATIONAL INTELLIGENCER (Daily), 1824 to 1857 inclusive (except Jan. to June 1834 and Jan. to June 1837); such a long set seldom occurs for sale. 68 Vols. all bound except half of 1841 and 1845, and 1848 to 1857. *Folio, Washington*, 1824–57

2519 NICHOLLS (J. F. *City Librarian, Bristol*) The Remarkable Life, Adventures, and Discoveries of Sebastian Cabot, of Bristol, the Founder of Great Britain's Maritime Power, Discoverer of America, and its first Colonizer. *Cloth. Portrait and map.* 4° *London, Sampson Low & Co.* 1869

We confess that we cut the leaves of this beautiful book, from the *Chiswick Press* of Whittingham, with an eagerness that has seldom been ours. We read it through. and through, and through, and closed it with a profound disappointment which has never before been ours. We interleaved it delicately with our historic litmus papers and found, to our great regret, that it would scarcely in any part stand the test of impartial criticism. We had long hoped some day to find time, with reverent hands, to mouse round and bring to light some hidden documents in Bristol that might throw light on the Cabots. Mr. Nicholls, as a thorough-going antiquary, has dispelled that hope. He has found nothing in Bristol that properly pertains to that family, and has been compelled to rehash Biddle, Tytler, Humboldt, seasoning the dish with the discoveries of Mr. Rawdon Brown in Venice, and Mr. Bergenroth in Madrid, flavoring the whole with a portrait of Sebastian Cabot, exquisitely engraved by Rawle, and an extract from 'Sebastian Cabot's Map,' of 1544, now in the Imperial Library at Paris. Mr. Nicholls, as a painstaking chronicler, has used all the materials that the active research of many antiquaries has turned up in the present century, and the result is the above remarkable title-page, and the following passages from his conclusion, on pp. 187, 188: "Even where his [Sebastian Cabot's] ashes lie is a mystery; and he who gave to England a continent, and to Spain an empire, lies in some unknown tomb." . . . . "This man, who surveyed and depicted three thousand miles of a coast which he had discovered; who gave to Britain, not only the continent, but the untold riches of the deep, in the fisheries of Newfoundland, and the whale fishery of the Arctic Sea; who broke up a monopoly that, vampire-like, was sucking out England's infant strength, and unlocked for her the treasures of the world, saying, 'Go, win and then wear them;' who is never reported to have struck an aggressive blow; who made enemies into friends, and whose friends were ever warmly attached to him; who, by his uprightness and fair dealing, raised England's name high among the nations, placed her credit on a solid foundation, and made her citizens respected; who was the father of free trade, and gave us the carrying trade of the world: this man has not a statue in the city that gave him birth, or in the metropolis of the country he so greatly enriched, or a name on the land he discovered. Emphatically, the most scientific seaman of his own or, perhaps, many subsequent ages — one of the gentlest, bravest, best of men — his actions have been misrepresented, his discoveries denied, his deeds ascribed to others, and calumny has flung its filth on his memory."

Now, without attempting to become a champion of "Historic Truth," being familiar with all the materials used in compiling this book, and much more of kindred character, we cannot forbear, here, for the want of a better place, to book our earnest protest in behalf of the memory of John Cabot and Christopher Columbus, against such wholesale assumptions. There is no warrant in the documents that Mr. Nicholls has used to justify him in placing Sebastian Cabot on this pedestal. What we know of him is very slight. It is only by making his hero tell a flat lie that Mr. Nicholls makes him an Englishman instead of a Venetian, and in the face of the most valuable contemporary papers brought to light by Mr. Rawdon Brown and Mr. Bergenroth, he appropriates honors to the son which rightfully belong to the father, John Cabot. The simple truth is that all those papers of 1497 and 1498 refer only to John Cabot, and the voyage of 1497. They allude to the larger expedition of 1498 as having gone forth, John Cabot with it, but not yet returned. That Sebastian Cabot was in both voyages there is little doubt, but in a subordinate capacity. As nothing more is heard of John Cabot it is not unlikely that he died during the voyage of 1498, and so his son took command — but this is not certain. We have no distinct account of the voyage of 1498, nor have we of any subsequent voyage from England of Sebastian Cabot. If he 'surveyed and depicted 3000 miles of a coast,' it must have been in the Gulf of St. Lawrence.

In the fall of 1512, having received no further encouragement from Henry VII or VIII, Sebastian Cabot took service under the King of Spain, where he remained for a great number of years, though, perhaps, visiting England occasionally. If he made the voyage of 1517 it 'took none effect,' and we have no account of it. In his old age he returned to England after the death of Holbein and was made use of in getting up a trading company to Russia, but of this honorable enterprise very little has come down to us of a character to lift him to the high position claimed by the author of this book. Documents may turn up hereafter, justifying in a degree the high encomiums of Mr. Nicholls, but at present we know of them not. Nor do we know of any one whose "calumny has flung its filth on his memory." On the page of history, if one finds very little in favor of Sebastian Cabot to raise him far above the level, yet no one has found anything against him. His record, so far as we know it, is honorable.

To all intents and purposes Christopher Columbus was the discoverer of America, and is entitled to that honorable distinction. The grand idea of sailing west to find the east was his, and the success was his; let the honor be his. It is true he did not first see the Island of Cape Breton nor the northern coast of the Gulf of St. Lawrence, yet he pointed out the way to his friend and fellow-townsman, John Cabot.

As to the excellent portrait in this book it is a welcome contribution, but it ought perhaps to be explained that what may have been true forty years ago is not true now, "from the original in the possession of Charles Josh Harford Esq." Nearly 40 years ago the original portrait passed into the hands of Mr. Biddle, it is understood at the cost of £500, and was brought by him to this country. A good copy was taken and is now preserved in the Massachusetts Historical Society. The original was destroyed by the great fire in Pittsburgh. There appears to be a mistake in ascribing it to Holbein, as that celebrated painter is now proved to have died before S. Cabot returned to England from Spain. The Latin inscription on the portrait to us seems to point to John Cabot as the first discoverer of the new land [primi inventoris terræ novæ] and not to the son Sebastian.

As to the extract of the map of Sebastian Cabot which Mr. Nicholls has given, it is difficult to account for the errors that have crept into and all over it. Out of 65 names given in and about the Gulf of St. Lawrence and Nova Scotia, more than 40 of them are misspelled, and several of them hopelessly disguised. The typographical errors and literary slips throughout the book are as unpardonable as they are numerous. They are such as properly belong to the author and not the printer, witness the date 1474 in heading of Chap. III and repeated, the dates 1543 on page 67, &c. &c. Still with all its faults the book is an interesting one.

2520 Parcel of odd volumes of Old English Magazines, *etc.* 20 *large volumes.* 8° *Lond. v. y.*

2521 Patiño (*Fr.* Pedro Pablo) Disertacion Critico-theo-filosofica sobre la Conservacion de la Santa Imagen de Nuestra Señora de los Angeles, que se venera extramuros de esta Ciudad de México, y con motivo de un Novena que se ha dispuesto apropiada á la dicha conservacion, se considera necesaria para prevenir la sabia critica de las personas doctas. *Fine copy, calf.* 4° *Mexico,* 1801

2522 Puente (Pedro de la) Reflexiones sobre el Bando de 25. de Junio ultimo, contraidas a lo que dispone para con los Eclesiasticos Rebeldes, &c. *Fine copy, calf.* 4° *Mexico,* 1812

A very interesting and important book. See note under No. 1739 of this Catalogue.

2523 San Antonio Abad. Flores del Yermo, Pasmo de Egypto, Assombro de el Mundo, Sol del Occidente, Portento de la Gracia, Vida, y Milagros de el grande S. Antonio Abad. Escrita por el Maestro Blas Antonio de Cevallos. Vltima impression, corregido y emendada. *Vellum, margins of some leaves slightly mutilated. Scarce and curious.* 4° *Madrid,* 1713

2524 San Anastasio (*El R. P. Fr.* Juan de) Coloquios Canonico de Regulares. Compuestos por el R. P. Fr. Juan de San

Anastasio, Provincial que fue de los Carmelitas Descalzos, en esta Provincia de Nueva España, &c. Obra póstuma. *Fine copy, calf.* 4° *Mexico,* 1816

An interesting book of 226 pp. with 10 preliminary and 5 sequent leaves. Preceding the text are 8 pages containing *Breve Noticia del Autor de esta Obra.*

2525 SOLIS (Antonio de) Historia de la Conquista de Mexico. *Fine copy, vellum.* 4° *Madrid,* 1790

This excellent edition, in good type, contains a Life of the Author and a good Index. No book has yet appeared to supersede de Solis's "Conquest of Mexico."

2526 TESTAMENT. Das Neue Testament unsers Herrn und Heylandes Jesu Christi, nach der Deutschen Uebersetzung D. Martin Luthers, mit Kurtzem Inhalt eines jeden Capitels, und vollständiger Anweesung gleicher Schrift-Stellen. Wie auch aller Sonn-und Fest. tägigen Evangelien und Episteln. Zweyte Auflage. *Fine clean copy, original binding.* 8° *Philadelphia, bey Carl Cist,* 1796

This very rare edition is not noticed by O'Callaghan.

2527 TIJADA (Miguel Lerda de) Comercio Esterior de México desde la Conquista hasta hoy. *Small folio, Mexico,* 1853

The historical portion (63 pp.) of this valuable work is divided into three periods: 1st, 1519–1777; 2d, 1778–1821; 3d, 1822–1853. Then follows the main bulk of the volume, entitled, "Documentos que se citan en esta obra."

2528 THACKERAY (Wm. Makepeace) La Feria de las Vanidades, por W. Thackeray. 638 *pp. uncut.* 4° *Mexico, Andrade y Escalante,* 1860

2529 ULLOA (*Don* Antonio de) Noticias Americanas: Entretenimientos Fisico-Historicos sobre la America Meridional, y la Septentrional Oriental: Comparacion General de los territorios, Climas y producciones en las tres especies vegetal, animal y mineral: con una relacion particular de los Indios de aquellos paises, sus costumbres y usos, de las petrificaciones de cuerpos marinos, y de los antiqüedades. Con un discurso sobre el idioma, y conjeturas sobre el modo con que pasáron los primeros pobladores. *Fine copy. Calf.* 4° *Madrid,* 1792

2530 UNIVERSAL MAGAZINE (The) of Knowledge and Pleasure, containing news, debates, poetry, history, biography, geography, voyages, criticism, mathematics, cookery, trade, navigation, architecture, *etc., from* 1749 *to* 1792, 39 *vols. Maps and plates, many of which relate to America. Not uniform, and some volumes imperfect and duplicate.* 8° *London,* 1749–1792

2531 VALLEJO (*Don* Josef Ignacio, *Presbiterio, Natural del Obispado de Guadalaxara en el Reino de Mexico*) Vida de la Madre de Dios y siempre Virgen Maria. *Fine copy on thick paper, half calf.* 4° *En Cesena,* 1779

Fine line engraved portraits of the author and the Virgin, by Angelo Ferri, inserted. On the portrait of Vallejo his death is recorded as having taken place on the 30th May, 1785, six years after the publication of this volume.

2532 VALLESIUS (Franciscus) Francisci Vallesii Covarrvbiani, Professoris Complutensis, in Aphorismos, & libellum de Alimento Hippocratis, Commentaria. *Vellum, scarce.* 8° *Compluti, Andreas ab Angelo,* 1561

The first aphorism commented upon is our old friend *Vita brevis, ars longa,* etc.

2533 VELASCO (*El Dr. Fr. D.* Pedro Andres de) VIDA, y Milagros de San Juan Nepomuceno, canonigo de la cathedral de Praga, Proto-Martyr del Sigilo de la Confession, singularissimo Abogado de la Honra, buena Fama, y Credito, y Protector de la Esclarecida Religion de la Compania de Jesus. *Fine copy, calf.* *Thick* 4° *Madrid,* 1736

2534 VERMONT REGISTER and Almanac for the years 1812, 1814, to 1822, 1825 (imperfect), 1826 to 1835, 1837 to 1849, 1852, 1854, 1857 to 1861, and 1863, *in all* 42 *vols. A very scarce and unusually full set.* 16° *Burlington and Montpelier,* 1812–1863

2534* VERMONT REGISTER, *another set,* for the years 1812, 1815, 1817 to 1819, 1827 to 1836, 1838 to 1846, 1848, 1852, 1858, *in all* 27 *vols.* *Burlington and Montpelier,* 1812–58

2535 WASHINGTON. EULOGIES AND ORATIONS on the Life and Death of General George Washington, first President of the United States of America. *Portrait inserted, fine copy, calf.* 8° *Boston, Manning & Loring,* 1800

2536 WATTS (ISAAC) THE PSALMS OF DAVID Imitated in the Language of the New Testament, and apply'd to the Christian State of Worship. *Fine clean copy, calf.* 12° *London, for J. Clark, and others,* 1719

FIRST EDITION, of excessive rarity. It is permitted to but few in these days even to see, much less to possess, a fine copy of the first edition of Dr. Watts's Psalms. No English book probably, except the Bible, has passed through so many editions, and taken so strong a hold of the people of New England as this book.

2537 WATTS (I.) Psalms of David, Imitated, *etc.* The Second Edition. *Good copy, but wanting one leaf, pp.* 125, 126. 12° *London, for J. Clark and others,* 1719

2538 WATTS (I.) Psalms, *etc.* The Seventh Edition [with 4 leaves of tunes inserted, engraved by F. Hoffman.] *Half roan.* 12° *London, for John Clark,* 1729

2539 WATTS (I.) Psalms, *etc.* The Fifteenth Edition, with the Preface and Notes. [The Tunes in the First Part, engraved by F. Hoffman, inserted.] *Very fine large clean copy, half roan.* 8° *London, J. Oswald,* 1748

2540 WATTS (I.) The Psalms, *etc.* *Fine copy.* 16° *London, for J. & F. Rivington,* 1773

This copy possesses peculiar interest from the fact that Dr. Rippon has gone carefully through it and noted the many variations he found in collating this with the first and many other editions. This copy has at the end four leaves of Tunes, engraved.

2541 WATTS (I.) Psalms of David, imitated, *etc.* Together with Hymns and Spiritual Songs. *Printed in double columns, sheep.* 8° *Boston, by Thomas & Andrews,* 1791

2542 WATTS (I.) Hymns and Spiritual Songs. 9th Edition. 4 *leaves mutilated, and table at end imperfect. Calf.* 16° *Lond. for R. Ford,* 1725

2543 XALISCO (*State of, Mexico*) Catecismo Politico é instructivo, para uso de los habitantes del Estado libre de Xalisco. Su autor el Ciudadaño Victoriano Roa.
142 *pp.* 16° *Guadalaxara*, 1823

CONSTITUCION politica del Estado de Xalisco, formada y presentada al Congreso Constituyente del mismo Estado por su Comision de Constitucion.
100 pp. 16° *Guadalaxara*, 1824

REGLAMENTO para el gobierno Interior del Congreso Constituyente del Estado de Xalisco. 28 pp. 16° *Guadalaxara*, 1824

MAXIMAS de Prudencia que escribió un sabio, y las dán nuevamente à la luz pública dos Ciudadaño de Xalisco. 12 pp.
4 vols in 1, fine copies, half calf. 16° *Guadalaxara*, 1824

2544 ZIMMERMAN (Mr.) Strictures on Natural Pride.
8° *Philadelphia*, 1778

2545 ZODIACO MARIANO, en que el Sol de Justicia Christo con la salud en las alas visita como Signos, y Casas proprias para beneficio de los hombres, los templos, y lugares dedicados à los cultos de su SS. Madre por medio de las mas celebres, y Milagrosas Imagenes de la misma Señora, que se veneran en esta America Septentrional, y Reynos de la Nueva España. Obra posthuma de el Padre FRANCISCO DE FLORENCIA, de la Compañia de Jesus, reducida à compendio, y en gran parte añadida por el P. Jvan Antonio de Oviedo, *etc.* 12 *preliminary leaves and* 328 *pages, fine copy, vellum.* 4° *Mexico*, 1755

A work of considerable importance for the Ecclesiastical history of Spanish North America, like all the works of this distinguished author, Father Florencia. The work is divided into five parts. Part I, contains the history of the miraculous appearances of Our Lady in the Province and Bishopric of Yucatan; II, in the City of Mexico and its neighborhood; III, in the Cities of Puebla, Oaxaca, California, etc.; IV, in the Kingdom of Guatemala; V, in the Provinces of Michoacan, Guadalaxara, and Guadiana. The details are narrated with great fullness, with names, dates, and circumstances, with authorities and bibliographical citations.

Τέλος

Riverside Press

Printed by H. O. Houghton and Company

CAMBRIDGE, MASS

Feb. 1870

MESSRS LEONARD & CO AUCTIONEERS

NOS 48 AND 50 BROMFIELD STREET BOSTON

Who undertake to execute all Commissions intrusted to them

CATALOGUE SENT POST PAID ON THE RECEIPT OF ONE DOLLAR

TWO DOLLARS WILL SECURE A LARGE PAPER COPY

SALES MORNINGS AT 10 AFTERNOONS AT 2 O'CLOCK

TUESDAY APRIL 5TH WEDNESDAY 6TH THURSDAY 7TH

AND FRIDAY THE 8TH 1870

www.ingramcontent.com/pod-product-compliance
Lightning Source LLC
LaVergne TN
LVHW010253110826
845151LV00004B/1459

* 9 7 8 1 4 2 5 5 2 2 0 0 1 *